The World of the Medieval Shipmaster

Despite a background of war, piracy, depopulation, bullion shortages, adverse political decisions, legal uncertainties and deteriorating weather conditions, between the mid-fourteenth and the mid-fifteenth centuries the English merchant shipping industry thrived. New markets were developed, voyages became longer, ships and cargoes increased in size and value, and an interest in ship ownership as an investment spread throughout the community.

Using a rich range of examples drawn from court and parliamentary records, contemporary literature and the codifications of maritime law, this book illuminates the evolving management and commercial practices which developed to regulate the relationships between shipowners, shipmasters, crews and shipping merchants. It also brings to life ship performance, navigation, seamanship, and the frequently harsh conditions on board.

The World of the Medieval Shipmaster
Law, Business and the Sea c.1350–c.1450

Robin Ward

THE BOYDELL PRESS

© Robin Ward 2009

All rights reserved. Except as permitted under current legislation
no part of this work may be photocopied, stored in a retrieval system,
published, performed in public, adapted, broadcast,
transmitted, recorded or reproduced in any form or by any means,
without the prior permission of the copyright owner

The right of Robin Ward to be identified as
the author of this work has been asserted in accordance with
sections 77 and 78 of the Copyright, Designs and Patents Act 1988

First published 2009
The Boydell Press, Woodbridge

ISBN 978 1 84383 455 7

The Boydell Press is an imprint of Boydell & Brewer Ltd
PO Box 9, Woodbridge, Suffolk IP12 3DF, UK
and of Boydell & Brewer Inc.
668 Mt Hope Avenue, Rochester, NY 14620, USA
website: www.boydellandbrewer.com

The publisher has no responsibility for the continued existence or accuracy
of URLs for external or third-party internet websites referred to in
this book, and does not guarantee that any content on such websites is,
or will remain, accurate or appropriate.

A CIP record for this book is available
from the British Library

This publication is printed on acid-free paper

Printed in Great Britain by
CPI Antony Rowe Ltd, Chippenham Wiltshire

Contents

List of illustrations	vi
Acknowledgements	vii
Abbreviations	viii
Introduction	1
1 The shipmaster and the law	9
2 The shipmaster and the rise and fall of the admirals' courts	27
3 The shipmaster as owner, partner and employee	48
4 The shipmaster's on-shore responsibilities	69
5 The shipmaster's off-shore responsibilities	95
6 The shipmaster at sea: navigation and meteorology	122
7 The shipmaster at sea – seamanship	157
Conclusion	179

Appendices

1	Transcription and translation of the MS *Liber Horn* copy of the *Lex d'Oleron*	183
2	Transcription and translation of the *Inquisition of Queenborough*	206
3	A partial transcription and translation of *Les Bons Usages et Les Bonnes Costumes et Les Bons Jugemenz de la Commune d'Oleron*	219
4	Transcription and translation of a 1323 charter-party	229
5	Transcription and translation of the chapter 'de regimen transfretantium' from Gilbertus Anglicus' *Compendium Medicine*	235

Select Bibliography	239
Index	255

Illustrations and Tables

Figures

1. The first folio of the *Lex d'Oleron* from MS *Liber Horn* — 21
2. Front and back of a 1323 charter-party — 79
3. Ships in a haven — 125
4. An early 32-point compass with 'lunar times' — 131
5. Hypothetical passage across the Bay of Biscay — 149
6. The first folio of the rutter from MS Lansdowne 285 — 153
7. A ship sounding — 168

Tables

1. Comparison of wages and portage values — 111
2. The moon as an analogue clock — 137

Acknowledgements

This book is the result of my curiosity of how they did things at sea six hundred years ago. Many useful conversations have been had during the preparation of this book with scholars, sailors, lawyers and boat builders, to all of whom I am indebted. I owe particular thanks to Wendy Childs, Richard Gorski, Vanessa Harding, Gillian Hutchinson, Maryanne Kowaleski, Susan Rose, Albrecht Sauer and Richard Unger from various universities and maritime museums in Europe and America.

Most authors thank members of their families for their understanding and forbearance during the long and painful gestation of their work; I now understand why. I salute Kit, my long-suffering wife, for her help with proofreading and in untangling more than usually opaque sections of text, and her constant support. My children should also be mentioned – apart from everything else, sailing with them on the west coast of Scotland and in the Mediterranean has always been the pleasantest of escapes from libraries. And without the generous help and advice of Caroline Palmer, Rohais Haughton and Vanda Andrews at Boydell and Brewer, this book would never have reached the printer.

Despite all that assistance and advice, the errors and omissions remain my responsibility.

Abbreviations

BIHR	*Bulletin of the Institute of Historical Research.*
Brit. Chron.	*Handbook of British Chronology*, ed. E.B. Fryde, D.E. Greenway and I. Roy (3rd edn, London, 1986).
CCR	*Calendar of Close Rolls, 1272–1500*, 47 vols (London, 1892–1956).
CLB	*Calendar of Letter-Books Preserved Among the Archives of the Corporation of the City of London at the Guildhall*, Books A–L (1275–t. Henry VII), ed. Reginald R. Sharpe (London, 1899–1912).
CLMC	*Calendar of Letters from the Mayor and Corporation of the City of London, c.1350–1370*, ed. Reginald Sharpe (London, 1885).
CLRO	City of London Record Office.
Coutumier	*Les Bons Usages et les Bonnes Costumes et les Bons Jugemenz de la Commune de l'Oleron*, MS Douce 227, Bodleian Library, Oxford, published as *Le Coutumier de L'Ile d'Oléron*, ed. Charles Bémont (Paris, 1919) and in Twiss, *Black Book*, II, pp. 254–401.
CPMR	*Calendar of Plea and Memoranda Rolls of the City of London Preserved Among the Archives of the Corporation of the City of London, 1323–1482*, 6 vols, ed. A.H. Thomas (vols 1–4) and P.E. Jones (vols 5–6) (Cambridge, 1926–61).
CPR	*Calendar of Patent Rolls*, 52 vols (London 1891–1916).
CRR	Chester Recognizance Rolls
Customs	*Customs of the Sea*, Paris, Bibliothèque Nationale, MS Espagnol 124; Twiss, *Black Book*, III, pp. lix and 35–657
DCRS	Devon and Cornwall Records Society.
EcHR	*Economic History Review.*
EHR	*English Historical Review.*
EETS; OS, ES	Early English Text Society; Ordinary Series, Extra Series.
Foedera	*Foedera, Conventiones, Litterae ... etc., 1066–1383*, ed. Thomas Rymer, 4 vols (London, 1816–69): 1383 AD ff., 10 vols (The Hague, 1793–1845).
MM	*Mariner's Mirror.*
NRS	Navy Records Society.
OED	*Oxford English Dictionary*, Compact Edition (Oxford, 1971).

ABBREVIATIONS

Oleron	MS *Liber Horn*, Corporation of the City of London Records Office, Guildhall, fos 355v–60r.
Ordinances	*A Collection of Ordinances and Regulations for the Government of the Royal Household*, The Society of Antiquaries (1790).
PP	*Past and Present*.
PRO	The National Archives – Public Record Office.
PROI	Public Record Office of Ireland.
Queenborough	*The Inquisition of Queenborough*, published in Twiss, *Black Book*, I, pp. 132–73
Rot. Parl.	*Rotuli Parliamentorum ut et Petiones et Placita in Parliamento, Edward I–Henry VII*, ed. J. Strachey, 6 vols and index (London, 1783–1832).
RS	*The Rutter of the Sea*
SRS	Southampton Record Society.
Statutes	*The Statutes at Large from Magna Charta to the End of the Eleventh Parliament of Great Britain, Anno 1761*, ed. Danby Pickering, 28 vols (Cambridge, 1762–9).
Twiss, *Black Book*	*Monumenta Juridica, Black Book of the Admiralty*, ed. Sir Travers Twiss, 4 vols, Rolls Series 55 (London, 1871–76).
Year Book	*Year Books of Edward II, Edward III, Richard II, Henry IV, Henry V. and Henry VI*; variously Selden Society, Chronicles and Memorials of Great Britain and Ireland during the Middle Ages, and The Ames Foundation.
York Sessions	*The Year Books of Yorkshire Sessions of the Peace, 1361–4*, ed. B.H. Putnam, Yorkshire Archaeological Society Record Series C (Wakefield, 1939).

The abbreviations listed above are used throughout the text. Other citations in the text are printed in full in the footnotes at first occurrence and in an abbreviated form in subsequent reference. All cited works and those for suggested further reading are given in full in the Bibliography.

Except in the Introduction and in the transcriptions and translations of manuscripts included in the Appendices, footnotes are collated by paragraph and indicated by a single reference number at the end of that paragraph.

This book is produced with the generous assistance of a grant from
Isobel Thornley's Bequest to the University of London

Introduction

Despite a reduced population, perennial war, endemic piracy, shortage of bullion, recurring plague, sporadic famine, deteriorating climatic conditions and little or no encouragement from the crown, the English shipping industry not only survived, but in certain sectors prospered, in the hundred years between c.1350 and c.1450. During that period there was a marked change in the pattern of goods imported and exported, an increasing sophistication in the management of shipping, and an awakening interest in ship-ownership for both mercantile expansion and for capital investment. At the centre of the shipping industry was the shipmaster on whose ship-handling and commercial skills the viability of every overseas enterprise depended. To be successful, a shipmaster, necessarily endowed with the initiative, courage and physical strength to overcome the inherent *risica maris et gentium* of his profession, also had to have an extensive array of non-physical skills. Alone, in partnership or as an employee, he had to negotiate for cargoes at profitable freight rates, victual and maintain his ship, recruit and manage his crew, and navigate in all weathers through unmarked seas. This wide range of skills was mediated by a protean system of laws, contradictory political policies, a paucity of navigational instruments and unreliable equipment. Although there has been much research on English seaborne trade and commercial organisation in the late Middle Ages – encompassing the economic, legal, political and social dimensions of the subject – there has been no thorough or consolidated examination of the work of the medieval shipmaster.

Unfortunately there appears to be insufficient evidence to build a prosopographic portrait of a typical shipmaster, but while his origins, private life and views on the world around him remain largely opaque, occasional pieces of information indicate that he could be young or old, literate or illiterate, very skilled or less skilled, lucky or unlucky. This book takes as its central theme the expertise required of the men of the sea who prospered or failed by their acumen in business and lived or died by their decisions.

The legal background

During the period under examination, litigation was not uncommon at the bar of a court practising any one of the several codes of law available. Furthermore, it appears to have been increasing in frequency. Common law in medieval England was concerned primarily with property, and in the fourteenth century was ill-prepared to deal with commercial problems. Merchant law, on the other hand, with a positive attitude towards trade, was equipped to serve the needs of the international commercial community. Although practised generally on the continent, in England it was found mainly in the courts of fairs and markets, and in port towns. Maritime law, distinct from the other codes, embodied rules for the conduct of ships and shipping and offered the quick and realistic decisions sought by transient shipmasters and freighting merchants; it too was practised in the courts of port towns. Through the fourteenth and fifteenth centuries the various law codes and their courts competed for business, competition which forced common law to recognise the requirements of commerce, the precepts of merchant law to become more generally recognised, and maritime law to acquire its own admiralty courts.

The commercial background

Most English ships were confined to coastwise sailing within the Bay of Biscay, English Channel, North Sea and Irish Sea during this period, while long-distance trade with southern Europe was handled largely by Italian shippers. Operations northward and eastward were restricted to Iceland and its stockfish trade, under the careful scrutiny of the Danish and Hanseatic authorities. The problems that beset England in the fourteenth and fifteenth centuries, and the industries whose pattern of imports and exports radically changed, have been thoroughly examined by generations of economic historians. Records of exactions levied on imported and exported commodities such as wool, woolfells, wine and cloth provide information which, although not always complete nor continuous, have been used to give a measure of the movement of goods. Of all cargoes carried, wool, cloth and wine were of the greatest importance to merchants and shippers. It has been shown that as bulk wool exports steadily declined from an average of over 25,000 sacks per year in the 1350s, much of it handled by alien merchants, to c.6,000 in the 1450s, exports of cloth grew in the same period from fewer than 2,000 pieces per year to an average of over 35,000, the majority handled by English merchants Although the combined export tonnage of raw wool and woollen cloth halved from c.4,200 tons in 1350 to c.2,300 tons in 1450, the added value of the cloth allowed the total value of those exports to double from about £250,000 to perhaps £500,000 per year.[1]

The very different bulking characteristics and packaging requirements of cloth and wool prevent these tonnages being translated into comparable cargo volumes but the increase in cargo value allowed shipmasters to raise their freight rates and

---

[1] Based on 364lbs of wool per sack, 85lbs of cloth per piece, and average prices of £8 per sack of wool and £13 per piece of cloth. Because of wide variations, those prices and weights can be only approximations.

so improve the viability of the shipping industry. While English merchants and ships were gaining a larger share of the diminishing wool export business (after the negative effect of a royal embargo on the use of English ships between 1353 and 1357), they also held the larger share of the growing cloth export trade.

The customs records of wine imports from Gascony reveal a decline from a peak of $c.20,000$ tuns per year in the early fourteenth century to the smaller but still considerable volume of $c.10,000$ tuns per year in the middle of the fifteenth century. During that period an increasing number of the ships engaged in the wine trade were English, carrying wool and cloth out and bringing wine back. Other English ships took similar cargoes to Iberia and brought back oil and soap for the growing textile industry and iron for agriculture and domestic uses. The quantities of imported chemicals destined for the textile industry, alum from Asia Minor and Italy, dyestuffs from Castile and Toulouse and potash from Scandinavia, grew in volume commensurately with cloth production although those products were generally carried by foreign ships. Until early in the fourteenth century there was a small export of surplus salt from England, but increased requirements for the preservation of fish, particularly after the development of double salting and the decline of local salines, reversed the flow. Thereafter large quantities of salt were imported from Bourgneuf Bay, either directly in foreign ships or by transhipment from the Low Countries, sometimes in English vessels. Apart from the bulk cargoes discussed above, other goods shipped out of England included relatively low-volume cargoes of finished metal and pewter work and sporadic bulk loads of grain or beans in the years of good harvest.

The import from the Baltic of timber, naval stores, fish and fur was encouraged by the 1370 Treaty of Stralsund and continued until later in the century. Hanseatic opposition proved to be too strong however, although some English ships continued to trade well into the fifteenth century. By 1408 trading privileges had been secured by England with Norway, Sweden and Denmark and soon after, but for only a short period, with Iceland, where cloth, grain and other necessities were exchanged for stockfish. English attempts to trade in the Mediterranean during the first half of the fifteenth century failed and it was not until the next century that regular sailings were attempted.

Ships and shipping

Coastal shipping, the essential means of bulk transport before the construction of reliable roads, was complementary to the deep-sea fleet engaged in overseas trade; many cargoes were broken down and transhipped after arrival in England to be distributed around the coast. Ships of average size or larger could be deployed coastwise and deep-sea in a single season, sailing, for example, to Bordeaux for the October wine harvest and then reverting to fishing or coasting on their return.

The type of ship used by the English in the fourteenth and fifteenth centuries has been the subject of much debate. More than 60 names of ship-types have been found in English records between 1200 and 1520; many of these were undoubtedly boats, lighters and barges not engaged in off-shore work, and alternative and duplicated type-names were common. Early work on town seals and more recent work using customs accounts, court records and archaeological remains, has shown that many, perhaps most, of the overseas trading ships of the fourteenth century were 'cogs'. Those were the workhorses of the northern seas; they had flat bottoms of edge-butted planking and raised sides of clinker construction of overlapping planks, squared transoms and straight stem and stern posts. They were fitted initially with one mast carrying a large rectangular sail athwart the ship and, after about 1400, a mizzen mast with a fore and aft lateen sail. For defence, cogs could carry castles at the bow and stern and platforms at the mast-head and, when impressed for naval service, were used as military vessels. They could be fitted out specifically to carry bulk cargoes, barrels, sacks, bales or pallets, but when fully loaded they had a poor windward performance and were generally slow. The alternative design for commercial ships was the 'hulk', a double-ended ship of finer lines and curved stem and stern, with one mast again carrying a rectangular sail, later supplemented with a mizzen and lateen sail. Information about the hulk-type ship is based largely on iconography and is therefore very insecure, but their appearance indicates that they would have been able to sail faster and probably closer to the wind than cogs, but did not have the same carrying capacity nor could they be beached for cargo handling. It is now thought that there was a process of cross-fertilisation in the fourteenth and fifteenth centuries between cogs, hulks and perhaps other vessel types resulting overall in hybrids that were generally more effective. The introduction of a second, and later a third mast to cogs, hulks and cog-hulk hybrids allowed a split sail plan of a larger total area while the mizzen-rigged lateen sail improved the ship's windward performance. About the same time, clinker construction gave way to the carvel method of edge-butted planks, a construction method borrowed, as was the lateen sail, from the Mediterranean.

English ship sizes in the period 1327–1451 have been tabulated. Although there may have been a differing distribution of ship tonnages in the fleets working the several routes and markets, by dividing the total tonnage of impressed fleets by the number of ships involved, a steady rise in average size may be seen: 36 tons in 1359, 65 tons in 1409–10 and 100 tons in 1450. The hypothetical shipmaster whose life and work are studied in this book may be taken to have had an 'about average for deep-sea voyages' ship with a capacity of 80 ± 20 tons.

Except for a lead-line for sounding the depth and for sampling the seabed, a sand-glass for indicating a fixed time lapse and a primitive compass, the medieval northern shipmaster sailed without navigational instruments. For the literate who could afford them, sailing directions, or 'rutters', became available towards the end

INTRODUCTION

of the fourteenth or early in the fifteenth century but most shipmasters had to rely on their own experience and on what they had gleaned from other mariners. For the rest, it was a question of memory, skill, nerve and luck.

Organisation of the book

Chapter 1 examines the precepts of common, merchant and maritime law which were relevant to mercantile shipping, while chapter 2 recounts the rise and fall of the admirals' courts and their uncomfortable relationship with those of the port towns and the crown. In chapter 3, the position of the shipmaster as sole owner of his ship, as a member of a partnership or as an employee of the owners is examined. The increasingly complex clauses of the financial and business instruments available to the shipmaster, in particular the charter-parties which were, in effect, his service contracts, are discussed in chapter 4. Chapter 5 looks at the shipmaster's responsibilities on board his ship as an employer and as a supplier of transport services to merchants, and chapters 6 and 7 review the craft of the shipmaster at sea, looking at his methods of navigation, his skill and his use of meteorology as a seaman. The first three Appendices are new transcriptions and translations of the *Lex d'Oleron*, the *Inquisition of Queenborough* and relevant parts of the *Coutumier* of the island of Oléron; Appendices 4 and 5 are transcriptions and translations of the oldest known English charter-party and a tract by the physician Gilbertus Anglicus on avoiding and treating seasickness.

Sources

The development of law in England in the fourteenth century as the country recovered from the combined effects of the disastrous reign and murder of Edward II, the ravages of the Black Death and the expense of Edward III's war against France, is succinctly explained by Musson and Ormrod. To discover the attitudes of common, merchant and maritime laws towards commerce and business in general, and to establish the legal status of the shipmaster as sole owner, partner or employee, the published histories of law by recognised authorities were used. Those included works by Holdsworth and Baker on common law, Hanbury and Martin and Avery on equity, Pease and Chitty, Gross and Hall, Goode and Bateson on merchant and commercial law, and Cheshire and Fifoot on contract. That background information was expanded and illustrated by evidence from the calendared records of court proceedings of the Chancery Court, King's Bench and London mayoral and other aldermanic courts.[2]

---

[2] Anthony Musson and W.M. Ormrod, *The Evolution of English Justice: Law, Politics and Society in the Fourteenth Century*, British Studies Series (Basingstoke, 1999). W.S. Holdsworth,

The works of Twiss, Sandborn and Bémont were used as basic texts on maritime law, and the new transcriptions and translations of the codifications of maritime law printed here in the Appendices were sifted for information. Many records of litigation heard before admirals' courts were taken from Marsden's work, and of the proceedings concerning West Country shipping heard in the Chancery Court from Gardiner's calendar.[3]

Information about imports and exports in the fourteenth and fifteenth centuries is readily available in the published works of scholars analysing the records of the various trades and industries. These include Bolton and Hatcher for economic overviews, Carus Wilson and Coleman and Lloyd for wool and cloth, James for wine, Childs for Anglo-Castilian trade and Bridbury for salt.[4]

There is a paucity of information about medieval business methods but the works of Postan, Gras and others offer a good general description. Roger and the de Roovers offer more specialised information on accountancy, insurance, sales credit and partnership; those aspects of business are expanded here from evidence in records of court proceedings. The edited individual accounts of Maghfeld, de la Pole and the Celys give a more personal view of the methods of merchant practitioners, and analyses of surviving freighting agreements give insights into the business relationship between merchants and shipmasters.[5]

A History of English Law, 17 vols, ed. J. Burke et al. (London, 1903–72). J.H. Baker, *An Introduction to English Legal History* (3rd edn, London, 1990). Jill E. Martin, ed., *Hanbury and Martin: Modern Equity* (14th edn, London, 1993). Margaret E. Avery, 'The History of the Equitable Jurisdiction of Chancery before 1460', *BIHR* 42 (1969), pp. 129–44. Edward F. Cousins and Robert Anthony, eds, *Pease and Chitty's Law of Markets and Fairs*, ed. (4th edn, Croydon, 1993). *Select Cases Corncerning the Law Merchant, 1239–1633*, ed. Charles Gross and Hubert Hall, 3 vols, Selden Society, 23, 46, 49 (London, 1908–32). R.M. Goode, *Commercial Law* (rev. edn, London, 1995). Mary Bateson, ed., *Borough Customs*, 2 vols Selden Society 8 and 21 (London, 1904–6). *Furniston's Law of Contract*, ed. Cheshire and Fifoot (13th edn, London, 1996).

[3] *Monumenta Juridica, Black Book of the Admiralty*, ed. Sir Travers Twiss, 4 vols, Rolls Series 55 (London, 1871–76). Frederic Rockwell Sandborn, *Origins of the Early English Maritime and Commercial Law* (New York and London, 1930). *Oleron and Coutumier. Select Pleas in the Court of Admiralty, The Court of Admiral of the West, 1390–1404 and the High Court of Admiralty, 1527–1545*, ed. R.G. Marsden, 2 vols, Selden Society 6 and 15 (1892, 1894). *A Calendar of Early Chancery Proceedings Relating to West Country Shipping, 1388–1493*, ed. Dorothy M. Gardiner, Devon and Cornwall Record Society NS 21 (Exeter, 1976).

[4] J.L. Bolton, *The Medieval English Economy, 1150–1500* (rev. edn, London, 1988). J. Hatcher, *Plague, Population and the English Economy, 1348–1530* (London, 1977). E.M. Carus Wilson and Olive Coleman, *England's Export Trade, 1275–1547* (Oxford, 1963). T.H. Lloyd, *The English Wool Trade in the Middle Ages* (Cambridge, 1977). M.K. James, *Studies in the Medieval Wine Trade* (Oxford, 1971). Wendy R. Childs, *Anglo-Castilian Trade in the Later Middle Ages* (Manchester, 1978). A.R. Bridbury, *England and the Salt Trade in the Later Middle Ages* (Oxford, 1955). Charles L. Cutting, *Fish Saving: A History of Fish Processing From Ancient to Modern Times* (London, 1955). E.M. Carus-Wilson, *Medieval Merchant Venturers* (Oxford, 1954).

[5] M.M. Postan, *Medieval Trade and Finance* (Cambridge, 1973). N.S.B. Gras, 'Capitalism – Concepts and History', *Bulletin of the Business Historical Society*, XVI, 2 (1942). James Steven Roger, *The Early History of the Law of Bills and Notes* (Cambridge, 1995). R. de Roover, *L'Evolution de la lettre de change, XIVe–XVIIIe siècles*, Ecole pratiques des hautes études (Paris,

INTRODUCTION

The seminal work on English medieval shipping is that by Burwash, written some 60 years ago. In that work navigation, conditions of employment, the types and sizes of ships and the *Lex d'Oleron* were examined in the light of the evidence then available. The present book extends Burwash's work on maritime law and examines in more detail navigation, the role of the shipmaster, seamanship and conditions on board the ship. It does not attempt to analyse types and sizes of hulls, ship construction and maintenance costs, nor the effectiveness of ship use, all of which have been examined variously by Friel, Hutchinson, Scammell, Unger and others.[6]

For detail of the history of navigation, sea-marks and navigational instruments, the works of Taylor, Waters, Naish and dos Reis were used. Analyses of the Low German and Middle English sailing directions by Sauer and the present author were used to assess the navigational information available to the northern medieval shipmaster.[7]

Most of what little is known about the personnel at sea and their recruitment and training has been collected by Kowaleski who prefaces her paper: 'the scarcity of notarial records, diaries, and admiralty courts for the period before 1500 have stymied efforts to analyze in much detail how seamen were recruited, employed and paid.' It has been possible to add something to her work: information about conditions at sea was gleaned from references to personnel in the codifications of maritime law, in contemporay accounts of life on board ship and in Middle English alliterative poetry, a genre characterised by accurate, if anach-

---

1953). Florence Edler de Roover, 'Early Examples of Marine Insurance', *Journal of Economic History*, 5, 2 (1945), pp. 183–4. F.W. Maitland, 'Trust and Corporation', in *Collected Papers* (Cambridge, 1911). H.A. Miskimin, 'Monetary Movements and Market Structure', *Journal of Economic History*, 24 (1964), pp. 170–90. M.K. James, 'Gilbert Maghfeld, a London Merchant of the Fourteenth Century', *EcHR*, 2nd series 8, 2 (1955–56), pp. 364–76. E.B. Fryde, 'The Wool Accounts of William de la Pole', in *Studies in Medieval Trade and Finance* (London, 1983). Alison Hanham, *The Celys and Their World, An English Family of the Fifteenth Century* (Cambridge, 1985).

6 Dorothy Burwash, *English Merchant Shipping, 1460–1540* (Toronto, 1947, reprint Newton Abbot, 1969). H.H. Brindley, 'Medieval Ships', *MM* 12 (1926), pp. 211–16 and 14 (1928), pp. 76–7. Richard W. Unger, *The Ship in the Medieval Economy, 600–1600* (London, 1980). Detlev Ellmers, 'The Cog as Cargo Carrier' and Timothy Runyan, 'The Cog as Warship', both in *Cogs, Caravels and Galleons, The Sailing Ship 1000–1650*, ed. Richard W. Unger (London, 1994). G.V. Scammell, 'English Merchant Shipping at the End of the Middle Ages. Some East Coast Evidence', *EcHR*, 2nd series 13, 3 (1961), pp. 327–41. Ian Friel, *The Good Ship* (London, 1995). Gillian Hutchinson, *Medieval Ships and Shipping* (London, 1994). Björn Landström, *Sailing Ships* (London, 1978).

7 E.G.R. Taylor, *The Haven-finding Art* (London, 1956). D.W. Waters, ed., *Rutters of the Sea* (London and New Haven, CT, 1967). John Naish, *Seamarks: Their History and Development* (London, 1985). António Estácio dos Reis, *Medir Estrelas* (Lisbon, 1997). Albert Sauer, ed., *Das Seebuch* (Hamburg, 1996). Facsimiles of the original text, transcriptions and translations into German and English by Albrecht Sauer and Robin Ward are available at www.dsm.museum /seebuch /_html. Robin Ward, 'The Earliest Known Sailing Directions in English', *Deutsches Schiffahrtsmuseumarchiv*, 27, pp. 49–92 (2004).

ronistic, detailed descriptive passages. Contemporary literature which has been found fruitful includes *Richard Redeless*, Barbour's *Bruce*, the *Complaynt of Scotland* and the works of Geoffrey Chaucer, whose role as an official in Customs brought him into frequent contact with shipmasters and merchants.[8]

Notes on translations

Translations from older languages such as Latin, Anglo-Norman French, Middle Low German and Old and Middle English, mostly made by the author, are not always literal but in all cases the sense has been retained. Translations from modern languages, also by the author, are literal. When considered relevant, the original text has been included in a footnote.

---

[8] Maryanne Kowaleski, 'Working at Sea: Maritime Recruitment and Remuneration in Medieval England', *Ricchezza del Mare, Ricchezza dal Mare, Secc. XII –XVIII*, Atti della 'Trentasettesima Settimana di Studi', 11–15 April 2005 (Florence, 2006). Appendices 1, 2 and 3. *Expeditions to Prussia and the Holy Land made by Henry, Earl of Derby, 1390–1391 and 1392–1393*, ed. L. Toulmin Smith, Camden Society (London, 1894). *The Stacions of Rome, the Pilgrims Sea Voyage*, ed. F.J. Furnivall, EETS OS 25 (London, 1867). Michael Jones, 'Le Voyage de Pierre de Lesnerac en Navarre, 1386', *Mémoires de la société d'histoire et d'archéologie de Bretagne*, LXI (1984), pp. 83–104. *The Poems of the Pearl Manuscript*, ed. Malcolm Andrew and Ronald Waldron (London, 1978); *Morte Arthure*, ed. Edmund Brock, EETS OS 8 (London, reprint 1961); William Langland, *Richard Redeless*, ed. W.W. Skeat, EETS OS 54 (London, 1873). *Barbour's Bruce*, ed. Matthew P. McDiarmid and James A.C. Stevenson, The Scottish Text Society, 3 vols (Edinburgh, 1985). *The Complaynt of Scotland wyth ane Exortatione to the Thre Estaits to be Vigilante in the Deffens of their Public Veil*, 1549, ed. J.A.H. Murray, 2 vols, EETS ES 17 and 18 (London, 1872–3). *The Vision of Piers Plowman*, B text, ed. A.V.C. Schmidt (London, 1978); Geoffrey Chaucer, *The Complete Works of Geoffrey Chaucer*, ed. F.N. Robinson (2nd edn, Oxford, 1957).

I

The Shipmaster and the Law

Background

From the thirteenth century the development of English overseas trade made necessary a body of laws to regulate commerce which, reflecting the practices of the markets, would be acceptable to denizen and alien merchants and shipmasters. Common law was peculiar to England and had grown out of customary usage; merchant law, on the other hand, had developed from the Roman *corpus juris* and was accepted, with local variations, throughout the rest of Europe. Merchant law followed the concept that the sea was outwith national jurisdiction, or *nullius territorium*, and was described by a fifteenth-century English chancellor as 'secundum legem naturam qu'est appell par ascuns ley Marchant, que est ley universal per tout le monde' ('following natural law which is called by some Merchant Law which is the universal law for the whole world'). In addition to common and merchant law, for problems which arose aboard ship or between one ship and another, mariners were subject to maritime law, a code of international application derived from the sea laws of the classical Mediterranean states and related to merchant law. For felonies committed ashore or at sea, mariners, as any other person, were subject to criminal law.[1]

In late medieval England, these and other legal codes in use were the result of disparate decisions handed down by a bewildering diversity of courts, each reflecting the differing expectations and needs of a section of society. Pleas could be brought to the county courts or to the Common and King's benches, to the King's Council or to Chancery, all practising common law; or to the aldermanic courts and the courts of markets and fairs of the Staple and of the Cinque Ports, all practising variants of merchant law. There were also the local manor courts, the specialised courts of the admirals practising maritime law, the courts of the Church practising canon law, and the courts of the universities. Very few decisions running contrary to the precepts of common, merchant or maritime laws have been found, and it appears that the various courts consistently followed variants of one of the three major codes throughout England.

---

[1] Holdsworth, *History*, 5, p. 62; *Year Book 13 Edward IV*, Pasch., pl. 5.

Because English common law jurists were reluctant to accept the precepts of the Roman *corpus juris*, merchant and maritime laws flourished independently in their different courts. Doubts sometimes arose about the relevant choice of code, and when the principles of one body of law favoured one litigant, the choice of code could become part of the dispute. The competition for business between merchant, maritime and common law courts was an important contributory factor in the development of the legal codes which regulated English overseas trade and shipping in the fourteenth and fifteenth centuries.

The Court of Chancery

Medieval common law was a formulary system developed from writs which, since the time of Henry II, litigants had had to obtain from Chancery to initiate litigation in the royal courts. Each writ gave rise to a particular manner of proceeding, or to a defined form of action with its own rules and procedures, and no plea could be brought to court without a writ. This procedure restricted the business of common law courts to complaints which fell within an existing form of action, and by the fourteenth century the range of writs had become too narrow for the increasing variety of commercial disputes. Ever more convoluted formulae had to be devised to pursue such complaints within the form of an existing writ; actions of account, for example, were used to claim not only unpaid debts, but also penal bonds arising from broken service agreements. Because common law courts could decide that the writ as presented disclosed no claim recognised by the law, plaintiffs in commercial litigation often found that there was no remedy for them at common law. The increasing complexity of mercantile transactions required either a broadening of the scope of common law or a higher jurisdiction which could make decisions and award fair remedies beyond the scope of existing procedures.

In theory, the chancellor could influence the development of the law by introducing new forms of writ to encompass new situations, but by the middle of the fourteenth century the categories of writ were closed. Frustrated by the inadequacies of common law, an aggrieved plaintiff looking for remedy in a commercial dispute then had three options, all expensive and sometimes uncertain. He could petition the King's Council, with the risk that a writ might be issued and the petition returned to a common law court; he could present a bill to Parliament in the hope of legislation; or he could ask the chancellor for an ad hoc decision by decree *ad personam*, binding only the parties in that suit. Of these, the procedure which was the simplest, quickest, and most satisfactory, was to petition the chancellor on whom the responsibility to award equitable jurisdiction fell.[2]

---

[2] Avery, 'Equitable Jurisdiction', *passim*.

The chancellor's jurisdiction grew from that of the King's Council, of which he was the representative, and it was partly through the issue of writs and partly due to their limitations that the chancellor became associated with the administration of justice. The chancellor did not see himself as administering a new body of law but rather as trying to give relief in hard cases, not by precedent but according to his own sense of right and wrong – 'equity is according to the conscience of him that is chancellor, and as that it is longer or narrower so is equity'. The Court of Chancery, as the court both of first application and of appeal, remained separate from and superior to the other common law courts and was able to hear suits which were deemed to be too difficult for lower courts, or where one or both of the disputing parties were aliens. It was less inhibited by the precepts of common law, had the power to oblige witnesses to attend, and could deal with actions with an overseas element. When the chancellor accepted a plea, he ordered the defendant to appear before him by subpoena, the penalty to be forfeited for non-appearance. Examination was under oath and was not necessarily restricted to specific questions raised in the complaint; issues of both fact and of law could be decided by the chancellor. His decision, which he could back up with an order for contempt, might well have differed from that which would have been reached in common law, but because it was *ad personam*, it did not necessarily (but could) affect common law.[3]

Maritime cases presented special difficulties to common law courts because of their technical content, the transient life-style of the witnesses, and the rule that cases had to be tried by a jury drawn from the place where the complaint had been laid. By the beginning of the reign of Richard II, plaintiffs in maritime suits, caught in the cumbersome and restrictive procedural net, were frequently obliged to direct their petitions to the chancellor, entreating him personally for remedy. That procedure offered many inherent advantages to seamen engaged in overseas trading: speed, no jury requirement (and therefore no geographical limitations), no restriction to specific questions raised in the complaint, and the power to oblige even foreign witnesses to attend without a royal warrant. Those advantages had to be weighed, however, against the additional expense incurred in pleading in the Chancery Court.

Common law

One important result of equity decisions made in the Court of Chancery was the acceptance by common law of the precept of 'trust', concomitant with 'use'. Trust was frequently used de facto amongst medieval merchants, and probably

---

[3] Martin, *Modern Equity*, p. 7, citing Frederick Pollock, ed., *Table Talk of John Selden* (1927), p. 43; e.g. PRO, *Ancient Petitions*, SC8/81.

between shipowners and their shipmasters, when passing the custody of goods (or a ship) over to another for trading 'to the use of' or 'to their best avail'; in other words putting the goods into trust. The *de jure* acceptance of trust at common law avoided the necessity of a formal partnership between the parties involved, but the absence of written evidence of such agreements has the effect of making this *commenda* type of partnership appear to be less common in England than on the continent (there was no English word for this type of agreement). In fact, *commenda*-like arrangements between partners for service were not uncommon and were *commenda* partnerships in all but name. The use of trust also deferred the recognition at common law of the obligations of service contract, at considerable cost to the courts in lost business. The concepts of trust, contract and partnership in relation to the ownership of ships are explored further in chapter 3.[4]

The recognition of commerce by common law
Title to goods, their quality, and the enforcement of payment terms were three of the pillars of commerce; another was the problem of recognition of the obligations of service contract. Medieval common law's view of ownership of movables, or 'title', was grounded on possession, and its view of responsibility for the soundness of the product was justified, in effect, by the negative. As the courts of markets and fairs practising merchant law declined in number in the mid-fourteenth century, commercial complaints had to be pursued at common law. Thus, litigation arising from, as examples, bona fide purchases of stolen property, loans, debts, breaches of contract, faulty goods and failure to meet the terms of a financial obligation, went to courts practising common law, but only through the less than adequate procedure of Chancery writs. As common law courts took over the jurisdiction of the fair courts however, they began to absorb some of the precepts of the law merchant, recognising at the same time the legal privileges which had been extended to merchants. An important example of this absorption was the eventual acceptance of legally binding contracts. Eventually, common law courts gave full recognition to the law merchant, not by way of a judicial notice of a proposition of law, but by accepting evidence of mercantile custom as a question of fact. Merchant law continued to be practised by the Staple courts and so controlled the legal aspects of English foreign trade for at least a further century, but because of the osmosis from merchant to common law, it became well established that

---

[4] Postan, *Medieval Trade, passim*; and Maitland, 'Trust and Corporation', III, p. 333 and *passim*. A *commenda* contract was an agreement between a sedentary investor, the *commendator*, and a travelling associate, the *tractator*. The *commendator* risked only the capital advanced and was exposed to no other losses. The contract ended when the *tractator* returned and profits were distributed. It was a convenient tool used to circumvent restrictive usury laws and reduce capital risk.

merchants could withdraw their suits from the former and submit them to the latter.[5]

Criminal, common, merchant and maritime law, each to a varying degree, recognised evidence, backed by compurgation, as acceptable proof. In this procedure, the plaintiff or defendant and six to eleven witnesses swore to the truth of a statement in a formal ritual; if it was carried out correctly and precisely, then the evidence was accepted as true, the fear of spiritual punishment for perjury being so profound. Compurgation could not be used to prove a negative and so the process, also known as 'to wage one's law', was frequently limited to the plaintiff. In common law, compurgation was used by the defendant in trials of debt and detinue raised on informal contracts, but the complex and intimidating procedure could easily fail by a simple mistake. A defendant in a complaint heard at the fair court of St Ives in 1287 attempted to wage his law, but one of his compurgators named the defendant Robert instead of Henry and so the defendant lost the suit. Compurgation was used at maritime law in 1382 in *Hamely* v. *Alveston*, a plea heard in Padstow and discussed in the next chapter. Compurgation lingered in civil actions until seen to be farcical and abandoned in the reign of William IV.

The common law attitude to 'service contract' and to 'title' through the fourteenth and fifteenth centuries, is important in an examination of medieval partnerships, trading agreements, credits and loans, charter-parties and other obligations. It is first necessary, however, to differentiate between formal and informal, or *parol*, agreements. The latter had intrinsic and important deficiencies: although actions arising from informal agreements for debts *sur contract* could be brought to common law courts, breaches of agreement to do something, such as to make a delivery of goods, were not actionable. Other deficiencies in the law's view of informal contracts, including rules which could not be questioned, were that debts of this type died with the debtor and so freed the executor from liability, and that there could be no recognition of informal guarantees. These and other defects led to the development of equitable remedies by the Court of Chancery and since equity effectively supplemented common law in commercial matters, the defects may have been the catalyst required for common law jurists to begin to take more interest in such affairs.[6]

Informal contracts were therefore of restricted use for general business purposes until the introduction for private citizens of actions for wrongs or torts early in the second half of the fourteenth century. Such actions for 'trespass', as they were known, were initiated by a 'writ on the case' which was flexible and could be drafted for the special circumstances of the case. Trial was by a jury which

---

5   *The Little Red Book of Bristol*, ed. F.B. Bickley, 2 vols (Bristol and London, 1900), 1, p. 68: 'De feoffatis infra bundes etc', and pp. 57–8: 'Incipit lex mercatoria, que, quando, ubi, inter quos et de quibus sit.' See also Goode, *Commercial Law*, p. 32.
6   Cheshire and Fifoot, *Contract*, pp. 2–6.

assessed the remedial damages. Amongst the trespasses brought for remedy were actions of *assumpsit* in which the plaintiff alleged that the defendant had failed, by negligence, to complete the obligations which he had undertaken in exchange for 'consideration', an entirely new concept of 'contract' distinct from 'use': 'Verily if this action be maintainable on this matter, for every broken covenant in the world a man shall have an action of trespass', as Justice Martin said in 1425. Because in such actions the plaintiff was not required to produce evidence under seal, the procedure was open to abuse until, finally, in the first half of the fifteenth century a compromise was devised whereby *assumpsit* was taken for misfeasance (doing something badly), but not for nonfeasance (not completing the undertaking). Nevertheless, the first tentative step towards the recognition of 'service contract' had been taken.[7]

Although common law was becoming more flexible, it could also be harsh. Because it was a standard premise that a document was firm proof and that an unsupported *parol* agreement could not stand against it, an informal agreement could be without remedy. Important agreements were therefore made in writing and authenticated by sealing; early written 'contracts' then became actionable at common law following one of two forms of action. First, an action of covenant, which had come into use in the thirteenth century as an action for the specific performance of agreements to do something, such as to deliver certain goods to a determined place, developed into an action for damages, assessed by a jury, for the wrong of breaking a covenant. In the early fourteenth century, this action came to be limited to agreements under seal and hence the term 'covenant', originally meaning simply an agreement, came to mean an 'agreement under seal'. The seal was, therefore, virtually essential in common law, a requirement set out by Fleta, whether it were simply a blob of wax impressed with a fingernail or something more elaborate.[8]

The action of covenant was little used, however, and important contracts were generally reduced instead to agreements whereby the parties entered into bonds to pay penal sums of money unless they carried out their side of the bargain. If a written and sealed obligation was fulfilled, the penal bond became void (a condition of 'defeasance'); if it was not fulfilled then the terms of the bond had to be honoured. Disputes as to whether the conditions, which contained the real agreement, had been fulfilled or not, were to be decided by a jury. Such penal bonds with conditional defeasance could be adapted to cover virtually any transaction and were widely used as early contractual instruments. In the vast preponderance of medieval common law cases concerning contract, the dispute was over the bonds, their illegality or impossibility and the rules which governed them; the

---

[7] *Year Book* 3 Henry VI, fo. 36, pl. 33.
[8] 'Non solum sufficiet scriptura nisi sigilli munimine stipulantis roboretur cum testimonio fide dignorum praesentium', Holdsworth, *History*, 3, p. 417, quoting Fleta, ii, 60, 25.

law's approach to the disputed contract was, therefore, from a 'reverse angle'. Also, as in the treatment of informal agreements, the law of formal agreements could be harsh; a lost bond or one which had lost its seal was without remedy; for example a debtor who had paid but had failed to have his copy of the bond endorsed, remained liable. A debtor remained in the hands of his creditor, who could have him committed to prison for default until he had paid – and could prove it.[9]

It was as late as the third quarter of the fourteenth century before common law courts could be relied upon to give a hearing, fair in the view of merchants and shipmasters, to cases which involved service contracts and the other basic instruments of business. Until then, those engaged in commerce who wished to pursue a perceived wrong, had to find a suitable court elsewhere. They could try the court of the local fair or market (by then disappearing), or the mayoral court (where their pleas would be heard at merchant law), or one of the developing admiralty courts should their business be maritime (see the next chapter). If all else failed, there were the more expensive options of the Court of Chancery or of presenting a bill to Parliament.

Merchant law

For hundreds of years merchant law subsisted in England as a distinct source of law administered by its own mercantile courts, until it was ultimately absorbed into common law. Until the fourteenth century, the English-owned mercantile fleet was comparatively small and generally confined to coastal or cross-Channel work. The few denizen mariners with commercial grievances pursued them locally, using the market, fair or borough courts practising merchant law. Statutorily, the *Carta Mercatoria* of 1303 gave aliens the right to be tried in local courts without delay by a jury made up of equal numbers of their compatriots and of denizens, and many suits in which that privilege was used have been recorded. Some alien merchants and mariners had alternative, and usually preferable, recourse to their own courts granted by charters and treaties; members of the Hanseatic League, for example, were given the right in 1282 in the city of London, and in 1310 in Lynn, to be tried in commercial litigation before two burgesses of the city and two Hanseatic merchants.[10]

It was probably not uncommon for native and foreign mariners and merchants, when they had to turn to litigation in minor disputes, to appear with the local traders in the 'piepowder' courts of the markets and fairs. Those courts were informal in nature, the name deriving from the Norman-French *pieds pouldres* ('dusty feet'), and were required to produce a verdict before the end of the day, a

---

[9] Cheshire and Fifoot, *Contract*, p. 3.
[10] *Statutes*, 27 Edward III, st. 2, cc. 1–29. *CPMR*, I, p. 359.

requirement similar to that in the port towns' courts where, 'for straunge marynerys passaunt and for them that abyden not but her tyde [pleas] shuldene ben pleted from tyde to tyde'. The courts, similar to those of northern Europe, were held before the mayor and bailiffs; some boroughs had such courts as part of the municipal judiciary even without a market or fair, specifically to try without delay suits in which transient merchants were involved. In Bristol, for example, a piepowder court was held during the annual 14-day fair and during the rest of the year the tolsey court administered justice. Pleas were begun without a writ and there were few formalities; all types of plea could be heard including trespass, debt and contract, but not those concerning land nor serious crimes which were reserved for royal justices. The law the courts administered was derived from the customs of English and continental merchants and in the fourteenth century was still relatively unevolved. It reflected enough of the continental *lex mercatoria* to be acceptable to both native and foreign litigants, stood apart from common law, was specifically for mercantile transactions rather than for merchants, and was in effect a body of rules of required evidence (proof of sale, for example) in a disputed agreement.

Although the law merchant was of such importance to merchants and appears to have had a considerable effect on the law practised in local courts, direct reference to it by name is strangely absent from borough custumals. The only sure surviving evidence of the influence of merchant law on the workings of local courts comes from before the fourteenth century. Examples include the pleas of persons passing through London in 1221 who were unable to wait for the Hustings, the pleas over debts to be heard without writs in Bristol in c.1240, and the necessity of immediacy in hearing pleas of strangers (from hour to hour, after dinner as well) and mariners (from tide to tide) in Ipswich in 1291.[11]

Because of the natural association between port towns, merchants and ships, the laws merchant and maritime had aims and problems in common. In addition to their remote common ancestor, to a certain extent they grew up together although their appearance in England was probably neither synchronous nor sudden; both codes arrived in an elementary form and developed individually with use and experience. That they marched together may be seen in the frequent instructions to justices to proceed in piracy claims 'following the law and customs of Oleron and similarly the law merchant'. Both were seen as species of *jus gentium* available across frontiers and both were victims of the jealousy of common law courts.[12]

The rationale of merchant law was that, unlike common law, decisions should

---

[11] *The Acts of the Parliament of Scotland*, I, part 2, p. 725 (*t*. King David, 1124–53): 'De placito inter piepoudrous.' Gross and Hall, *Law Merchant*, I, p. xiv, citing Bracton, fo. 34. Twiss, *Black Book*, I, pp. 16–20; Bateson, *Borough Customs*, pp. 183–5, as in a case before the mayor and bailiffs of Bristol in 12 Edward III.

[12] 'secundum legem et consuetudinem de Oleron et similiter legem mercatoriam'; Twiss, *Black Book*, I, pp. lxi–lxii.

be in the interests of commerce. 'In what way the law merchant differs from common law' is explained in a treatise in the *Little Red Book of Bristol*. In common law, proof of purchase in good faith merely relieved the innocent third party from the possibility of punishment for theft, and the goods had to be returned to the true owner without restoration of the purchase money. In the law merchant, with the interests of commerce in mind, the true owner had to refund the purchase price to the bona fide purchaser on the return of the stolen goods, in effect a repurchase by the owner of his own property. Also in merchant law, whoever pledged for anyone to answer for trespass, covenant, debt or detinue of chattels, pledged for the whole of the damages and expenses, which was not the view at common law. Further, in common law the precept *caveat emptor* ('buyer beware') prevailed and there was no obligation on the vendor to reveal defects in his goods (unless they were victuals); in merchant law the responsibility for the quality of the goods remained with the vendor.[13]

Yet another important difference between the codes of law was in the master/servant relationship, which in the context of shipowner/shipmaster or shipmaster/crew is particularly relevant. In merchant law the principle was that 'no merchant ... shall lose or forfeit his goods or merchandise for any trespass or forfeiture incurred by his servant, unless his act is by the command and consent of his master'. The philosophy behind that was clearly that if a master was to be held responsible for the acts of his servant, especially if they had been perpetrated against his instructions, there would be a considerable brake on trade and the appointment of agents would be a hazardous affair. A master was held responsible however, when his apprentice or servant, publicy known to be trading for him, bought on credit for his master's use. Similarly, if a merchant creditor could prove that the apprentice or servant who bought certain goods was with his master at the time and conveyed the goods to him, the master was responsible for the debt. An example may be seen in a plea brought before the mayoral court in London in 1389. John Forteneye, an apprentice of John Mokkyng of London, bought from John Costace of Gascony 10 casks of Gascon wine in Sandwich for £57 18s. 4d. (from the price, the casks appear to have been tuns). The casks were landed, gauged and filled in London but Forteneye refused delivery and would not pay for them on the grounds of some unreported irregularity; the jury were divided in their opinion but four vintners decided in favour of Costace, and Forteneye was gaoled. The latter then brought a bill against his master, Mokkyng, alleging that Mokkyng had approved the purchase of the wine but had refused to accept it when it reached London, and that the profit from the bargain was not for himself but for Mokkyng. The court decided in Forteneye's favour, released him from gaol

---

[13] 'Quomodo lex mercatoria differt a lege commune': Bickley, *Red Book*, 1, p. 58. Bateson, *Borough Customs*, 2, pp. lxxvi–lxxix. A further complication was the rules of 'market overt'.

and ordered Mokkyng to pay Costace after deducting 51s. 8d. for gauging and other expenses.[14]

The question of a shipowner's responsibility for the actions of his ship's master, or a shipmaster's responsibility for those of his crew, is extremely important. Although merchant and maritime law generally saw questions in a similar light, in the area of a shipmaster's responsibility there may have been a point of difference. The decision in the 1351 case of *Pilk v. Vener(e)* heard in the Bristol 'tolsey' court is puzzling. The hearing was in a local court which would normally have worked in merchant law, but both parties to the dispute agreed to the case being heard at maritime law and the 'law of the country'. The dispute was whether a shipmaster could be held responsible for theft from the cargo by members of his crew; the theft itself was not in dispute. The plaintiff claimed that the shipmaster was always responsible for the conduct of his crew; the defendant pleaded that only if the shipmaster had given a surety for the goods could he be held responsible. The court decided in favour of the plaintiff making it clear that a shipmaster is responsible for any criminal act perpetrated by his crew even if they were not acting under his instruction. Since the case was heard at maritime law and the 'law of the country', the court appears to have accepted the position of the latter.[15]

The case went to appeal, the result of which is unfortunately not known; it may be that the lower court decision was reversed and that the position at maritime and merchant law was seen to be identical. There are two pointers suggestive of disagreement by the superior court with the lower court's decision. First, the king instructed the mayor and bailiffs to certify the case, which had been heard *sine brevi nostro*, together with their decision, to the chancellor. That unusual order may have reflected jurisprudential disquiet at the decision or it may have been reaction to complaints from the defendant and possibly other shipmasters. Second, in the report on the case three textual corrections are apparent: in the introductory passage, the words 'secundum legem de Olerun deducta' are superscript and not on the text line, and in the body of the report, the words printed here in square brackets were inserted in the following phrases: 'secundum legem et consuetudinem [regni domini Regis Anglie ac leges] de Oleron' in one place and 'quod lex [Anglie et de] Oleron' in another. It appears that in the writing of the report there was some doubt about which code had been used at the hearing – or, *ex post facto*, common law was seen as best explaining the apparently anomalous decision of the lower court. *Pilk v. Vener(e)* remains an important case without a satisfactory conclusion or explanation.

Merchant law's view of the master/servant relationship was confirmed in 1442

---

[14] *Statutes*, 27 Edward III, st. 2 (Statute of the Staple), c. 19; Bickley, *Red Book*, 1, p. 66: 'Quod mercatores respondeant etc.', and *CPMR, 1381–1412*, pp. xxx and 162–3, 4 July 1389.
[15] PRO C 47/59/2/48 mm. 1, 2 and 5–7.

in a petition to Parliament, in which a statute of Edward III and the law merchant were quoted as holding that

> no ... possessor or owner of ships ... lese nor be enpeached, constreyned nor put to answer ... by any officer or minister of the Kyng for the deedes, trespasses or offences doon upon the water by any other person beying in shippes ... than by hymself, but if it be hys commaundement, abettement or consent.

The 1353 Statute of the Staple extended the terms of the *Carta Mercatoria* of 1303, providing special courts in which merchant law was administered 'to give courage to merchants strangers to come with their wares and merchandise into the realm'. The English, Welsh and Irish Staple towns introduced Staple courts in which a chosen mayor and two constables administered justice swiftly, 'from day to day and from hour to hour', according to the law merchant, for all merchants coming to the Staple. The statute prescribed paramountcy for merchant law in mercantile disputes, expressly excluding common law where it conflicted with merchant law. Merchant plaintiffs, and presumably shipmasters, had the choice of suing in a Staple court at Staple law or elsewhere at common law for debt, covenant or trespass (although pleas of land or for felonies still had to be tried in common law courts). The king's justices and officers were to stay out of Staple affairs but there was to be a right of appeal to the chancellor or the King's Council. The composition of an inquest could be wholly alien, half alien and half denizen, or wholly denizen reflecting the origins of the parties in a dispute, and the mediators of a question were to be two of 'Almaigne', two of Lombardy and two of England.[16]

The new courts' procedure, the law to be applied and the control by the merchants themselves, reflected the procedures that prevailed all over the continent. Bargains made at the Staple were to be recorded by a Corrector and the mayor of the Staple was to take 'recognizances' and seal letters of obligations of debts (promissory notes), which gave the creditor statutory rights to a defaulting debtor's property, a development of the provisions of the earlier acts of 1283 and 1285. However, there was a further important innovation in the Statute of the Staple: 'And in cases that no creditor will have letters of the said seal, but will stand to the faith of the debtor, if after the term incurred he demand the debt, the debtor shall be delivered upon that faith.' In other words, after the Statute of the Staple, English merchant law was prepared to accept the concept of good faith, including unsealed letters recognising debt. This adaptability of merchant law was especially important in the development of acceptance of negotiable instruments. Long before it became acceptable in common law, merchant law recognised that the right to a sum of money embodied in a bill of exchange or promissory note

---

[16] *Rot. Parl.*, 1439–68, pp. 55–6, 20 Henry VI, no. IX: 'That masters of ships may not be punishable for the servant's faults.' *Statutes*, 27 Edward III, st. 2, cc. 1–28 (1353), Statute of the Staple.

could be conferred, even although the instrument was not under seal. When common law did eventually accept the binding force of executory instruments, it imposed restrictions which had not operated under merchant law. The Commons' reaction to the statute was immediate and inevitable; they complained 'that in many cases the Commons would be judged and ruled by the Laws and Usages of the Staple which are all unknown to the Commons'; which elicited the royal *Responsio* that the 'usages would be openly declared'.[17]

Maritime law

Northern European medieval maritime law was based largely on the *Lex d'Oleron* [hereafter *Oleron*], reputedly formulated by Richard Coeur de Lion some time after his return from the Holy Land in 1194. The history of *Oleron*, its origins in the classical Mediterranean sea laws *Lex Rhodia* and *Consolate del Mare*, and its development into the several versions used around the coasts of western and northern Europe, have been explored by, among others, Twiss in the 1870s, Studer in 1913 and Krieger in 1970, following the pioneering work from the seventeenth century onwards of Selden, Cleirac, Verwer and Pardessus. The consensus of scholarly opinion posits two versions of *Oleron* descendant from a twelfth-century southern French compilation derived from the ancient Mediterranean maritime laws. From one version the Flemish and German codes, and from the other the Castilian and Anglo-Norman codes, descended. The Anglo-Norman version of *Oleron* is the most relevant to English medieval shipping. Studer believed that it was drawn up about 1200 and was probably in operation from then, perhaps only locally. From references to the *loy doleron*, the *statuta de Olerona* and the *lex maritima* in local and admiralty courts, it is clear that by at least early in the fourteenth century *Oleron* had been generally accepted in England. For example, in 1339 the mayor and bailiffs of Bristol certified to the lord chancellor that the hearing of *Pilk v. Vener(e)* (discussed above) conformed to the 'lex et consuetudo de Oleron'. The articles of *Oleron* are presented as court decisions; in the Anglo-Norman manuscripts they start with the formulaic 'Ceo est la copie de la chartre Doliroun de jugemenz de la mer' ('This is the copy of maritime judgments in the charter of Oleron'), and each article ends with 'Et ceo est le jugement en ceo cas' ('And this is the judgment in this case').[18]

---

[17] *Statutes*, 11 or 13 Edward I, Statute of Acton Burnell; 13 Edward I, st. 3, Statute of Merchants, c.1; and 27 Edward III, st. 2, Statute of the Staple, cc. 9 and 22; 'q'en plusurs cases les Communes serront juggez & reulez par les Leys & Usages de l'Estaple, queles sont de tout desconuz a les Communes': *Rot. Parl.*, 2, 28 Edward III, p. 261, no. 47.

[18] Twiss, *Black Book, passim*; *The Oak Book of Southampton, c.AD 1300*, ed. Paul Studer, SRS, 2 vols and suppl. (Southampton, 1910–13), II, *passim*; *Ursprung und Wurzeln des Rôles D'Oléron*, ed. Karl-Friedrich Krieger, Quellen und Darstellungen zur Hansischen Geschichte, Neue

1 The first page of the *Lex d'Oleron* from the *Liber Horn*. The first line reads 'Ceo est la copie de la chartre Doliroun des iugemenz'. Folio 355v of MS *Liber Horn*, reproduced with the kind permission of the City of London Metropolitan Archives.

The two earliest known copies of *Oleron* in England are in the Guildhall, London. Studer agrees with Twiss in suggesting that the copy bound into the *Liber Memorandum* [LM] is the earlier because the marginal and superscript additions and corrections to the copy in the *Liber Horn* [LH] appear to be later. Krieger awarded seniority to LH because of certain earlier grammatical characteristics (for example, the plural of *il*) and because he believed that LM was a copy of LH, written before the corrections were made. Twiss and Krieger agreed, however, that both the manuscripts had been copied around 1315, their inclusion in the *Libri* indicated that the *Lex* was recognised in London at least as early as the first quarter of the fourteenth century, that they are of sound provenance and that they are copies, directly or indirectly, of an Anglo-Norman original.

The number of articles in the surviving copies of *Oleron* varies considerably: 24 in LH and LM, 24 or 26 in other Anglo-Norman manuscripts, 27 in the version in the *Oak Book of Southampton*, 35 in the fifteenth-century MSS Selden, Vespasian and Whitehall and 47 in the Breton version. The last three articles in the *Oak Book* do not occur elsewhere and concern pilots, the beginning of a Letter Patent from Edward I and a re-statement of the 1275 statute on wreck.[19]

The extra articles in the other manuscripts were added to reflect local practices or changes in maritime procedure; for example, the additional 11 in the 35-article manuscripts were added for the use of admiralty after the period here considered. They cover the definition of wreck and the rights, obligations and duties of the finders and the care of survivors. Interestingly, article 32 in the expanded versions amends an existing provision for jettison and general average (the earlier article 8) and is based on an ordinance of Edward I of 1285. Of the additional 11 articles Twiss writes:

> It was ordained and established for a custom of the sea that their authority rested upon something more than mere usage, but there is nothing which indicates directly the occasion of their being adopted as part of the system of maritime law to be administered in the maritime courts of England.

Folge/ Bande XV (Cologne and Vienna, 1970), *passim*; and, as quoted by Twiss and Krieger, John Selden, *Mare Clausum seu de Dominio Maris* (London, 1635); Cleirac, *Us et Coustumes de la Mer* (Bordeaux, 1661); A. Verwer, *Nederlants Seerechten* (Amsterdam, 1730); and *Collection des lois maritimes antérieures au XVIII siècle*, ed. J.M. Pardessus, 6 vols (Paris, 1828–45).

[19] The manuscripts mentioned here and below are: MS Bodley 462, Bodleian Library, Oxford [MS B]; MS Whitehall in Twiss, *Black Book* [MS W]; MSS *Liber Memorandum* and *Liber Horn*, Corporation of London Records Office, Guildhall, London [MSS LM and LH]; MS Rawlinson B356, Bodleian Libary, Oxford [MS R]; MS Selden B27, Bodleian Library, Oxford [MS S]; MS Cotton Vespasian B XXII, British Library, London [MS V]; MS *Liber Rubeus*, City of Bristol Archives, Bristol [MS LR] and MS 1386 Troyes, Bibliothèque de Troyes [MS T]; The texts of MSS LH, LM, LR and R are essentially the same and with B are fourteenth century; MS T gives the Norman version of the Laws, the *Coustume de Normandie*, and is also fourteenth century. MSS S, W and V, with 35 articles, are fifteenth century; *Statutes*, 3 Edward I, st. 1, c. 4.

The concluding words of the additional articles, however, indicate that they too were judgments handed down by a court or inquisition as were the original 24 articles, confirmation that the additional articles had been adopted in the maritime courts and that they reflected the needs of the expanding shipping industry.[20]

The material in the 24 articles of MSS LH and LM overlap to a certain extent, but may be divided into groups: the rules governing the shipmaster's conduct and responsibilities (1–12, 15, 16, 18–20 and 24); the crew's responsibilities (3, 6, 8, 11, 15 and 21); discipline (5, 6, 12 and 14); terms and conditions of employment (17–21); health and safety considerations (7, 8, 10, 16 and 17); general points of management and seamanship (4, 8, 9, 11, 13, 15, 16 and 22–4); and dealings with the freighting merchants (4, 8–11, 13, 15, 22 and 23). Noticeable deficiencies are any mention of felonies, which presumably were to be dealt with ashore, and any rules for the avoidance of collision at sea, although responsibility for accidents in havens is defined. MS LH, which is the clearer of the two Guildhall manuscripts, has been transcribed and translated, and is printed in Appendix 1 with a commentary; the first folio is shown in Figure 1.

As a code of law, *Oleron* became inadequate when confronted with the increasing complexity of fourteenth-century commercial shipping. To cope with that, the Inquisition of Queenborough was set up by Edward III in 1375 'to make certain the points written below in the manner they were used in ancient times'. The commission sat intermittently until 1403, crystallising certain aspects of maritime law by recording opinions on a number of practical questions posed to the jurors, who sat under oath. By its constitution, the commission brought considerable practical experience to its deliberations. The members, initially, were the Warden of the Cinque Ports, the Admiral of the North, and 19 mariners drawn from ports along the south and east coast of England. Although listed as one inquisition, the articles fall into three groups, each collected at a different time and covering rather different ground. In the first section, articles 1 and 2 concern finds and jettison, 3–15 and 17 set out wage and 'portage' (the crew's freight perquisite) rates, and 16 refers to pilots. In the second section, articles 18–70 list a miscellany of matters into which admirals should inquire or for which they have responsibility: prizes, piracy, aiding the enemy, felonies, deaths, mayhems, desertions, affrays, fishing, customs evasions, discipline, claims to wreck, forestalling and regrating, and misappropriation of ships' buoys and buoy-ropes. In the third section, articles 71–81, there is an extension of the duties and responsibilities of the admirals and, tellingly, their sources of income and rates of charges. In Appendix 2, I give a transcription and translation of the relevant articles from a fifteenth-century Anglo-Norman text preserved in MS Cotton Vespasian Bxxii (hereafter cited as *Queenborough*) and

---

[20] *CPR, 1281–92*, p. 168. Twiss, *Black Book*, I, p. 121 n.3.

reproduced in *The Black Book*, together with a commentary and a summary of the less relevant articles.[21]

A third contribution to an understanding of English medieval maritime law is a collection of court judgments and decisions made on the Isle of Oléron and preserved as *Les Bons Usages et les Bonnes Costumes et les Bons Jugemenz de la Commune d'Oleron* of which a unique copy has survived in MS Douce 227. It is written in a fourteenth-century hand in the Oléronais dialect, a variant of the *langue d'oïl* with affinities with Saintongeaise (the island was in the diocese of Saintes). Twiss transcribed and translated the manuscript in his *Black Book* because a number of the chapters were related to articles in *Oleron*. The manuscript was also transcribed, but not translated, in 1919 by Bémont who added notes on the provenance of the manuscript, the language used and the laws and procedures recorded in what he describes as the *Coutumier* (the title by which it is referred to hereafter). The dating of the manuscript is indicated by the end colophon: 'et fuit completus a. D. m°. cccxl. quarto, scilicet decima die mensis Februarii' ('completed on 10 February 1344'), but the provisions it contains are believed by Bémont and Twiss to be older.[22]

Although most chapters of the *Coutumier* are not relevant to the present review, some are especially useful. In chapter 88 the responsibilities of the shipmaster are more clearly defined than in *Oleron*; chapters 63, 64, 83, 86 and 87 define the mutual responsibilities in law of shipowners in partnership, information which occurs nowhere else; chapter 86 touches on the master/servant relationship which between merchant law and common law had become confused in England; chapter 94 concerns the shipmaster's contribution to general average and chapter 95 defines the responsibilty for hiring pilots. A translation of the relevant chapters of the *Coutumier* may be found in Appendix 3, with a commentary.

Given the obvious importance of the Island of Oléron as a source of maritime jurisprudence, its geographical and historical credentials from the twelfth to the fifteenth centuries is of interest. The island lies off Saintonge in the duchy of Aquitaine, the south end being about 15 nautical miles north of the mouth of the Gironde. Its position on an important trading route no doubt contributed to its prominence in matters concerning maritime law, and its magistrates and *prud'hommes* appear to have built up a reputation as reliable jurists. Its courts were, from the evidence in *Coutumier* chapter 87, available even to those from outside the island seeking equitable solutions to maritime legal problems.

With Eleanor of Aquitaine's marriage to Henry II, in 1154, the island came under English control. It remained so until 1214 when, because of the failed marriage arrangements planned for Henry III's daughter (aged three) to the younger son

---

[21] 'pour mettre en certain les points apres escript en manere comme ilz ont este usez dancien temps': Twiss, *Black Book*, I, pp. 132–7.
[22] Twiss, *Black Book*, II, pp. 254–401; *Coutumier, passim*.

of the count of la Marche, the ownership of Oléron, which was part of the dowry, was in dispute. Henry retrieved his infant daughter, but control of the island was argued until the Conference of Bourges in 1224 when Henry was able to negotiate an agreement with Louis VIII. In 1249 Henry gave the whole of Gascony to his son Edward 'to be held by the king and his heirs as they themselves had held it', a gift which was confirmed several times, latterly with the condition 'that [Oleron] would not be separated from the English crown'. Edward I's well-known ordinance defining the total loss of a ship as that from which no living creature has escaped, not even a cat or a dog, particularly mentions 'the coasts of Saintonge, the Isle of Oléron and of Gascony'. The people of the island remained *fidèles partisans* of England during the Franco-English wars at the end of the thirteenth century, for which the king ordered a payment to them of £1,000 *tournois*.

As he had received the island from his father before succeeding to the throne, so Edward I passed it, with the duchy of Aquitaine, to his son in 1306, to allow him to 'sustain his estate better and more honourably' – provided that he did nothing to alienate the island nor the duchy. Edward did not respect the interdiction and with other territories, gave Oléron to Piers Gaveston in 1308 until the latter's death in 1312, when it reverted to the crown. Following a period of unrest on the island it passed into French protection between 1324 and the 1360 treaty of Brétigny. Edward III then reclaimed possession and in 1362 incorporated Oléron in the principality of Aquitaine under his oldest son. By 1373 the island was again in French hands, a position finalised by the loss of Gascony in the middle of the next century.

The Island of Oléron was therefore under English control for 220 years, with two interruptions in *de facto* governorship from 1214 to 1224 and from 1324 to 1360, although *de jure* sovereignty was still claimed. The date of the MS Douce copy of the *Coutumier*, 1344, is during the second of these breaks in English control of the island; it is not possible to know if the copying of the judgments, which was by order of the mayor of London, was merely a routine municipal administrative matter or an attempt to preserve the island's legal inheritance during a period of political instability. Whatever the reason for making the copies, they make a valuable contribution to the understanding of early maritime law.[23]

A further document of interest, if only indirectly, in any examination of maritime law in medieval England, is the Catalan *Lo Libre de Consolat* (The Book of the Consulate). Two late fourteenth-century Catalan manuscript copies survive in Paris, one of which was printed and published in 1494. A 1791 Castilian edition of the same work, *Codigo de los costumbras maritimas*, has been transcribed and translated by Twiss and it is this translation which is used for reference here, with

---

[23] CCR, I, pp. 345, 386 and 389; *Foedera*, 1, part 1, p. 374, 11 July 1258; *Statutes*, 3 Edward I, st. 1, c. 4; *Gascon Rolls*, PRO C61, III, no. 4914. *Foedera*, 2, part 1, p. 48, 7 June 1308; *Coutumier*, pp. 44–5.

the abbreviated title of *Customs*. *Lo Libre de Consolat* comprises over 300 chapters of legal decisions and opinions by juries and judges on maritime situations. It was known in the thirteenth century, and almost certainly earlier, and was the code of maritime law widely accepted by Mediterranean coastal towns and cities. It is of only limited value to the present work as it does not have an English or Norman provenance, but it does share a common twelfth-century ancestor with the Anglo-Norman *Lex d'Oleron* and many of its chapters are similar in content to articles in that, and to chapters in the *Coutumier*. The similarities are most marked in the rules for the handling and stowage of cargo, jettison and general average; terms and conditions of employment of seamen; seamanship in anchorages; and the rules for partnerships in ship-ownership. There is also a considerable amount of commercial material in *Customs*, particularly referring to responsibility for damage to cargo, the relationship between merchants and shipowners, and dealing with a permutation of examples of frustrated contracts. Although there is a general similarity to what is known of English practices, there are several situations where significantly different legal views are held, some more and others less favourable to one or other of the parties.[24]

The next step

With the existence of a reasonably comprehensive code of maritime law and with the increasing complexity of litigation arising from maritime enterprises, it might be expected that specialised courts would be set up, dedicated to the quick and equitable settlement of disputes between mariners and merchants. The admiralty courts established in the mid-fourteenth century were intended for that purpose but, although for brief periods they worked effectively, within a century the pressure of political, commercial and personal interests contributed to their impotence in all but a narrow range of subjects. Their rise and fall are discussed in the next chapter.

---

[24] Twiss, *Black Book*, III, pp. lix and 35–657; the manuscript is Paris, Bibliothèque Nationale, MS Espagnol 124; *Customs* was published as *Codigo de los costumbras maritimas de Barcelona*, ed. Capmany (Madrid, 1791).

2

The Shipmaster and the Rise and Fall of the Admirals' Courts

Background

Merchants, shipmasters and shipowners who were involved in overseas trade all wished for protection from piracy and spoilage, for rules for the conduct of maritime business and for assurance that action would be taken against those who did not operate within the law. As discussed in the previous chapter, there were available to them many local courts administering justice in commercial and maritime matters. In Bristol, for example, the city custumal specified that actions 'between merchants and ships, or between merchants and merchants, or between ships and ships, on land or sea, whether between denizens or aliens ... could be heard following the laws and decisions of the town'.[1]

By the end of the thirteenth century, however, the increasing amount of business arising from maritime litigation, its technical difficulties and the nomadic life of the appellants, began to prove too much for the non-specialised courts. A good example of the complications which could arise from the lack of a specialised court may be seen in a 1293 *placita in Parliamento* concerning the case of *Helemes* v. *Opright* in which Jacob Helemes and others claimed that a failure to deliver wine was in breach of the terms of a charter-party made under seal. Walter Opright, master of the ship *All Saints*, said in his dramatic defence that, having been driven by storm onto the coast near Helford, his ship was looted by men of the sea and all 36 tuns of wine aboard had been taken. In the course of the proceedings the Warden of the Cinque Ports was instructed to bring the spoilers *Coram Rege*, whence they were passed to the justices assigned to hear cases of spoil. The primary case concerning the breach of the charter-party (in reality a service contract, as yet unrecognised by common law) was heard in Chancery. What had started as a relatively straightforward suit had spread over several judicial authorities. In contrast,

---

[1] 'inter mercatores et nautas, sive inter mercatores et mercatores, sive inter nautas et nautas, sive per terram sive ... mare, utrum fuerint burgenses vel extranei', could be heard 'secundum leges et consuetidines ville': Bateson, *Borough Customs*, 2, p. 193. CCR, 1354–60, pp. 441–2.

in the following year, a case of piracy, *Mulard* v. *Hobbe*, was tried before the King's Bench, perhaps because Walter Hobbe, a shipmaster and alleged pirate, proved to be an extremely elusive witness. Courts, run by judges skilled in merchant and maritime law and appointed by admirals, situated in seaports, working with the alacrity of market courts and with the authority to oblige witnesses to attend and to accept their judgments, were clearly necessary.[2]

The inception of the admirals' courts

The title of 'admiral' is not to be found in the records of English-controlled regions before 1295 when, in Gascony, Barrau de Sescas was appointed 'Admiral of maritime Bayonne and captain of our ships and sailors in that town'. Sescas' title was not confirmed the following year; he was described then as 'captain of the Bayonne fleet' under Sir William Leyburn (probably a Gascon) and John Botetourte, both of whom were described in a royal writ as 'admirals of our English navy'. Despite these Gascon titles, the word 'admiral' appears not to have been used in England until 1300 when Gervase Alard was appointed 'Admiral of the fleet of the Cinque Ports', a responsibility confirmed in 1303 and extended to 'all other ports from the port of Dover by the sea coast westward as far as Cornwall etc.'. Because the title of admiral was not in general use in England before 1300, there could have been no earlier eponymous court.[3]

Further, even after the appointment of the first admiral, there appears to have been no judicial role for him as work which should have been within his scope was directed to officials with no maritime experience. In 1304, a professor of civil law, the Constable of Dover Castle and two representatives of the French king were sent to Calais to inquire into the recurrent reciprocal depradations at sea by men of Calais and of the Cinque Ports. Part of the French defence to charges of piracy was that the spoilers were acting under the orders of Reyner Grimaud, a Genoese who, 'calling himself Admiral of the sea', was exercising the French king's prerogative of defending the ships of his nationals. The inquisition was similar in constitution to an earlier deputation which had included the bishop of London and a professor of civil law and had been sent to France in 1293 to negotiate a settlement over French piracy claims. It is interesting that the 1304 inquisition was apparently not seen as an admiralty responsibility, nor was an admiral appointed to take part even for such an obviously maritime problem.[4]

---

[2] *Rot. Parl.*, 1, 21 Edward II, p. 125 and 128.
[3] *Gascon Rolls*, PRO C61, 3, p. 290, no. 3883 and pp. 322–3, no. 4134. Marsden, *Select Pleas*, p. xii. *Brit. Chron.*, pp. 134–5. *CPR, 1301–7*, p. 111. *Brit. Chron.* p. 136.
[4] 'Admirallum maritime Baionensis et capitaneum nautarum et marinariorum nostrorum in ejusdem [sic] ville': *Gascon Rolls*, 3, p. 290, no. 3883.3 and pp. 322–3, no. 4134. For admirals' dates,

An apparent attempt to remove a maritime case from the Court of Common Pleas in 1296–97 may be less of a signpost to an admiralty court than has been suggested. In *de Beuso v. Crake*, which concerned piracy, counsel for the defence objected to the jurisdiction because no certain venue had been assigned. Further, interestingly, because an admiral had been nominated by the king specifically 'to hear and conclude the pleas of anything done at sea', the counsel wanted none other. Although this implies the existence of an admiral's court, the Justice's reply was 'We have general jurisdiction throughout England but of the Admirals' jurisdiction of which you speak, we know nothing', which either denies the existence of such courts or indicates that Crake and his counsel had run into non-cooperative judicial jealousy. The original manuscript is now lost and the case has to be seen through secondary sources which do not agree amongst themselves about the implication of the Justice's remark, or even on the date of the case. In the absence of any other evidence, it is safer to conclude that there was neither an admiral nor an admiral's court in 1296 and that the plea of the defence counsel has been misunderstood.[5]

During the first 40 years of the fourteenth century, however, courts were certainly held by admirals. The surviving records indicate that their duties were largely, probably wholly, administrative or military rather than legal; admirals were responsible for a wide range of administrative duties ranging from overseeing the navy and maintenance of the Statute of the Staple, to the conservation of oyster beds. From about 1340 admirals appointed by the king were authorised to hear in their own courts at maritime law, cases involving piracy, the retention and distribution of prizes and disputes over wrecks and reprisals. The decision to extend the authority of the admiralty courts to hold judicial inquiries may have arisen from two factors other than the problems of overworked local courts. The first of those factors was the king's growing confidence in English mastery of the seas. In 1321 Edward II had written to the king of France demanding restitution of goods pillaged from an English merchant freighting on a Genoese ship off Sandwich. The merchant was described by Edward as merely 'under assurance of our protection and safe conduct' with no hint of a royal claim to sovereignty of the sea. In the following year Edward appears to have claimed *superioritas maris* because the king of France, in a letter to Edward, reported that English sailors who had assaulted French ships 'described themselves to be custodians of the sea on your behalf'. The concept, or perhaps the rhetoric, of English naval supremacy may thus have begun rather hesitantly in the early 1320s, but it was certainly more apparent after the decisive battle of Sluys in 1340. By 1372, in a petition to Parliament to

---

see *Brit. Chron.*; *CPR*, 1301–7, p. 111; *Foedera*, 1, part 2, p. 961, 28 Jan. 1304: *Ad Regem Franciae*; and *CPR*, 1301–07, p. 208; Marsden, *Select Pleas*, 1, pp. xxxi; xxxii and xvii.
5 'Nous avons poer general per my tut Engleterre mes del poer des Admirals dont vous parles ne savons rien': Marsden, *Select Pleas*, 1, p. xvii.

reduce the duration of impressments, Edward III was described as 'le Roi de la Mier' not only to his own subjects but also to those of other countries, marking a substantial expansion of his claim. The rather laconic *Responsio* to that petition about impressments was that it was the king's pleasure that the navy should be maintained and protected to increase the ease and profit within its power.[6]

The second factor in Edward III's decision to give his admirals authority to hold judicial inquiries arose from the painful results of his subjects' piracy. He had felt obliged to pay, from his own purse, large amounts of compensation to Genoese and Venetian merchants and shipowners, for losses at the hands of English pirates during the 1330s and was anxious to curb these instincts for pillage. The control of his subjects' piratical tendencies was urgent also for political reasons and Edward's immediate solution was to pass the problem of control to his admirals. A commission was appointed in 1339 to consider, *inter alia*, the settlement of outstanding Flemish, French, Spanish and Portuguese claims, the preservation of peace and the maintenance of the king's sovereignty of the sea. Although the appointment of the commission and its remit are recorded, no record has survived of any initial directive to the commission nor of its deliberations and final conclusions. It is probable that, by the use of specialised courts presided over by admirals, a tightening of the control of denizen and alien pirates roaming the trading routes was recommended. The subsequent expansion of the authority of the admirals' courts reflects the commission's contribution to the debate on maritime lawlessness. The three members of the commission who were to advise on the enforcement of the fittest laws to control piracy and on the consequent claims following piracy were ecclesiastics, who brought to the meetings knowledge of the canon and civil codes but not necessarily of common or maritime law. Also in 1339, Edward claimed both a criminal and a civil jurisdiction 'over all people of whatever nationality passing through the English sea', not only to keep the peace but to administer justice according to the *Lex d'Oleron*, the laws and statutes ordained by his forbears. Whatever the situation before the battle at Sluys, there can be no doubt that the claim of jurisdiction *inter omnes gentes* carried more weight abroad after that victory.[7]

The maritime legal situation and the work of courts in which admirals were involved before Edward's claim in 1339, can be discerned faintly from contemporary references in port books, Chancery and Parliamentary records and other archives. For example, in 1323, an admiral was ordered to hold an inquisition on

---

[6] Twiss, *Black Book*, I, pp. 2–87: 'Rules for the Lord Admiral'; 'Instructions what the Lord Admiral is to doe, at sea and land in tyme of war'; and 'Rules or Orders about Matters Belonging to the Admiralty', all transcribed from MS V. *Foedera*, 2, part 1, pp. 455–6, 25 Aug. 1321: *Ad Regem Franciae*, and p. 475, 17 Feb. 1322: *Littera Regis Franciae*. *Rot. Parl.*, 2, part 1, 46 Edward III, p. 311, n. 6.

[7] 'inter omnes gentes naciones cujuscumque per Mare Angliae transeuntes': Marsden, *Select Pleas*, 1, pp. xxxv–xxxvi, xxx–xxxiii and lxi–lxii.

alleged pillage at sea and to seize and restore to the owners the captured alien ship and her cargo, if spoil was established. The inquisition found that there had indeed been pillage and the king issued a writ to the sheriff of Gloucestershire to arrest the spoilers and their ship for trial in the Bristol local court before a jury of merchants and mariners. The admiral's powers at that time appear to have been restricted to holding inquisitions ordered by king's writ and to arrest ships as necessary.

Admirals, however, did not necessarily deal with all cases of piracy. In 1325, Thomas Rente of Pontise alleged in a petition to the King's Council that his ship and cargo of wheat en route to Newcastle had been pillaged by men of Yarmouth, who had justified themselves by claiming that there was a state of war between the kings of England and France. Rente demanded the return of his ship and cargo which was then being held under guard. The *Responsio* was that the petition should be passed to the chancellor for him to inquire into the matter, including the cause of the incident, the value of the spoil and every other circumstance felt to be necessary, and then for him to certify thereon to the king by the third day of Christmas. The outcome of the inquiry and the fate of the petition are not known but, significantly, no admiral was involved. Rente may have hoped to improve his chances in an English court by playing the 'export card' as he claimed that he had intended to load his ship with sea coal for his return passage.[8]

Rente's status as an alien was not a likely reason for bypassing the admiral, for there were other similar cases involving denizens. An Englishman, Hugh Sampson, owner of the ship *Portpays* which had been taken off Brest with 140 tuns of Bordeaux wine, by Frenchmen who had killed her crew, petitioned the Council for restitution in 1327. The Council's response was to deliver the petition into Chancery and there to let 'right be done according to the Law used in the case of arrest'. There were two similar pleas at the same time, a petition by Francis Maffe (or Maffy) and another by Henry (later Geffrey) le Lacer, both London merchants who had been robbed while abroad (although perhaps not at sea) and for whom the Council offered the same redress: that 'justice bee done, according to the Law in such case used', to wit, that the foreigners responsible should have their goods in England impounded. The similarities between the case of Sampson, which had already been resolved, and the others may have persuaded the Council and Chancery not to pass the suits to a lower common law court or to an admiral's court; in the first case perhaps because the question was one of diplomacy, and in the others because to obtain redress from defendants who were abroad was difficult. The conclusion has to be that, at least until 1327, cases of piracy

---

[8] Marsden, *Select Pleas*, I, p. xxiv: *Coram Rege*, Trinity, 18 Edward II, rot. 18, Rex. Appendix 2, *Queenborough*, articles 19, 20 and 70 for the later codification of an admiral's duties. *Rot. Parl.*, I, 19 Edward II, p. 433, no. 9.

involving denizens or aliens, whether as plaintiffs or defendants, were heard before the King's Council or in Chancery.[9]

In 1327 an admiral was called upon to perform a legal if not a judicial duty in a criminal matter. The Admiral of the North was directed by writ to act as one of two commissioners to inquire, by jury drawn from Great Yarmouth, into a case of piracy and murder on the ship *La Pelarym* of Flanders at Whitby, the master, Walter called Fose of Lescluse (Sluys), being one of those killed. The inquisition was required to certify to the crown that justice could be done 'following the law and customs of our king'; the return of the inquisition appears to have been made to Chancery and the indicted were later tried at common law. Later in the century the position of the ship at the time of the murder would have been decisive; at sea, off Whitby, the admiral would have claimed jurisdiction whereas, in Whitby harbour, the regional criminal court would have been paramount. By 1338 the admirals' interest in matters of piracy was increasing, particularly when the malefactors were English, although they still lacked judicial authority. That year, the two Admirals of the Northern and Western fleets and five others were directed by writ to inquire into the pillage of Flemish ships. They were to identify and arrest those responsible by taking evidence on oath from merchants and mariners and other honest and lawful men of Southampton, and to certify the result to the king. The king added a note to the writ that the spoilage was 'to the grave damage and manifest dishonour of us' and that he was concerned that he might have to make good the claims himself.[10]

The result of cases being passed to the chancellor, to the Council or, significantly, for an admirals' inquiry, was that the use of common law courts for allegations of piracy declined. One of the last cases in which piracy was tried as a common law criminal charge was in 1343. Following an inquisition by the Admiral of the Northern fleet concerning the spoil of the ship *Tarryce* of Flanders in the previous year, Sir John Beauchamp, then Constable of the Tower (and to be appointed Admiral of all the fleets in 1360) was ordered to deliver the pirates, whom he had in custody, to the justices in Norfolk. The result of the hearing was that some of the accused were hanged and others, for a variety of reasons, were pardoned. One alibi certified by the admiral was that four of them had equipped ships and served the king on an expedition to Brittany.[11]

Even after admirals' courts had been authorised to hear cases of piracy, there is evidence that at least some still appeared before the Council or the chancellor

---

[9] *Rot. Parl.*, 2, 1 Edward III, p. 435, no. 57; p. 437, no. 66 (Maffy); and no. 67 (le Lacer).
[10] *CPR*, 1324–7, p. 354 (1327). Appendix 2, *Queenborough*, articles 29–34 for the later clarification of an admiral's duties in cases of alleged murder, mayhem, etc. *Foedera*, 2, part 2, pp. 1055–6, 28 Aug. 1338.
[11] Marsden, *Select Pleas*, 1, pp. xxxvii–xxxviii. *Coram Rege*: 16 Edward III, Trinity, rot. 25; 17 Edward III, Trinity, rot. 14; same year, Easter, rot. 5; same term, rot. 28; and same term, rot. 36. In these the legal processes are set out as if there had been two incidents rather than one.

without any admiral's presence. In a letter to the king of Aragon in 1343, Edward III wrote that, in complaints of piracy, the chancellor and Council were to call the parties together and that, in a particular case current at the time in which two Bayonese *naves armatae* had spoiled two Aragonese *cochae*, judgment had been made that the attack was covered by maritime law. A few years later, in 1347, a mandate from Chancery to the sheriff of Devonshire and others ordered them to restore certain wines to Spanish merchants who had had them taken at sea. The wines had been hidden at Dartmouth by John Gordon and others who were required to make full restitution or be taken to the Tower and have their property impounded. In that case there was also a political motive: Edward was anxious not to be seen to violate the treaty with Spain.[12]

An early record of judicial proceedings before an admiral acting alone is of a 1347 certification by the *locum tenens* of the Admiral of the West, Richard, earl of Arundel. A ship, *Le Michel* of Fowey, had been forfeited to the king for robbery at sea by her owner and she was to be given as a gift to Peter Foulk of Winchelsea whose own ship had been sunk, apparently deliberately, in Calais harbour while on the king's business. In the account of the proceedings it certainly appears that Arundel had acted alone in a judicial capacity in what was, in effect, an admiral's court. The year 1347, therefore, might be taken as the year of the conception, if not the birth, of admiralty courts. However, very shortly afterwards, in 1349–51, the Bristol tolsey court heard the case of *Pilk v. Vener(e)*, the somewhat perplexing case discussed in chapter 1, concerning a shipmaster's responsibility for theft by two of his crew. Another example of a maritime case heard in a local court at about the same time concerned a claim for compensation for cargo taken from a captured ship.[13]

At about this time the problem of ownership of goods taken at sea became an issue; the principle in merchant and maritime laws frequently differing from that in common law. In 1349 a common law court decided that the original owners of goods taken at sea retained ownership, a clear enough statement of the position in common law, unfortunately somewhat clouded by a condition in the last sentence which declared that it would be an offence to recover one's goods by force. Four years later, in 1353, it was decided, in a case heard before the Council with the admiral present, that ownership was not lost in maritime law unless the goods remained in the possession of the spoilers for 24 hours. It might be thought, however, that the chances of an owner recovering his pillaged goods from pirates within 24 hours must have been slim. The 1353 decision is known because of a surviving order to Robert de Herle, captain of Calais, to arrest all the wool in a certain ship and to deliver it to a number of London merchants who claimed that the wool was theirs, taken by the king's enemies and then cast up in

---

[12] *Foedera*, 2, part 2, p. 1229, 19 July 1343. CCR, 1346–9, pp. 10–11 (1346).
[13] CPR, 1345–48, p. 260 (1347). PRO C 47/59/2/48 mm. 1, 2 and 5–7.

a storm. In their plea, which had been accepted, the merchants claimed that their serjeants, who had guarded the wool since the wreck, had never been driven off and had asserted the merchants' right of ownership; in short, the wool had not been abandoned.[14]

In 1357, the king of Portugal claimed from Edward III the restitution of goods which had been taken at sea by a French ship and then later by Englishmen. Edward replied that the decision, made by the admiral before whom the Portuguese owner had sued for restitution, was 'rightfully constituted', and that the goods were a good prize and therefore belonged to the Englishmen. It is possible that the plea was merely a summary decision by a local admiral and had not been heard in an admiral's court, but an admiral acting alone, perhaps without writ, appears to have made a legal decision. Strangely, although there was perhaps an argument at merchant law for returning the goods to the owners on payment, that does not seem to have been discussed. The decision would have done nothing to encourage alien merchants.[15]

Other cases heard at this time, in courts presided over by admirals apparently acting in a judicial capacity, include a 1358 case relating to average. In that, as a result of a decision by an admiral sitting alone, the sheriffs of London were ordered to hold under arrest certain merchants until they had each paid Saier Scoef a share of £100, in proportion to the value of their cargo in a total of more than £1,000 freighted on a ship which had been attacked. The £100 was the value of food belonging to Scoef, who was a merchant of London, which had been given by the shipmaster in an attempt to buy off the men who had attacked the ship. The original decision was made by Guy Lord Brian, the Admiral of the West, acting 'in accordance with maritime law' in what appears to have been the earliest case of average to be heard by an admiral.[16]

When the Council or other courts, with an admiral present, could reach the decision that in several areas of complaint the principles of maritime law should be followed, the stage had been set for the appearance of a specialised admiral's court with, perhaps limited, judicial authority. In 1360, John de Pavely was appointed admiral with express powers to hear maritime plaints and punish those found guilty, according to maritime law. Later that year, Sir John Beauchamp, the first High Admiral of all the fleets with deputies responsible for each fleet, had the authority to appoint a further deputy, probably to act as judge in the new admiralty court working in maritime law. That court, it should be noted, was not the somewhat later High Court of the Admiralty.[17]

---

[14] *Law Reports*, 22 Edward III, Mich., pp. 16–17, n. 63; and CCR, 1349–54, pp. 424–5.
[15] *Foedera*, 3, part 1, p. 354, 29 April 1357: *Ad Regem Portugalliae etc.*
[16] CCR 1354–1360, pp. 441–2.
[17] *Foedera*, 3, part 1, p. 479, 26 March 1360: J. de Pavely 'admirallus constituitur': his remit is interesting: 'querelas omnium et singulorum armatae praedictae audiendi et delinquentes incarcerandi castiganti et puniendi et plenam justitiam ac omnia alia et singula quae ad hujusmodi

Despite the Scoef case of 1358, disputed maritime 'business' matters such as average and wages were not included in the remit of the new admirals' courts but remained under the jurisdiction of the existing courts. This may have been because of the expense to which litigants were put in preparing even a relatively small claim, for example for unpaid wages or for a small salvage find, for presentation to an admiral's court and for the principals and witnesses travelling to it. The problem of the expense involved in having recourse to an admiral's court appears to have been perennial; later, complaints of the costs were made to the king and Parliament, particularly when a case was moved up to London from the provinces. Other maritime commercial matters which appear not to have been taken to admiralty courts include disputed contracts, partnership agreements and financial instruments, perhaps because such litigation was reserved by their nature for the courts practising merchant law.[18]

As a further complication to the question of maritime jurisdiction, by the middle of the fourteenth century the court of the Constable and Marshal (the 'Court of Chivalry') had also evolved. Even after the authorisation of the admiralty courts' judicial functions, the Court of Chivalry too was concerned in maritime misdeeds; the case of *Roches v. Hawley*, which dragged on from 1386 to 1402 (with an apparent lull between 1388 and 1393), is an example. John de Roches, who had been engaged by Richard II to guard Brest, attempted to recover from John Hawley of Dartmouth three ships and a quantity of wine and other goods taken from Breton merchants off Pontcroix. This was within Roches' area and the ships had been attacked despite safe-conducts and without the justification of warfare. Hawley was of the family identified as supplying the model for Chaucer's Shipman who 'of nyce conscience took no keep'. Statements were obtained from witnesses in Brittany, London and the West Country but the hearings were disrupted by the deposition of Richard II, and by the disappearance or death of several of the participants. *Roches v. Hawley* may have been sent originally to the Court of Chivalry because it involved aliens and had political undertones, but Richard's use of civil law in that court instead of common law in a common law court, gave rise to fears of absolutism. These fears led, in 1385, to parliamentary complaints that the practice was to the great damage and disquiet of the people. Hawley's lawyer declared in his plea in 1399, before new court officers, that the case should have been heard before an admiral's court, a suggestion which, despite the removal of Richard, was rejected. The visible trail of the case ends in 1402 with an agreement by all parties to take the case to the king and to accept his decision. The

---

capitaneum et ductorem pertinent ... secundum legem maritimam fuerit faciendum.' *Foedera*, 3, part 1, p. 505, 18 July 1360: J. de Bello Campo, comes Warrewici 'admirallus omnium flotarum constituitur'.
[18] *Rot. Parl.*, 3, 17 Richard II, p. 322, no. 49; 4 Henry IV, p. 498, no. 47; 11 Henry IV, p. 642, no. 61.

evolution of the admiralty courts was thus a gradual affair with several judicial processes operating in parallel for some time.[19]

The flourishing of the admirals' courts

The jurisdiction offered by the admirals' courts amounted to discretionary and flexible equity, and something of that and of the working of their courts is visible in the surviving records of two early cases. In *Smale et al. v. Houeel et al.*, heard in the admiral's court at the Wool Quay in London in 1361, the French defendants pleaded that their capture of an English ship was an act of war; if there had been a truce in operation they were unaware of it and anyway the recent treaty (of Brétigny, in 1360) precluded any claims made for wartime capture. The English plaintiffs objected that the defendants had given three responses of which each one would have been sufficient, in other words, multiplicity.

The admiral's court was not impressed by that objection and, importantly, claimed 'this court, which is the office of the admiral, will not be governed as narrowly as other courts of the kingdom which follow the common law of the country, but decides by equity and maritime law'. This statement demonstrates remarkable independence and confidence and makes clear how an early admiral's court saw its duty. Further, that it overruled a denizen's plea in favour of an alien must have further enhanced its reputation abroad. After a postponement, the plaintiffs produced evidence of a truce at the time of the incident and were awarded damages. The defendants, who did not dispute the award, had to remain in custody until they had paid but no action was taken against them for the act of piracy or for the deaths of the crew of the captured ship.[20]

An example of the flexibility of an admiral's court may be seen in the 1369 order to the earl of Devon and others, to set free and to make restitution to Hugh Peyntor, a merchant of Vannes, who had been cleared of allegations of adherence to the king's French enemies. The case was transferred on the king's instructions to the jurisdiction of the Admiral of the North from that of the Admiral of the West, in whose bailiwick the arrest had been made but who was engaged elsewhere on the king's business. The Admiral of the North was commanded to call before him the merchant and anyone else he required, and to deal with the former, his ship, goods and seamen, according to maritime law. With him he had three common

---

[19] Michael Jones, '*Roches contre Hawley*: la cour anglaise de chevalerie et un cas de piraterie à Brest, 1386–1402', *Mémoires de la société d'histoire et d'archéologie de Bretagne*, LXIV (1987), citing PRO C47/6/4 rolls 1–9 and C47/6/6 rolls 8–9.

[20] 'pur ceo qe ceste court qest office dadmiralle ne serra pas rulle si estroit come serront les autres courtz du roialme qe sont rullez par comune ley de la terre, mes est reullable par equite et ley marine': Charles Johnson, ed., *An Early Admiralty Case*, Camden Miscellany, 3rd series XV (1929).

law lawyers and the constable of the Tower of London. During his examination (in the port of London), the defendant claimed he was in no wise guilty and put himself upon the country; the sworn jury found him and his crew not guilty. The willingness of the king to move the hearing from one admiral's area to another so that the merchant should not be detained longer in prison was perhaps a reflection of the merchant's influence in high circles, but it also demonstrates the flexibility of working of the admirals' courts. The use of a sworn jury and of legally qualified assistants in an admiral's court is also of interest; it must be presumed that the lawyers and jurors had experience of maritime affairs even if not qualified in maritime law.[21]

Once established, the admirals' courts did their best, despite competition from merchant and common law courts, to attract all the business they could within their 'Rules or Orders about Matters belonging to the Admiralty' of c.1340, and later confirmed at the end of the fourteenth or very early in the fifteenth century in the second section of the *Inquisition of Queenborough*, both of which have been discussed above. The scope of the admiralty courts was summarised in the sentence 'Every contract made between merchant and merchant, or merchant and mariner, overseas or within the tide mark, will be tried before the admiral and no-one else, by order of king Edward and his lords'. Further, 'divers lords' were forbidden from trying pleas in ports if they concerned merchants or mariners, including cases concerning charter-parties, obligations and other matters of fact. An inquiry was to be held into anyone who sued at common law, a merchant, mariner or any other person in a matter belonging to the *marine auncien droit*. If they were indicted and convicted by a jury of twelve men, they were to be fined and have to withdraw their suit from common law and bring it into an admiralty court if they wished to proceed further. An example of the esteem in which an admiral's court was held at that time was an order by the king in 1371 to John Lord Nevill, Admiral of the North, and Guy Lord Brian, Admiral of the West to resolve by inquiry the tangle of complaints from Flemish merchants who had been spoiled at sea.[22]

The High Court of Admiralty was probably formally constituted during the sitting of the Inquisition of Queenborough, but unfortunately cases heard before the High Court were recorded only from about 1524, despite an express instruction to keep a record 'according to maritime law and the ancient customs of the sea'. The admirals' courts did not get off to a flying start and, indeed, there were many missed opportunities in maritime legal affairs when admirals could have

---

[21] CCR, 1369–74, pp. 369–370.
[22] 'Chascun contract fait entre marchant et marchant ou marchant ou mariner outre la mer ou dedens le flodemark sera trie devant ladmiral et nenient ailleurs par lordonnance du dit Roy Edward et ses seigneurs.' For the constitution of the Inquisition of Queenborough, see p. 23; Appendix 2, *Queenborough*, articles 18–80 and especially 51 and 52. Foedera, 3, part 2, p. 907, 1 Jan. 1371: 'Pro mercatoribus Januae, etc.', and p. 917, 24 and 25 May 1371, 'Pro mercatoribus de Bruges, etc.'.

been called to assist. Commissions of *oyer et terminer* were appointed on two separate occasions without admirals in 1376 to examine petitions for the restitution of losses to English pirates in English waters, although in both cases Guy Lord Brian, by then no longer the Admiral of the West, was a member, either as a quondam admiral or as a reliable committee member. Significantly, one of the commissions was instructed 'to determine the premises according to law and the customs of the realm and [specifically] maritime law but our [the king's] intention is that the office of the Admiral shall be in no way prejudiced under colour of these presents'. In the following year there were two more commissions of *oyer et terminer* to examine maritime incidents on neither of which was there an admiral, current or former. Both of those cases concerned Hansa ships wrecked by storm on the coasts of Lincolnshire, Norfolk, Kent and Essex and afterwards pillaged; the king had already decided to pay compensation, no doubt under the pressure which alien merchants could exert.[23]

There were other cases which unexpectedly did not go before an admiral's court and are worth considering in some detail because of that and because of their content. In 1381, in the case of *Hamely v. Alveston* heard in the 'maritime court' of Padstow, John Alveston was found guilty of pillaging Osbert Hamely's ship in Plymouth harbour when she was fitted out and ready to sail to Bordeaux for the wine harvest. John failed to pay the 200 marks awarded to Osbert and because the former did not have anything within the bailiwick of Padstow which could be arrested, the latter appealed to the king for an order against him. For this petition to be heard, a full account of the trial in Padstow had to be sent up to London and this has most usefully survived in the *Coram Rege* Roll. The case was not heard in an admiral's court at the first instance, although tried according to maritime law, but before a 'maritime court' with a jury of merchants, the justification for the hearing in that court being that the assault took place 'in Plymouth harbour where the tide ebbs and flows'. Compurgation (see p. 13) was used by the plaintiff with six trustworthy men to substantiate his plea; and the appeal for execution of the judgment was heard before the King's Bench, the complaint having mutated into one of trespass for non-compliance with a court order.

The Padstow hearing reveals the workings of a port town's maritime court; it first sat on a Friday at the first hour of the flood tide and was postponed until the following day at the same tide-time in accordance with maritime law and custom (in other words, 48 minutes later). The petitioner duly appeared at the third hour of flood-tide on the Saturday but the defendant sent along his shipmaster who asked for a further postponement until Tuesday. Having missed Tuesday's scheduled appearance, Alveston finally turned up on the Wednesday at the first hour of the flood-tide; the court's tolerance of the accused's failures to appear is remark-

---

[23] *CPR, 1374–1377*, pp. 408, 410 and 417.

able. In the subsequent litigation before the King's Bench, Alveston claimed that the local court had no jurisdiction, that Padstow was not an ancient borough, the mayor and burgesses had no authority to hear pleas and they had not been deputed by the admiral to try such cases. Hamely disputed all those criticisms of the Padstow court and maintained his claim. The case ended with something of a whimper when the King's Bench reserved judgment followed by a *sine die* postponement while Alveston served under the command of Sir John de Roches, captain of the castle of Brest.[24]

The case of *Hamely* v. *Alveston* may have been one of those, together with the cases of *Gernesey* v. *Henton* and *Sampson* v. *Curteys*, both of which are discussed below, to which reference was made in the petitions to king and to Parliament and which led to the statutes defining and restraining the admirals' jurisdiction. Other piracy cases which were not heard by an admiral include the 1383 trial of William Wilton and John Gloucester before the King's Council on a charge of contempt arising from piracy against a merchant of Lombardy, and a 1384 complaint by Gunsales, a Portuguese merchant, of spoilage in Southampton, aggravated by the subsequent loss of the ship at sea to pirates. The latter case was referred from Chancery to the King's Bench in 1384 where the jury was half alien and half denizen and the plaintiff, perhaps somewhat unfairly, lost the case.[25]

While it is possible to find examples of maritime cases which did not go before an admiral, there remains considerable uncertainty about the unrecorded activities of the admiralty courts from their beginnings in the mid-fourteenth century until about 1524 when the High Court of Admiralty records began. By the chance recording in the Patent and Close Rolls and elsewhere of actions resulting from the courts' decisions, something of the early operation of admirals' courts can be seen. The surviving evidence confirms that most of the cases heard concerned piracy, prize or reprisal, with very little mercantile work. It is not known if the commercial business was truly small, and if so by chance or by deliberate exclusion, or was in fact larger but has left no trace. Examples of the few commercial cases which were heard in admirals' courts in the period 1350–1450 are discussed below.

A number of cases brought before the courts of the Admiral of the West, John Holland, earl of Huntingdon, appointed In 1389, have been recorded because they were passed *a certiorari* or for other reasons to Chancery. One, in 1390, was *Sampson* v. *Curteys* in which John Sampson accused Curteys of stealing goods from his ship in Lostwithiel while she was on passage from Plymouth to London. The king, in his writ to Huntingdon, referred to the court as 'coram vobis in curia Admiralitatis vestre' which indicates that the admiral had a court of independent jurisdiction

---

[24] Marsden, *Select Pleas*, 1, pp. xvii and xlix: *Coram Rege*, 7 Richard II, Hil., rot. 51.
[25] *Foedera*, 4, p. 168, 8 April 1383: 'De venire faciendo certas personas *coram* concilio.' Marsden, *Select Pleas*, 1, p. xlviii: *Coram Rege*, 8 Richard II, Hil., rot., 18.

within his admiralty and that it sat in Lostwithiel and in Fowey, sittings timed, no doubt as usual for maritime courts, by the tide. The return of the commission to take evidence, however, was made to the 'subadmirallus nobis et curie nostre ... apud le Wolkey, London', a move which would have added considerably to the expenses of the litigants and was to become one of the complaints against the admirals' jurisdiction. The case was not entirely straightforward; the defendant was the seneschal of the Lostwithiel court and his defence was that he was acting in an official capacity in taking some of the goods and that he knew nothing about anything else that was missing. The judgment has not survived.[26]

Another recorded case, *Gernesey v. Henton*, was an extraordinarily long-drawn-out and complex affair stretching from *c*.1389 until 1404. It was initially a commercial matter, an attempt by Gernesey to recover money from Henton for freight and for salt and herrings which Gernesey had bought. It was heard before William Thomer the *soi-disant* deputy admiral at Bridgewater but it spawned another case, *Henton v. Kedewelly*, the latter being Thomer's bailiff. In that case Henton sued Kedewelly for breaking into his house to recover goods to the value of the debt. From then the complications multiplied until, by Marsden's count, there were 29 separate legal steps including appeals to the Admiral, to the Privy Council and five to the king, and five different commissions had been appointed. Curiously, the chancellor himself does not appear to have become involved at any point in this arachnoid web of litigation. The case is interesting because it illustrates a challenge to an admiral's authority, albeit an admiral's pretended deputy who was probably acting *ultra vires*.[27]

The decline of the admirals' courts

Sampson v. Curteys, *Gernesey v. Henton* and the consequent case of *Henton v. Kendewelly* were all before the courts while the earl of Huntingdon was the Admiral of the West, and all demonstrate unsatisfactory legal practices. These and other irregularities committed by judges in admiralty courts during Huntingdon's tenure, led to a general dissatisfaction with the judicial role of the admirals. In addition to the improprieties of the courts, there was also still doubt about the range of authority allowed to the admirals. Further, there is indirect evidence of dissatisfaction in the records of appointments of judges to hear appeals against the courts' judgments. Cases considered to have been handled unsatisfactorily include

---

[26] Marsden, *Select Pleas*, 1, p. 54: the court 'apud Orton's Quay juxta pontem Londinensem loco vid' dicte curie solito'; the wolkey ('wool quay') was usually on the north bank of the Thames, but Horton's Quay was in Southwark.
[27] Marsden, *Select Pleas*, 1, pp. 1–27 and pp. 149–72: Chancery Rolls, Misc., bundle 18, nos 10 and 11; also *CPR*, 1391–6, p. 339, etc.

Beche v. *Nyweman*, a case of debt in 1391; *Nocolt* v. *Appe Hacche*, a question of part-ownership of a ship also in 1391; and *Draper* v. *Stillard*, concerning a freight contract in 1394 in which it was complained that two of the lawyers involved had been suborned. None of those three was a straightforward maritime law case, although indirectly involving ships or freight, but all were heard during the period of admiralty of the earl of Huntingdon. The judge in the first case was Nicholas Maclefeld who, like Thomas Thomer in *Gernesey* v. *Henton*, appears to have been a *soi-disant* lieutenant 'claiming to supply the place of the admiral'.[28]

The case of *Yter et al.* v. *Haule* [Hawley], was heard in an admiral's court by Sir Nicholas Clifton in 1389. Although Hawley was alleged to have taken a hulk and a cog laden with wine, iron and other merchandise belonging to Frenchmen and Flemings, interestingly, the competence of the court to hear a case of piracy was not questioned. The confusion surrounding the admiralty courts' responsibilities is epitomised in the 1393 case of *Copyn* v. *Snoke and Saxlyngham* in which John Copyn, master of the ship *Gabriel*, sued the two merchants for the payment due on the freight of a cargo of wine carried from Bordeaux to Essex. Copyn began his suit in a common law court, then in the court of the Admiral of the North, both without remedy, and finally before the court of Constable and Marshal with whose decision he did not agree. In the common law court the judges had declared that they had no jurisdiction (perhaps because Copyn had no written proof of agreement?) but it is not known why the admiral's court could not offer remedy. It may be that by 1393 the admiralty courts were too demoralised to hear cases with a commercial element.[29]

Port town courts resented the loss of commercial business and no doubt resisted attempts to take such cases to an admiral's court. Further, litigants were unsure of the outcome of their pleas before an admiral's court, at least during the tenure of the earl of Huntingdon, and were unhappy about the expense of moving their cases to London. There had been complaints from the city of London in 1345 about the jurisdiction of the Admirals of the North and of the West but more general unrest grew towards the end of the century with repeated petitions to the king and to Parliament from towns in the west of England from 1391 to 1410. The burden of the complaints was that the admirals' courts were encroaching on the franchises of the towns, that the expense of litigation before an admiral was too great, and that wrong judgments were being given. Following what appears to have been a pre-emptive strike by Huntingdon, an inquiry was ordered to be made by John, duke of Lancaster in 1391

> to hear and examine complaints by the earl of Huntingdon, Admiral of the West, that the mayor and sheriffs of London and others had done divers

---

[28] CPR, 1388–92, pp. 412, 425, 459, 473 and 491 (all 1391); and 1391–96, p. 388 (1394).
[29] CPR, 1388–92, p. 159 (1389). CPR, 1391–96, pp. 340 and 378 (1393–4). See also chapter 3.

duresses, grievances, disobediences or rebellions and prejudices to the officers and courts of the admiral and to certify to the king and council.[30]

The result of the dissatisfaction with the admiral's courts was that two statutes were passed which drastically restricted their judicial powers to hear pleas, quarrels or anything else under the laws of the country. The remit of the courts was limited specifically to inquiries concerning deaths and mayhem in ships at sea, or in the main stream of great rivers below the bridges. The admirals were, however, empowered to arrest ships for the king's use, provided that all forfeitures and profits arising there from went to the king, and to exercise jurisdiction on those impressed fleets during their voyages, subject to the franchises and liberties of the lords, cities and boroughs. They were also authorised, when the evidence was too technical for non-seafaring lawyers and they had secured pledges from both parties, to pass a dispute to arbitration by nominated experts or *aimables compositeurs*. An example of such arbitration, from the papers of John Holland (earl of Huntingdon, later duke of Exeter), is a case which ended in 'coram vobis pendente indecisa' – a telling phrase. Such use of *aimables compositeurs* in arbitration is discussed by Marsden, who gives as an example a rare hearing of a case of collision at sea, and by Rawcliffe in connection with non-maritime commercial disputes.[31]

The statutory restriction of the admirals' powers was seriously at odds with the admirals' own view of their responsibilities as set out in *Queenborough* less than 25 years earlier. There the admirals were charged with responsibility for inquiries into death and mayhem on ships, for false weights and measures within their jurisdiction, for wrecks and, most relevantly, to have sanction over those who sued at common law when 'by ancient right' the case should have been tried by maritime law, and over any judge who heard a plea belonging to an admiralty court. The admirals' status had been secured, they felt, by the *Queenborough* authority to punish any who should oppose the office of admiral. The 1390 and 1392 statutes proved inadequate and had to be followed by a further statute in 1400 which confirmed the restriction of the admirals' jurisdiction and threatened the admirals and their lieutenants with the sanctions of statute and common law. That statute also offered anyone who felt aggrieved, the possibility of action by writ grounded on the case heard against them in an admiral's court, with double

---

[30] *Rot. Parl.*, 3, 17 Richard II, p. 322, no. 49; 4 Henry IV, p. 498, no. 47 and 11 Henry IV, p. 642, no. 61.

[31] *Statutes*, 13 Richard II, st. 1, c. 5; and 15 Richard II, c. 3. Twiss, *Black Book*, I, p. 246–80: 'Documents Connected with the Admiralty of John Holland, Duke of Exeter, 1443–1446'; Holland died in 1447. Marsden, *Select Pleas*, pp. lxix and 90–1. Carole Rawcliffe '"That Kindliness Should Be Cherished More, and Discord Driven Out": The Settlement of Commercial Disputes by Arbitration in Later Medieval England', in *Enterprise and Individuals in Fifteenth Century England*, ed. Jennifer Kermode (Stroud, 1991), pp. 99–117.

damages from the pursuant, the latter also paying £10 to the king if attainted. As late as 1409–10 there were two more petitions to Parliament complaining that the admirals' courts, coupled, in the first petition, with the court of the Constable and Marshal, were still hearing cases which should have been heard at common law. In the second petition there were also much broader based complaints of all sorts of dishonesty in the collection of customs, in false weights and measures, overpayment of employees, bad judgments, deliberate delays and 'of all other things by which they can illegally gain some money'. The second petition went on to say that none of this happened before Huntingdon was appointed admiral, and that an inquiry should be held. To all of which the king replied 'Soient l'Estatutz ent faitz tenuz & gardez'.[32]

During their short life in the late fourteenth and early fifteenth centuries, the admirals' courts had stirred up sufficient enmity to be reduced to handling little more than violence at sea. This may well be attributed to the laxity or dishonesty of Huntingdon as Admiral of the Western Fleet over a period of 12 years (from 1389 to 1401) but, whatever the reasons, the results were clear. The admirals' judicial powers were rendered inadequate for maritime commercial litigation; and, more often than not, merchants and mariners had to go elsewhere for justice.

As the spirit of the 1360 treaty of Brétigny evaporated, and Edward III reclaimed the title of king of France in 1369, the sea became increasingly dangerous until the beginning of the next century. The mayor of Sandwich confiscated a ship of La Rochelle which had been driven in by bad weather in 1396 and many vessels were taken by both sides over the next three years, 1399 being a particularly hazardous year for English seafarers. By 1402 losses at sea, through direct action and reprisals, were so heavy that maritime trade was crippled, but neither Paris nor London did anything much to calm the situation and probably encouraged the attacks under the guise of reprisals. During this period the ambassadors of both sides evaded and postponed the restitution of captured ships and cargoes and anarchy spread at sea. By the second half of 1403 hostile marine activity appears to have become less intense, although until 1406, there was a series of raids on the south coast of England by French, Breton and Castilian fleets, followed inevitably by English retaliatory raids. In that year, at their despairing request, the merchants were themselves entrusted with the custody of the sea for which they nominated two admirals to be responsible for the North and the West. Nothing is known of this experiment except that it was of brief duration and it has to be assumed that for whatever reason the merchants' control of admiralty failed and John Beaufort, earl of Somerset, was appointed admiral by the king later in the same year. In 1407, without admitting that the 1396 truce of Paris had failed, a new tripartite truce

---

[32] Appendix 2, *Queensborough* articles 29 (death), 30 (mayhem), 51 (suing at common law), 52 (judges wrongly hearing pleas), 54 (weights and measures) and 72 (opposers of admiralty), etc. *Statutes*, 2 Henry IV, c.11. *Rot. Parl.*, 3, 11 Henry IV, p. 625, no. 24 and p. 642, no. 61.

was agreed at Gloucester. The fullest part of the truce, which held until 1412 and during which the admirals were able to deal with infractions, was that which had the express purpose of protecting maritime trade.[33]

Little is known of the work of the regional admiralty courts after their statutory emasculation in the 1390s; that they did continue to hear some commercial suits may be conjectured from the appointments of commissions to investigate appeals. As early as 1390 the *Sampson* v. *Curteys* appeal, discussed above, had been moved to Southwark and there was certainly a *curia principalis* in Southwark from 1408 when Thomas Beaufort, earl of Dorset, was appointed Admiral of England, Ireland and Aquitaine. The Southwark court may have had a chequered career for while, in 1410, there was a complaint in Parliament that (*inter alia*) witnesses were summoned 'a Loundres a le key de William Horton, Southwerke', in 1422 there is mention of courts held in turn in Dartmouth, Plymouth and Kingsbridge.[34]

During Beaufort's admiralty, the amount of work coming before admiralty courts appears to have increased despite the statutory restrictions, confirmed, ironically, by the number of appeals against the decisions of his lieutenants. Beaufort himself did not escape complaint; in 1409 John Byrkyn and three others alleged that after a judgment against them by the admiral's lieutenant, Beaufort exacted excessive fees for himself and the office of admiralty. In December 1409 (too late to have been one of the subjects of the 1409–10 petitions to Parliament), a commission was appointed to hear an appeal in the case *Watertoft* v. *Jonesson* which concerned a debt arising from a freight agreement. The original plea had been heard by Henry Bole, a lieutenant general of the court of Admiralty, and should have been held on the quayside at Boston with a jury of 12 merchants, shipmasters and mariners. Watertoft's appeal was on the grounds that it was held in the town (outside the admiral's jurisdiction), that the jury were not merchants, shipmasters or mariners, and that he and his counsellors had been too intimidated to complain at the time. Other appeals against admirals' courts' decisions in commercial disputes were heard in the same period: concerning freight payments in 1412 and in 1414; the withholding of a ransom payment in 1415; the management accounts of a ship in 1418; and money due on the sale of a ship in 1422.[35]

At this time, cases of piracy were the occasional subject of petitions to Parliament. There were, for example, two in 1410; that of John Trebeel who had captured a ship out of St Malo loaded by merchants who had a safe conduct from Richard of York – 'which they had forgotten'(!) – and that of John Kedwelly who, during a truce between France and England, had lost his ship and cargo to pirates from

---

[33] *CCR*, 1396–9, pp. 113, 165; 1399–1402, pp. 119, 319, 395; 1402–5, p. 48. *CPR*, 1399–1401, p. 164 etc. *Rot. Parl.*, 3, 7–8 Henry IV, p. 571, no. 26. *Foedera*, 8, pp. 507–9.
[34] *Rot. Parl.*, 11 Henry IV, p. 642, no. 6. *CPR*, 1416–22, p. 427.
[35] *CPR*, 1408–13, pp. 139, 154 and 422; 1413–16, p. 204; 1408–13, p. 407; 1416–22, pp. 174 and 427.

Harfleur and St Malo, and had been imprisoned. In 1414 a statute was passed authorising the admiral to appoint conservators of truces in various seaport towns. Their duties included inquiry into, and determination of, piracy cases, an area which had, in any case, escaped the statutory restrictions on the jurisdiction of the admirals. There had always to be present at the inquiries men learned in law, and that obligation may mark the end of lay judges in the admiralty courts; it is curious, however, that the type of law in which they were to be learned was not specified. The conservators were able to appoint ships and crews, operating with 'letters of marque', to assist them but, perhaps inevitably, this led to such gross exploitation that the statute had to be reduced by partial repeal, suspended for seven year after that, and finally abandoned in 1435. A further blow to the admirals' authority was struck in 1450 when the 1414 statute was revived but with the chancellor and chief justices being given the powers of the conservators. Throughout the remainder of the fifteenth century conservators, or envoys with similar powers, appear to have been the usual judges of cases of piracy, perhaps further confirmation that the admiralty courts had not worked satisfactorily.[36]

In 1426 the restriction of the admirals' legal franchise was repeated in the Letter Patent appointing John, duke of Bedford, as Admiral of England, Ireland and Guienne, but despite that, commercial suits continued to be heard. Four appeals against decisions by the admiral's lieutenants between 1428 and 1442 confirm that such cases were still being taken to an admiralty court.[37]

Sometime before 1429, qualified lawyers began to be appointed to sit judicially in the admirals' courts, which therefore became somewhat more reputable resorts for litigants to receive as fair a hearing as they might reasonably expect in common or merchant law courts. The rehabilitation of the admirals' jurisdiction had begun, but there was a problem in that professional counsel was in short supply in the more remote districts. In 1429, after John Kelke complained that he could not find counsel in Norfolk or Suffolk to defend him against a charge of wrongful arrest, the admiral's lieutenant decided that the case should be heard in 'his principal court at Southwark' where, presumably, counsel were available in plenty. In the interim, a *soi-disant* deputy awarded Kelke's goods to the other party involved and Kelke had to make an appeal for help.[38]

With the courts of the conservators, and occasionally the admiralty courts, hearing cases of piracy, the criminal jurisdiction of common law felt the lack of such business. That may have been the subtext in a petition to Parliament in 1429,

---

[36] *Rot. Parl.*, 3, 11 Henry IV, pp. 628–9, no. 35 and pp. 643–4, no. 66. *Rot. Parl.*, 4, 2 Henry V, pp. 22–4, no. 2. *Statutes*, 2 Henry V, st. 1, c. 6. *Rot. Parl.*, 4, 2 Henry V, pp. 22–4, no. 23. *Statutes*, 2 Henry V, st. 1, c. 6; 4 Henry V, c. 7; 14 Henry VI, c. 8; and 14 Henry VI, c. 8; 29 Henry VI, c. 2.
[37] *CPR, 1422–29*, pp. 349–50.
[38] *CPR, 1422–29*, p. 470; 1436–41, p. 203; 1441–46, p. 133; 1429–36, pp. 32–2 and 37; 1436–41, p. 203; 1441–46, p. 133; 1429–36, pp. 32–3.

in which the commons asked that piracy be made a felony and that justices of the peace of the county in which the 'Roveres sur le Mere' were taken could enquire into their aiders and abettors with a view to *oyer et terminer*. The king was not immediately disposed to help, his *Responsio* being 'Le Roi s'advisera'. The intention of the petition seems to have been to curb once again the admirals' courts' powers, and it was no doubt encouraging to the admiral and his staff that Henry VI's council in 1429 was less disposed against them than Richard II and Henry IV had been in 1391 and 1410. The rehabilitation of the court of admiralty continued.

Throughout the first half of the fifteenth century the admirals' courts' work was largely maritime, concerned with discipline and seamanship, and with an occasional commercial suit. At least one case combined both commercial and maritime interests: in 1437 an appeal was made for the restoration of wrongly sequestered goods which had been sold following a decision by an admiral's court on a (rare) collision dispute involving *le Antony* of London, freighted with merchandise from Prussia. Meanwhile, the port town courts, for example that at Ipswich, in competition with the admiralty courts, continued to be available for hearings of marine issues under maritime law: 'The pleas yoven to the lawe maryne, that is to wyte, for straunge marynerys passaunt and for them that abyden not but her tyde, shuldene ben pleted from tyde to tyde.' Sometime in the fifteenth century, the Fordwich and Sandwich custumals made it clear that whenever a denizen or alien came to the mayor's court asking for settlement at maritime law of a dispute concerning damage at sea 'the mayor shall give him two jurats who know such like law, and two shipmasters of the vill who ... shall allot to each what by law he ought to have ... provided that both parties submit to his judgement'. If one of the parties did not agree with the judgment, then he could plead in the hundred or the mayor's court but, if the decision went against him, it would go badly for him – a blatant threat![39]

Aftermath

After half a century of active and successful jurisdiction over matters maritimo-commercial, the admiralty courts in the late fourteenth and the first half of the fifteenth centuries, despite their professional judges and recent record of equitable decisions, gradually ceased to be of much use to denizen or alien shipmasters and merchants. Haunted by the malpractices of Huntingdon's deputies, hounded by the port towns guarding the franchises of their own courts and harried by common law jurists looking for business, they were unable to extend their jurisdiction or even to exercise their own franchise as set out in the articles of *Queenborough*. The

---

[39] CPR, 1436–41, p. 94. Twiss, *Black Book*, I, pp. 16–209: the *Domesday of Gippewyz* [Ipswich]; Bateson, *Borough Customs*, 2, pp. 193–4.

admiralty courts continued to hear technical cases in maritime law concerned with discipline, collisions, seamanship, pilots, jettison and so on, but maritime commercial suits were generally taken to common or merchant law courts.

To the hardy and practical shipmaster, the rise and fall of the admiralty courts together with the jealousies and intrigues of the practitioners of the several codes of law, must have been a source of considerable frustration and bemusement.

3

The Shipmaster as Owner, Partner and Employee

Ship-ownership

In the twelfth century, most shipmasters owned their own ships, either participating in joint commercial ventures with a group of merchants assembled for each voyage, or arranging at their own expense the purchase and sale of cargo, the fitting-out of the ship and the hiring of a crew. As a member of a cooperative, the owner/master commanded the ship, acting as *primus inter pares* with the participating merchants working as crew, and would have received a charter fee or an enhanced share of the profits of the voyage. When working alone, all the risks and any profit (or loss) on the voyage were his. Vestiges of the rules of cooperative ventures which appear to pre-date its codification may be seen in certain articles of the *Lex d'Oleron*.[1]

The earliest English shipowners known to employ professional shipmasters were civil and religious institutions and the crown. In 1224 Margam Abbey in South Wales owned a ship which was arrested in Bristol, and in the following year Neath Abbey obtained a safe conduct for their *hulc* to trade in England. In 1242 Robert Elye of Winchelsea handed over £20 *bordeaux* as the king's share of the booty taken while he was shipmaster of *La Brette*, which is described as a 'king's ship' and was therefore neither a privately owned nor an impressed vessel. At about the same time, individual continental merchants were already owning ships with professional shipmasters. In 1234 John Blundus and William, both merchants of Antwerp, obtained a safe conduct for their ship *Benalee* and her shipmaster Terricus, also of Antwerp. Terricus was described as 'leading' the ship and may have been a professional seaman with no share in the ship, which belonged to the merchants. By 1250 shipmasters were being employed by private individuals in England. Ellen Lambord of Bristol obtained safe conducts for two ships, the *Lambord* and *La Sauvee*, to go to Bordeaux, presumably with professional shipmasters. She may have been a widow carrying on her deceased husband's busi-

---

[1] Appendix 1, *Oleron*, articles 1, 2, 14, 18.

ness or, somewhat ahead of her time, she may have regarded shipowning as an investment.[2]

Shipowning purely as an investment, with no mercantile interest, appears to have been uncommon before the second half of the fifteenth century. By the early fourteenth century, however, ships were frequently owned by merchants, singly or in partnership, to expand their business interests. In addition to the returns, largely paid in England, and to the 'in-house' advantageous freight rates, shipownership also offered alternative opportunities when occasional royal restrictions were imposed on their activities or trading areas. As early examples of such marine diversification by merchants, two impressment indentures for Exeter ships show that *La Sauveye* had five owners in 1303 and the *Seinte Marie Cog* also had five in 1310; the shipmasters of both ships are listed as part-owners, the others being local merchants actively engaged in overseas trade. From London, Richard and Bartholomew Denmars, the latter a corder, owned *La Katerine de Hope* in the 1340s; Thomas le Northerne, a vintner, sold *La Marie* of Boulogne; and Richard de Preston, a grocer, owned the *Michel* of London and half of *Le Thomas* of Calais in the 1360s. Some 15 London merchants, including John Chirche, a mercer who owned four or five ships, were granted letters of marque for their ships in 1436 and 1438. There were many Bristol shipowning merchants, amongst whom William Canynges and Robert Straunge had fleets of 10 and 12 ships respectively. Vintners and fishmongers appear to have been amongst the most diligent investors in ships although, as wine was the best recorded of imports, that view may not be entirely objective for the former.[3]

Shipowning gradually came to be seen as a sound 'arms-length' investment to the point that, in a muster of 63 vessels at Plymouth in 1450–51 to take part in an expedition to Gascony, only 13 were owned by the shipmaster, although almost all (61) of the ships had single owners. Later, those who wished to invest in shipping and had sufficient funds to buy a ship, probably spread their risk by joining partnerships in the ownership of several vessels. A petition to the chancellor in about 1467 concerning certain ships of Dartmouth shows how widespread shared ownership had become: a list of 23 'partners and victuallers' included a shipmaster, two knights, a priest and an esquire. If the ships listed at Plymouth and Dart-

---

[2] CCR, 1231–34, p. 360; 1232–47, pp. 108 and 328. CPR, 1232–47, p. 85; 1247–58, p. 72.
[3] Restrictions on trading included: *Statutes*, 37 Edward III, c. 5: 'Merchants shall not engross merchandizes to inhance the price, nor use but one sort of merchandize'; 38 Edward III, st. 1, c. 2: 'Any merchant may use more sorts of merchandize than one; English merchants not to export wool, gold, silver etc.'; 42 Edward III, c. 8: 'English merchants shall not pass into Gascoigne to fetch wines, nor shall buy any wines until they be landed'; 43 Edward III, c. 2: 'English, Irish and Welshmen, not being artificers, may import wine from Gascoigne … he shall buy an hundred tuns of wines and no less … and bring the same into England … and to no place elsewhere.' Exeter Deeds M/196 and M/214, transcribed by Michael Jones, 'Two Exeter Ship Agreements of 1303 and 1310', *MM* 53, 4 (1967), pp. 315–19; CPMR, 1323–64, p. 207 and 1364–81, pp. 35 and 43. CPR, 1436–41, pp. 1 and 166–7. Childs, *Anglo-Castilian Trade*, pp. 163–4.

mouth were representative of the merchant fleet, and allowance must be made for unrepresentative sampling, then by mid-fifteenth century there was a wide demographic range of people investing in ships. The legal and financial aspects of ship-ownership are discussed below, pp. 000–00.[4]

The shipmaster's options

A shipmaster in the fourteenth and fifteenth centuries could have been the sole owner of his ship, a waged employee, a part-owner, a charterer or an experienced mariner brought into a *commenda*-type arrangement (as discussed in chapter 1), formally or in trust, by the partners. The co-existence of self-employed and employed shipmasters may be seen as early as 1315: William Ribald, owner and master of the ship called the *Godyer* of Spalding, and John Irpe, owner, and Amisio Ethoun, master, of the ship called the *Godyer* of Ipswich, occur in the same account. The number of employed rather than self-employed shipmasters grew with the increase in demand for English ships, and by or before 1315, the date of the London manuscripts of the *Lex d'Oleron*, there were sufficient of them to require a specific definition of their obligations and authority. These conditions were amplified in the *Coutumier*, of which a 1324 copy survives and in the 1378 *Inquisition of Queenborough*. In the 1450 Plymouth muster mentioned above, the number of shipmasters who individually owned their vessels was less than 20 per cent.[5]

In the accounts of the king's ships between 1422 and 1427 shipmasters are seen in several and changing rôles. John William, employed by John Hawley of Dartmouth as shipmaster of the balinger *Craccher*, 56 tons, entered service with the Crown first as shipmaster of the cog *John*, 220 tons, and then of the king's flag-ship *Jesus*, 1,000 tons. During his royal service he acquired a half share with the Crown of the *Margaret*, 70 tons, based in Beaumaris and in 1423, when the royal ships were being sold off, he and two others bought his old ship the *Craccher*, which had been either forfeited or given to the Crown by Hawley, and with others, the *Swan* of 20 tons. By 1436 he was trading on his own account in wine, possibly as shipmaster on his own ship, and by 1440 he had another vessel employed either in coastal work or as a lighter in Southampton harbour. John William, therefore, worked progressively as an employed shipmaster, as an investing partner with the Crown in one ship and then as a part-owner of a number of ships, on one

---

[4] Gardiner, *West Country Shipping*, no. 79, pp. 95–6, a translation of PRO C1/33/179; the ships had taken Burgundian goods which had to be returned.
[5] Friel, *The Good Ship*, p. 30: an analysis of the Plymouth muster, and PRO E364/92, A, m. IV and B, m.1r. Also *CPR, 1429–36*, p. 471; PRO C1/7/186; *CLB Letterbook A*, p. 6; PRO C1/7/291; and PRO E101/16/40. Appendix 1, *Oleron*, articles 1, 3, 23. Appendix 2, *Queenborough*, article 64. Appendix 3, *Coutumier*, chapters 86, 88.

of which he may have been master, and finally as a full- or part-time merchant employing a shipmaster.[6]

Friel has suggested that, paradoxically, single ownership favoured technical development whereas shared ownership appears to have been more conservative; further, the largest and therefore the most capital intensive ships, were owned by one person. Possibly a committee of partners would have had a more cautious investment policy than an entrepreneurial 'loner', or maybe partners with different interests found it difficult to agree on further investment.[7]

Ship-owning partnerships and service agreements

All merchants engaged in buying and selling at home or overseas had to be experienced in striking bargains and entering various forms of partnership and trading agreement. They were practised in pursuing debtors and recognising embezzlers and would know the advantages and disadvantages, to them, of common, mercantile and maritime law in matters of commerce and contract. The risks for a possibly illiterate and initially naïf shipmaster bargaining with, or putting his ship and savings into a partnership with, such men must have been considerable. Until the last quarter of the thirteenth century, when most shipmasters owned their own vessels, they arranged their cargoes and freight rates, relied on their own resources against weather and enemies, sometimes in convoy but usually alone, and repaired, manned and victualled their ships without outside assistance. Although a partner with available funds would have covered periods of poor cash flow, diluted the risk and made possible the purchase of a bigger ship, shipmasters were probably men who valued their independence and saw little reason to share their enterprise with anyone else. Although cooperation on a legal basis between merchants and shipmasters existed in England in the early fourteenth century, there is little in the records of common and merchant law courts on that subject. From Chancery records of appeals in the fifteenth century some detail of the arrangements in such ventures may be gleaned, but it is not clear what type of association was usual – whether legal partnership was necessary or if participation by shareholding sufficed.

Commercial partnerships were known in Saxon times, and later there were early attempts to form primitive industrial partnership-type arrangements in the Stanneries and in the clothing industry. Sharing in the ownership of a ship would almost certainly require a legal partnership, or something very similar, to define

---

[6] Susan Rose, *The Navy of the Lancastrian Kings, Accounts and Inventories of William Soper, Keeper of the King's Ships, 1422–1427*, Naval Records Society, 123 (London, 1982), pp. 245, 247, 249, 250–1.
[7] Friel, *The Good Ship*, pp. 30–1.

the responsibilities and privileges of the participants. Possible evidence of formal partnerships in shipowning may be seen in testamentary records. In the 1340s, Henry Graspays, a fishmonger, left his half of *Le Lancastre* and her rigging, and fractions of two other ships, to his son; and Roger de Bernes, another fishmonger, left his share of *le Andreu* and 20 silver marks for her maintenance, to his son and his apprentice.[8]

What might be regarded as a proto-partnership in ship management, although not ship-ownership, is seen in the charter of a ship in 1282. Walter Clerk, boatman, and his partner received from Henry Herford a *batell* for a period of two years in return for 1d. out of each 3d. profit. Walter's honesty was guaranteed by the threat of gaol for any transgression. In effect, all three men were to share the trading risks for that period; one had contributed his ship and the other two were to manage her and presumably to arrange cargo, while all were to share the profits.[9]

There were in the Middle Ages, as now, two principal purposes for setting up a partnership. First, a combination of investors with funds and tradesmen with skills could be put to use for their mutual reward, a situation summed up by the phrase 'al use et common profit de lui [the shipmaster] et du dit suppliant [the sleeping partner]', quoted in a dispute in Chancery sometime around 1400. In that partnership, Nicholas Blakeburn and Richard Newland, a tailor of York, shared the ownership of a ship which was 'en la possession et en la governaunce' of Newland. The second principal purpose was simply to combine the investments of several people in order to spread the risks of a venture, an arrangement of which there are many examples. A partnership also offered other advantages, for example as a form of insurance. In an agreement made as early as 1292, before partnerships were fully recognised in law, Walter le Mounier acknowledged receipt of 10 marks from Geoffrey le Norton for trading in merchandise 'for which he [Mounier] will answer within the quinzaine of Easter unless prevented by tempest of the sea ... which peril will rest with the said Geoffrey, and at his risk'. Norton had contracted with Mounier for a service at the former's risk and Mounier had, in effect, been insured against risks at sea for one particular venture and voyage. No example within a formal shipowning partnership has been found, but it might be expected that one partner would accept the financial risks of a venture for a higher share of

---

[8] Roy C. Cave and Herbert H. Coulson, *A Source Book for Medieval Economic History* (New York, 1936, reprint 1965), p. 186 and Benjamin Thorpe, ed., *Ancient Laws and Institutes of England* (London, 1840), p. 552: *Leges Henrici Primi*, *Liv*. 1 concerns the dissolution of partnership and *Liv*. 2 covers the obligations of partners. If partners had to choose between friendship and the law, the former may stand but there could be no return to the law; *Calendar of Wills Proved and Enrolled in the Court of Hustings, London, 1258–1688*, ed., Reginald R. Sharpe, 3 vols (London, 1889–90), I, 627 and 485.

[9] CLB, Letterbook A, p. 61.

the profits. Less reputable reasons for forming partnerships, such as camouflage for interest on loans or for avowry, are discussed below.[10]

Postan has described the mechanism of three types of partnership: that in which 'capital' hired the services of another (here read 'shipmaster') to form a 'service partnership'; that in which 'labour' (the shipmaster) raised capital to form a 'finance partnership'; and the 'complete' or 'real' partnership into which all the partners were prepared to contribute both capital and service. These partnership models, which were well known in Italy in the fourteenth century, are relevant here. The *commenda* arrangement in which one investing, or sleeping, partner delivered goods or money to an active partner who was then expected to employ the capital profitably, was close in function, although not in legal constitution nor in financial distribution, to that of a service agreement. The active partner was usually but not always rewarded by a share of the profits or, less usually, by commission, so that both partners enjoyed the profit or bore the loss of the venture. As in a service agreement, the investor contributing no labour hired the active partner, who contributed no capital, to perform a service for one transaction only, or for a defined period. The important difference was that the active partner, against a share of the risks, enjoyed more independence and more responsibility than if he had been a hired servant or an apprentice. Within this definition, 'service partnership' was a common arrangement between English merchant shipowners and shipmasters in the late fourteenth and the fifteenth centuries.[11]

Although a service agreement between a master and an agent or servant not in partnership could also be occasional or temporal, the rules governing their relationship and responsibilities were fundamentally different from those relating to partners. Litigation at common law during the fourteenth century, including that between partners or concerning a service agreement, had to be initiated by one of a number of formalised Chancery writs (as discussed in chapter 1), which unfortunately render the true burden of the litigation somewhat occult. That, together with common law's reluctance to recognise contract and partnership until the second half of the fourteenth century, has led to two difficulties. First, the difference between a service agreement and a partnership is not always clear and second, some writers, failing to recognise the *actualité* behind the protocol of the writs, have believed that commercial litigation was the exclusive preserve of the law merchant. Once the writs issued in commercial disputes have been deciphered, however, it is apparent that many commercial cases were indeed heard at common law and from amongst the reported cases, sufficient may be identified as disputes concerning partnerships or agreements.

Two examples of disputed service agreements make clear how they differed from partnerships. In 1351–52 the mayor of London wrote to the constable of

---

[10] PRO, C1/7/186 (*t.* between 15 Richard II and 10 Henry VI). *CLB*, Letterbook A, p. 139.
[11] Postan, *Medieval Trade*, p. 66.

Dover Castle certifying that Thomas de Leycestre, who had been arrested on suspicion by a bailiff in Dover and was found to be carrying 56 florins of gold (nobles) and his travelling expenses, had indeed been sent to Flanders to trade on behalf of a merchant, John de Knyghtcote, and that the money he was carrying should be returned to his master or his attorney. Similarly, in 1366, when William Conteshale, an apprentice, died in Normandy, the mayor of London certified that the deceased had no share in the goods and merchandise which had been seized on his death and that they should be returned to William de Tudenham, his master, or his attorney. Both cases not only make it clear that a servant acting for his master had no share in the capital of the enterprise but also show that sworn evidence, certified by a municipal authority, was sufficient to prove the master/servant relationship. Such decisions are of particular relevance in the dealings between shipowner and shipmaster when a formal partnership had not been arranged.[12]

In contrast, there is an example of a service partnership in a petition to the chancellor in 1416 by Richard Bokeland, a citizen and merchant of London. He and John de Boys, a merchant of Brittany, had agreed by indentures to be *compaignons de marchaundie* in any type of venture and Bokeland had accordingly given de Boys £80 working capital. De Boys returned to Plymouth from overseas with a miscellany of goods and chattels for trading purposes which he apparently refused to give up. Bokeland claimed the goods, but because de Boys held a safe conduct from the king, Bokeland dared not take the goods nor apprehend him and so looked to the chancellor for help. In that formal partnership, which appears to have had no time limit nor restriction of range of goods to be traded, Bokeland was the investor or sleeping partner and de Boys the active partner, and the former clearly believed that the law would uphold his claim on the goods allegedly purchased with his money. Unfortunately it is not known how the case was determined but it is interesting that even in 1416, in the matter of partnerships at common law, Bokeland had to take his plea to Chancery for a decision.[13]

Relationships within partnerships
'Actions of account', discussed in chapter 1, were generally used during the fourteenth century as a means of enforcing the obligations of all types of agents to their principals, and for the recovery of credit extended in a commercial transaction. Until common law recognised the obligations of partnership late in the fourteenth century, actions of account were also used in disputes between partners. The question of an investor's legal responsibility for his colleague, whether as master to servant, as principal to agent or as one partner to another, has been explored by Postan. A defaulting partner could be pursued at common law only

---

[12] *CLMC*, I, no. 56; and II, no. 6.
[13] Gardiner, *West Country Shipping*, no. 17, pp. 19–20: a translation of PRO C1/6/290.

as a master could seek remedy from a servant, the action of account requiring the defendant to account for his dealings. Similarly, in a finance partnership the legal remedy could lie in actions either of debt or of account, depending on which of the parties was the aggrieved. In both types of action any reference in the plea to a sharing of the profits arising from a venture may be taken as a prima facie indication of the existence of a partnership agreement rather than a loan which had been arranged for the venture. Absence of any mention of profit sharing, however, does not necessarily preclude the existence of a partnership. Although Postan's work was not concerned with the shipowner/shipmaster relationship, such evidence as has survived indicates that where the shipmaster was a partner in the ownership of the vessel, the partnership between him and the other owner(s) was no different from that in other medieval mercantile or industrial partnerships.[14]

A shipmaster-partner who had to render account to his investing partner appeared in a case heard in London in 1386. Hugh Richardesson, master of *Le Marie* of Exeter, was ordered by the London mayoral court to go to the Calais court to satisfy the shipowner, John Bedon. Bedon owed Richardesson £6 for ship's expenses but Richardesson had 40 francs ransom money for a prisoner which Bedon said was his, plus 10 marks and certain freight monies from Middleburg to London which Bedon claimed he was owed by Richardesson. Richardesson was awarded the £6 by the London mayoral court, presumably following merchant law, but was required to go to Calais to have the rest resolved by rendering account to Bedon. The business arrangement between the two men was identified at merchant law by the London court as a service agreement and not as a partnership, which it almost certainly was. Paradoxically, by 1386, it could probably have been recognised as a partnership at common law.[15]

Another example of a problem within a shipowning partnership may be seen in the 1388 case of *Burwell v. Horne*. Burwell, the investing partner, claimed from his shipmaster partner Horne, 86 tuns 1 pipe of Rochelle wine. The mayor and aldermen of London decided that Burwell was entitled to the cash equivalent of 78 tuns, assessed at £36 5s. 2d., which Horne had sold at Middelburgh and five eighths of the value of the wine still unsold; Horne was to receive the value of the remaining three eighths. A further claim by Burwell, which is of interest because it could have revealed maritime law's view of partnership, was for Horne's contribution towards the ship *Cristofre*'s expenses, including rigging, victuals and wages which Burwell valued at £7 8s. ¾d. Unfortunately, because of a lack of information, this was not settled. In the first claim, neither partner was required to render account and the court appears to have accepted the obligation of each partner to the other. The second claim depends in part on the nature of the ownership of the vessel, whether the partners were part- or joint-owners. The difference is

---

[14] Postan, *Medieval Trade*, p. 68.
[15] *CPMR, 1381–1412*, pp. 121–2.

explained by a chapter in the *Coutumier* which deals with a partner who cannot or will not contribute to the ship's expenses; in such a case the hull is to be bound to the partner who has prepared the vessel for sea until the other partner has paid a proper proportion of the costs. It would appear that Burwell had paid for the fitting out of the ship himself and expected to have the profit of the voyage; Horne may have made a contribution amounting to the value of the five tuns of wine which he was awarded.[16]

The rôles of partners
When both (or all) partners contributed capital, or value in kind, to an enterprise and shared the profit or loss, and with one or both (only the shipmaster in the present discussion) contributing labour, then the partnership was complete and known legally as a *societas maris* of which the partners were *socii*. The active partner could contribute his expertise, in lieu of capital, as his entry fee to the partnership; a shipmaster without funds, therefore, was able to enjoy a share of the profits without any financial investment. A possible variant was where the shipmaster, already the active member of the partnershipowning his ship, invested his own funds, as well as his time, for an increased share in the profits of the enterprise. A shipmaster's financial involvement in his ship was in the interests of all the partners, since a high degree of personal motivation could be expected when he had the opportunity to enjoy a greater share of the profits. Entrepreneurs wishing to spread their risk could, of course, participate in several such *societates* investing in other ships.[17]

An example of the active member of a complete partnership working as shipmaster, a situation in which he is described in the Catalan *Customs* as 'senyor de nau' (translated by Twiss as 'managing owner'), may be seen in a letter from the mayor of London to the mayor and bailiffs of Faversham in 1352. In 1349, two partners jointly owned a 'crayer' (a type of small merchant ship). One of them, Nicholas Dagh of Faversham, was master and the other, John de Hatfield, was a chandler and citizen of London; the latter had invested further money in the enterprise. The letter required Dagh, or his attorney, to appear and satisfy de Hatfield to the tune of half the profits of the ship. A further letter concerning the same case was sent from London to Faversham again asking the mayor and bailiffs to compel Dagh to appear before them, this time to 'render account' of the money received, which was to have been used to trade until the following Easter for the profit of de Hatfield. There is no doubt that the men were partners in joint-ownership and that that appears to have been understood at merchant law in the mayoral court. Unfortunately for Dagh his petition pre-dated the recognition

---

[16] CPMR, 1381–1412, p. 136. Appendix 3, *Coutumier*, chapter 83.
[17] Despite its name, the *societas maris* was not exclusively for maritime purposes.

under common law of the contractual nature of partnerships, a recognition which could have enabled him to control more effectively his partner's activities.[18]

The understanding of partnership at merchant law may be seen in another letter from the mayor of London in the late 1350s to the mayor and bailiffs of Winchelsea concerning a complete partnership in joint-ownership of a vessel, one partner acting as shipmaster. Roger, a servant (perhaps the factor, agent or apprentice) of the non-working partner, John Bridport, had had a row with the shipmaster and active partner, John Gyles, who abandoned his ship *Hardebolle* at Rye, apparently in a huff. Bridport and Gyles then claimed that Roger had falsely made it known that Gyles had sold his share of the ship to him and that the mayor and bailiffs of Winchelsea had claimed the share as forfeit to the king, to the great loss, as they claimed, of the two Johns. Gyles meanwhile had found a buyer for his share and had paid the custom on the sale; both he and Bridport wanted the bogus sale to the servant to be annulled, and the forfeited share to be returned to allow the second sale to proceed. Apart from the alleged dishonesty of Roger, there is an interesting further dimension to the dispute which was not raised in the action. As joint-owner of the *Hardebolle*, Gyles was bound by the rules set out in the *Coutumier* to offer the other part-owner, Bridport, first refusal of his half before the ship was put on the open market. John Bridport, therefore, could have asked to have John Gyles's alleged sale to Roger annulled on the grounds that he had not been offered the chance to buy.[19]

It may have been the late recognition of the status of a sleeping partner that delayed common law's acknowledgement of the obligations of partnership. As discussed in chapter 1, when common law began to absorb the concept of contract from merchant law, a breach of contractual conditions could be pursued at common law as a trespass. At about the same time, the legal concept of trust evolved, perhaps from decisions of the Court of Chancery which had become the source of judicial equity as common law courts failed to cope with the complexities of commercial actions. To possess goods 'to the use of', that is, to employ them for the profit of the owner, was the rationale of trust; a shipmaster managed a ship for the owners and was expected to make profitable use of her for them, on a basis of trust. The early development and recognition of trust in English common law made it possible to commit goods to others, without the risk of losing the rights of ownership and without the need for a formal contract of partnership. In fact, the use of the concept of trust often dispensed with the necessity of forming a legal corporation. Although it was perhaps not legally necessary for a shipmaster, who had been assisted financially by non-active investors, to be either a partner of the financiers or to have exchanged with them a formal recognition of the debt, it would have been prudent for the investors to have had some legally recognised

---

[18] CLMC, I, no. 100.
[19] CLMC, I, no. 81. Appendix 3, *Coutumier*, chapter 64.

confirmation of their investment. The paucity of the surviving evidence, however, suggests that written agreements in matters of trust were rare.[20]

It may be that the lack of surviving agreements between shipowners and shipmasters from the fourteenth and fifteenth centuries is because the transfer of the management of a ship was generally an act of trust and very few, or perhaps no, agreements were written out. The absence of any documentation is at the heart of a petition to the chancellor in 1465 by William Brewer and William Dawe, two shipowners, who asked for the return of a ship, the *Davy*, with all her tackle, which they had given to John Treyouran, the master, 'for ever to the use and behoveth of your said oratours, trusting to his good faith'. They had since asked many times for the return of the ship, but Treyouran had refused and continued to take the profits from her for his own use. Brewer and Dawe asked the chancellor to consider the evidence, as they had no remedy at common law to recover the ship, and to grant them a writ to oblige the shipmaster to appear before the king in Chancery. They had no remedy at common law, presumably because of the lack of written evidence, and were obliged to fall back on the hope of an equitable decision in the Chancery Court.[21]

The responsibilities of partners

The touchstone of true partnership, of whatever type, is the acceptance by all the partners, singly and jointly, of responsibility for the debts of the partnership and the authority of each partner to bind the partnership. These precepts may be seen in many cases recorded in the London Plea and Memoranda Rolls. For example, in a case in 1363 before the mayor, aldermen and recorder, John Wroth sued William Tong for £617 10s. declaring that, by merchant law, when one of two partners bought goods for their common profit, the other was equally responsible for the debt. Tong offered to wage his law that he did not owe the money, to which Wroth replied that as Tong did not deny that he was a partner and was therefore responsible for the debts of the partnership, he was not entitled to clear himself by waging his law. While the court was adjourned for consultation, the plaintiff and defendant came to an agreement, but it is clear that by 1363, at least at merchant law, partners were recognised to be singly and jointly responsible for the debts of the partnership. A legal curiosity in this case, and perhaps the reason for the out-of-court settlement, is that at merchant law a defendant could not wage his law to affirm a negative. Postan quotes this case but appears not to have noticed the out-of-court settlement nor the one-sided nature of waging one's law.[22]

Investors spread the risks of ship-ownership by sharing in a number of ships,

---

[20] There is still some discussion (Professor P.S. Atiyah) as to whether a contract is a promise or an obligation. Maitland, 'Trust and Corporation', III, p. 333 and *passim*.
[21] Gardiner, *West Country Shipping*, no. 81, p. 97: a translation of PRO C1/36/109.
[22] Bickley, *Little Red Book*, 1, p. 58: 'Quomodo lex mercatoria differt a lege commune.'

just as merchants spread their risks by distributing their cargoes over more than one vessel. Such practices may be seen as a form of insurance, but as they do not remove the risk, but merely reduce it by dilution, they are not strictly insurance. Evidence of such risk distribution by shared ship-ownership and by split cargoes may be found in customs records where the shipowners are identifiable. The five partners in ownership of the cog *Seinte Marie* of Exmouth in 1310 have been mentioned above. Several of those shipped wine from the 1312 harvest on a number of ships, particularly Philip Lovecok who had 45 tuns and 34 tuns on two voyages of the *Seinte Marie*, 24 tuns and 29 tuns on two voyages of the *Margarete*, and 24.5 tuns on one voyage of the *Bonan* – about half of his total importation carried on the ship known to be partly his. In 1319–20, Lovecock's wine purchases were spread over four ships, two carrying the autumn vintage and two the early spring 'rack' wine. In this case only about one third of the total purchase was carried by the *Seinte Marie*. It is probable, given the even distribution of cargoes, that Lovecock was also part-owner of the other ships. The master of the *Seinte Marie*, Peres Godlok, was another of her part-owners but he appears to have shipped wine exclusively on her, taking advantage only of his portage and customs allowance.[23]

Investment in a commercial venture has to be distinguished from a loan; the former implies the sharing of any profit or loss from the venture while the latter requires the eventual repayment of the capital and accrued interest, regardless of the fortunes of the venture. As discussed in chapter 4, interest-bearing loans were illegal in the Middle Ages, but partnerships could be used dishonestly to avoid accusations of usury, by disguising interest payments as dividends, in other words, *usuria occulta*. To what extent loans to buy ships were concealed as partnerships between financiers and shipmasters cannot be known. The receipt of regular and equal payments in the accounts of a merchant or financier provides strong circumstantial evidence of money lent to, rather than invested in, a partnership (provided that the ship was not chartered or 'farmed' for regular rent payments). Irregular payments into an account are more likely to be shares in the trading profit of the ship.[24]

Another dishonest use of partnership was the exploitation of the privileges of one partner to 'colour' the goods of another, who was without the privileges, to evade by 'avowry' national or local restrictions and customs on imports and exports. This type of deception appears to have been not uncommon and may be seen in cases heard before the City of London courts in which local merchants

---

[23] *Local Customs Accounts of the Port of Exeter, 1266–1321*, ed. Maryanne Kowaleski, DCRS NS 36 (Exeter, 1993), pp. 122–6 and 173–7.
[24] Usury was any charge made for the use of money and was illegal. Interest was a penalty and not a charge for the use of the money. The church allowed payment of a penalty (*id quod interest*) if the lender suffered loss, or failed to make a gain, because of a delay in repayment.

were accused of 'colouring' goods passing through the docks. For example, in 1368 Thomas Serland, a freeman of London living in Flanders, coloured six bales of goods for import to Nicholas Sarduche who sold them on as 'duty paid'. In 1427 there appears to have been an attempt to clamp down on avowry with several cases appearing at about the same time. In one of these, John Lyng, a draper and freeman, allegedly coloured for an alien two packs of wool shipped for export, the two men, described as partners, using common funds for shared profit. Avowry could be organised within a quasi partnership with recompense to the local merchant on an agreed commission basis, or within a true profit sharing partnership of the *societas* type. Of the two cases above, one was a true partnership and the other may have been. At Lynn, too, in the fourteenth century, aliens were apparently in the habit of delivering their goods 'with their letters from various burghers in the wool-trade for their said merchandise' to avoid the high customs charges that would otherwise be levied on them. This abuse of partnership became sufficiently common to cause resentment amongst those merchants who, because of morality, fear of the law or lack of initiative, were not themselves engaged in avowry. Although no corroborative evidence has been found, unscrupulous shipmasters must have succumbed at times to the temptation of avowry when sailing to, or out of, a port town of which they had the freedom. Petitions in Parliament led to a prohibition of business liaisons between denizens and aliens by a 1340 statute which decreed that 'none cocket Wools, but in the Name of him that shall be Owner of the same'. That sanction was expanded in 1390 by a further statute forbidding denizens to clear wool and other merchandise belonging to aliens and so deprive the king of his customs, under threat of forfeiture of the goods. Such restrictions, however, do not appear to have deterred the avowers in the cases described above.[25]

Ship-ownership by several investors within a partnership could be in two forms. The joint-ownership type of partnership, in which each partner owned a fraction of the ship, made contributions to expenses and received a *pro rata* share of the profits derived from the ship's trading activities. This was characterised by the responsibility of every partner, singly or jointly, for all the partnership's debts. The alternative to part-ownership was an arrangement in which each investor held a share in what was effectively the company which owned the ship, receiving a share of the profits in the form of a dividend but without responsibility for the day-to-day expenses of operating the ship. In the *Coutumier*, which may be taken as a guide to common practice, it can be seen that both joint- and part-ownership existed. It may also be seen that it was possible to move from one to the other, either because of the default of one partner, or by mutual agreement when the partners differed in their proposals for the use of the ship. Joint-owner-

---

[25] *CPMR, 1364–81*, pp. 103–4; Serland and Sarduche appear to have been close business associates, perhaps partners *de facto* if not *de jure*. *CPMR, 1413–37*, pp. 212–13. *Statutes*, 14 Edward III, c. 21. *Rot. Parl.*, 14 Richard II, 3, p. 281, no. 26.

ship appears to have been the norm with part-ownership as the less common alternative, but unfortunately there is little surviving firm evidence for this. The *Coutumier* is concerned largely with joint-owner-partners all of whom are singly and jointly responsible for the venture, and share proportionally in the profits. The only clear reference to part-ownership is in the 1388 case of *Burwall v. Horne*, discussed above, in which the defaulting partner later decided to rejoin a venture but was to be allowed to do so only as a part-owner, with a restriction on his share of the profit. Part-ownership became common, of course, as shipping became accepted purely as an investment.[26]

As would be expected, the costs of running a ship were obligatorily shared between partners in joint-ownership. The case of *Bedon v. Richardesson*, also discussed above, may be seen as merely an extension of the concept of mutual responsibility as expected at merchant law. By the same token, the use of the ship had to be shared fairly amongst the partners, as emphasised in the *Coutumier*.[27]

The *Coutumier* explains the procedure for the sale of a partner's share in a ship. All partners had the option of buying another partner's share and the ship had to be made available to all the partners for a valuation survey. The price of any share to be sold was controlled by a reverse option rule by which the selling partner could buy the share of a bidding partner at the price offered by the latter. Offers by third parties, that is, by those outside the partnership, were precluded, except perhaps with the agreement of the whole partnership, since that would destroy the entity of the original partnership and because of the risk of price fixing between the selling partner and an outside bidder. An example of that provision in action has been discussed above, in the case of *Bridport v. Gyles*. When the sale had been effected, the terms of payment were laid down in the *Coutumier* as seven days from taking possession, an unusually precise condition.[28]

The sale of half of a ship and her cargo was disputed in Chancery in 1483. Thomas Croppe and Harry Hornbroke, both merchants, owned between them the ship *Andrew*, which was attacked on her way back from Nantes loaded with wine and other merchandise, and taken into Penmarc'h by Bretons. The two owners had been landed at Brest and they afterwards struck a mutual bargain at Plymouth that, for 100 *écus*, Hornbroke would take over Croppe's share of ship and cargo. In the event, Croppe allegedly returned to Brittany to claim everything as his own, refusing 'contrary to reason and conscience' to return the money or Hornbroke's half share. Two interesting points arise from this case; since the two men appeared to have had equal rights to ship and cargo, they were almost certainly legal partners in joint-ownership of the ship and, following the *essec* rule of options, Croppe could have reversed the sale and bought Hornbroke's share

---

[26] See chapter 1 and Appendix 3, *Coutumier*, chapter 83.
[27] Appendix 3, *Coutumier*, chapters 63, 64a, 83.
[28] Appendix 3, *Coutumier*, chapter 64b.

for 100 *écus*. Second, Hornbroke took his plea to Chancery because, he said in evidence, he had no remedy at common law. By 1483 partnerships and commercial obligations (the sale of the half share) were well recognised at common law, so the impediment must have been that the ship was abroad, beyond the reach of the common law courts.[29]

The participants in the ownership of a ship are referred to in *Customs* as *personers*, which Twiss has translated as 'part-owners'. A better translation would be 'partners', as their legal position was that of 'joint-owners' and the word is cognate with the Oléronais *parconners* used in the *Coutumier* to identify partners. Similarly, the position of the partner who in Catalan is described as *senyor de nau*, translated by Twiss as 'managing-owner', is the active partner working as shipmaster. The rules in *Customs* relating to multiple ownership are similar to those in the *Coutumier* when the shipmaster is one of the owners of the ship. The sale of a share in the ship by a sleeping partner requires the active partner's approval and *Customs* describes the steps to be taken by the active partner to defend his position. In the case of the active partner wishing to sell his share, he has an obligation to set up a reverse option deal with the other partners, a process similar to the *essec* in the *Coutumier*. *Customs* also covers the situation where the active partner sells the ship while away from the home port, without the prior permission of the other partners: he must 'render account' on his return and compensate the others for their shares.[30]

The advantages of partnership
Apart from the possibilities of participation in the profits of the ship, joint-ownership by partnership offered another advantage to the shipmaster – that of surety. In 1423, James Boudenson, master of the *Jacobknight* of Sluys, was released from gaol, where he had been held for trespass and account, when he swore that he owned half of the ship. He agreed to accept the court's decision at merchant law and entered in his own recognizance of £72 (the amount in dispute was £72 8s. 2d.) which was secured against the ship and the goods on board. Boudenson, who apparently not only owned half the vessel but had also contributed to the cargo, clearly had the authority to pledge at least part of the partnership's capital as collateral for himself. According to *Oleron*, if he had been a shipmaster with no share in the ship, he could have offered only equipment as security for a loan, and that only with the crew's consent, and not the ship's hull. In this case, although the ship was not in distress and he appears not to have consulted the crew, he was

---

[29] Gardiner, *West Country Shipping*, no. 94, pp. 115–6, from PRO C1/60/116.
[30] Twiss, *Black Book*, III, pp. 35–657: *Customs*, chapters ii, iii, x, xi, clxxxiv, ccii, ccxi and ccxlii:. Appendix 3, *Coutumier*, chapter 64b.

able to use the vessel as security for his release, precisely because he was a partner in her ownership.[31]

Whole-ship charter

The discussion on shipmasters has so far referred only to those who were partners in the ownership of the vessel and to professional masters who had been hired in a service agreement by the owning partnership. There was also a third category: the shipmaster of a chartered ship which had been put out 'to farm' by the owners. Such a shipmaster could be one of several partners who had accepted the full responsibility of the ship, with its profit and loss, in exchange for a fee; he could be acting on his own in a hiring agreement with the owners; or he could be subcontracted with the ship by the owners. The 'farming' of a ship to third parties was not uncommon and may be seen in the case mentioned above, p. 58. One example concerns two men, Walter Clerk and his partner, who took over a *batell* for two years for two thirds of the profits, with one third for the owner, an arrangement which would now be known as a 'bare-boat' charter. Something similar appears to have been arranged by Thomas and Margaret Stoon, husband and wife (interestingly described as 'partners'), who had to sue with a writ *corpus cum causa* for the return of their barge which had been 'let'.[32]

The charter of a 'skippered' vessel (i.e. with master included) was, for merchants, the alternative to paying freight, ton by ton, voyage by voyage. All the expenses and risks of the voyage, except those covered by warranty, presumably fell to the charterers. Such chartering would have been less expensive for merchants with sufficient goods to fill the vessel (or with colleagues with whom to share the ship's hold); it would also have allowed more flexibility in routes and timing, but could lead to having 'too many eggs in one basket'. In 1439 William Payne, citizen and ironmonger, chartered with warranty, *la Marie*, a lighter or 'kele' and her gear, for a year and a day from Roger Pye, a waterman, 'according to the *law of Olroms*'; this may have been a skippered time charter, with the owner (and perhaps his crew) accompanying the ship. Charters which included the master and crew, fed and paid by a third party (although still in the service of the owner), may be seen in the 1420s, when two of the ships belonging to the Crown were sent out on charter. It is clear from the accounts that the charterers were responsible for all the running expenses of the ships plus a fee due to the king; £20 for the *Holyghost of Spain*

---

[31] *CPMR, 1413–1437*, p. 169. Appendix 1, *Oleron*, article 1.
[32] *CLB*, Letterbook A, p. 61. PRO C1/31/234.

(290 tons) for two and a half months to sail to Zealand and back, and £10 for the *Valentine* (100 tons) for three months to sail to Calais and back.[33]

Shipowning as an investment

When participation in ownership of ships became an investment for financial rather than commercial reasons, the investors bought shares in the ships without entering partnerships. A share could be as small as a thirty-second part, but four or six part-owners were more common. Although there were considerable risks at sea, most ships returned safely and profitably and it was perhaps possible to recoup an investment relatively quickly except when the seas, and those sailing on them, were more than usually dangerous. Then, as a consequence, freight rates rose and with them, the potential profit. It has been suggested that the initial outlay in a ship on the Bristol–Spain run could be recovered within a year, and William Crathorn of York estimated in 1440 that the loss of his ship for 17 months had cost him at least £200. In contrast, the Celys appear to have been unconvinced that shipowning was profitable despite the preferential freight rates in their own ship, and without their incurring the loss of the ship or suffering any serious damage. The form of the brothers' partnership is not identifiable but each traded on his own account as if the ship were part-owned. Although merchants and merchant families were the largest single group of shipowners in the fourteenth and fifteenth centuries, at Dartmouth in 1467, 23 diverse 'partners and victuallers' of ships indicate how widely investment in ships had spread by the middle of the fifteenth century. The use of the word 'partner' in this context is confusing and may be wrong – it is more probable that the investors were shareholders in the ships. As the development of investment in shipping for purely financial motives evolved after the codification of *Oleron* and the *Coutumier*, no evidence of the workings of a shipping company may be gleaned from them. Disputes over commercial or contractual matters arising within a group of shareholders would have been heard in courts of merchant or common law whichever was considered to be more relevant to the argument.[34]

---

[33] CCR, 1435–41, p. 287. Surviving copies of *Oleron*, however, make no reference to ship chartering. Rose, *Lancastrian Navy*, pp. 64, 88–91.
[34] Jennifer Kermode, *Medieval Merchants, York, Beverley and Hull in the Later Middle Ages* (Cambridge, 1998), p. 212 citing Probate Registers, Borthwick Institute of Historical Research, York, III, fo. 556 (Joan Gregg), Hull Records Office, D81 and Hull Bench Book I, fo. 11. Enemy action in the mid-fifteenth century led to an acute shortage of English ships; freight rates were high and most imported wine was carried in alien ships: James, *Wine Trade*, p. 171; Childs, *Anglo-Castilian Trade*, p. 162; Kermode, *Medieval Merchants*, p. 213, citing Hanserecesse, 1431–76, II, pp. 542–5; Hanham, *Celys' World*, pp. 365 and 397.

The shipmaster's relationship with the ship's owners

So long as the master of a ship was her owner, acting on his own account and using his own money, or was a member of the partnership owning the vessel and was acting with the authority of the other partners, the only constraint on his business activities was his own, or the partnership's financial standing. On the other hand, when a shipmaster was an employee of the ship's owner(s), there must have been doubt about the extent to which he could be authorised to accept commitments on behalf of his employer(s) and how he could be restrained from commercial ventures beyond their means or wishes, a situation well recognised by merchant law. A couplet from Langland's *Piers Plowman*, written in the last quarter of the fourteenth century, illustrates the feudal restrictions placed on a servant or agent employed by his lord: 'For may no cherle chartre make, ne his chatel selle, / Withouten leave of his lord – no lawe wol it graunte.' If the master/servant relationship at sea were similar to that ashore, which is probable, then 'shipowner' may be read for 'lord', and the shipmaster's authority was severely restricted. This retention of responsibility by the owner for the legal, financial and administrative work of ship management can be seen in a charter-party of 1453 drawn up between John Heyton, a merchant, and Clement Bagot, the owner of the *Julian*. In the agreement it was stipulated that the freight money should be paid at the end of the voyage to the owner or his factor or attorney but not to the master, John White, although he had the authority to reserve space for Bagot's and Heyton's wine along with six tuns of wine for himself.[35]

Sea loans, taken out by a shipmaster to allow him to continue a voyage, at a fixed rate of interest for an agreed term, and more especially 'bottomry', where the loan was against the security of the ship's hull at an uncontrolled rate of interest with repayment due on completion of the voyage, were commitments of potential risk for the owners. Sea loans and bottomry, and their use as forms of insurance, are discussed in chapter 4 under 'Loans'. In 1486, the *Margaret Cely* was delayed in Plymouth for 11 weeks with a partially unloaded cargo. To pay for repairs, William Aldridge, the purser, borrowed 25s. 8d. against the ship as collateral, accepting all the risks that bottomry entailed rather than sell part of the cargo, and went up to London to collect more money from the owners. As such a loan contravened *Oleron*, it must be assumed that Aldridge had the Celys' authority for the loan. Similarly, a shipmaster's use of the ship, the cargoes he found, the freight rates he negotiated, the voyages he undertook, the terms and conditions of service he arranged for his crew, and the duration of his own period of service, must all have been pre-defined and agreed, if not in writing then at least by solemn undertaking, following generally accepted rules.[36]

---

[35] *Piers Plowman*, passus xi, lines 125–6. CPMR, 1381–1412, pp. 133–4.
[36] Hanham, *Celys' World*, pp. 370–1. Alison Hanham, ed., *The Cely Letters 1472–1488*, EETS OS 273 (1975), p. 226. Appendix 1, *Oleron*, article 1.

When a shipmaster was himself a partner in the ownership of the vessel, then the rules of the partnership, both those generally recognised and those specific to that agreement, defined his obligations and his authority. When a shipmaster was an employee, however, in effect acting as the agent of the shipowners, the problem of controlling his aspirations might well have fallen between the differing views under common and merchant law, on the master/servant relationship. Despite the perceived difficulties, there is remarkably little evidence of attempts to control a shipmaster, beyond a few articles in the surviving collections of maritime law. No indenture or other contractual agreement between owners and shipmaster has been found; indeed, in 1465–68, as mentioned above, William Brewer and William Dawe, petitioning for the return of their ship, *Davy* of Fowey by the master John Treyouran, could produce no written evidence of the original transaction, saying that they trusted to Treyouran's good faith. That this occurred as late as the mid-fifteenth century suggests that written agreements of employment were perhaps unusual in the fourteenth and first half of the fifteenth centuries.

The authority that could be delegated by shipowners to their employed shipmaster was severely restricted in *Oleron* by a blanket prohibition on the sale of the hull or equipment, and by permitting the pledging of equipment only to raise funds to complete the voyage or to return the crew to their home port if the ship were unable to continue (provided the crew had assisted during the crisis). There appears to have been a readily available pawnbrokerage or money-lending service in port towns to cater for the pledging of equipment. In 1404 Nicholas Bygge pled in Chancery that he had pledged most of his ship's tackle to raise cash to keep his crew together while the ship was under arrest on the Thames for naval service and, as mentioned above, the Cely's purser raised a loan in Plymouth in 1486. In *Queenborough* there is no reference to a shipmaster's responsibilities, authority or conditions of service, except for the oblique threat of an inquiry into any excessive payments made to him or his crew. In the *Coutumier* there is a reference, and that only as an aside in the definition of the responsibilities of the pilot, to a shipmaster's responsibility for the management of the ship; he is required to be in command of the ship from the port of lading to the port of discharge. There is also a somewhat confused statement elsewhere in the *Coutumier* about the responsibility of an owner who has put on board the ship a man who causes damage. Here, it is not clear if the reference is to an ineffective shipmaster or to a careless seaman. The general silence on the subject of the shipmaster's responsibilities, particularly as an employee, is one of the several puzzles encountered in an examination of medieval ship management.[37]

---

[37] Appendix 1, *Oleron*, articles 1, 3, 23. Gardiner, *West Country Shipping*, no. 8, pp. 7–8, from PRO C 1/69/312. Hanham, *Celys' World*, pp. 370–1. Appendix 2, *Queenborough*, article 64. Appendix 3, *Coutumier*, chapter 88.

Customs contains much more information about the shipmaster's responsibilities although, if Twiss's translation of *senyor de nau* as 'managing partner' is correct, he has to be seen generally as one of the owners. The rules include a variety of situations: the responsibilities of the master towards the merchants and passengers; an obligation for the master to apply for permission from the other owners to arrange freight in a dangerous place; and the placing of responsibility on the master if he delays a sailing. *Customs* also contains an oath to be taken by the *notxer* (translated by Twiss as 'mate') and authorises him to sail the ship at sea, but not in and out of harbours, without the owners' consent. It specifies the skills he should have, including measuring and cutting sails and stowing cargo, an interesting list as it is the only job description and measure of competence of a ship's officer that has been found. There is no reference to a mate or second-in-command in *Oleron*, *Queenborough* or the *Coutumier* although one would expect that position to have been an essential step in the training of future shipmasters.[38]

It may be that the absence of a definitive list of the shipmaster's responsibilities in the English legal maritime codes was due to an assumption that either he would always be the sole owner, and could do what he pleased within the rules for the treatment of the crew, or he would be a member of the shipowning partnership, working within its rules and pretensions. Several articles in the codes, and in particular *Oleron*, appear to have been drawn up in the days of shared maritime trading ventures, while others refer to the responsibilities of an employed shipmaster. As a result, the collection of rules that makes up *Oleron* is a miscellany of instructions to a shipmaster in three possible roles: as the *primus inter pares* of a cooperative, as the whole or part-owner of the ship, or as the waged employee of the owners. The layers of articles added over many years reflect the evolution of the shipping industry from cooperatives to individual shipmaster/owners to waged shipmasters employed by shipowning investors. The articles of maritime law were not revised as the status of the shipmaster changed but rather additional articles were added, as in the decisions of the *Inquisition of Queenborough*, to cope with the increasing complexity of the industry.

A summary of the shipmaster's options

A man wishing to become a shipmaster after acquiring the necessary knowledge and experience had to obtain a ship. There were several options, each dependent on his financial situation, his business contacts and his reputation. He could be an employee of a ship's owners, perhaps a useful starting point for his career, enter one of various types of partnership to share the financial burden or the work load,

---

[38] Twiss, *Black Book*, III, pp. 50–657, *passim*; *Customs*, chapters ii–xi, xvi, xvii, clxxxiv and cxc.

or become the sole owner. By and large, the money to be made as a shipmaster reflected the degree of responsibility he had accepted; sole ownership risked his all but brought undiluted rewards, employment earned him a fixed wage, and the various degrees of partnership dictated his share of the trading profit of the ship. In the period 1350–1450 the shipmaster's position achieved some security as common law came slowly to recognise the concepts of contract, trust and partnership and the responsibilities inherent in each. Despite that, the possibility of accumulating wealth as a shipmaster, whether as sole owner, partner or employee, depended on his overcoming the many risks, natural, commercial and financial to which he and his ship were to be exposed.

4

The Shipmaster's On-Shore Responsibilities

Credit

The borrowing and lending of money by participants in the fourteenth- and fifteenth-century maritime industry has to be viewed in the light of contemporary mercantile practices. There was widespread use of credit, in the form of extended repayment terms, in all branches of English home and overseas trade from the thirteenth century onwards. Chaucer's remark, in 'The Shipman's Tale', about the merchant 'Ther wist no wight that he was in dette, / So estatly was he of his governaunce' suggests a generally recognised lack of solvency amongst merchants around 1400. Further, as Sloth confesses in *Piers Plowman*, written about the same time: 'If I bigge and borwe aught, but if [unless] it be ytailed [recorded] / I foryete it as yerne [immediately], and if men me it axe / Sixe sithes [times] or sevene, I forsake it with othes [deny it with oaths]', not all debts were repaid in time. Edward I's and Edward's III's legislative attempts to protect creditors by the registration of debts led to the enrolment of many agreements. These registrations, and the records of litigation against debtors, in a variety of court rolls and fourteenth- and fifteenth-century letterbooks and recognisance rolls, are evidence of the wide use of credit. Since many less formal credit arrangements were made and agreed with only a handshake, the tally stick, an exchange of earnest money or the giving of 'God's penny' (all in the presence of witnesses), the full extent of the use of credit cannot be known.[1]

Fourteenth-century wool merchants traded in wool futures as well as from stock in hand, buying anticipated clips up to three years ahead against credit extended for six or more months. Final payment was not made until the proceeds of overseas sales had been received, and was subject to the liquidity of the Calais mint and the availability of bullion. Sales credit was also common for other commodities; the account book of the London ironmonger, general merchant and shipowner Gilbert Maghfeld, shows that in the 1390s over 75 per cent of his trading

---

[1] *Statutes*, 11 Edward I, Statute of Acton-Burnell; 27 Edward III, st. 2, Statute of the Staple, c.; *Denarius ad deum* gave divine sanction to a transaction, accepted as validation by the *Carta Mercatoria* of 1303.

was against deferred payment, often with renewed letters of obligation extending the credit beyond six months. In the fifteenth century, the accounts of the Celys, a merchant family who also owned a ship, show that they sold wool on credit in all of their recorded transactions. These merchants' arrangements were, of course, only the visible links in the chains of credit and there may well have been unrecorded cash sales. Although it is not possible to quantify the overall ratio of cash to credit, nor to be sure of the prevalence of credit offered for different commodities, by the late fourteenth century the amount of business done on credit extending to several months was considerable.[2]

Because credit sales were so common in all trades, it is probable that much of a ship's cargo of wool, cloth or agricultural produce for export, and wine, salt, textile chemicals and other goods for import, had been bought on deferred payment terms. Shipmasters also offered extended credit by requiring only part, 25 per cent upwards, of the freight charge on lading, the rest to be paid either immediately on arrival at the destination or within a specified time after unloading. With the cargo and much of the freight cost caught in this web of credit, doubts about title to the goods in marine exigencies such as lost cargo, a call for contribution to general average, or a lien on the cargo for outstanding freight payment, must have led to many broken credit chains and the ruin of the financially stretched. The astute shipmaster could retain the initiative in such cases by refusing to unload his ship until he was satisfied or had sold the cargo for his own profit.

Financial and commercial instruments

For shipmasters, freighting agreements (or 'charter-parties') made with shipping merchants constituted a complete record of the service and financial obligations of both parties; they are discussed in detail below, pp. 78–93. For merchants offering and demanding credit and giving and taking loans, a formal legal procedure for the registration of debts together with recognised negotiable instruments for the transfer of funds in the same or different currencies were also required. In the fourteenth century, when a line of credit was formally arranged, the terms of repayment with dates and locations were commonly recorded as a debt in an obligatory, or in effect, a promissory note, a *scriptum obligatorium*. Any interest agreed between the parties was concealed in the transaction by falsifying the sales price, or by adjusting the rate of exchange between currencies, to avoid accusations of usury. A *scriptum* concerning a loan, produced as evidence and accepted at merchant law in the London mayoral court in 1386, demonstrates a general acceptance of

---

[2] E. Power, *The Wool Trade in English Medieval History* (Oxford, 1941), pp. 41–57. Lloyd, *Wool Trade*, pp. 295–313. James, *Wine Trade*, p. 203–4. Postan, *Medieval Trade*, pp. 21–2. Hanham, *Celys' World*, p. 137.

scripta and their remarkable flexibility. The loan had been effected in Zealand by representatives of the lender and borrower but was pursued by the principals in London.[3] Alternatively loans could be registered as debts under the several provisions of the *Carta Mercatoria* (1303) and the Statute of the Staple (1354) with its various additions. Such statutory bonds were less formal than obligatory letters but were recognised nationally; although valid only within England, they were, in effect, the forerunners of bills of exchange. However, the number of disputes concerning statutory bonds in the plea rolls perhaps indicates that the traditional enrolment of debts continued to be used for trade debts and loans.[4]

Bills of exchange evolved from the *scriptum obligatorium*, perhaps in the light of experience with statutory bonds, for credit or loan transactions. For international money transfers, *scripta* were sent with instructions to an associate of the borrower for him to recognise the *scriptum* and to repay the debt to the creditor in the required currency. The 'letter of payment' which accompanied the *scriptum* gave the details of the act or bond which had formalised the debt, and it was this letter which evolved into the bill of exchange. Bills of exchange were also used as security for an agreement which otherwise might be considered unsure. Although they were negotiable and could change hands several times, such bills required authorisation by notaries public or some other empowered official, and generally had to be backed by sufficient security. The earliest known reference in England to their use is a delivery of bills of exchange to Antwerp for Flemish merchants in 1303. Despite opposition from the Crown, who saw bills of exchange as a means of exporting bullion, they became increasingly popular. By 1330 bills of exchange were fully developed as part of what de Roover has described as a commercial revolution, and from that time bills were freely used in foreign transactions whenever greater flexibility and security than that offered by cash were required. Transferable *scripta* and bills became, in effect, paper money; they relied on the continuation of commerce to ensure their value and at the same time facilitated and therefore encouraged commercial transactions.[5]

Initially the bills were for the genuine transfer of money but it was soon discovered that, as they generally did not show the rates of exchange used, such transfers offered convenient cover for illegal interest on loans or sales credits. By buying and selling bills, lenders could receive more money abroad than they had lent at home. The Celys frequently used bills of exchange, sometimes with a bearer clause, and very variable rates of interest can be seen in their records, for example: a rate

---

[3] *CPMR, 1381–1412*, p. 125.
[4] *Statutes* 27 Edward III st. 2 and 28 Edward III cc. 13, 14 and 15. Gross and Hall, *Law Merchant*, III, p. xii.
[5] PRO C 47/13/3 is an obligatory letter detailing repayment in another currency: 2,430 Florentine florins and 15d. sterling with an exchange value *pro precio et cambio* of 600 marks sterling – which may have concealed interest. Marsden, *Select Pleas*, I, p. xxxi. R. de Roover, *Lettre de change*, p. 40. Bolton, *Medieval English Economy*, pp. 302–5.

of 8.5 per cent for a five-month loan (an APR > c.19 per cent) and 7 per cent for an eight- or nine-month loan (an APR of c.9.5 per cent). Interest rates were influenced by the reliability of the borrower, the stability of the money markets, the political situation, the amount borrowed and so on. Currency exchange rates were also manipulated for profit alone without any commercial transaction, as the merchant in Chaucer's 'Shipman's Tale': 'Wel koude he in eschaunge sheeldes selle', to profit from illicit currency deals. Shipmasters were, of course, accustomed to working in several currencies, for example in overseas payments of crew's wages, victualling, repairs, various dues, and in receipt of freight payments and they, no doubt, similarly played the currency markets.[6]

Loans

To what extent shipmasters became involved in loans in the course of their business cannot be quantitatively assessed from the information available. To buy a ship, or a share in a ship, shipmasters would often necessarily have to borrow money, unless they had entered a partnership agreement with financiers prepared to put up the capital required, as discussed in chapter 3. When buying a ship without the support of partners, a shipmaster could use the ship herself as security, the loan becoming, in effect, a mortgage. Although no documentary evidence for this has been found, such loans, which should not be confused with sea loans or bottomry, would have been enrolled in a local court with details of the security and the period of the loan, probably with one or two guarantors.

Sea loans were a specialised form of bills of exchange against which a shipmaster or merchant borrowed money at the port of lading and undertook to repay the loan at the ship's destination in the currency of that place, the interest perhaps being lost in the rate of exchange used to calculate the amount to be repaid. Such loans are discussed below under 'Insurance' (p. 75).

An important factor in such transactions was that the risk was borne by the lender; if the ship failed to arrive, the loan was not repaid. Sea loans given under those terms, therefore, were a form of insurance against loss at sea, and the rate at which the loans were offered had to reflect not only the interest but also the element of risk for the lender. Bottomry, a mortgage taken out against the security of the hull and to be repaid on arrival of the ship, was only for those *in extremis*. It had no insurance element; if the ship were lost, the loan went too, and if the ship returned safely, the loan was repayable at a high rate of interest which, on the grounds of necessity, was not seen as usury. As mentioned in chapter 3, in 1486, the *Margaret Cely* was delayed in Plymouth for 11 weeks with a partially unloaded

---

[6] Hanham, *Celys' World*, pp. 190–2 and 194–202. Chaucer, *Complete Works*, 'The Shipman's Tale', p. 156. *Statutes*, 25 Edward III, st. 5.

cargo of wine belonging to Tibbot Oliver. To pay for repairs, William Aldridge, the purser, borrowed 25s. 8d.; using the ship as collateral, he accepted the risks of bottomry rather than sell part of the cargo, although the risks were reduced by the ship remaining in harbour. The wine was eventually unloaded and the loan repaid. As the arrangement of such a loan contravened *Oleron*, it appears that Aldridge had authority from the owners, the Celys.[7]

Accountancy

Throughout most of the fourteenth century, accounts were kept in narrative or diary form; dealings being entered as they occurred, whether debits or credits, for each venture. The use of roman numerals, which are not easy to employ in calculations, compounded the problem; every arithmetical process of any complexity had to be made on an abacus or other calculating device. The lack of transparency of the accounts made it extremely difficult to assess the liquidity of a business and calculations of such fundamental ratios as profit to capital employed were probably never made. Chaucer describes the merchant (incidentally cuckolded) in 'The Shipman's Tale' laboriously balancing his books:

> And up into his countour-hous gooth he
> To rekene with hymself, as wel he may be,
> Of thilke yeer how that it with hym stood,
> And how that he despended hadde his good,
> And if that he encressed were or noon.
> His bookes and his bagges many oon
> He leith biforn hym on his countyng-bord.

Later his wife asks "'what, sire, how longe wol ye faste? / How longe tyme wol ye rekene and cast / Youre sommes, and youre bookes, and youre thynges?'" and later still urges, "'Com doun to-day, and lat youre bagges stoned.'" Bookkeeping was clearly an intricate operation and recognised as such by Chaucer and his audience.[8]

Towards the end of the fourteenth century, arabic numerals began to be used in commercial accounting and later the diary type of record evolved into a single column ledger. In this the transactions were separated into groups by customer or supplier, by credits or debits, and by venture. Slowly, with Italian examples to copy, double entry bookkeeping came to be adopted, until, with systematic and readable accounts available, it became possible for the first time to calculate accu-

---

[7] Hanham, *Celys' World*, pp. 370–1 citing File 13, fo. 32; the merchant, Tibbot Oliver, was unsurprisingly 'nott well content that sche tarryth soo longe'. Appendix 1, *Oleron*, article 3.
[8] Chaucer, *Complete Works*, 'The Shipman's Tale', p. 156.

rately and quickly the surplus earned from a venture and to measure the return on the capital employed.⁹

Gilbert Maghfeld used arabic numerals in his accounts (except for the month in the date) in the 1390s, but his bookkeeping consisted only of day-to-day journal-type entries. He merely cancelled the debts due to him after settlement – if he remembered or wanted to – and there was much clearing up to do after his death. John Balsall, purser of the *Trinity* of Bristol, drew up the ship's accounts for a seven month voyage to Oran via Irish and Spanish ports in 1480–81. They are divided into sections for payment and issues of clothing to the crew, purchase of equipment and victuals for the ship, and running expenses such as pilotage and gifts to local dignitaries. The cash sums are entered in roman numerals (as late as 1480) in sterling or Spanish *maravedis* converted from Spanish *reales*, *enriques* and *castellanos*, Portuguese *cruzados* and gold florins. Although the accounts are not compiled chronologically, it is possible to construct an approximate chronology from the occasional inclusion of dates. Even by the late fifteenth century it was not always possible to assess the liquidity of a business from the accounts available; the decline and failure of the Cely family enterprise was partly due to an unawareness of the dangers of expensive money bought through ever increasing loans, although the major factor was probably the difficulties they encountered in releasing funds in Calais and Bruges.¹⁰

The widening interest in investment in shipping, which was probably the most capital-intensive medieval enterprise, is usually explained by there being a more general availability of funds. Access to meaningful accounts may have been the catalyst that encouraged people who had little or no interest in investment in land to look at ships as alternative financial opportunities, in addition to merchants looking to expand their interests.

Insurance

Insurance, the covering of risk, should not be confused with the dilution of risk, commonly effected by the distribution of a merchant's goods, or the spread of a shipowner's investment over several ships. The rationale of cargo-spreading was summarised by Shakespeare two centuries later in the *The Merchant of Venice* in which Antonio says: 'My ventures are not in one bottom trusted … Therefore my merchandise makes me not sad.' The Staplers loaded an average of only two

---

9 Edward Peragallo, *Origin and Evolution of Double Entry Bookkeeping* (New York, 1938), *passim*.
10 James, *Wine Trade*, p. 204 citing Maghfeld's ledger PRO E101/509/19 fo. 23r. *The Accounts of John Balsall, Purser of the Trinity of Bristol, 1480–1*, ed. T.F. Reddaway and Alwyn A. Ruddock, Camden Miscellany, 4th series, XXIII, 7 (London, 1969), pp. 1–27. Hanham, *Celys' World*, pp. 398 ff.

sarplars of wool per ship: William de la Pole shipped his 1337 wool export in 12 separate lots from Hull and two from Boston, and in 1365–66, 217 merchants sent 1359 separate shipments in 178 shiploads from London. The 1319–20 wine loading arrangements of Philip Lovecock and other importers are discussed on pp. 58–9.[11]

A shipmaster, with only his skill and strength as protection against *risica gentium et maris* when caught at sea by enemies, storms, tidal currents or the consequences of poor navigation, had no means of spreading his risk. Losses due to enemy or piratical action were often the subject of claims for compensation, and could lead to authorised or unauthorised reprisal seizure of property belonging to co-nationals of the perpetrators. Although not insurance, when such compensation was arranged in a legal manner, it was a form of state aid. An alternative for a shipmaster was collaboration, perhaps partnership, with someone able and willing to accept the financial risk in exchange for a high proportion of the profits. The financial partnership of the type seen in the 1292 arrangement by Geoffrey le Norton and Walter le Mounier, discussed in chapter 3, p. 52, might be described as an early example of insurance for the active partner who had invested less in the venture. Similarly, a shipmaster who chose not to buy the whole of his own ship could take advantage of the financial cover of his investing partner. For a shipmaster participating in a shipowning partnership in consideration of a labour-only contribution, insurance cover for financial loss was irrelevant. For the shipping merchant with credit liabilities for cargo and transport and for the partner with money invested in a ship, her loss might well threaten both with bankruptcy; for them, insurance cover of any sort, rather than merely a spreading of the risk, would have been of great interest.

Other possibilities that existed for insurance cover for merchants and perhaps for shipowners included various forms of contingency loans, exploitation of currency exchange differences, false or adjusted sales contracts, port town municipal arrangements and premium insurance. All of these may have been used, but there is little surviving evidence of any before the early fifteenth century. A modification of the straightforward loan was the 'sea loan' which made use of a specialised bill of exchange valid for the single or return voyage of a ship. If she or her cargo failed to complete the voyage, then the bill was not repayable, but if all went well, the loan had to be repaid in the currency of the intended place of arrival. An example of such a deal, known because it went wrong, is that of *Gaspar Sculte*

---

[11] PRO, E 122/55/5 and 6. Distributing consignments over several ships is described in H. Bradley, 'The Datini Factors in London, 1380–1410', in *Trade, Devotion and Governance*, ed., D.J. Clayton, R.G. Davies and P. McNiven (Stroud, 1994), p. 67. Hanham, *Celys' World*, pp. 129–30. E.B. Fryde, 'The Wool Accounts of William de la Pole', in *Studies in Medieval Trade* (London, 1983), pp. 3–31 citing PRO E101/457/9 and E122/7/6. Vanessa A. Harding, 'The Port of London in the Fourteenth Century, Topography, Administration and Trade', unpublished PhD thesis, University of St Andrews, 1983, pp. 259–60 citing PRO E122/70/18.

et al. v. William Long et Thomas Hoo Esq., Sculte being the shipmaster-owner of *Le Berie*.[12]

To avoid any accusations of usury, the mechanism of the loan would be the advance of an amount less than that registered, the whole declared loan being repayable on successful completion of the venture. The lender then recovered not only his capital but also, as compensation for risk, the concealed interest on the bill and any profit arising from a good rate of exchange on the currency of repayment. The danger for the shipmaster or merchant taking out a sea loan was that the rate of exchange could be so low that it took up all the profits of the venture whether earned by the resale of the cargo or from the freight charges levied by the shipmaster. A further disadvantage for those with sufficient funds, but who wished to arrange insurance against certain risks by a sea loan, was that they were obliged to accept the expense and risks of borrowing unnecessarily.

Repayable loan arrangements may have been the earliest form of marine insurance; such cover was known to classical Greek and Roman traders. No evidence has been found of overt insurance loans in England in the fourteenth and fifteenth centuries, but the necessarily clandestine nature of the transactions required effective and impenetrable camouflage.[13]

In contrast to sea loans, bottomry, which has been discussed above, was terminal, repayable at the end of the voyage, and inevitably carried high interest. Mortgaging of the ship in this way was a hazardous arrangement for both lender and borrower and did not offer insurance for either party. If the ship were lost, the lender had no redress on the loan and the shipowner lost the ship without compensation; if she returned safely, the lender received back the sum ventured plus a high premium justified by the risk, and the shipowner retained his ship, but at the high cost of the loan.

Premium marine insurance was probably developed in Italy in the late thirteenth or early fourteenth century by merchants trading overseas who required cover but were disenchanted with the available types of loans and bills. The risks involved were calculable empirically from their experience over long periods and, provided the premiums offered sufficient return to the insurer, it would not have been impossible to find financiers prepared to accept the risks. The earliest known premium insurance contracts, excluding those disguised as *in mutuo gratis et amore* (interest-free loans), date from 1350 and were drawn up in Palermo. Since that port was one of the less important commercial centres, marine insurance was probably already being practised in the more important centres of Pisa, Florence and Venice. The contemporary Genoese form of insurance appears to have resembled a loan or a sea loan but, instead of the insured promising to repay the loan if

[12] PRO C1/26/193 and *Year Book* 21 Edward IV, Pasch., pl. 23.
[13] A.D.M. Forte, 'Marine Insurance and Risk Distribution in Scotland before 1800', *Law and History Review*, 5 (1967), p. 395, footnote 8.

he arrived safely, the insurer promised to pay him if he did not arrive safely; a true insurance policy disguised as a loan only by name. This pseudo-loan gave way in Genoa after 1365 to a contract of purchase and sale; the insurer undertook to buy any goods lost at sea, thereby obtaining undisputed title to anything that might be found later, except perhaps at English common law, where right of title was less clearly defined than in merchant law, a subject discussed in chapter 1.[14]

The earliest premium marine insurances in England were probably underwritten by Italians using the Florentine or Genoese formulae described above. A surviving example of a Florentine-type policy is that taken out by Alexander Ferrantyn in 1426 for his ship *Seint Anne* of London, master John Starling, which was then lying in Bordeaux laden with wine. For a premium of £22 (8.8 per cent), cover was arranged for £250, of which £200 was for the ship, until she had anchored in the Thames. She was captured at sea by Spaniards who took her to Sluys and there sold her to two Flemings. Ferrantyn claimed the £250 from the 17 Venetian, Genoese and Florentine merchant underwriters according to merchant law and the 'manner, order and custom' of the Florentines under which the insurance had been arranged. He did not deny that he had bought back the ship and her cargo through the agency of a certain John Waynflete. The underwriters refused payment on the grounds that, again according to the manner, order and custom of the Florentines (although those were not included in the bill of contract), if the owner brought back the ship and merchandise at 'second, third, fourth or thousandth hand' then those who had assumed the risk were 'quit and absolved therefrom'. In court Ferrantyn stood on the plain terms of the contract, and the defendants on the unwritten custom of the Florentines; in the end the insurers failed to produce written proof of their defence and forfeited both the £250 and a further bond of £100. A later example of premium insurance may be seen in a hearing before the mayor of London in 1480, by which time such business was probably better organised. John Pecok, attorney for the Genoese Antonio Spynule, a merchant, formally acknowledged receipt of £6 13s. 4d. from Marco Strozze, due under a bill of assurance for goods recently loaded as cargo in *Le Francesse*. Pecok claimed that his copy of the bill was lost and could not be cancelled. Those cases may have been only the tip of an iceberg of premium insurance in England in the fifteenth century but no further evidence has been found.[15]

The premiums for insurance cover would have depended on an assessment of the perceived risks of the voyage, including the type of ship, distance and season, the state of war or peace prevailing, the incidence of piracy along the route and, perhaps, the reputation of the shipmaster and his crew. It is not known how much 'historical performance' information was available to the insurers, nor with what accuracy the risks were calculated. Ferrantyn's premium was 8.8 per cent of the

[14] F. de Roover, 'Marine Insurance', pp. 183–4.
[15] *CPMR*, 1413–1437, pp. 208–10, and 1458–82, p. 139.

value of his ship and cargo for the journey from Bordeaux to the Thames at an unknown time of year (since the cargo was wine, it could have been autumn or early spring). Known Florentine rates include 8 per cent from Cadiz to Sluys or Southampton in August 1384 and 12 to 15 per cent for London to Pisa in 1442. Neapolitan rates were 9 per cent for English wool ships sailing from Southampton to Leghorn and 10, 12 and 14 per cent from Southampton to Pisa, Piombino and Talamone. All of those rates are high and reflect the hazards to which the insured were exposed in their slow, fully laden and vulnerable ships.[16]

An evolving descending line of cover against risk may be traced from financial partnerships, particularly those of a terminal nature, to sea loans, bills of exchange, the Genoese purchase system and finally to premium insurance. All required a financier to place his capital at risk in exchange for a consideration – but only in the last two, the most evolved, did the merchant or shipowner have to pay for his cover in advance, leaving the financier with no outgoings unless and until the venture failed. A further type of insurance, although not known to have been practised in England, was that offered municipally or nationally. As early as 1293 Dinis, king of Portugal, ordered the merchants of Oporto to contribute to a fund to cover losses incurred through weather or enemy action when sailing to foreign parts. The premium was 20 *soldos distillis* for each ship of more than 100 tons, and half that for ships under 100 tons. Sometime before 1380, king Fernando ordered by *carta régia* the setting up of a Companhia das Naus, first in Lisbon and then in Oporto, to which every ship had to pay two crowns per cent of the profits of every voyage, in return for which they were completely covered against shipwreck or capture. Unfortunately, the fund in Oporto was found to have an 'activity, irregular or in some way ephemeral' (!) and in 1397 the council and *homens bons* asked for authority to revert to the earlier fixed premium scheme, which appears to have continued for some time. Municipal insurance of that type clearly worked; it is curious that no similar scheme is known to have been attempted in English port towns.[17]

Charter-parties and freighting agreements[18]

An agreement to ship goods which do not fill the entire vessel is, in current English, a freighting agreement, while a charter-party is a contract to hire the whole ship either for a fixed period (a time charter), or for a specific voyage (a

---

[16] F. de Roover, 'Marine Insurance', p. 190.
[17] António Cruz, 'Quadros da vida social e económica da cidade do Porto no sêculo quinze', *Anais da Academia Portuguesa de História*, 2nd series, 26, 2 (Lisbon, 1980), pp. 202–13.
[18] Much of the material in this section may be found in two papers by R.M. Ward, 'A Surviving Charter-Party of 1323', *Mariner's Mirror* 81, 4 (1995), pp. 387–401 and 'English Charter-Parties in the Fourteenth and Fifteenth Centuries', Association for the History of the Northern Seas, *Yearbook 1999*, pp. 1–22, in both of which there are more detailed discussions.

THE SHIPMASTER'S ON-SHORE RESPONSIBILITIES

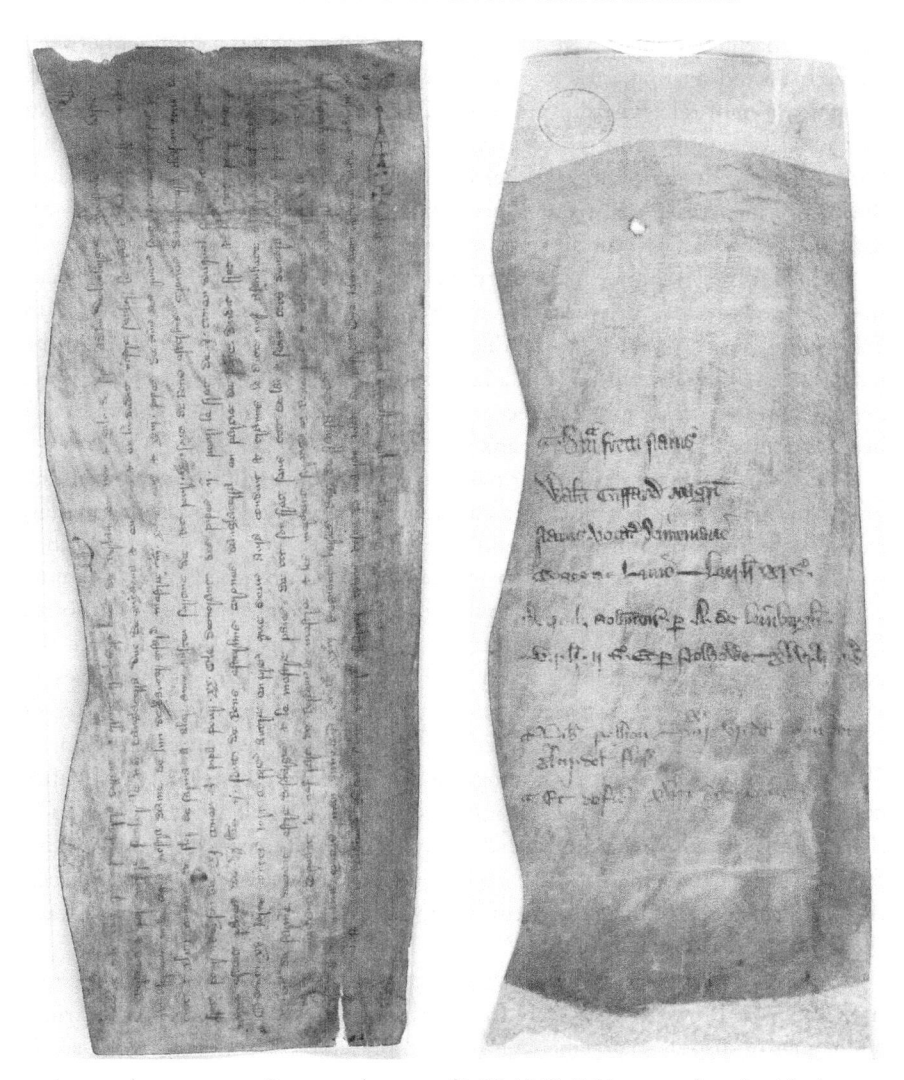

2 A 1323 charter-party. Recto and verso of MS AML/M/1, reproduced with the kind permission of the National Maritime Museum, Greenwich.

terminal charter). In the late Middle Ages, a charter-party was a contract between a merchant and a shipmaster to deliver a quantity of goods to a certain port at an agreed freight rate, whether the goods filled part or the whole of the ship. An individual merchant's ventures were unlikely to fill the whole cargo space of a ship, but several merchants acting together could justify the cost of chartering a ship, the voyage being covered by one charter-party. In this chapter the term 'charter-party, is used generically for all types of medieval shipping contract.

Although they were not mandatory, written agreements were sensible precautions for transactions between merchants and shipmasters. The signatories to fourteenth- and fifteenth-century English charter-parties expected them to be recognised as legal documents and a late fourteenth-century cynical Dutch jingle demonstrates the need for such recognition: 'It lasted a while, but not long, as I heard, because it was an Englishman's word.'[19]

Charter-parties were written out twice on a membrane of parchment or vellum, or later on paper, and separated by a cut along a sinuous line into a pair of indentures, sometimes with an inked doodle across the cut for added security. They were drawn up by a notary, signed or marked by the contracting parties, solemnly witnessed by several others, and often registered with the local legal authority. Each party kept the half with the other's signature, or 'mark manual', until the completion of the undertaking when they signed and exchanged the halves as quittances. In Figure 2, a 1323 charter-party, the mark manual and signatures of the contracting parties may be seen recto, with the signed quittance on the dorse; also visible is the hole made by a filing spike. The formal exchange of halves after completion was often recorded in court records. For example, a memorandum in the London mayoral court notes that Henry Field, shipmaster, had received his freight payment from John Waryn, a merchant, for a completed delivery of salt on the cog *Seinte Marie* from Bourgneuf Bay to Bristol, and that all matters between the two men had been cleared up.[20]

By their nature, charter-parties were ephemeral and few original manuscripts have survived. However they were frequently used as evidence in court hearings and copies of disputed agreements have been preserved in court records. Usually only the plaintiff's plea has been recorded, although sometimes, after mid-fifteenth century, the defendant's answer appears. Only rarely can the court's judgment or decision be found in the records, but occasionally the result of a hearing may be seen in subsequent happenings recorded elsewhere, for example, in the confiscation of a ship or cargo or in an order for arrest. Caution has to be exercised when

---

[19] 'Dit ghedverde ene stont, / Maer niet langhe, als ic verhoerde, / Want het was Ingelsche vorworde':: H.P.H. Jansen, 'Holland's Advance', *Acta Historiae Nederlandicae*, X (1978), referring to the moves of the Staple.
[20] *CPMR*, 1364–8, p. 120: 'Et super hoc liberavit coram eisdem Maiore et Aldermannis in plena Curia cartam bipartitam inter eos de frettagio predicto confectam cancellandam.'

using court proceedings as evidence of common practice because, although court records throw much light on the law in operation, the cases heard were atypical by their very appearance in court. Further, without a decision, the contemporary understanding of the law may not be precisely known, and an unknown amount of illegal activity might have been going on 'behind the law's back'.

As attested legal documents, charter-parties could be used by shipmasters as evidence of their commercial bona fides. John Berthe, shipmaster of the *Gracedieu* of Brittany, his ship, cargo and crew were seized and taken to Dartmouth by John Hawley, jnr, in 1413 despite the fact, as he said in evidence, that he had produced his safe conduct, his papers of ownership under the seal of the mayor of Bristol *and* his copy of the charter-party to establish that he was going about his lawful business.[21]

The wording of 'terminal' charter-parties was largely fomulaic, setting out the agreed terms of the contract for a particular voyage. The earliest contracts contain little more than an invariable minimum but with time and the growing complexity of the commercial world, there was an accretion of detail in the agreements with many variations to suit individual situations. Appendix 4 is a transcription and translation of the 1323 charter-party shown in Figure 2, the earliest English example known to have survived. By the end of the fifteenth century charter-parties had become considerably more comprehensive, containing some or all of the clauses listed below; those marked with an asterisk were invariably included.

legal clauses:	names of the contracting parties*
	name of the ship*
	date and place of the agreement*
	relevant code of law
	names of witnesses*
financial clauses:	freight rate and discount*
	advance payment
	terms for final payment*
	currency to be used*
	penalties for various failures
	distribution of finds, salvage and prizes
voyage:	route and ports to be visited, optional destinations*
	specification of master
	pilotage, provision and payment
	maximum time to be taken and penalty for delay
	towing, cargo handling, port and other charges

---

[21] Gardiner, *West Country Shipping*, no. 16, pp. 18–19: from PRO C1/6/123.

cargo:	description and weight of goods*
	time limit for loading and unloading and penalties for delay
	specification of stowage, dunnage and protection
	specification of acceptable damage and loss
	provision of lighters in port
crew:	payment and feeding of the crew
	compensation in case of delay
	provision for defence
other items:	accommodation, food, water and light for passengers
	individual idiosyncrasies of shipmaster or merchants
	distribution of finds.

The contracts usually ended with a statement of trust and good faith all round and were signed with great solemnity by the contracting parties, the notary who had drawn up the agreement, and normally two to four witnesses.

From the available evidence, time charters, as described in chapter 3, pp. 63–4, appear to have been rare. An unusual example occurred in 1439 when a waterman, Roger Pye, chartered his whole ship and her equipment to William Payne, an ironmonger, for a year and a day 'according to the law of *Olroms*' (although *Oleron* has no article concerned with charters). It is not known if the shipmaster accompanied the ship or if the charter was 'bare board' but the intention of the agreement was clearly to hire the whole ship for a fixed period to undertake any voyages and carry any cargoes the charterers wished.[22]

Legal clauses
Once signed and sealed before a notary, charter-parties were usually, but not always, recognised at law – although there could be confusion over which law was relevant. Because of the differing views on commercial matters held by common, merchant and maritime law which have been discussed in chapters 1 and 2, situations could arise in which the appellant saw some advantage to himself in one code while the defendant preferred another. Competition between the courts compounded the problem and even the legal validity of the agreement itself could be argued between courts. Problems may have been fewer when pleas were submitted to an admiral's court, since they were frequently referred for arbitration to two or more experienced *aimables compositeurs*, both the parties in dispute lodging bonds with the court.[23] As has been discussed in chapter 1, the 1393–94 case of *John Copyn v. William Snoke et Thomas Saylyngham* (hereafter, the *Copyn* charter) demonstrates the potential for trouble even when an admiral's court was involved. Copyn, master of the *Gabriel*, brought a cargo of wine from Bordeaux, where the charter-

---

[22] CCR, *1435–41*, p. 287.
[23] Twiss, *Black Book*, I, p. 275.

party had been signed, to Gadeness in Essex, but Snoke and Saylyngham, who owned the wine, refused to pay the freight. The shipmaster sued first at common law, and then in the Admiralty Court of the North at maritime law, but without result because both courts held that they had no jursdiction. He then tried the Court of the Constable and Marshall, where the judge also denied jurisdiction but nevertheless gave judgment against him with heavy damages. With remarkable spirit, Copyn then appealed to the king who appointed judges to hear the appeal; unfortunately the final outcome is not known. Copyn's tribulations illustrate the confusion which could arise over disputed charter-parties, but as they coincided with the period in which the admirals' courts were being criticised by their competitors it may be that he was the victim of a political struggle.[24]

Because of anticipated problems, disputes over frustrated charters were frequently referred directly to the Court of Chancery rather than to lower courts, even although that incurred greater expense and more delay. In 1453 a plea was heard in Chancery in which Clement Bagot, defendant and owner of the ship *Julian*, and the appellant, John Heyton, a merchant shipper, differed in their opinion of which law was relevant (the *Bagot* charter). Bagot claimed that his plea could be heard at common law but Heyton submitted that there was no recourse for him in that code, presumably because there was no writ suitable for his requirements. In 1467 a London draper sought the chancellor's intervention against a Southampton merchant and shipowner who had covenanted to bring his wine from Spain but had failed to do so. Although other merchants' wines had been shipped, the draper claimed that his had been left behind, and he had had to sell his wine at a loss in Spain because there were no other ships available. Interestingly, whereas the *Bagot* charter plea asked the chancellor to define the relevant law, in the draper's case that was not in dispute; it was a straightforward mercantile quarrel, both parties were English, and common law had by then recognised the obligations of service contract.[25]

Even when complications might be expected there was not always doubt about the law or the court. In 1393 the London mayoral court heard a plea of debt by Robert Normant, a shipmaster, against John Lotolli, a merchant of Bordeaux (the *Normant* charter), alleging that the latter had contracted to load his ship with wine for delivery to London, Southampton, Sandwich or Middelburg, but had failed to do so. Normant further alleged that Lotolli had bound himself to pay half the freight (£30) in default of the cargo, but had not done so, denying that the signature on the agreement was his, despite there being five witnesses and the seal of the mayor of Libourne on the agreement. The case, which involved an alien, a complex charter-party and allegations of forgery and breach of contract, might be expected to have caused trouble. In the event however, the jury, who

[24] CPR, 1391–1396, pp. 340 and 378.
[25] PRO C1/24/211–217; PRO, C1/44/160.

were half Gascon (as was then customary when hearing cases involving aliens), found the case proved and awarded the shipmaster his claim and damages. The plea was heard at merchant law, as a frustrated commercial transaction, with no apparent problems.[26]

The rôle of witnesses was no sinecure since, to substantiate the signing of a disputed agreement, they could be called upon at any time in person or by deposition. That is illustrated in a successful plea by Bernard Bensyn, merchant of Bordeaux, who accused Bernard Brennyng, merchant and shipowner of Bristol, of delivering his wine to Bristol instead of to Ireland, as had allegedly been agreed in the charter-party. Brennyng denied all knowledge of the wine and of the charter-party, which was produced in evidence by Bensyn; the court accepted written statements from the three witnesses to the charter-party, which had been signed in the church of St Peter, Bordeaux, and found for Bensyn.[27]

Freight rates and payment

The freight rate, discounts and terms of payment were agreed in advance by the shipmaster and merchants for each voyage, and were always confirmed in the freighting agreement. The wide fluctuations of rates within a background of steady increase during the period under examination, reflect the effect of enemy and piratical activity on the availability of ships and crews, often a national political issue. There was an English shipping monopoly for English-owned goods in 1382, modified the following year to allow alien ships to be used if no English ships were available, and then a further period of English monopoly from 1390.[28]

When things were relatively quiet in the Bay of Biscay and the Channel, the rates dropped to 7s. or 8s. per tun (for example in 1416) while in times of open warfare they rose to 22s. (in 1372, 1414 and 1487). There was also a variable subsidy to be paid for convoy defence against *risicum gentis* which amounted, for example, to 6d. per tun in 1340, 1s. in 1350 and 3s. 4d. in 1360. Within each year there was also a seasonal variation in rates, reflected in the specified crews' wages and 'portages' in *Queenborough* for the vintage and rack wine deliveries from Bordeaux, but no doubt applicable on other routes. James gives examples of summer and winter rates, too few to analyse statistically, which she felt were significantly different, but it is difficult to discern the seasonal effect amongst the much larger perturbations due to hostile activity.[29]

It is clear that with changing circumstances in the shipping market, the commercial initiative oscillated between the shipmasters, when they could raise the freight

---

[26] *CPMR, 1381–1412*, pp. 199–200.
[27] PRO C1/26/474/2.
[28] *Statutes*, 5 Richard II, st. 1, c. 3; 6 Richard II, st. 1, c. 8 and 14 Richard II, c. 6.
[29] James, *Wine Trade*, pp. 128–33 and appendix 18, pp. 151–3: freight and subsidy rates from the King's Butler's accounts E101/77/2, also p. 145, citing E364/54/4. Appendix 2, *Queenborough*, article 5; vintage wine transport was in late summer, rack in early spring.

rates, and the merchants, when they could force them down. The volatility of the rates also indicates that there was good communication within the separate communities of shipmasters and merchants and that both received a flow of intelligence about hostile activity at sea, ship availability and the current freight rates and discounts. Such exchanges of information between shipmasters may be seen in the alliterative poem *Morte Arthure*: 'Thane the marynerse mellys [mixed], and maysters of chippis, / merily iche a mate menys tille other [chatted to another], / of theire termys thay talke, how thay ware tydd [what had happened to them]', and undoubtedly the merchants did the same.[30]

The *Coutumier* specifies a discount on the freight rate of 21 tuns for the price of 20 (5 per cent), for Oléronais merchants shipping in Oléronais bottoms, but discounts appear to have been fairly common, although not invariable, away from Oléron. For example, the 1323 charter-party shows that Walter Giffard offered his shipping customers 7.5 per cent discount for carrying wine and flour from Bordeaux to Newcastle (the *Giffard* charter), and in 1485 Tibbot Oliver was given 5 per cent discount on his 50 tuns of wine on the *Margaret Cely*. In the 1453 *Bagot* charter any discount is expressly ruled out 'paying for every ton and tonlode accomptyng j ton for j ton'. Not all merchants lading a ship were offered the same freight rate and *Queenborough* stipulates that varying rates have to be averaged for the calculation of payment to members of the crew who had opted for their portages to be *au fret de la nef* (see chapter 5, pp. 107–8). The owners and their favoured customers enjoyed reduced rates; other merchants negotiated the best rate they could, presumably based on the volume of their cargo. The Celys' accounts for their ship on the Bordeaux run show that when they and the purser paid 18s. per tun, other merchants paid 20s., and when the 'in-house' rate was 19s., the others paid from 20s. to 24s.[31]

The terms of payment of the freight charges varied. In times of peace and low piratical activity, shipmasters generally did not expect their shippers to pay the freight charge until the end of the voyage, except for an advance to victual the ship or to pay a proportion of the crew's wages. Part-payment to the crew at the outboard port enabled them to buy goods for their own ventures utilising their freight-free portages, but it would appear that shipmasters were generally too illiquid to put up the money before receiving an advance on the freight. In the 1323 *Giffard* charter, £7 2s. (13.25 per cent of the total charge) was paid in advance at Bordeaux; in 1387, 40s. (26.2 per cent) was advanced to William Prophet, a mariner, before a coastal passage from Fossdyke to London by William Jay, a sum

---

[30] *Morte Arthure*, lines 3652–4.
[31] Appendix 3, *Coutumier*, chapter 55. Ward, *Surviving Charter-Party*, pp. 389–391 and 395. Hanham, *Celys' World*, pp. 372–3 citing File 13, fo. 52. The terms portages (a crew perquisite) and *au fret de la nef* (profit sharing amongst the crew) are explained in chapter 5, pp. 107–13, and in Appendix 2, *Queenborough*, article 18. Hanham, *Celys' World*, pp. 372–3.

which was said to be borrowed (the *Prophet* charter); and in 1392 Thomas Lynne, shipmaster, received 200 francs (29.6 per cent) at Seville, also described as a loan, before departure (the *Lynne* charter). In the 1453 *Bagot* charter, a payment of 20 marks was to be made to the crew from the freight money, within six weeks of arrival at whichever Irish port was chosen by the merchant. When the dangers of enemy or piratical action at sea were higher than usual, for example after the start of the Hundred Years War, it was not unknown for shipmasters to require payment of the freight and pilotage charges in advance.[32]

The timing of the final payment of the freight was generally related to the ship's arrival or to the completion of unloading. While for both the shipmaster and the merchants it might appear that the sooner the ship was unloaded the better, the situation became complicated if the merchant had neither local agent nor warehousing. To use the ship as a warehouse from which to sample and deliver, provided that he could persuade the shipmaster to agree to a reasonable charge for the delayed unloading, was an ideal solution for the merchant. In Sanlúcar in 1478, Philip Wawton sold his cloths from the *Mary Asshe*, the ship in which the delivery had been made, using her as a travelling showroom. Unfortunately, the shipmaster had not agreed to such a course and took his complaint to Chancery.[33]

For delayed payment, or protracted unloading which led to delayed payment, there was often a stipulated penalty in the charter-party and, if it came to the worst, the shipmaster always had the possibility of refusing to allow unloading until cash or pledges to cover the freight were given. A very large pledge combining the freight charge and a penalty for delayed payment may be seen in a dispute over a 1485 agreement. This had been signed by a group of merchants who undertook to pay £86 12s. if they had not paid the freight charge within 21 days. In the event, they paid neither freight nor penalty and the shipmaster, a Breton, had to plead in Chancery for his money.[34]

A typical contractual penalty was the payment of the shipmaster's expenses while waiting for the late completion of unloading at a rate of, for example, half a silver mark per day. In the 1387 *Prophet* charter, the merchant was contracted to pay within seven days after coming alongside in London, with a penalty of 3s. 4d. per day thereafter. Neither the freight nor the penalty were paid and the shipmaster asked in court for the arrest and sale of the remainder of the cargo of salt to meet his debts. In the *Lynne* charter of 1392, the merchants were to pay a 300 *doubles* penalty plus expenses for any delay beyond four weeks in loading at Seville, beyond four days in partially unloading at Southampton and beyond 25 days in unloading at London, where payment of the freight charge was due on arrival. In the question of cargo-handling and payment times, no doubt the same

---

[32] CPMR, 1381–1412, pp. 133–4 and pp. 194–8. PRO E101/78/19(3) (a butlerage account).
[33] Childs, *Anglo-Castilian Trade*, p. 170 citing PRO C1/66/430–1.
[34] Appendix 1, *Oleron*, articles 22 and 23 concern delays. PRO C1/59/70.

market forces that controlled freight rates were in operation; when conditions were more competitive for one party than the other, there was scope for negotiation for the latter.

Shipmasters were themselves occasionally put under pressure to effect a speedy turn-round. For example, a group of Chester merchants who chartered a ship in 1393–94 to go to Bordeaux to load wine for Ireland, stipulated that she should not be in Gascony more than than 21 days. To place those and Lynne's time allowances in context, information from customs accounts indicates that two days in harbour appears to have been possible, two weeks was about average and five weeks was not unusual. Longer delays were occasioned by a need for repairs or re-fit or simply waiting for cargo.[35]

The currency to be used was always specified in a charter-party. In the 1392 *Lynne* charter signed in Spain between Genoese merchants and an English shipmaster, the currencies used were neither Genoese nor sterling but gold francs and Spanish *doblas Moreskes dor*.[36]

The *Giffard* charter signed in Bordeaux in 1323 specifies payment in *bons esterlins corones dAngleterra* and not in the local *solidi burdegalenses*. Merchants probably carried up-to-date tables of rates of exchange, but varying currency values (not to mention the necessary arithmetic) may well have posed problems for shipmasters. Suitably adjusted rates of exchange were almost certainly used as cover for interest on loans or on credit, and as a form of non-premium marine insurance, as discussed above under 'Insurance'.[37]

There were several different, and changing, sets of rules in operation for the distribution of prizes and finds in the fourteenth and fifteenth centuries. It is not surprising, therefore, to find in a charter-party a specific allocation of finds: in the 1392 *Lynne* charter, which covered a voyage down the Guadalquivir then to Southampton and finally round to London, all finds at sea or in fresh water were simply to be divided into three, one share each for the merchants, the ship and the shipmaster.[38]

Concerning the voyage
The time allowed for the voyage was generally, but not always, left unspecified in charter-parties, presumably on the assumption that the shipmaster would complete the voyage as quickly as possible. An example of an agreed time clause

---

[35] James, *Wine Trade*, pp. 134 and 137 citing *Chester Recognizance Rolls*, 2/66, m. 3 and 2/74, m. 2d. Harding, 'Port of London', pp. 268–9: figures for London, July–September 1384, citing PRO E101/71/8.
[36] *CPMR*, 1381–1412, pp. 194–8.
[37] George Cely listed the value in francs of English and other coinages: Hanham, *Celys' World*, p. 375.
[38] *Foedera*, 1, part 2, p. 654 (1285) and 10, 367 (1426). Appendix 2, *Queenborough*, articles 1, 18. *Rot. Parl.*, 5, p. 59 (1442).

is in the 1323 *Giffard* charter, in which the ship is to travel from Bordeaux to Newcastle-upon-Tyne in 15 days from departure to discharge, a strangely confident promise by the shipmaster given the uncertainties of a passage of over 1000 miles. The ship did arrive safely at Newcastle but unfortunately it is not known when, as the quittance is undated. Another example, which was perhaps more of a management dispute, concerns Richard Bye's ship the *Gost* of Lynn which in the late 1460s arrived a month late after a shuttle voyage Zealand–Bordeaux–Winchelsea–Bordeaux–Ireland. The delay was allegedly because there had not been a change of shipmaster at Winchelsea as Bye had ordered.[39]

Many charter-parties specified several destination ports, or included provision for a decision of where to go, to be made at some point along the route. As an example, in 1381 a shipmaster agreed to carry wine from Bordeaux to England, the merchant shippers to choose between Southampton, Sandwich and London when they reached the 'Sea of Brittany'. No doubt the merchants expected to meet in St Mathieu, or elsewhere, outward bound merchants from England who would pass on the latest market intelligence. A more complicated list of options was arranged in 1393 by the group of Chester merchants who planned to send a ship to Bordeaux, from where, within 21 days. she was to return reloaded to Dalkey and then, possibly, to Drogheda, a decision to be taken by the merchants within three or four days of arrival at Dalkey. A similar agreement was made between another group of Chester merchants and a shipmaster, but only one day was allowed in Dalkey and the alternative port was to be Chester. This last charter must have been successful because in the following year the same merchants planned a more ambitious voyage from Ottermouth to Ile de Rhé, La Rochelle, Libourne or Bordeaux and then back to Waterford, Dublin, Drogheda, Beaumaris or Chester, the decision about the final destination to be made at Bellisle. In 1449, John Motte of London freighted in Drogheda the *Patrick* of Waterford to sail to Bordeaux and return to either Dublin or Drogheda, the decision to be made *en voyage*.[40]

Clearly, flexibility was an integral part of maritime commerce and much of the success of a trading voyage must have depended on the decision taken by the leading merchant on board (chosen by the value of his cargo) when there were contractual options open to him. Extra-contractual changes of route or of ports of call, perhaps because of weather or in the light of new market intelligence, had to be with the consent of both the shipmaster and the merchant shippers, and could require revision of the freight rate. The *Normant* charter of 1393 lists as possible destinations London, Southampton and Sandwich, all at 15s. freight per cask, or for Middelburg at 20s. In 1465, Arnold Makenham, a merchant, contracted with Sir John Lisle, the owner of the *Anne* of Hampton, to freight cargo from South-

---

[39] James, *Wine Trade*, p. 134, citing PRO C1/45/230.
[40] PRO C1/45/230 and C47/24/9. CRR, 2/66, m. 3 and 2/68, m. 2. Timothy O'Neill, *Merchants and Mariners in Medieval Ireland* (Dublin, 1987), p. 50.

ampton to Bayonne, from where the ship was to return to London in 32 days (the *Lisle* charter). Makenham took the ship on to Spain, claiming to have a second charter, which was disputed by Lisle implying, perhaps, that the shipmaster had been talked into the changed destination by Makenham while at sea.[41]

A charter did not necessarily commence at the port of lading; the agreement could require a ship to sail to the starting point for loading; in such cases the freight rate presumably had to cover the passage to the start. An example of one such pre-loading delivery voyage concerned Mathew Andrewe, owner of the *James* of Ottermouth, who had contracted in 1474 with Harry Denys, grocer of London, to sail under ballast from Topsham to London, there to pick up cargo and return to Topsham, at an inclusive rate of £9 per tun. The details of the charter survive because it went badly wrong, leading to allegations in the Court of Chancery of a non-existent safe conduct countered by a complaint of non-delivery of cargo to the London quay.[42]

Additional charges for pilotage, cargo handling and other items
According to the terms of *Oleron* and the *Coutumier*, additional costs, such as deep-sea pilotage, pier dues, stowage and river tolls should be on the ships' accounts while costs associated with the cargo, such as local pilotage, cranage, special dunnage (wood for supporting and bracing cargo) and unloading were to be charged to the merchants. The allocation of expenses was, however, sometimes specifically listed in charter-parties: in the 1323 *Giffard* and 1392 *Lynne* agreements it was confirmed that *petit lomnage* (local pilotage) was to be charged to the shipper, exactly as specified by law. In 1394 the shipmaster who had agreed with the Chester merchants that he would accept the cost of pilotage from Milford Haven to Beaumaris or from Dalkey to Chester, refused to pay when the time came. It may be that the pilotage charges had been included in the freight rate, a fact which the shipmaster 'failed to remember', or that he changed his opinion about what constituted sea pilotage and felt that the Irish Sea, which was not included in the *Oleron* geographical definitions, should be seen as 'local' and therefore on the merchants' account. A letter to the mayor of Winchelsea in 1350 indicates that the shipmaster may sometimes have paid towage and other charges for the shipping merchants in expectation of repayment later: Gamelin atte Watere, a merchant, freighted salt from Bourgneuf Bay to Winchelsea at 15d. per quarter plus towage and 'petty lading' but failed fully to recompense John Maydekyn, shipmaster of the *Nicholas* of Romene. Although the terms of the charter-party should have ensured that the shipmaster recovered his expenses without argument, in the event, the salt was arrested in Winchelsea to be sold for compensation to

---

[41] PRO C1/26/300.
[42] Gardiner, *West Country Shipping*, nos 89a, b, c and d, pp. 104–9 citing PRO C1/51/151–153 and C1/45/88.

Maydekyn. Many important ports, for example Seville, Bordeaux, London and Newcastle, are several miles up-river from the open sea. Towage by oared boats was necessary for taking ships up and down the rivers, and in and out of harbours and docks. In the 1323 *Giffard* and 1392 *Lynne* agreements the merchants accept towing costs, following the precepts of *Oleron*.[43]

What might be seen as an idiosyncrasy of a charterer was the inclusion 'of a doge and a cat with all other necessaryes' in a later charter of 1532. The animals were required ostensibly as ratters but the possibility of their survival from an accident would, in the terms of Edward I's well-known statute defining total loss, circumvent any attempt to write off the ship as a wreck and so preserve title of ownership to anything of the ship or cargo that was salvaged.[44]

A century of charter-parties
The 1323 *Giffard*, the 1392 *Lynne* and the 1453 *Bagot* charter-parties demonstrate how freighting agreements evolved during the 130 years from the first to the last. The *Giffard* contract, which is written in Norman French with Gascon variants, is the oldest known surviving English charter-party; it is shown in Figure 2 with the transcription and translation in Appendix 5. In summary, the contracting parties were Sir Hugh de Berham, acting on behalf of Sir Adam de Limbergue, constable of the castle of Bordeaux who was, in turn, acting on behalf of the king, and Walter Giffard, the shipmaster. The ship was the cog *Nostra Dame* of Lyme (although she had become the *Sainte Marie* on arrival at Newcastle), loaded with 102 tuns of wine, of which three tuns were *vin tint* (possibly red wine cosmetically improved with colouring) and 44 tuns of flour, all destined for the army mustering in Newcastle for an expedition (later abandoned) against Scotland. The freight rate of 9s. per tun was discounted at 21.5 tuns for the price of 20, and payment was to be in sterling crowns. £7 2s. was paid in advance and acknowledged by the shipmaster; the ship was to go straight to Newcastle, and Giffard promised a 15-day delivery. The terms of payment were 'immediate on delivery' without demurrage and the merchants were to pay towage and local pilotage. The charter-party ends, encouragingly, with 'when the ship left Bordeaux the master and the merchants were at peace and in a good relationship and without any quarrel' and everyone, including four witnesses, signed on 23 May 1323, Giffard making his mark manual.

The quittance on the dorse of the charter-party confirms the total freight cost of £53 11s. of which Limbergue had paid £7 2s. in advance. Polhowe (keeper and receiver of the king's victuals in Newcastle), acknowledged receipt of 86 tuns of wine and 43 tuns of flour, although 102 and 44 tuns of wine and flour had been

---

[43] Appendix 1, *Oleron*, article 13. Appendix 3, *Coutumier*, chapters 76, 95, 97. CRR 2/66, m. 3. CCR, 1349–54, p. 197.
[44] Marsden, *Select Pleas*, 1, p. 37. *Statutes*, 3 Edward I, c. 4.

THE SHIPMASTER'S ON-SHORE RESPONSIBILITIES

loaded, and paid £46 10s. There appears to have been a loss of 16 tuns of wine and one tun of flour *en voyage*, and the accountancy appears to be awry in that Giffard was underpaid by 7s. Some of the missing wine might be accounted for by spillage, evaporation (ullage) and crew's perquisites, although a 15.6 per cent loss is large. A fuller analysis of the accounts is given in Appendix 4. Because the indenture bears the mark manual of the shipmaster, and the quittance endorsement is signed by the recipient of the cargo, this surviving copy of the charter-party was probably the shippers' and was either given to the shipmaster as his receipt in Newcastle or retained as evidence for later litigation, of which there is no trace. The agent in Newcastle would have received the shipmaster's copy, acknowledging payment and authenticated with his mark.[45]

The 1323 charter-party is a straightforward, uncomplicated agreement with a minimum of clauses and without threat of penalties. In addition to the names of the parties, the destination and the terms of the contract, details are given of the cargo which is already loaded; this charter-party is, in effect, a 'bill of lading' acknowledging receipt of the goods and embodying an agreement to transport them to the destination.

The 1392 *Lynne* charter-party was written in Norman French, and a transcription survives in the records of a dispute heard in the London mayoral court. Two Genoese merchants, acting for themselves and two other partners, contracted with Thomas Lynne, master of the barge *Seintmarie* owned by John Hawley, to ship 150 tons of merchandise down river from Seville to Sanlúcar de Barrameda then to Southampton and finally to London. In court, Lynne alleged that he had not been paid and each party produced a version of the agreement which, although essentially the same, differed in detail and was not acceptable to the other party. The clauses in the charter-party are complex and interesting: the lading at Seville was to be completed within four weeks; the freight rate was 4½ francs per ton amounting to a total of 675 francs; and there was to be a further payment of 25 francs *chaux* (?shoemoney) to the shipmaster (apparently a gratuity, worth 3.7 per cent of the freight). The ship was to remain in Southampton for four days while part of the cargo was unloaded, then she was to sail to London to discharge the rest of the cargo (within 25 days in the defendants' version of the agreement). If the ship were not loaded at Seville within four weeks, through delay by the merchants, they were to pay the shipmaster 300 *doubles Moreskes dor* plus his expenses while there. It was agreed that the merchants would provide (i.e. pay for) a pilot from Seville, presumably for the 60 miles down the Guadalquivir to the sea, and pay for any other local pilotage and towage, an arrangement conforming to *Oleron*. The merchants had to caulk the cabin of the ship, and the shipmaster had to provide a boat equipped, manned and ready to load or unload in any harbour,

---

[45] Appendix 1, *Oleron*, article 17 for the ration of wine. A loss of c.6% of the wine was common.

and to pay the boat crew. He also had to supply the merchants with fresh water, salt, firewood and lamps fore and aft and be prepared, with his crew, to defend the ship against everyone except compatriots.

The terms of the charter-party are considerably more sophisticated than those in the 1323 *Giffard* agreement in that they include penalties for unloading delays, more than one currency, a gratuity for the shipmaster, a list of the responsibilities of the two parties and a requirement for the crew to defend the ship and cargo. Further, unlike the *Giffard* charter on which the shipmaster/owner had made his mark manual on his own responsibility, the *Seintmarie*'s master signed the agreement acting as agent for the owner. It is not known if he had full authority to engage the vessel or had to work within defined parameters. The voyage was completed but led to claim and counter-claim between the shipmaster and the merchants because of non-payment of the freight. Unusually, the court's interim decision on the question of outstanding payments is recorded – in Lynne's favour – but there was a postponement *sine die* of the other matters, because of a writ of protection for Lynne while he was on the king's service provisioning the town of Cherbourg. Of happenings thereafter, no record has been found.

The 1453 *Bagot* charter-party, written in English, binds John White, the shipmaster, with the assent and agreement of Clement Bagot, the owner of the *Julian* of Bristol, to carry cargo for John Heyton, a merchant of Bristol, on a circuit of ports at which the ship was to be unloaded and reloaded. The proposed route was from Bristol to Lisbon with 'diverse merchaundisez' belonging to Heyton but allowing space for ten tons for Bagot (the owner), six tons for John White (the master) and five tons for Nicholas Mody (the purser). After Lisbon, loaded with 85 tuns of wine, 15 tons of honey and with the remaining space filled with salt, the ship was to sail to one of three ports in Ireland, the selection to be made by Heyton (the merchant). The freight rate from Lisbon to Ireland was to be 20s. per ton without discount, the other units of cargo being defined as two pipes, four hogsheads or five quarters of salt (Bristol measure) to be charged at the wine tun rate. Within six weeks of arrival in Ireland the crew were to be paid 20 marks. In the Irish port the ship was to be discharged and reloaded with hides; she was then to sail to Plymouth, wait there for three tides (*c*.18 hours) then sail on to a port in Normandy, Zeeland or Brittany, again to be selected by Heyton, at a rate of 40s. per last.

According to Heyton, all went well until they left Plymouth when White took the ship to Winchelsea and then to Sandwich where the ship was discharged by order of Bagot. Unfortunately, to Heyton's 'grete losse and undoyng', the price of Irish hides compared to the Welsh was uncompetitive in England at that time. Bagot however, maintained that the unloading at Sandwich was with Heyton's written consent and that the latter owed him the freight and a penalty for delayed loading. The reason for the diversion, as set out in the depositions of John White, Nicholas Mody and other crew members, was that reprisals being exacted by the Duke of Burgundy made it too dangerous to sail to Flanders, so they sailed instead to Calais with Heyton's consent, were caught in a storm, almost lost the ship on the Goodwin Sands, broke their best anchor and took refuge in Sandwich. Heyton had then signed a notarised agreement that the ship should be discharged there, leaving on board sufficient of the cargo to cover the freight if that had not been paid within 32 days.[46]

The *Bagot* charter shows further advances in complexity together with a considerable amount of commercial detail. A ship's purser is mentioned; there is a reservation of cargo space for the ship's owner and officers; the destinations are to be decided *en voyage* by the charterer; the cargoes to be loaded at various ports are listed; the timing and amount of payment to the crew is specified and the tun equivalents of other weights and measures are defined. Of significance is a legal point, revealed in the court hearing following the voyage: the document which altered the terms of the original charter-party had to be signed and sealed by a notary, indicating that the contractual status of the original agreement was accepted by both parties, although at which law is not clear. The position of White, as agent for Bagot, is not denied by Bagot nor questioned by Heyton, which perhaps points to merchant law. Heyton stated in his plea to the chancellor that he had no remedy at common law, that is, there was no writ available to plead breach of service contract. Why he did not direct his plea to a merchant law court where contractual obligations were recognised, but decided to seek equity from the Court of Chancery, is not known. Bagot maintained that the matter was determinable at common law where a service contract and its notarised alteration would be recognised. The differing views reflect the confusion in mid-fifteenth-century England arising from the reluctance of common law to accept the obligation of contract (a subject examined in chapter 1), and demonstrate the advisability of defining in the charter-party the code of law under which any dispute is to be heard. In view of Copyn and Snoke's troubles in the 1390s and, half a century later, those of Bagot and Heyton, merchant law was the safer option for those engaged in a service industry.

The shipmaster's bureaucratic load

In addition to finding cargo for the next voyage, the shipmaster had to arrange credit in such a way that accusations of usury were avoided. He had to agree to, and sign, financial instruments sometimes in foreign languages and often involving

---

[46] Heyton was right about hide prices; the few Irish hides imported at that time were probably seamen's freight-free portages of three dickers each. In 1436 a ship arrested at Southampton for king's service was given special licence to unload and later reload Irish hides because of the difficult market. The claim of a later, over-riding contract is reminiscent of *Lisle v. Makenham*, discussed above.

different currencies, try to keep a record of his various transactions, and investigate the possibilities of some form of insurance cover. When in partnership with men or women experienced in business affairs, his bureaucratic load would have been considerably reduced and that may have been a factor in the selection of partners. Although it may have been possible to appoint a shipping agent to work on his behalf, no evidence of such assistance has been found.

Of all the financial and commercial instruments available to the medieval shipmaster, the best-known are charter-parties because of their survival in the records of court hearings. These offer useful windows on the developing English medieval shipping industry, and on the business life of the mercantile shipmaster. The completion of the charter-party before each voyage could be quite straightforward, even formulaic, but nervous or cunning merchant shippers were capable of demanding complex clauses involving an unacceptable flexibility of route, an impossible timetable, or a mixture of currencies at different rates of exchange. Just as the growing complexity of commercial transactions, and the increasing risks to which shipmasters were exposed, required the *Lex d'Oleron*, dating from before 1315, to be supplemented by the additional articles of the Inquisition of Queenborough, sitting from 1375 to 1404, so the content of charter-parties also had to be expanded during the fourteenth and fifteenth centuries to cope with new situations. Particularly pertinent are those clauses which seek to defend the shipmaster after jettison or collision, defend him from the consequences of delay caused by a shipping merchant, and define the terms of payment.

With the necessary bureaucracy completed, it is probable that the late medieval shipmaster welcomed his return to the sea which he understood better, and on which he was more at ease.

5

The Shipmaster's Off-Shore Responsibilities

Relationships with merchant shippers

In addition to their mutual obligations set out in the charter-party, the shipmaster and the merchants who travelled on his ship with their goods, had further legal responsibilities to each other while at sea. Those are set out in *Oleron* and to a lesser extent in the *Coutumier* and follow practices developed by 'long use and wont'.

Delayed and frustrated voyages
If a ship foundered between ports, the shipmaster had the option of repairing her or of transferring himself, with the cargo, to another vessel to continue the voyage. If the merchants did not accept his decision, the shipmaster was still able to claim his freight payment for that part of the voyage that had been sailed. When weather conditions delayed a ship in port for so long that the shipmaster ran out of money, he was permitted to send home for more funds. Alternatively, he could sell as much as necessary of the cargo to revictual or repair the ship and, on arrival at their final destination, compensate the merchants for the 'borrowed' cargo at the same prices as they had obtained for the cargo which had arrived safely. The shipmaster nevertheless received his freight payment for the whole cargo for the whole voyage. These arrangements appear to be complementary to the prohibition on the shipmaster selling the ship without the owners' authority, although he could pledge equipment to borrow money for his necessary expenses, with the consent of his crew.[1]

Jettison and general average
Before ordering jettison or cutting away rigging in an emergency, the shipmaster had to consult the merchants. By giving their consent to any action which led to loss or damage of the cargo, the merchants reduced their title to their goods. The risk to the merchants in accepting responsibility for the drastic remedial action was balanced by their being able to call together the crew, after the voyage, to ask them to swear that the shipmaster's decisions had been correct and without alternative. This provision was available to the merchants not only when there

---

[1] Appendix 1, *Oleron* and Appendix 3, *Coutumier, passim.*

had been jettison, but also if other aspects of the shipmaster's seamanship was in doubt.

If the merchants, through caution, fear or cupidity, were slow to agree to approve jettison, and such procrastination caused damage, the shipmaster's cargo was exempted from contribution to general average (see below). No litigation arising from such a situation has been found to indicate how long merchants might reasonably be allowed to consider their options in a storm-tossed ship on a lee shore. If any merchant later attempted to deny his alleged agreement to jettison, the shipmaster had the right to ask one third of his crew to swear that his actions were necessary during the emergency. The *Customs* rules on jettison are generally similar to those in *Oleron* but with two additional rules: that the merchant had to throw overboard the first item, presumably to confirm his agreement to jettison; and that extra-contractual agreements made on the open sea under the duress of fear or seasickness were not necessarily valid later.

If jettison saved a ship and part of her cargo, then the value of each merchant's goods, as a proportion of the total value of the items saved, was made to those whose cargo had been sacrificed for the general good, a process known as 'general average'. *Oleron* exempted crew portages (see below, pp. 107–13) from contribution, even those portage allowances which had been subcontracted to merchants. *Oleron* also gave the shipmaster the option of contributing the ship or his own cargo, but in a 1285 Letter Patent of Edward I, it was ruled that the ship, her rigging and the crew's personal belongings, food and cooking utensils should be 'quit of contributing aid towards the jettison into the sea' but that everything else belonging to the merchants and the crew had to be included. The letter also ruled that the mariners should have the freight money for the cargo that was saved, but the shipmaster should forfeit the freight for the lost cargo. The reason for the differing views on what was to be included in contribution may be chronological; the *Oleron* article was probably formulated before 1285. The *Coutumier* ruled that the hull, tackle and stores of the ship, and the beds and chests of the crew, were exempt, but everything carried as merchandise must contribute; a rule virtually identical to Edward's, and reflecting the later date of the *Coutumier*. Although the 1285 decision precluded obligatory inclusion of the ship in the contribution, it apparently did not specifically prevent a master choosing to offer the ship rather than his cargo, as suggested in *Oleron*. To be able to contribute the ship, the shipmaster would have had to own her or have had authority from his fellow owner/partners; to want to contribute his (or their) cargo implies that it was of lesser value than the ship. Further, to contribute the ship, he would have had to persuade the merchants that he was legally entitled to choose the smaller contribution – not an easy proposition.[2]

---

[2] Appendix 1, *Oleron*, articles 8 and 9; Appendix 3, *Coutumier*, chapter 94.

With the exemption from contribution of the crew's portages, a shipmaster might be sure that they would cooperate in the jettisoning of cargo. However, that provision may have made collusion between shipmaster and crew more likely when there was a dispute with aggrieved merchants. Mariners might be prepared to swear that the shipmaster had had no option but to jettison if their own investments were not at stake. The shipmaster also had further means of ensuring the cooperation of the crew: in order to qualify for a share of the salvage from the wreck of their ship, the shipmaster had to agree that the crew had 'defent en la meer cum un homme'. The articles concerning jettison, wreck and any damage to the cargo were therefore potentially very much to the benefit of the shipmaster rather than the merchants. The introduction of general average may have been a sensible precaution when the merchants themselves had to assist in the jettisoning of their cargo, but a contemporary (c.1375) poem describes the reality of a storm. In the unsurprising general panic there is non-selective jettisoning of anything that comes to hand:

> And then the cry arises, they cut the ropes and throw everything out; many men jump about to bale and to throw – scooping out the dangerous water when they would rather escape – for however heavy a man's load, life is always sweet. They were busy throwing bales overboard, their bags and their feather beds and their best clothes, their cases and their chests and all their casks, and all to lighten the ship in the hope that calm should fall.[3]

Resposibilities for the cargo

As discussed in chapter 1, one of the strengths of the law merchant was its encouragement of commerce. Similarly maritime law favoured the shipmaster as a supplier of a service to merchants trading overseas. If the shipmaster were to be held generally responsible for any damage to or loss of cargo, then there would have been, at best, a substantial increase in freight rates and, at worst, a cessation of shipping services. There appears to have been a *caveat emptor* situation for shipping merchants – there was no money-back guarantee if a voyage was not completed, a situation aggravated by the absence of premium insurance facilities before the fifteenth century. The shipmaster, however, was not entirely immune from claims; according to *Oleron*, damage to the cargo because of bad loading or badly placed dunnage could be claimed against him and the crew, unless they were prepared to swear that the dunnage supplied was faulty or that there were other extenuating circumstances. Given the few personal belongings of the shipmaster

---

[3] Appendix 1, *Oleron* and Appendix 3, *Coutumier*, passim. Twiss, *Black Book*, III, pp. 148–57, 444–9: *Customs*, chapters l–liv and ccviii. *Liber Albus*, ed. Henry T. Riley (London, 1861), pp. 421–2; *CPR* 1281–92, pp. 168–9; *Pearl*, 'Patience', lines 152–60 (in modernised English).

and his crew, any worthwhile compensation would have had to be found from the cargo that each man had loaded. The responsibility for damage to the ship and cargo when a shipmaster was ordered by a merchant to take his ship against his will into a hazardous situation, is not entirely clear. An interesting argument about responsibility surfaced in a case in 1376 when Arnald Pope, master of the *George*, lost his ship and cargo when, against his better judgement, he took her closer to the town of Blakeney on the instruction of Robert Rust, who had freighted the ship with salt at Bourgneuf and wanted to discharge her in a quiet place nearer the town. Unfortunately the decision of the court is not known.[4]

Loading and unloading times are frequently mentioned in freighting agreements and the rules for compensation for delay are dealt with in both *Oleron* and *Customs*. Claims against merchants who delayed a sailing may be found in pleas before Chancery and other courts and are discussed in the section on freighting agreements in chapter 4, pp. 78–93. Customs records indicate that although unloading and reloading could be completed in a few days, at other times, several weeks were required. An analysis of the time spent in London by ships with customable, and therefore recorded, cargoes between July and September 1384, shows that in summary, 11 turned-round in 4 days, 19 in between 5 and 12 days, and 18 in between 14 and 23 days, with two spending 29, and one other 52 days, in harbour. An averaged turn-round time has to be treated with caution since not all ships carried customable goods and their arrivals and departures were not recorded. Further, cargoes varied in ease of handling, ships may have required repairs while in harbour, or they may have had to wait for favourable weather. Also, although the shipping merchants were subject to the late delivery penalties set out in *Oleron* and, additionally, were often bound by the charter-parties to load and unload within a given time, there may have been delays awaiting cargoes. The average turrn-round, however, appears to have been about two weeks, confirmed in the contemporary *Libelle of Englyshe Polycye*. In this essentially political poem, the importance of a speedy turn-round is emphasised:

> Conceyve well here, that Englyssh men at martes
> Be discharged, for all her [their] craftes and artes,
> In Braban of all here marchaundy
> In the xiiij. dayes and ageyne hastely
> In the same dayes xiiij. are charged efte.
> And yf they byde lengere, all is berefte;
> Anone they shulde forfet here [their] godes all
> Or marchaundy, it shulde no bettere fall.

Furthermore, shipmasters were occasionally bound by the charter-party to a schedule for their voyages, as discussed in chapter 4.[5]

[4] Appendix 1, *Oleron*, articles 4, 8, 9, 11, 23; CCR, 1374–77, p. 404.
[5] Appendix 1, *Oleron*, article 22. Twiss, Black Book, III, pp. 162–3, 196–7, 366–9: *Customs*,

THE SHIPMASTER'S OFF-SHORE RESPONSIBILITIES

Responsibility for payment of incidental expenses and of pilotage
For the payment of incidental expenses, the *Coutumier* defines more fully than *Oleron* or *Queenborough* the respective responsibilities of the merchants and of the ship. Assiage (stowage), planchage (landing dues), quillage (pier or perhaps anchorage dues), and rivage (tolls on tow paths), were all charged to the ship. According to *Oleron*, the costs of lodmanage (pilotage) were split; the merchants to pay for petty, or local, pilots and the ship to pay for sea pilots (see chapter 7, 'Pilots' (pp. 175–7) for further information). The *Coutumier* adds that additional pilots (or crew) taken on at the merchants' request were to be on their account if the ship were already well crewed and carried a pilot.[6]

When a ship was handling cargo with lighters alongside, or with carts brought down the beach at low water, then her own lifting gear would have had to be used. If she were working against a quay or a dock then either her own lifting tackle or shore cranes could be used. Use of the ship's lifting tackle, operated by the crew, could incur primage charges to be paid by the merchants; the use of dock-side cranes, sometimes stipulated by the local authority, would incur a guindage (cranage) charge and require shore-side stevedores, again to be paid by the merchants. As examples: in Dublin in 1332–33, the hoisting of wine aboard the *Margaret* from barges cost 2d. per tun and 1d. per pipe and in 1480–81, the crew of the *Trinity* were paid 200 *maravedis* for bringing aboard a cargo of 33.5 tuns of wine from the ship's boat. Cranes were available on the London wharves from the fourteenth century and on Southampton quay from the early fifteenth century, and the crane garth at York is first mentioned in a document of 1417. In 1431–32 over 25s. were spent on repairs (indicating that it was of some age) to the 'machine' at Topsham; it may be assumed that by the fifteenth century other important port towns had similar facilities. When using the ship's own lifting tackle, the shipmaster could avoid responsibility for damage to the cargo by insisting that the merchants inspected the ropes before unloading began. If equipment failure caused damage to the cargo after the merchants had given approval, the shipmaster and crew were not culpable. They could still be held responsible for damage in the hold due to faulty stowage, however.[7]

Customs confirms much of the above and defines more closely the responsibili-

---

chapters lx, lxxxix, and clxxxix. Harding, 'Port of London', pp. 268–70, citing PRO E101/71/8. *Libelle of Englyshe Polycye*, ed. Sir G. Warner (Oxford, 1926), chapter 7, lines 512–19.
[6] Appendix 3, *Coutumier*, chapters 55, 76, 95, 97. Appendix 1, *Oleron*, article 13. *Local Customs Accounts of the Port of Exeter*, p. 6; keelage at Topsham in the early fourteenth century was 2d. per vessel and by the mid-fifteenth century *bushellage* and *plankage* were also being charged, probably to the merchants' account.
[7] O'Neill, *Merchants and Mariners*, p. 54 citing PROI: *43rd Report of the Deputy Keeper*, p. 60. Reddaway, *Accounts of John Balsall*, p. 23. Gillian Hutchinson, *Medieval Ships and Shipping* (London, 1994), p. 112. *The Local Port Book of Southampton for 1439–40*, ed. Henry S. Cobb, SRS V (Southampton, 1961), p. xxxvi. Appendix 1, *Oleron*, articles 10, 11.

ties of the *senyor de nau* towards his merchant freighters and passengers, and the consequences of damage to the cargo arising from jettison, damp, rats or other spoilage on the ship when loading, unloading or lying on or under the decks. There is also provision for living space for the merchants and their servants (the merchant paying the highest freight was allocated the best accommodation), and penalties are specified for keeping a ship waiting. As in *Oleron*, the right of the merchants to obtain sworn testimony from the crew, when in dispute with the shipmaster, is confirmed. As mentioned under 'Jettison' above, agreements made at sea, when, it is said, a frightened or seasick man will agree to anything, are invalid later on dry land, except if the ship had been anchored or moored. Other example of promises which might be treated as revocable later include those made to armed enemies, offers of rewards to the crew when aground or to avoid jettison, and offers of compensation for a change of course, unless the last was entered in the ship's log as soon as convenient. There is no such provision in *Oleron*, *Queenborough* or the *Coutumier*; merchants on English ships were held to any promises they made even when *in extremis* although, presumably, such promises would have had to be substantiated.[8]

It was customary for one of the shippers to be regarded as chief merchant, probably he with the largest cargo. The chief merchant represented the others, paid the dues, tolls and charges owed by them, and guaranteed payment to the shipmaster of the freight and other expenses, against later repayment. From the Exeter customs accounts it appears that he may occasionally have paid, or given pledges for, local customs dues on the cargoes of unenfranchised merchants. Unfortunately, it is difficult to separate such payments from pledges given by local worthies who were also importing merchants. *Customs* recognised the chief merchant's position by stipulating that he should have the best accommodation on board and defines him as the merchant with the most cargo, but it does not list his responsibilities.[9]

Personnel and man-management

Crew strengths varied with the need for defence and the size and rig of the vessel; in 1324 ships over about 120 tons were manned at four tons per man, under 120 tons at something over three tons per man and under 80 tons at less than three tons per man. A typical 100-ton ship, therefore, would have had a crew of around

---

8 Twiss, *Black Book*, III, pp. 88–91, 102–5, 106–7, 162–3, 242–7, 270–5, 336–43: *Customs*, chapters xvi, xviii–xx, xxii, xxvii–xxix, xxxi–xxxiii, lx, cxli, cli, clxxviii–clxxx, clxxxiv and ccviii.
9 James, *Wine Trade*, pp. 135–6. *Local Customs Accounts of the Port of Exeter*, p. 9: pledges for payment were given only by the larger merchants, confirmed by the attempts in court by the customs receivers to recover money from the sureties. Twiss, *Black Book*, III, pp. 106–7: *Customs*, chapter xxxi.

30 men. The simplification of sail handling following the introduction of a split sail plan early in the fifteenth century may have allowed an increase in the tons per man ratio, but the long yard and the lateen sail rigged on the mizzen mast would have required considerable man-handling. The total number of men working on ships was probably around 15,000 in the late fourteenth century, calculated from the number of ships involved in the wine trade or in troop movements during the Hundred Years War.[10]

The backgrounds and demography of seamen are difficult to trace. The average age of 80 men from Dartmouth ships who gave evidence in an enquiry into piracy off Brest in 1386 was around 30, with three quarters of them below 40 years of age. Seamen were mostly men from port towns or the surrounding countryside: again from the Dartmouth ship enquiry, 68 of the 80 men were from Dartmouth itself or the estuarine villages of the Dart, with a further eight from port towns within 12 miles of Dartmouth. There was a familial seafaring tradition, especially amongst shipowners /masters such as the Hawleys of Dartmouth, and this may well have been a common path towards the position of shipmaster. For ordinary mariners, the cyclical nature of fishing, farming and the Bordeaux wine trade also offered men opportunities of gainful work throughout the year, and a degree of trade interchangeability amongst seamen can be seen. Amongst the men of the Dartmouth ships were 14 tradesmen including four tailors, two barbers and a carpenter, plumber, armourer, cutler, skinner, goldsmith, baker and mason. Their shore-side trades were perhaps laid aside when they needed additional capital to expand their businesses or their land holdings by the possibilities of portages and prizes available at sea.[11]

There were difficulties for men who were still in feudal servitude who wanted to go to sea and there is evidence of those difficulties even in impressment. In 1335, for example, Thomas Springer, master of the *Cogge Edward*, was, exceptionally, ordered to seize men 'whether in or outside liberties' to make up his crew and again, as late as 1416, Haukin Pytman of the *Weathercock of the Tower*, was instructed to seize any man he could find as crew. This instruction may well have been difficult to carry out, as the king's officials theoretically could not deliver or enforce writs to those within liberties, and usually had to rely on the officials of the liberty. Manumission was still necessary in the fourteenth century but since it was an opportunity for a lord to exploit his serfs financially, as feudal service became meaningless, high costs restricted the purchase of freedom to only the wealthiest of the unfree. In view of the number of men who went to sea in the fourteenth century, it is strange that only two records have been found of permis-

---

[10] Ratios calculated from *British Naval Documents 1204–1960*, ed. John B. Hattendorf, *et al.*, NRS (Aldershot, 1993), p. 39.
[11] For fuller analyses of seamen's ages, trades and backgrounds from the limited information available, see Kowaleski, 'Working at Sea'.

sion granted to leave feudal servitude specifically for work at sea. One is the only known manumission of a mariner; Thomas Knollyng, a villein of Ashburton manor was released by the Bishop of Exeter in 1355 to practise more freely his *ars navalis*. Thomas was 50 years old, childless and had been at sea since he was a child. Why he should have required manumission when of an age when most men gave up sea-going, is not clear.[12]

The other record is of Richard Fouke, 'who withdrew from the craft of ploughman, out of the service of Emere of Shernborne [Norfolk], and is received and hired by Ralph Pibel, crossing the sea in the craft of mariner'. Nothing is known of the cost of his manumission, if anything, and the fact that his departure was noted, makes more mysterious the lack of other records. For men not within liberties there was the risky alternative of de facto freedom by escape to sea, but the 1351 Statute of Labourers and later legislation further reduced their opportunities. There are records of many prosecutions of men and women who had tried to move (although not necessarily to sea) but were arrested; the Yorkshire East Riding Roll from 1363 to 1364, for example, records 46 thwarted attempts to depart from a locality and a further 11 attempts to leave a master. The Lincolnshire Peace Rolls of 1360–75 record many transgressions, and it is possible that when the shortage of manpower began to bite towards the end of the 1370s, greater attempts were made to stop a widespread movement of workers to higher paid jobs elsewhere. One of those caught was William Runfare, a fisherman, who was hired in 1371 by William Skott of Saltfleet Haven for a whole year but worked only from St Hilary's day until the following Purification day; the call of the deep-sea may have tempted him away. Despite the refusal of the Lords and Commons to accept enfranchisement of the serfs, servitude began to crumble. The 1381 revolt was another step towards general emancipation, and by the early fifteenth century increasing numbers of men were able freely to choose to go to sea. This freedom usefully coincided, more or less, with the growth of the English merchant fleet and the demand for mariners.[13]

---

[12] Letter Patent of Edward III, 14 Oct. 1335. CPR, 1416–22, p. 84. R.H. Hilton, *The Decline of Serfdom in Medieval England*, The Economic History Society (1969), pp. 51–5. The sums required for manumission varied considerably: in 1317, 50 marks was demanded by Sir John Botetourte; in 1335 Worcester Cathedral Priory received £20, and in 1414 £6 13s. 4d. was paid by a *neif* of Oddington, Gloucestershire. F.C. Hingeston-Randolph,ed., *The Register of John de Grandison, 1327–69*, 3 vols (London, 1894–9), II, p. 1159.

[13] Simon A.C. Penn and Christopher Dyer in 'Wages and Earnings in Late Medieval England: Evidence from the Enforcement of the Labour Laws', *EHR*, 2nd series 43, 3 (1990), pp. 356–76. *Statutes* 23 Edward III, st.2, cc. 1 and 2 and The Statute of Labourers; 25 Edward III, st. 5, c. 18. B.H. Putnam, *The Enforcement of the Statute of Labourers, 1349–59* (New York, 1908); *York Sessions*, p. xxxii. *Records of Some Sessions of the Peace in Lincolnshire*, ed. R. Sillem, Lincoln Record Society, XXX (1936), pp. xlvi and 20. Bolton, *Medieval English Economy*, pp. 213–15. Hilton, *The Decline of Serfdom*, pp. 51–9. J. Hatcher, 'England in the Aftermath of the Black Death', *PP*, 144 (1994), pp. 3–35. E.B. Fryde, *Peasants and Landlords in Later Medieval England, c.1380-c.1525* (Stroud, 1996), pp. 8–53.

Training and promotion

There is a complete absence of evidence of indentured apprenticeship or formal training for the position of shipmaster. Adolescent boys could begin their life at sea as cabin boys, receiving half a man's wage, and such arrangements were probably frequently made within a family. There were certainly advantages in having familial connections, the Hawleys of Dartmouth offering such an example. Otherwise, the path to becoming a shipmaster appears to have been open to any intelligent, assertive and ambitious young man who informally learned the skills of a ship's officer by working his way up from deck-hand. The first step after mastering the basic skills of sailing the ship and handling the cargo, would have been to persuade a master to accept him informally as an apprentice or assistant, and so to learn the art of navigation on the job. There is no reference to a mate or second-in-command of an English ship in *Oleron*, *Queenborough*, the *Coutumier* or elsewhere, although one would expect that position to have been an essential step in the training of future shipmasters. Thereafter, for a man to improve his lot, he would have had to find a merchant, or wealthy patron, prepared to invest in a ship. The business and managerial skills required of a shipmaster would then have to be acquired, perhaps under the guidance of the shipowner, before the tyro could be considered fully qualified to work alone.[14]

There was visible 'class mobility' and a considerable overlap between the roles of owner, shipmaster, merchant and crew. That a shipmaster or a merchant could be part or sole owner of a ship has been shown in chapter 2, but it was also possible for a member of the crew to be a part-owner or to be a merchant working the ship that was carrying his cargo. The shipmaster appears, not infrequently, to have shipped more cargo than his free allowance, perhaps in the process of accumulating sufficient capital to become a fully fledged merchant or, if he were an employee, to buying his own ship. There was no impermeable barrier between the categories of those engaged in sea ventures, and a man could, if he wanted, act in several capacities at the same or at other times. Clear evidence for this mobility may be seen in the loading details for the shipmasters and crew in the Exeter customs accounts. One example is Paye Hardy who, as a crew member in 1305, brought in only his one tun portage allowance. The following year he brought in four tuns and was perhaps establishing himself as a merchant before his luck changed; in 1315 he had to revert to being a mariner again with only his one tun portage allowance.[15]

---

[14] Twiss, *Black Book*, III, pp. 50–657, *Customs*, chapters ii–xi, xvi, xvii, clxxxiv, and cxc.
[15] *Local Customs Accounts of the Port of Exeter*, passim.

Relationship with crew

The first commercial ventures at sea were probably informal cooperatives using a ship belonging to one of the members. The group worked the ship, caught fish, bought and sold goods (trading individually or together) and shared the expenses and profits of the voyage, although the shipowner, acting as *primus inter pares*, presumably received a higher proportion of the profits. The corporate responsibility demanded in such cooperative ventures sufficed until it became necessary to employ waged seamen; thereafter inducements and sanctions had to be introduced. Whether the master owned the whole or part of his ship or was an employee of the owner(s), he was responsible for the hiring and firing of crew and pilots, for their terms of employment, and for discipline on board. The shipmaster was also responsible for the ship's housekeeping, victualling, the issue of rations, the conservation of water and so on. *Oleron* shows traces of mutual endeavour by defining the need for consensual decisions by the shipmaster and his crew in such matters as the pledging of equipment, suitability of weather, salvage and jettison. Interestingly, when such cooperation is required, the crew are referred to in *Oleron* as *compaignouns*, a degree of equality reminiscent of Ulysses' last voyage on which he addressed his loyal crew as *compagni*. In contrast, in the *Oleron* articles which concern matters of discipline, hiring and firing crew, paying them and feeding them, the seamen are described more formally as 'mariners'. The relationship between master and crew was symbiotic; complementary to the situations in which the former had to consult the latter about certain maritime decisions, he might have to ask them to swear to his professional ability by confirming the necessity of jettison, the soundness of the lifting tackle, the careful stowage of cargo or the 'no fault' nature of an accident.[16]

Discipline

According to *Oleron* 'a shipmaster hires his sailors and must hold them in peace and be their judge'; he therefore had to try to maintain an orderly calm on the ship, know how to deal with arguments amongst the crew and with defiance of authority, and be aware of the approved scale of punishments for a variety of offences. There were, however, several gaps in the shipmaster's disciplinary armoury. *Oleron*, the *Coutumier* and the early section of *Queenborough* make no mention of punishments for theft by the crew from colleagues or from the cargo. This was possibly a sensitive subject when even the shipmaster could be guilty, as in the case of Chaucer's shipman: 'Ful many a draughte had he [the shipmaster] ydrawe / Fro Burdeux-ward, whil that the chapman [the merchant] sleep. / Of nyce conscience took he no keep.' Theft is covered in the later, fifteenth-century section of *Queenborough* but in only a general way and without reference to any

---

[16] Appendix 1, *Oleron, passim*; Appendix 3, *Coutumier*, chapter 95.

responsibility on the part of the shipmaster. That the shipmaster appears to have had no defined authority to deal summarily with thieves in his crew is curious, given the importance of the security of the cargo, and the unsettling effect on a crew within which a thief lurked. The case of *Pilk* v. *Vener(e)* (see chapter 2, p. 32) had been through the courts some 15 years before the later section of *Queenborough* was compiled; absence of any reference to a shipmaster's responsibility for the wrongdoings of his crew is therefore even more mysterious. Theft, however, is dealt with in *Customs* which prescribes for a man who has been found guilty three times, three duckings from the yardarm, a spell in irons, loss of wages and delivery to a magistrate ashore, if further punishment was felt necessary.[17]

When there was a dispute between a shipmaster and a member of his crew, the former could take away the *towaile*, translated as 'cloth', from in front of the wrongdoer while at the mess table. This may have meant either that the defaulter's rations were to be withheld for a specified period, or it was a form of social exclusion. Any repetition of his misbehaviour after the third withdrawal could lead to the man being sent ashore, at the crew's decision. If any seaman should denigrate another, he had to pay a fine of 4d. (a day's wage) whereas denigration by the shipmaster cost him 8d. If the shipmaster struck any member of the crew, then the latter had to take the first blow but thereafter he could defend himself. If it were the sailor who struck the first blow, then he must pay 100s. or lose a fist, the choice again being left to the crew. As manual abscission would render a man unfit for further work, it seems unlikely to have been practised. The table was the forum where the crew assessed a defaulter's contrition after his third and final warning or after an assault on the shipmaster, and it appears to have had a symbolic significance on board ship. The apparently democratic involvement of the crew may have been because they had to live and work with the accused, or it may have been another survival from the days of cooperative ventures.[18]

The most frequent breaches of discipline were almost certainly drunkenness and falling asleep while on watch, neither of which are mentioned in *Oleron*. The most likely explanation for such omission is that the shipmaster had at his disposal generally recognised sanctions for unspecified common offences. Desertion was another potential problem; both *Oleron* and *Queenborough* insist on the sailors remaining with the ship until she reaches her home port, the former advising shipmasters to retain some of the wages as security for men who have no belongings, and the latter threatening severe punishment to those who leave the ship too soon. For breaches of discipline, *Customs* offers the shipmaster the

---

[17] Appendix 1, *Oleron, passim*; Appendix 2, *Queenborough*, articles 2–13, 15 and 21. Chaucer, *Complete Works*, 'General Prologue', lines 396–8. See Chapter 2 for the responsibility of master for servant in common and merchant law, and for *Pilk* v. *Vener(e)*. Twiss, *Black Book*, III, pp. 36–345: *Customs*, chapters cxiii and cxxii.
[18] Appendix 1, *Oleron*, articles 12 and 14.

choice of withholding the man's food and wine for an unspecified period, or of ducking him three times from the yard with additional soakings from a bucket; it also, significantly, forbids wine for those about to go on watch.[19]

The serious crimes of murder, mutiny, sexual offences, arson, treason and deliberate damage, are not mentioned in *Oleron* or in the first section of *Queenborough*. Felonies committed at sea were covered by the criminal law applied ashore however, and the later section of *Queenborough* specifically lists murders, mayhems, mutinies and affrays as crimes to be the subject of inquiry by an admiral. A man suspected of a serious crime could no doubt be incarcerated on the ship until delivery to the shore authorities was possible, and there are records of prosecutions in port towns' and admirals' courts for murder and mayhem which had happened at sea. For example, the Yorkshire assize rolls record trials in 1361 and 1362, of two groups of men who, in one case, had robbed a ship off Scarborough and in the other, had killed a fisherman at Whitby.[20]

The *Coutumier* deals with damage on board a ship by a member of the crew in a rather confusing chapter. The responsibility for compensation, it suggests, lies in the master/servant relationship, but that, of course, is exactly where common and merchant laws had differing views, as discussed in chapters 1 and 2. A part-owner who placed on the ship the man who caused the damage (merchants, at their own expense, could place additional crew on board, even if the ship were fully manned) may be held responsible, unless the man had come to some concordance with the owner of the damaged property. A shipmaster who had some share in his ship, therefore, could be held responsible for any damage wrought by a member of the crew whom he had recruited.[21]

There is no mention in *Oleron* nor in *Queenborough* of a formal 'signing on' by the crew. In *Customs*, after a handshake with the shipmaster on joining the ship, a sailor is bound to obey him as if the agreement to serve had been made in writing before a notary. If a mariner should have a quarrel with, or strike, the shipmaster, he must lose half or all of his wages and goods and be dismissed the ship; the punishment for a mariner found guilty of theft for the third time has been discussed above. Additionally, *Customs* includes a ban on the crew undressing while at sea, sleeping ashore or leaving the ship without permission, and the punishments for those who fall asleep on watch.[22]

---

19   Appendix 1, *Oleron*, article 19; Appendix 2, *Queenborough*, articles 2 and 17. Twiss, *Black Book*, III, pp. 36–345: *Customs*, chapter ccvi.
20   Appendix 2, *Queenborough*, articles 29–34, 45, 46. York Sessions, pp. 90 and 128.
21   Appendix 3, *Coutumier*, chapters 86, 95.
22   Twiss, *Black Book*, III, pp. 186–7, 216–19, 220–1, 228–9, 230–3, 234–5, 436–9: *Customs*, chapters lxxx, cix, cxii, cxviii, cxix, cxxi, cxxiv, cxxv, cxxix and ccvi. Appendix 1, *Oleron*, articles 5, 12, 14.

The shipmaster's duty of care

To a marked degree the shipmaster's relationship with his crew was paternalistic. *Oleron* specifies that a sailor who falls ill as a result of service on the ship and is unable to work, has to be put ashore, supplied with food and light, and be cared for by a ship's boy or by a hired woman. While ill he has to receive the same rations as he would have received on board, any extras are to be at his own expense, but he is to receive no wages. If he dies, his belongings and unpaid wages are to go to his next of kin, perhaps discounted by the expenses incurred while he was sick, an hypothesis discussed in appendix 1. Men who leave the ship without permission, get drunk and are hurt, are to be left to their own devices, but if they are wounded ashore when on ship's business, the shipmaster has to look after them. If the ship founders and cannot continue the voyage, *Oleron* obliges the shipmaster to pay the fares for the crew's return home, provided they worked well during the crisis; if they had not done their best (in the shipmaster's opinion), their pay was to be stopped and they were to be abandoned wherever they happened to be.[23]

Customs, as *Oleron*, obliges the shipmaster to care for any member of the crew who has been wounded while on duty ashore and also to pay wages in full to a newly recruited mariner whether he turns out to be good or bad, unless he had misrepresented his skills, and all wages are to be paid however drastic the financial situation – 'even if there is only a nail with which it is possible to pay'. *Customs* also forbids the dismissal of a man to make room for a relative, or for another man at a lower wage. The shipmaster has to offer the crew portages, again as in *Oleron* and *Queenborough* but with certain restrictions, and to allow them time ashore to arrange and load their cargoes before the ship is fully laden, a provision reminiscent of *Queenborough* in which are set out the rules for compensation for portages unloaded to make room for merchants' cargoes.[24]

Remuneration of shipmaster and crew
On most routes, the shipmaster offered his crew the choice of cash (*a deniers*), an allowance of cargo space (portage) or payment *au fret de la nef* whereby, it would appear, the mariner made his portage space available for the ship's cargo, in exchange for a share of the ship's profit. Part of the crew's wages were paid in advance, in cash, at or before arrival at the ship's destination, enabling them to purchase goods for their own trading on return to the home port. Cash payment on a daily rate was not unknown; it may have been the method of payment intended in *Queen-*

---

[23] Appendix 1, *Oleron*, articles 3, 6, 7, but see Hanham, *Celys' World*, p. 371 for the *actualité* of the division of a dead man's wages between past and current pursers.
[24] Twiss, *Black Book*, III, pp. 188–9, 196–7, 198–205: *Customs*, chapters lxxxi, lxxxii, lxxxix, xciii–xcvi. Appendix 1, *Oleron*, article 6. Twiss, *Black Book*, III, pp. 35–165: *Customs*, chapters lxxxvi–lxxxix, xci–xciii. Appendix 2, *Queenborough*, article 2 and Appendix 1, *Oleron*, article 18.

borough where a *raisonable salaire* is mentioned for an 'open-ended' hire when the final destination had not yet been decided. Daily, weekly or monthly rates were also the bases of payment of crews on impressed ships, supplemented by a ration allowance known as *de regard*. There were variants of the portage option: a sailor could load his own cargo, he could make it available *au fret de la nef*, or he could sell the space to a merchant (a subcontract forbidden in *Customs*). According to *Oleron*, if cargo had to be jettisoned, portages were exempt from contribution to general average. That exemption held, even if the crew had shipped 'only water which was to be valued as wine', or if they had sold their space to a merchant (who would have paid more than the ship's freight rate in order to enjoy the exemption). Individual negotiations, plus the varying discounts offered by the shipmaster to some merchants, could lead to a number of freight rates obtaining on the ship. Because of this variety of rates, it was stipulated in *Queenborough* that the freight charges were to be averaged for the calculation of the profit for members of the crew whose portages were *au fret de la nef*. In contradiction of the *Oleron* privilege, the *Coutumier* is quite clear that all cargo is to be included in general average.[25]

Of the options available, filling his own portage space would be potentially the most profitable for the mariner but it meant risking his own capital; to share in the profits of the ship would be the least profitable, but the safest and easiest; to subcontract his space to a merchant, involved negotiation but no investment, and was therefore a middle course. Unfortunately it is not possible to know the distribution of choices. In the early fourteenth-century customs accounts of Exeter, where portages were customs-free, it is sometimes possible to identify a portage filled by a member of the crew and that which had been subcontracted to a merchant. Unfortunately the customs accounts do not identify merchants' cargoes shipped in crew's space *au fret de la nef*. Other ports' customs accounts appear not to record portage landings and it may be that customs exemption was not always available outside Exeter. In *Oleron* and *Queenborough* there are rules covering payment for portages that had been excluded to make room for ship's cargo, for averaging varying freight rates for payment to the crew, and for additional payment for extended voyages. Those who opted for portage, which was, in effect, a fixed rate, received no extra if the voyage was extended. In *Customs*, the crew have first claim for the payment of their wages, before even the moneylenders, and although, figuratively, there may be only a nail left of the ship, and payment has to be made at the home port or wherever previously arranged.[26]

The post-plague attempts to control wages ashore by means of the Statutes of

---

[25] Appendix 1, *Oleron*, articles 8, 18, 20. Appendix 2, *Queenborough*, articles 13, 14, 17. Hanham, *Celys' World*, p. 382. Appendix 3, *Coutumier*, chapter 94.
[26] Appendix 2, *Queenborough*, articles 2–15, 17. Appendix 1, *Oleron*, article 20. Twiss, *Black Book*, III, pp. 198–205: *Customs*, chapters xciii–xcv. *Local Customs Accounts of the Port of Exeter*, p. 92, for example: Henry de Rochevale: eight lasts customed, but he is allowed to have four men's portage.

Labourers in 1349 and 1351, meant that any wage negotiations by seamen risked an admiral's inquiry and subsequent prosecution. In 1390 however, claims were made in Parliament for wage increases because mariners were refusing to sail in English rather than foreign ships. The existing wage for the Bordeaux run was 8s. and one tun portage for mariners, and double that for shipmasters, precisely the rates stipulated in *Queenborough*. The wage demanded for shipmasters was 24s. and three tuns portage, an increase of 50 per cent. In a 1441 account for the ship *Christofer* which had taken Edward Hull to Bordeaux, wages, which appear to be only for the one-way voyage, had increased to 10s. for the crew and 40s. for the shipmaster. The greater shipmaster/crew differential, a multiple of 4, may have been the result of a private negotiation – 'ex certa convencione secum facta' – because the *Christofer* at 400 tons was a particularly large ship. In 1442 a ship's crew and her shipmaster were paid 8s. and 21s. 4d. respectively plus some additional reward for 'keeping of the sea' for a period of 16 weeks; here the differential has fallen back to 2.7. Again in 1442, a scheme was presented to the Commons for guarding the seas with a standing fleet. The rates of pay defined in the petition are 2s. per month plus 14d. per week making 20d. per week total for seamen, and for shipmasters 'eche of hem overe this in the month 40d.', making 30d. per week total, plus the same ration allowance, a drop in the differential to 1.5 (although on wages alone the differential is 2.7). After a prolonged period of stability from the time of *Queenborough*, it appears that in the 1440s there was some movement in mariners' wages, perhaps because a shortage of seamen gave them a negotiating advantage. The downward adjustment in the differential would appear to be anomalous.[27]

The wages and portages decreed in *Queenborough* are given per voyage. Since overtime payments were expressly forbidden, persistent contrary winds were expensive for everyone on the ship. In addition to the hazards of the weather, ships and crew were also subject to changes in the sailing plans of the merchants which might involve longer or shorter times at sea. So important was a favourable wind to medieval merchants and shipmasters with their ships of poor windward ability, that in the mid-fifteenth century the port of Sandwich was paying for a watchman to call out wind direction throughout the night. *Oleron*, confirmed by *Queenborough*, specifies that when, for commercial reasons, a voyage is longer in distance (but not in time) than expected, those who had opted for portages were to receive no more, but those on wages, *a deniers*, were to be paid extra, 'vewe par vewe et corps par corps', because they had been hired to stay with the ship to her final port of call. If, on the other hand, the voyage was shorter than expected,

---

[27] Appendix 2, *Queenborough*, articles 5, 64. *Statutes*, 23 and 25 Edward III st. 2; 12 Richard II, cc. 3, 4, 5 etc. *Rot. Parl.*, 3, p. 283. Hannes Kleineke, 'English Shipping to Guyenne in the Mid-Fifteenth Century: Edward Hull's Gascon Voyage of 1441', *MM* 85, 4 (1999), pp. 472–6, citing PRO E101/53/27 (the charter was for 16 weeks and Kleineke assumes that wages included the return voyage, but the amount makes that unlikely). PRO E404/56/295. *Rot. Parl.* 5, 1439–1468, p. 59, 'Safeguard of the Sea'. *Naval Documents*, p. 13; *CPR 1436–41*, p. 372.

they were still to receive their full wages. The question of additional payment for protracted voyages is covered, or perhaps concealed, by an article in *Queenborough* which makes it clear that a mariner was hired in a rather open-ended way. Provided that reasonable wages are to be paid, the ship may go anywhere – Bordeaux, Bayonne, Lisbon and Seville are expressly mentioned – especially if a full cargo were not obtained at the first port, and the crew may not refuse to work her. With persistent winds from one direction, to sail to a more distant port could, paradoxically, shorten the total time of the voyage; alternatives were often agreed between merchants and shipmasters in the charter-parties, as discussed in chapter 4.[28]

The owners of the *Bitchellse* of London attempted to short-pay the crew when a Bordeaux run terminated at La Rochelle; the crew protested to the High Court of the Admiralty, perhaps on the grounds that according to *Queenborough* the wage and portage rates for Bordeaux and La Rochelle were the same. An example of additional pay for a longer distance to crew sailing *a deniers*, is in a Cely account of the 1480s; the crew of the *Margaret Cely* were hired to go to Arnemunde but the ship went on to Antwerp, for which each man received an extra 2s. *flemish*. When the delay of a voyage was due to dilatoriness on the part of a merchant, he was obliged by *Oleron* to pay compensation, at an unspecified rate, after 15 days, two thirds of which went to the shipmaster (because he had expenses to pay), and one third to the crew. *Queenborough* makes no mention of compensation for loading delays, the crew apparently having to accept lost time as a commercial risk.[29]

Wages, the rate per mile, and the value of portage for the return voyage, have been tabulated for a number of common routes in Table 1. These remunerations have been taken from *Queenborough* (and are therefore mid-fourteenth-century) backed with the rather scant information about rates of pay to be found elsewhere. From the table, two main groups of wage rates may be identified: over 0.2d. per mile for Lisbon (direct route), Prussia, Berwick and Ireland, and under 0.15d. per mile for Lisbon (coastal route), all the Biscaian ports (direct or coastal routes) and Newcastle. The direct routes, across the Bay of Biscay instead of coasting, would have taken less time and have been less subject to attack but offered no shelter from storms. The Calais run attracted enhanced rates, perhaps because of the risks of piracy, and Flanders falls between the higher and lower rates, assuming in both cases that the wages were 'both ways'. The portages which can be compared with wages indicate that they were probably related to early fourteenth-century rates. In *Customs*, a mariner's 'venture' is restricted to a value of 50 *besants* less than the

---

[28] *The Travels of Leo of Rozmital*, ed. M. Letts, Hakluyt Society, 2nd series, 108 (1957), p. 50. Appendix 1, *Oleron*, article 20. Appendix 2, *Queenborough*, article 17. A *vewe* (or French *veüe*) was the same distance as a *kenning*, somewhere between 17 and 19 miles.
[29] PRO HCA 24, file 7: *Richard Audsley and others v. Umfray Knight and William Sawbderson*. Appendix 2, *Queenborough*, article 5. Hanham, *Celys' World*, p. 379. Appendix 1, Oleron, article 22.

THE SHIPMASTER'S OFF-SHORE RESPONSIBILITIES

Table 1 Comparison of wages and portages values

The table has been built from wage and portage rates given in *Queenborough* articles 3–13 (Appendix 2) and the freight rates from other sources. The approximate pence per mile column has been calculated as (wages) divided by (distance in nautical miles).

From	To	Wages outward	Portages return[3]	Equivalent freight value	Approx wage as d./mile
London	Lisbon	20s.	1 tun wine	20s./tun[5]	0.14*/0.20^
London	? Prussia (Danzig)	20s.	⅓ last of ?		0.20
London	Ireland (Waterford)	10s.	3 dickers hides		0.21
London	Ireland (Dublin)	10s. + 2s.	– do –		0.22
London	Bayonne	10s.	1 tun wine		0.13*/0.15^
London	Scone	8s. 4d.	⅓ last of herring		0.20
London	Berwick	8s.	?		0.22
London	Bordeaux (autumn)	8s.[1]	1 tun wine	8s.–22s./tun[6]	0.11*/0.13^
London	La Rochelle (autumn)	8s.	1 tun wine		0.12*/0.14^
London	Bordeaux (spring)	7s.	1 pipe wine		0.10*/0.12^
London	La Rochelle (spring)	7s	1 pipe wine		0.10*/0.12^
London	Bourgneuf	5s.	3 x ¼ salt	3s. 9d.–5s.	0.08*/0.10^
London	Bourgneuf with cover		– do – + ½ x ¼ salt	4s. 4d.–5s. 10d.[7]	
London	Newcastle	4s.	2 x ¼ coal[4]		0.13
London	Flanders	6s	nil		0.18
London	Calais	5s[2]	nil		0.32

* calculated from the distance on a direct route
^ calculated from the distance on a coasting route

[1] Hanham, *Celys' World*, pp. 370–3: for autumn voyages to Bordeaux in the 1480s. the Celys paid their crew 4fr. and shipmaster 12fr., (8s. and 24s. respectively), the portages for the return are uncertain but the freight rate was 18s. in 1488 and 19s. in 1499. Kleineke, 'English Shipping', p. 473 quotes 10s. wages in the 1440s.

[2] Hanham, *Celys' World*, p. 368: in 1486 the Celys paid their crew 10s. per man, the shipmaster 30s., the cook, carpenter and boatswain 5s. and the purser 10s. for there and back to Calais. Soldiers 'wafting' the convoy received 6s. 8d. plus 12½d. per week ration money (the voyage took two weeks).

[3] Hanham, *Celys' World*, p. 368: portages shown are for an ordinary seaman, shipmasters were entitled to double or treble and boys to three quarters. *Local Customs Accounts of the Port of Exeter*, appendix 4.

[4] Coal was carried in place of stone ballast; the portage allowance was therefore not generous.

[5] Childs, *Anglo-Castilian Trade*, pp. 170–1. The rate quoted is, *faute de mieux*, from northern Spain.

[6] James, *Wine Trade*, pp. 17, 25–6. The freight rate in the early fourteenth century was 8s.; war conditions had raised it to 12s.–13s. 4d. by the middle of the century and to 22s. by 1372. The period of truce and then the peace of 1396 allowed rates to fall but only to c.18s.

[7] CCR 1349–54, p. 197: in the mid-fourteenth century, the freight rate for salt from the Bay to Winchelsea was 15d. per quarter. Bridbury, *Salt Trade*, p. 133: freight represented from 33% to 50% of the retail price of salt in England in the fifteenth century, from 1378 to 1450 salt prices varied between c.4s. and c.7s. per quarter.

wages for the voyage, further evidence of such a relationship. As late as 1486, the able seamen of the *Margaret Cely* were still being paid 4 francs (= 8s. sterling) for the Bordeaux run, when the merchant Tibbot Oliver paid freight at about £1 per tun, after a 21 for 20 discount, for his cargo of 48 tuns. Here, the seaman's wage had remained at the *Queenborough* level of 8s. since the mid-fourteenth century although the value of his portage, if he were offered that option, had inflated to £1. Portage allowances continued to become relatively more valuable as freight rates increased through the century, and their almost complete disappearance towards the end of the fifteenth century was perhaps due to a reluctance on the part of shipmasters to offer such an expensive option to the crew.[30]

There were other emoluments for the shipmaster and crew. What appears to be a tip for the shipmaster is described as *chaux* (perhaps 'shoemoney'?) of 25 francs (3.7 per cent of the freight cost) in the freighting agreement of 1392 *Lynne* charter-party discussed in chapter 4. The differences to be seen occasionally between the agreed freight rate and the money paid may have been gratuities, for example in a disputed charter of 1387 for 30 weys of salt at 5s. per wey (a total of £7 10s.), the plaintiff shipmaster claimed £7 12s. 6d., the extra 2s. 6d. (1.67 per cent of the freight charge) being, it was claimed, supported by a covenant between merchant and shipmaster. By tradition, the crew were offered 'first refusal' to unload the cargo from their ship for a *primage* payment by the merchant shippers at a rate per ton, an arrangement sometimes agreed in the charter-party. In 1332–33, in Dublin, the crew of the *Margaret* were paid 2d. per tun and 1d. per pipe for loading wine from barges; the same amount was paid to load the barges by windlass from a quay. In 1480–81; John Balsall, purser of the *Trinity*, paid the crew 200 *maravedis* for loading 33.5 tuns of wine from the ship's boat; and in 1486 Giles Beckingham, Richard Cely's apprentice, paid 4s. *fleming* (c.2s. sterling) for 'premech and lodmannach' (loading and pilotage) on the *Margaret Cely*. The crew were expected to carry out repairs on the ship for which they were sometimes paid: while waiting in Bordeaux the 'fellowship' of the *Margaret Cely* were paid 6 sous (1.6d.) for sewing a sail.[31]

When ships were detained for caulking and repairs, the shipmaster and a few of the crew were retained as ship-keepers, earning less but enjoying certain extras and better rations. The Lancastrian naval accounts show that ship-keepers were

---

30 Twiss, *Black Book*, III, pp. 192–4: *Customs*, chapter lxxxvi. Hanham, *Celys' World*, pp. 370–9. Appendix 3, *Coutumier*, chapter 55. See also James, *Wine Trade*, p. 145, citing PRO E364/54/4.

31 *CPMR, 1381–1412*, pp. 194–8 and pp. 133–4: William Prophet, the shipmaster, claimed against William Jay, a merchant, for freight of salt. Prophet admitted he had received an advance of 40s. and was due a further £5 12s. 6d. *Primage* is mentioned in *Oleron*, article 10, in some manuscripts; Twiss, *Black Book*, I, pp. 88–131. PRO C 47/37/14, mm. 19–34, fo. 5 and mm. 49–60, fo. 10; C 47/37/11, mm. 22–3, fos 1–6d. O'Neill, *Merchants and Mariners*, p. 54 citing PRI, rep. DK, 43, p. 60. Hanham, *Celys' World*, pp. 23, 365, 370.

paid at 6d. per week for shipmasters (most often not paid as they were going about their own business, sick or in receipt of an annuity) and, for ordinary seamen, 3d. The ship-keepers of the *Margaret Cely* were paid 12d. per week and two of them helped with the caulking at a going rate of 11d. for two tides. They were also supplied with small quantities of meat, fruit and vegetables, in addition to whatever they had bought for themselves.[32]

In the list of portage allowances, *Queenborough* mentions payment of the outward voyage wages at the out-port (specifically, Berwick) to enable the crew to buy goods for their portages. That provision also occurs in another, somewhat complex, article concerning the putting out of crew's cargo to make room for ship's cargo; here the men are to receive at the out-port (specifically, Bordeaux) half of their total wages plus 50 per cent in compensation if their cargoes are not shipped, the remainder to be paid at the home port. According to *Queenborough*, if a ship is freighted and has a fixed time limit for payment, the crew are to be paid half of their wages on loading and the other half when the ship has reached the unloading port; that provision includes a safeguard against sailors jumping ship however, because if the shipmaster or owner does not wish to take the ship home, the wages are to be paid only when half of the freight money has been received.[33]

It is not possible accurately to compare the earnings of mariners with those of their peer group ashore because of the very different conditions of employment. Seamen's rations were supplied by the ship, and impressed sailors on the king's service received a ration allowance, the *regard*. Mariners had opportunities to fish and catch birds, and had some cushion against shortages after poor harvests, by sailing to regions where the crops had been better. In addition to their basic pay, merchant seamen could often speculate by shipping goods, freight-free, in their portages, and had a chance of sharing in finds and prizes.

The quality of life at sea

Accommodation on board
There is no known surviving first-hand account of the life of the shipmaster and his crew on board a medieval ship, but some parallel evidence may be obtained from passengers' tales, ships' inventories and contemporary illustrations and literature. However, it is known that English fourteenth-century cargo ships were not fitted out with living accommodation for the crew. The crew had to find shelter

---

[32] Rose, *Lancastrian Navy*, pp. 71 ff. M.A. Oppenheim, *History of the Administration of the Royal Navy, 1509–1660* (London, 1896), pp. 25–6, 34. Hanham, *Celys' World*, pp. 364 (a caulking rate of 8d. per day is given thrice) and 377.
[33] Appendix 2, *Queenborough*, articles 2, 13, 15, 17.

on deck or, in bad weather, if cargo space permitted, they might have preferred the dark, damp, noisome and rat-infested hold. The ship's officers, fare-paying passengers and the more important merchant shippers lived in the after part of the ship, in the stern castle or below the quarter deck, a tradition which still survives. In the *Lynne* charter-party of 1392, the merchants were to be responsible for caulking the cabin which they had been allocated, unfortunately in an unspecified area of the ship, while the shipmaster had to provide for them fresh water, salt, firewood and lamps, in other words, they were to be self-catering.[34]

Longer voyages, particularly towards the north, and in the deteriorating weather experienced as the Medieval Warm Period ended, demanded better accommodation for the crew. Voyages to Iceland, for example, must have exposed crews occasionally to very severe conditions. The shelter supplied for the crew was initially perhaps only a canvas *tilt* erected in the shelter of the high bulwarks at the bows. It is possible, however, that from the beginning of the fifteenth century something more permanent was built into ships to accommodate the crew; certainly, before her first voyage for the Celys, the *Margaret Cely* had work done in her 'foxle' which required 100' of board.[35]

There are several examples of temporary cabins being built for important passengers; an extreme case of ship modification being that for Henry, earl of Derby, later Henry IV, on his expedition to Prussia, when provision was made for cabins and a hall, chapel and chamber. The poem *Morte Arthure* (written 1370–1420) describes a cabin prepared for a king: 'The kynge was in a gret cogge, with knyghtez fulle many, / In a cabane enclosede, clenlyche arayede; / With-in on a riche bedde rystys a littylle.' Another contemporary poem, *The Pilgrims Sea Voyage*, confirms that temporary cabins were specialy built for non-royal but important passengers: 'Anone he [the shipowner] calleth a carpentere, / And byddyth hym bryng with hym hys gere, / To make the cabans here and there, / With many a febyll celle.' The accounts for the construction of private accommodation in a ship for Juana of Navarre's journey to Brittany to marry John IV in 1386, have survived. It took seven carpenters 24 days to construct a framed structure of wood to which was nailed a covering of linen or canvas with net and leather, waterproofed with fat and rosin. The cabin was positioned aft, on deck or on the bridge, and fitted out with new furnishings, eating utensils, pottery, linen cloths, candles and wax torches. Significantly, the accounts show that most of the diplomatic party and

---

[34] Klaus-Peter Kiedel and Uwe Schnall, eds, *The Hanse Cog of Bremen of 1380* (Bremerhaven, 1985), p. 12: the cog found in the Weser had what might have been two cabins under the quarter deck. CPMR, 1381–1412, pp. 196.
[35] The presence of increased sodium chloride in the Greenland ice core indicates higher wind speeds after c.1410. For early arrivals on Iceland, see G.J. Markus, *Conquest of the North Atlantic* (Woodbridge, 1980). Hanham, *Celys' World*, p. 366. It is interesting that 'forecastle' had already been abbreviated to 'foxle'.

many of the crew left the ship to live ashore while waiting for Juana because of the primitive conditions on board. The erection of such temporary cabins, rather than a cheaper refurbishment of existing accommodation, perhaps confirms that normally there were no permanent cabins on medieval merchant ships.[36]

Pilgrims' voyages are well documented and reflect something of the conditions in which the crew lived, although ships were more crowded when carrying the devout than when loaded with cargo. Sea sickness was a perennial problem, at least for passengers and perhaps for the crew, in the small and foetid ships. Some passengers were sick from the beginning: Leo of Rozmital and his companions, after being rowed out to their ship were 'so distressed by the waves that they lay on the ship as if they had been dead'. Sanitary arrangements were primitive and required the use of a bucket on deck or a box or barrel suspended over the side of the ship: 'the perilous perch and the splashing of the sea are both discouraging to your purpose and your only hope is to dose yourself with purgatives.' The Dominican monk Felix Faber of Ulm, who travelled twice to the Holy Land in the 1480s, wrote a picturesque account of the lavatorial problems encountered, quoting 'the poet': 'ut dicitur metrice: maturum stercus est importabile pondus.' The result of the lack of comfortable facilities was that organic compost accumulated in the bilges until even the shipmaster realised that something had to be done about it; analysis of the ballast of the early fifteenth-century Aber Wrac'h wreck found the remains of food and human faeces. It is no wonder that in the *Pilgrims Sea Voyage* it was complained that: 'when that we shall go to bedde / The pumps was nygh oure beddes hede / A man were as good to be ded / As smell thereof the stynk.'[37]

Health at sea

Compared with their peer group ashore, sailors had the advantage of regular meals but the disadvantage of continual exposure to the weather. Although they were isolated for much of their working life from infections passing through their home communities, they were exposed to others in the ports they visited. The risk

---

36 *Expeditions to Prussia and the Holy Land*, pp. 26–27, 157–8. *Morte Arthure*, lines 756–8. Furnival, *Pilgrims Sea Voyage*, p. 40; the poem was written c.1460. Jones, 'Le Voyage de Pierre de Lesnerac'.
37 The numbers of pilgrims that ships were licensed to carry indicate potentially horrific conditions: *La Marie* of Southampton, 100; *La Sainte Marie* de Blakney, 60; *La Garlond* of Crowemere, 60, etc., *Foedera*, 12 Henry VI (1434), 10, pp. 567–9; on occasions more were carried, *CPR*, 1422–9, p. 493. *Rozmital*, pp. 162–4. J.J. Simmons, 'The Development of External Sanitary Facilities Aboard Ships of the 15th to 19th Centuries', unpublished thesis, Texas A&M University, 1985: the voyage of Eugenio de Salazar from Spain to the New World in 1573. Georges Dubuy, ed., *A History of Private Life*, 2 vols (Cambridge, MA, 1988), vol. 2, *Revelations of the Medieval World*, pp. 587–8. *The Book of the Wanderings of Felix Faber*, ed. and trans. Aubrey Stewart, 2 vols (London, 1892). Hutchinson, *Medieval Ships*, p. 99. Furnivall, *Pilgrims Sea Voyage*.

of exposure to pandemics such as bubonic plague was similar for everyone, but seamen visiting Gascon and Iberian ports ran the additional risk of contracting malaria from infected Anopheles mosquitoes, and parasite-borne diseases new to their immune systems. In addition, their living conditions were inevitably conducive to pulmonary tuberculosis. The physician Gilbertus Anglicus devoted a chapter of his medical textbook to the health hazards faced by those going to sea based on his personal experiences; he lists seasickness, foul stenches, thirst and parasitic infestation but does not mention seamen's industrial injuries. Although his sea experience was towards the end of the thirteenth century, his work was printed and publishd in 1510 and presumably reflects the experience of fourteenth- and fifteenth-century mariners.[38]

The principal physical hazards for mariners were suppurating sores and injuries arising from their work or from defending their ship. The rough timbers of the hull and decks splintered into bare feet and hands, falling cargo and equipment crushed and broke limbs, and hernias were probably not uncommon when handling heavy sails and cargo. Because any wound or rotting tooth could progress to septicaemia and death, it was probably generally known that at the first sign of inflammation, wounds had to be opened and rotten teeth extracted. In addition, although voyages were short, the persistently wet and salty conditions almost certainly led to dermatological problems such as salt water rash and fungal infections. Scurvy however, was no more of a problem at sea than ashore as voyages were insufficiently long for vitamin C deficiency to present. Ashore, for those who could afford the fees, repairs to bones, the extraction of teeth and the treatment of flesh wounds were undertaken by barber-surgeons, tooth-pullers and physicians. At sea, injuries, serious or trivial, had to be dealt with on the spot by seamen no doubt practised in empirical first-aid. While physicians argued the question of whether to keep a wound open or to close it, men on board ship had little choice. They probably gave every wound a thorough searching, removing any foreign material they could find and withdrew arrow heads when necessary, perhaps by covering the barbs with quills before pulling the head back through the flesh. Wounds were then plugged with bandages perhaps soaked in egg albumen and covered; although the bandages would be far from sterile, the stimulation of bleeding would help to cleanse the wound. The reduction of dislocated joints and repair of hernias with subsequent supporting bandaging, were no doubt also attempted. Seamen who were too badly injured or too sick to work were put ashore where the shipmaster had an obligation under *Oleron* to arrange accommodation with a carer, food (but

---

[38] *Compendium medicine Gilberti anglici tam morborum universalium quam particularium nondum medicis sed et cyrurgicis utilissimum*, ed. Michael de Capella (Lyons 1510), 7, pp. 362–3 and see Appendix 4. Gilbert is amongst those mentioned by Chaucer in his cynical description of the Doctour of Phisik: *Complete Works*, 'General Prologue', line 434.

no better than aboard unless the sick man paid) and a light, but the ship was not obliged to wait for him. When an unidentified illness struck several members of the crew of Juana of Navarre's ship, mentioned above, lodgings and rations were paid for them in the town, as laid down in *Oleron*.[39]

Personal kit
The shipmaster and crew probably had little personal kit to take to sea, although the former might be expected to have accumulated more spare clothes than a first-time sailor, who no doubt suffered a great deal from the weather. Each man had a mattress stuffed with straw or heather or, if he could afford it, a feather quilt and a bed-cover of waterproofed cloth or of skins. He would also have had a box or canvas bag for his few belongings, all of which were liable to jettison as in the storm in the poem *Patience* quoted above. Although later than the period under examination, an inventory produced in the High Court of Admiralty in 1535 may be typical of a successful shipmaster's belongings a century before. John Aborough had a jerkin of frieze and another of canvas, two petticoats, two pairs of breeches, a shirt, a pair of short hose, a bed (presumably a mattress), a pillow, a coverlet of bever, a handline of 180 fathoms, two sets of sailing directions (one in English and the other Castillian, and a 'year and a half in the making') and four compasses. Other things which a shipmaster might have owned are listed incidentally in a Letter Patent of 1285 defining items to be exempted from contribution to general average, namely a bracelet, belt, ring, silver drinking cup and bedding. He would also have had various personal tools – a knife for eating and working (Chaucer's Shipman had a dagger on a lanyard) and a spike to undo knots. Other eating utensils appear to have belonged to the ship as there are several entries in the Celys' accounts for replacement dishes, cups, spoons, ladles and platters. In view of the paucity of their belongings, the authorisation in *Oleron* for the shipmaster to hold the crew's possessions against their return from leave appears to be optimistic; the lien must have included whatever goods they had shipped if the total were to attain any real value.[40]

---

39 C.R.W. Edwards *et al.*, eds, *Davidson's Principles and Practice of* Medicine (Edinburgh, 1995 ed.), p. 571: 'Body store [of ascorbic acid] lasts for about 2.5 to 3 months on a deficient diet'. Roy Porter, *The Greatest Benefit to Mankind* (London, 1997), p. 117. Gallen's *Book of Operations*, British Library Sloane MS 2463. Malory, *Works*, ed. Eugène Vinaver (2nd edn, Oxford, 1971), for example p. 656, lines 41–2: 'Than the knyghtes that were hurt were serched, and sofftе salves were layde to their woundis.' Tony Hunt, *The Medieval Surgery* (Woodbridge, 1992), p. 29. Appendix 1, *Oleron*, article 7. Jones, 'Le Voyage de Pierre de Lesnerac', pp. 83–104.
40 Burwash, *Merchant Shipping*, pp. 33–4. Riley, *Liber Albus*, pp. 490–2. Chaucer, *Complete Works*, 'General Prologue', lines 392–3. CPR 1281–92, pp. 168–9. Hanham, *Celys' World*, pp. 378, 389. Appendix 1, *Oleron*, articles 2, 3, 8, 10, 11, 14, 16, 19. Appendix 3, *Coutumier*, chapter 94.

Rations at sea

Oleron stipulates that when the ship is in a place where grapes are grown, the sailors must have wine and one hot meal each day, but when there is only water to drink, then they are to have two cooked meals per day. When beer was issued to English crews on outward voyages, it appears to have been counted as wine, with the men reduced to one hot meal daily, but they had a second meal of bread and salt-cured beef or salted or smoked fish with their wine or beer. A two-meal regime was generally followed ashore and would not have been seen as any hardship by the crew. As with their peer group ashore, the hot dinner would have been eaten at about 10 a.m. and the cold supper between 4 and 6 p.m., depending on work demands and whether it was summer or winter. No doubt the quality and quantity of the messing varied with the parsimony or generosity of the shipmaster and whether the ship was at sea or in harbour. It is probable that the master, and perhaps other members of the crew, purchased delicacies for themselves whenever they were able. The ruling in *Oleron* that a sick man who has been left ashore has to pay for any 'viaundes plus deliciouses' bought to supplement the ship's basic rations, confirms that the crew fortified their rations at their own expense. Items bought for the crew of the *Margaret Cely* when the ship was in port included fresh meat, eggs, butter, oil, oatmeal, smoked herring, mustard, mussels, medlars, figs, raisins, green peas and leeks but as these were not always bought in sufficient quantities for the full crew, they must have been only for those of the crew and any travelling merchants who could afford them.[41]

Difficulties of food preservation severely restricted the choice of food available at sea. Bread could not be kept fresh for more than two or three days, unsalted meat for little more, and water turned stale if the casks had not been well cleaned and aged. Vegetables were necessarily restricted to root crops which kept well, such as turnips, beets and onions but ships were not at sea long enough for any dietary deficiency to develop. In addition to victuals brought on board at the last port of call, fish and birds would have been caught *en voyage*; the Cely accounts include the purchase of fish hooks and line. There was no understanding of the need to balance the diet and little attention was paid to hygiene in the galleys; ships' cooks were probably no better than the scullions in the kitchens of Henry VIII who 'goe naked or in garments of such vileness as they now doe' or Chaucer's cook: 'But greet harm was it, as it thoughte me, / That on his shyne a mormal hadde he.'[42]

The bread on board was of two types; fresh when in harbour and for a day or

---

[41] Appendix 1, *Oleron*, article 17. PRO C 47/37/14 mm. 1–6, 7–12. *A Collection of Ordinances and Regulations for the Government of the Royal Household*, The Society of Antiquaries (1790), p. 151. Appendix 1, *Oleron*, article 7.

[42] Hanham, *Celys' World*, pp. 378 and 390–1. *Ordinances*, p. 148. Chaucer, *Complete Works*, 'General Prologue', lines 385–6.

two thereafter and biscuit or 'hard tack' when at sea. Only larger ships had ovens and it was not possible to bake on the smaller ships to maintain a supply of fresh bread. During Henry of Derby's voyage to Prussia in 1390, his ships were supplied with quantities of ship's biscuit in Danzig. The *Margaret Cely*'s 'koke rom' had a hearth which appears to have been unsuitable for baking at sea, as bread was bought (no doubt as biscuit) in dozens to be stored on the ship, but she carried flour to be baked when in port. In contrast, a larger ship operated by Sir John Howard had a sizeable brick-built oven in which bread could have been baked. *Oleron* and *Queenborugh* do not specify a bread ration for ships' crews but *Oleron* article 21, which may be corrupt, rather vaguely suggests that sailors going ashore may take with them any amount of bread. What can be said for certain is that, however made and in whatever quantity, indigestion after eating the cooks' 'bread hastily made, without leaven, from the dregs of the ale-tub, leaden bread, bread of tares', would have been considered normal.[43]

It has been calculated that medieval seamen expended something over 4,000 calories per day, much of the energy for English crews coming from beer. The protein in seamen's rations consisted principally of fresh or salted meat, 'white' (salted) and 'red' (smoked) herring and 'stockfish' (dried cod). The Cely accounts show the loading of large quantities of red and white fish and stockfish in barrels in March and two oxen salted down also in barrels and loaded just before a sailing in mid-May. The quantity of meat or fish to be issued to each man per day is difficult to extract from the accounts, as the number of days for which provisioning is intended is not given. Other evidence gives an idea of a minimum daily ration: in the *Liber Niger* of Edward IV, a messenger, whose wage of 3d. in court and 5d. out of court was close to a seaman's, received 'one loffe, one messe of grete mete, dim' gallon ale'; a seamen would have required more because of his hard physical work. Another indication of the quantity of food available is the 'cash in lieu' or *regard* paid by the crown to men on merchant ships impressed for service. Between 1327 and 1450, except in 1442 when other arrangements were made, the *regard* was 6d. per week, increased in 1460 (when naval pay was reduced from 3d. per day to 1s. 3d. per week) to 1s. ½d. per week. Hanham has calculated that the food costs on the *Margaret Cely* approximated quite closely to that allowance while the ship was on convoy duty in 1476. In the owner's accounts for the preparation of the *Christofer* of Dartmouth for a voyage to Guyenne with Edward Hull in 1440–41, the victuals bought consisted of wheat flour, a small quantity of oatmeal,

---

43 *Expeditions to Prussia and the Holy Land*, p. 347. Hanham, *Celys' World*, p. 379: the Celys' day book shows baking at Antwerp and elsewhere. 'Registres de grands jours de Bordeaux', 1456, 1459, ed. H.A. Barckhausen, *Les Archives historiques du départment de la Gironde*, vol. IX (Paris and Bordeaux, 1867). G.G. Coulton, *Medieval Panorama* (Cambridge, 1937) p. 233. Piero Camporesi, *Bread of Dreams: Food and Fantasy in Early Modern Europe* (London, 1989). Tares (red corn poppies) and other hallucinogenic and toxic grains were to be found in bread.

beef carcasses, three different types of salt fish and beer, the quantities indicating that all ranks, crew and retinue, were to share the rations. The accounts may be incomplete, in that last-minute purchases were probably made of fruit, vegetables and dairy produce. These victuals and the food purchased for several voyages of the *Margaret Cely* in 1488–89, break down in approximate percentages by value as follows:

	Christofer	*Margaret Cely*
meat	23%	15 to 34%
fish	30%	10 to 16%
bread, flour, oatmeal, etc.	26%	15 to 25%
drink	20%	30 to 34%
fruit and vegetables	–	0.2 to 2.2%
dairy products and eggs	–	0.2 to 2.8%

In addition, certainly on the *Margaret Cely* and perhaps on the *Christofer*, the casual purchases of the extras mentioned above. The only conclusions that may be drawn from the table are that, compared with the diet of their peer group ashore, sailors had more protein and bread but fewer vegetables and dairy products. The *Margaret Cely* anticipated good catches of fish and the crew of the *Christofer* appear to have been, perforce, relatively abstemious.[44]

The shipmaster's off-shore responsibilities in brief

As might be expected, a shipmaster's responsibilities increased when he put to sea. There were well established protocols for the management of a ship, covering the shipmaster's dealings with the freighting merchants and with his crew. His relationship with the merchants were commercial, reflecting the precepts of maritime and merchant law, while his relationship with his crew was both paternalistic and authoritarian, again based on articles in the several codifications of maritime law. Crisis and post-crisis management, remuneration, payment of incidental expenses, duty of care, a disciplinary code and a complaints procedure were all covered by those protocols.

The training of men to become shipmasters was one aspect of the working life at sea which was not centrally defined, and about which little is known. Acquisition of the necessary skills appears to have been accomplished on the job, often within a familial group. Accommodation on board ship was spartan, but the

---

[44] Michel de Jourdin Mollat, *Europe and the Sea* (Oxford, 1993), p. 158. *Ordinances*, pp. 48–9. Oppenheim, *Administration*, pp. 25–6, 34. Hanham, *Celys' World*, pp. variously 369–91. Kleineke, 'English Shipping', pp. 474–5, citing PRO E101/53/27.

health of the crew and their rations were, in general, no worse than those of their peer group ashore.

It is not known how closely medieval shipmasters followed the ordained managerial paradigms once they were at sea, but an ineffective, cruel or miserly skipper would be generally recognised and have encountered difficulties in manning his ship.

6

The Shipmaster at Sea: Navigation and Meteorology

Having found sufficient cargo, negotiated freight rates, signed the charter-party with, if relevant, the shipowner's authorisation, recruited a crew, fitted-out and victualled the ship, obtained up-to-date information about the risks of piracy and made his passage plan, the shipmaster was ready to put to sea. How he found his way to his destination is the subject of this chapter.

Direct navigation

'L'art & science tressubtillez & quasi divine du noble mestier de la mer' has been described as the 'haven-finding art'; it might also be described as the 'land-avoiding art' since any undesired contact with land could be fatal. Until navigational instruments became generally available, shipmasters followed the classical advice 'littus ama; altum alii teneant' ('love the shore; let others go to the deep') – holding a safe distance off, but always within sight of land, except for short off-shore passages preferably sailed in daylight. Shipmasters in the fourteenth century, in the absence of instrumentation, had only direct observational methods to know the time, their position and course, and the distance and direction to their next destination. Late fourteenth-century improvements in ship design made longer and safer voyages possible but there was no certainty of a safe return, nor of repeat visits, until the introduction of magnetic compasses in the second half of the century. Although astronomers ashore had long been able to take accurate astral sights and calculate both latitude and longtiude, the former was not used ar sea until the second half of the fifteenth century, and the latter not until three centuries later. A certain complacency amongst northern seamen, habitually navigating without measuring latitude, may have contributed to the delay but the cost and reliability of salt-resistant astral height measuring instruments usable on a moving platform, were a major problem. Measurement of longitude at sea was delayed until reliable time-keeping pieces were manufactured. Meteorology, similarly *faute de mieux*, relied on direct observational methods and folklore.

NAVIGATION AND METEOROLOGY

Direct navigation depends on the recognition of landmarks, visual assessment of the distance off the coast, and estimating bearings extrapolated from the positions of astral bodies. The fourteenth-century shipmaster had a lead-line to determine the depth and to bring up samples from the sea bed, both of which, with previously acquired knowledge, could be used to confirm the ship's position. He may also have had a sand-glass to measure regular periods of time and, perhaps, a primitive, ungimballed compass. For the rest, he observed the behaviour of animals, the direction, strength, humidity and temperature of the wind, the cloud formations over hills and even the smell coming off an invisible shore. With those natural aids, an experienced shipmaster could lay and hold a roughly correct course and estimate the ship's speed and distance run. He also observed the lunar cycle and carried a mental picture of the tidal flow on his route and in his havens. The skills attributed by Chaucer to his Shipman confirm the abilities of late fourteenth-century seamen:

> But of his craft to rekene wel his tydes,
> His stremes, and his daungers hym bisides,
> His herberwe [harbours], and his moone, his lodemenage [pilotage]
> ...
> He knew alle the havenes, as they were,
> Fro Gootland to the cape of Fynistere,
> And every cryke in Britaigne and in Spayne.

That he knew all the havens from the Baltic to Spain is extremely unlikely, but since Chaucer's work required frequent visits to the London docks, and he also undertook several missions abroad, his Shipman was certainly a representative, if caricatured, member of the seagoing fraternity.[1]

Sailing directions, or rutters, for northern waters, became available as handwritten copies at the end of the fourteenth or the beginning of the fifteenth century. Information from the oldest surviving directions, the mid-fifteenth-century manuscript copies of the English rutter and of the Hanseatic Middle Low German *Seebuch*, have been used in this chapter to assess the skills of a contemporary shipmaster, assuming, not unreasonably, that the navigational techniques of English and German seamen were identical. Although few mariners would have had their own copies of those directions, there was a lively exchange of information between shipmasters in havens and on port towns' quays, as described in the c.1400 alliterative poem *Morte Arthure* and quoted on p. 85. In addition to the latest news of piracy and current freight rates, information would have been exchanged about good anchorages and hidden rocks – items which were entered by the literate in their notebooks and later evolved into sailing directions. The eventual dissemination of these directions gave shipmasters access to the empirical

---

[1] Chaucer, *Complete Works*, 'General Prologue', lines 401–3 and 406–9.

information accumulated by others over many years, collated in the user-friendly format discussed below.

Land- and seamarks

Landmarks were indispensable to medieval seamen; the *Seebuch* lists over two dozen monasteries, churches, chapels and houses, and many hills, cliffs and promontories. For the entry to Yarmouth on the east coast of England, for example, the marks include a 'house where the sick live' – the local historian has confirmed that this was a leper colony – and a 'house with four oriel windows'. Even ephemera such as a large tree north of Harwich and a high wood to the west of Dartmouth are mentioned. Figures 3 and 7, which are from the Hastings MS copy of the English rutter, show a variety of landmarks, man-made and topographical, useful for in-shore navigation. Such marks were used alone for location identification, and with a second mark to give a leading line past a hazard or into an anchorage. Members of the crew with local knowledge helped to identify the marks, and canny shipmasters made mental notes of useful features along their routes.[2]

References to man-made seamarks on the English coast go back to the earliest surviving documents, many of them confirmed by archaeological evidence. The Romans built beacons at Dover and elsewhere as navigational aids, and the Vikings heaped stones into cairns on headlands for the same purpose. Excavation of a mound at Tywn Llewelyn, Glamorgan, revealed a cairn built on top of a rocky extrusion apparently marking the high water channel up the River Thaw. The eighth-century Old English poem *Beowulf* describes the construction of such a sea mark: 'The Wedra people had made a shelter on the headland, so high and so wide that it was seen by the seafarers from afar, and they built in ten days a beacon for the battle-brave.'[3]

The rutter lists churches and other large buildings as leading marks into Dartmouth, Harwich and Broadstairs and in both the rutter and the *Seebuch* there are buildings apparently sited specifically as navigational aids. Although no mention has been found in any sailing directions of the medieval church at Bosham (from where Harold sailed in 1064), it is built on the line of the channel up Bosham Creek, a site surely not chosen by chance. The *Seebuch* uses a church and a visible rock in describing the entrance to Dartmouth:

---

[2] Extracts from the Hamburger Commerzbibliothek, *Altes Seebuch*, saeculi, ut videtur, XIV, MSS A and B have been taken from the transcription and translation of both manuscripts into German and English by Albrecht Sauer and Robin Ward, see http://www.dsm.museum /seebuch /html. Extracts from the Pierpont Morgan Library, New York, Hastings MS 775 have been taken from the transcription in Ward, 'The Earliest Known Sailing Directions' (cited hereafter as Hastings). Seebuch, MS B, fo. 36r, item 1.

[3] Naish, *Seamarks*, pp. 15–24. Hutchinson, *Medieval Ships*, p. 170: citing D.M. Wilson and J.G. Hurst, *Medieval Archaeology*, 27, p. 170. 'Geworhton ða Wedra leode / hleo on hoe se wæs heah ond brad, / weg-liðendum wide gesyne, / ond betimbredon on tyn dagum / beadu-rofes becn': *Beowulf*, ed. C.L. Wren, rev. W.F. Bolton (London, 1973), p. 211, lines 3156–60.

3 Ships in a busy haven. Folio 130v of Hastings MS 775, reproduced with the kind permission of the Pierpont Morgan Library, New York.

whoever would sail into Dartmouth should sail by St Petroc's church which stands on the W side of the haven, and should sail in by the large rock [Mew Stone] which lies by the east shore because of the dangerous shallows that lie off the sandy bay.

Depths were often included in the instructions for entering havens, sometimes to delineate a route by isobathic (following a depth contour) navigation:

and hold the Helsingor church and the beacon-house so that you are able to see between them so that you will not sail the wrong course past Lappesand on the seven fathom line, and also so that you will not steer too close.

More sombrely, the best anchorage in Dieppe, according to the *Seebuch*, is when the gallows and the church are in transit, in seven fathoms at low water and in ten fathoms at high water.[4]

Navigational difficulties at estuary and harbour entrances led, from the end of the thirteenth century, to the construction of seamarks. Between 1299 and 1316, the merchants of Hamburg invested in a tower built on a sand island close to the Scharnoon reef, and towers were built at Nieuwpoort, at Hiddensee (Stralsund) and at Travemünde (although 'ubi signum eiusdem portus habetur' indicates that there may have been a beacon of some sort there much earlier). Lights were necessary on land and sea marks for ships arriving at night: Barbour tells of Robert the Bruce using a fire as a leading line in 1306 on his passage from Kintyre to Carrick (in modernised form): 'until night came upon them ... so that they did not know where they were ... steering all the time on a fire they saw burning light and bright, until they arrived at the fire and landed without more delay.' In 1314 a laden wine ship was wrecked on St Catherine's Point on the Isle of Wight and pillaged by local people. After litigation and an appeal to Rome, Walter de Godeton was ordered, as a penance and on threat of excommunication, to build an oratory and light-tower dedicated to St Catherine, the remains of which still stand. The Black Prince had a lighthouse built on what is now the islet of Cordouan in the Gironde estuary as a guide for the wine ships; during re-building, the ground subsided to make this the first light at sea. The importance of the man-made marks to sea-borne trade was recognised by the local and church authorities, who accepted responsibility for the construction and maintenance of marks and their top-hampers of baskets, barrels, fires or lamps, for which they levied a charge on passing ships. In 1261, the town of Winchelsea levied 2d. for the maintenance of fires from all ships entering the roads; Yarmouth similarly taxed visitors for two towers with fires on top; and in 1427 John Fitling organised a levy on shipping on the Humber to pay for a beacon at Spurn Head. Some marks were of

---

4   *Seebuch*, MS B, fo. 8v, item 4. Sauer, *Seebuch*; *Seebuch*, MS A, fo. 66r, lines 1–3; MS B, fo. 16r, item 2.

national importance: in 1398 all ships sailing from England to Calais had to carry stones as *lastage* (ballast) at 2d. per ton for the repair of the beacon and sea wall which were much decayed. It was as late as 1585, however, that Trinity House of Kingston-upon-Hull laid what appear to have been the first buoys marking the channel in the River Humber – again to be paid for by a levy on passing ships. The disappearance of natural and man-made marks was a serious matter and their removal was forbidden; the preamble to an Elizabethan Statute, referring to marks 'of ancient time', makes their importance clear.[5]

Initially, buoys were probably barrels – off Warnemüde as early as 1288 they were recorded as 'signum quod tunna dicitur' – but the nature of a buoy placed to seaward of the Scharnoon reef, at some time in the fifteenth century, to mark the approach to Hamburg, is not known. The earliest surviving chart recording of buoys is of those marking two channels in the River Swin, near Sluys; there is no differentiation on the chart between port and starboard marks, but the buoys may have been coloured or shaped to show on which hand they were to be held. Buoys would have been difficult to moor and maintain on station, but had the advantage of being easily removed in times of danger from enemy or pirate ships and it is probable that they were lifted in the winter to avoid the worst of the weather. There are no direct records of medieval English buoyage, but it is likely that the entrances to at least Lynn and Boston were marked, either by floating marks or by posts driven into the sand, following advice from Hansa ships sailing in from the well-marked northern German, Flemish and Danish ports where shifting sand was also a problem. There is indirect, later evidence of old navigational aids of some sort at Boston; the 1572 Charter to the burghers refers to marks 'nowe almost utterly decayed'. An example of the use of posts to mark shoals and to give a transit line occurs in the English rutter:

> And [if] ye goo oute of orwell waynis to the nase, ye must goo southe west fro the nase to the markis of the spetis [on a Thames sandbank]. Youre cours is weste southe west. Brynge yowre markis togedir that the parisshe stepill be ought be est the abbey of seynt hosies [St Osyth] than goo yowre cours ouir the spetis southe.[6]

---

[5] Sauer, *Seebuch*, pp. 155–6, citing *Hansisches Urkundenbuch*, I, no. 205. *Barbour's Bruce*, ed. Matthew P. McDiarmid and James A.C. Stevenson, The Scottish Text Society, 3 vols (Edinburgh, 1985), 3, Book V, pp. 104–6, lines 15–21, 29–30. Naish, *Seamarks*, pp. 26–7, 82. Sir Nicholas Harris Nicolas, *A History of the Royal Navy from the Earliest Times to the Wars of the French Revolution*, 2 vols (London, 1847), I, p. 237. Sauer, *Seebuch*, p. 155 citing Roger Degryse, 'De oudste vuurbakens van de Vlaamse kust en nabijgelegn Noordseeoevers' (1983). *Statutes*, 21 Richard II, c. 17, 8 Elizabeth c. 13: 'For as much as by the taking away of certain steeples, woods and other marks standing upon the main shores ... being as beacons and marks of ancient time accustomed for seafaring men ... divers ships ... have by the lack of such marks of late years been miscarried, perished and lost in the sea.'

[6] Sauer, *Seebuch*, p. 156. Naish, *Seamarks*, pp. 27–8, 51–2. A.W. Lang, *Geschichte des Seezeichenwesens* (Bonn, 1965). Hastings MS, fo. 131v.

The absence of early records of any marks in the Thames is curious. East of Herne Bay, Reculver church is known to have been used as a seamark, and it is possible that there was a very early fire beacon further to the east on the Isle of Thanet, but other references are few. It is possible that the channels were not marked, either because of the risk of attack, or because the local pilots wanted to keep their secrets to themselves. Ironically, in 1561, the Master of Trinity House himself said that 'in his tyme [he] hathe knowen meny shipps to have perisshid vnder pilottes of this Ryver', and as late as 1597 an Armada pilot reported that 'from the cape at North Foreland to the river at Rochester ... and then on to London, it is necessary to take on pilots ... since the shoals are shifting'. As in the Thames estuary, around the North Sea the topography made sea-marks very necessary, but the construction close to the water of cairns and beacons, some with lights, often obviated the need for marks below high water.[7]

Distance
Recognition of a landmark establishes a directional line from the shore, but to use that information to avoid hidden dangers it is necessary also to know the distance off. Shipmasters in the fourteenth and fifteenth centuries used the apparent sizes of trees, houses, humans and animals to judge distances and, further out to sea, the first appearance of hills or the line of the shore. They learned empirically the range of their vision, the theoretical limit of which, in clear conditions, is a function of the sum of the square roots of the heights above sea level of the observer's eye and of the object viewed. From a ship's deck and from her mast-head the distance at which objects become visible are:

height of on-shore object viewed	10m high	20m high	30m high
height of eye 3½m (on deck)	10 nM distant	12.5 nM distant	14.5 nM distant
height of eye 15m (at mast head)	15 nM distant	17.5 nM distant	19.5 nM distant

where m = metres and nM = nautical miles

Thus, very roughly, the top of a 100-foot hill becomes visible to a lookout atop a 50-foot mast when the ship is something short of 20 miles off-shore, a distance which became, perhaps not by chance, the *kenning* in Middle English, and the *veüe* in Middle French, the unit of measurement of long distances at sea.[8]

---

[7] Reculver church, built in 669, had towers added in *c.*1170. Naish, *Seamarks*, p. 34 citing W. Camden in 1620: 'the steeples whereof shooting up their lofty spires stand the mariner in good stead as markers whereby they avoid certain sands and shelves in the mouth of the Thames.' *The Concise Oxford Dictionary of English Place Names*, ed. Eilert Ekwall (Oxford, 1981): 'Thanet may have meant bright island or fire island suggesting a fire beacon'. G.G. Harris, *The Trinity House of Deptford, 1514–1660* (London, 1969), p. 102. A.J. Loomie, 'An Armada Pilot's Survey of the English Coastline', *MM* 49, 4 (1963), p. 299.

[8] Distance in nM = 2.072 x ($\sqrt{h_e} + \sqrt{h_h}$) where h_e and h_m are the heights in metres of eye and object.

That it was about 20 miles is confirmed by William de Worcestre's survey of the Bristol Channel in 1480: 'From the island of Holm to the island of Lunday, two kennings, that is two sights [where] each kenning [is] 20 miles [totalling] 40 miles', and by another reference in the same passage: 'in English, *vue* [is a] sight [a] kenning [of] 21 miles'. William, interestingly, sometimes translated the distance as an estimated sailing time: 'and the said Isle of Man is a distance of four kennings [80 miles] from Ireland, that is a day and night sailing [i.e. at 3.3 knots].' Flat Holm is actually 60nM from Lundy Island, and from Dublin to the south end of the Isle of Man is indeed *c.*80nM. In the Middle Low German *Seebuch*, multiples of the *myle* of three or four miles and also, on occasions, the kenning, were used: 'and watch out for the dangerous ground in the sea that lies 5 miles, or a good short kenning, to the NNE of the Schilt.'[9]

Shorter distances in the sailing directions were measured as long jumps (? 3–4m), bow-shots (? 100m), boat lengths (? 4m), and ship lengths (? 30m). The unit of length used for depths and for cordage was arm-spans, known in Germanic languages by cognates of Old English *fæðm*, the current English 'fathom' (*c.*1.85m) and in Latin languages by cognates of *bras* from the Latin *brachium*, 'arm'. A foot-length was sometimes used to indicate shallow water. While those measures were generally known and recognised, there was the usual medieval variation in unit size, although that perhaps was irrelevant in the overall inaccuracy of measurements assessed by the human eye. Distances that may be checked on a modern chart indicate that a 'sea mile' was between 5,000 and 6,000 feet, the present nautical mile being 6,080 feet. The length of the armspan and the foot also varied, which could be dangerous in the measurement of shallow depths but, so long as the shipmaster was using information related to his own or his peers' experience, or checked the depth in the sailing directions against his own measurement to establish the necessary correction, confusion could be avoided.

Direction
Recognition of a landmark, and an estimate of the ship's distance off-shore, gives one vector of a ship's position; the other, and more difficult, vector for the shipmaster to establish, is the direction being sailed by the ship, a vital component of his calculation when a course to the next destination is to be set and steered. Without a compass, the cardinal points had to be ascertained by direct observation of any indicators available to the shipmaster. The rise and set of the sun are accurate pointers to east and west at equinox but require a daily correction at other times of the year, an estimation which the medieval mariner could probably apply instinctively with variable accuracy. Similarly, the sun's direction when

---

[9] 'De jnsulis Holmys vsque jnsulam Londay [.40. miliria deleted] duo kennyngs jd est twey syghts continet quelibet kennyng.20. miliaria, .40. miliaria': *William Worcestre, Itineraries*, ed. John H. Harvey (Oxford, 1969), pp. 302–3. *Seebuch*, MS B, fo. 34v, item 4.

it appears to be at its zenith, indicates south. A sun compass depends on the changing length of shadow measured through the day. In its most primitive form, a trace is made of the diurnal track of the tip of the shadow of a vertical gnomon on a horizontal disc on which north has previously been marked with a notch. At sea, the disc is turned until the tip of the shadow fits exactly on the trace, before or after noon, the notch then again points towards north. Any significant change in latitude or longitude, or delay between zeroing and use, reduces the accuracy of the device, so that for long voyages it was of little value. If, as has been suggested, the sun compass was used by the Norsemen, it might be expected to have been used by medieval shipmasters, but there is no indisputable evidence that such an instrument was carried. Behind cloud cover the sun is difficult to locate but sun-stones, translucent trigonal crystals of calcium carbonate (occurring naturally as Iceland spar) polarise light and may have been used by Vikings and later, possibly, by some medieval seamen to locate the sun; there is, however, no reliable evidence that any early mariners used such stones.[10]

On a clear night the Pole Star (*Polaris* or α *Ursa Minor*), identified by the 'pointers' *Dubhe* and *Marak* in the constellation of *Ursa Major* (the 'Plough', 'Great Bear' or 'Big Dipper'); or the 'guards' β and γ of the constellation *Ursa Minor* (the 'Little Bear'), can be used to locate north. Although the former constellation is the more obvious and easier to use in northern latitudes, the latter appears to have been the constellation of choice for medieval mariners in northern waters, perhaps following the tradition of their Mediterranean predecessors: 'the North star is well enough known by all navigators and is the first of the seven stars of the Little Bear.' *Ursa Minor* was used not only to find north but also as an astral analogue clock with the outline of an imaginary human figure, a method described below, p. 142. When the pointers and the guides of the *Ursae* are hidden by cloud, *Polaris* may be identified, although not with the same accuracy, by extrapolation from other constellations such as *Orion* or *Cassiopeia*. *Polaris* is now circling the pole within a radius of about one degree of arc, in the late Middle Ages it was as much as four degrees off the pole, a drift due to the precession of the earth. This divergence was known to astronomers but unnoticeable to an observer without a compass and was, together with the difficulty of taking bearings and steering an honest course, yet another component in the overall inaccuracy inherent in non-instrumental navigation.[11]

Having established a cardinal point, by whatever method, a shipmaster without

---

[10] Bruce E. Gelsinger, 'Lodestone and Sunstone in Medieval Iceland', MM 56, 2 (1970), 219–26. Pliny described the *solis gemma* in his *Natural History* (first century AD); there are several references, possibly to sun-stones, in the Sagas; MM 78, 1 (1992), pp. 89–90.

[11] *L'Art de naviguer de Maistre Pierre de Medine, Traduit de Castillan en Françoys par Nicolas Nicolai du Dauphiné, Geographe du tres-Chrestien Roy Henri II de ce nom* (Lyon, 1554, facsimile edn, Milan, 1988), p. 84. In classical times, β *Ursa Minor* was the 'pole star' which may explain the constellation's original significance.

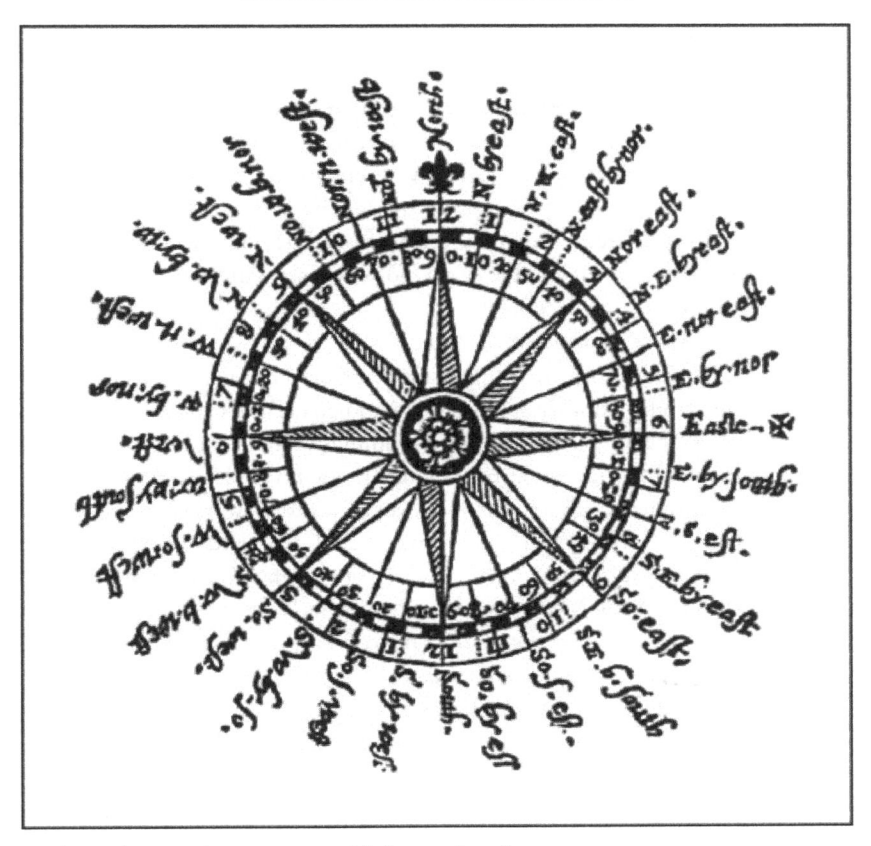

4 An early 32-point compass with 'lunar times'.

a compass had to extrapolate to left or right to find an approximate course bearing by holding his hand at arm's length. With the arm extended, the width of the fist with thumb alongside subtends at the eye c.10° (cf. 11.15° for one point of a 32-point compass rose) and with the thumb and fingers abducted, slightly less than 20°. It is doubtful if even an experienced seaman could consistently estimate bearings within ± 2 points of a 32-point rose, especially when estimating a wide angle on a rolling ship. Further, it is unlikely that even a conscientious helmsman, without a consistent wind or a visible landmark, could hold a ship to within two points of the required course because of the movement of the ship and the force of water against the unbalanced rudder. The resultant course made good, therefore, could have been up to four points either way away from that intended, in other words, somewhere within an arc of 45°. Because something more than two points is the best accuracy that can be expected of a naked eye, any reference to courses and bearings of two points or less, indicates the use of a graduated magnetic aid. In his *A Treatise on the Astrolabe*, Chaucer wrote 'Now is thin orisonte departed in 24 parties by thin azymutes in significacioun of 24 parties of the world; al be it so that shipmen rekene thilke parties in 32.' From that it is clear that sometime before 1391, when the *Treatise* was written, not only were there compasses on at least some ships, but also that some were capable of indicating a direction to within 11.25°. A 32-point 'rose' or 'card' is shown in Figure 4. There are many instances of reliance on astral navigation on medieval ships even after the introduction of compasses. For example, in 1465, Leo of Rozmital set off from Poole for Brittany only to be carried by pirates and unfavourable winds to Guernsey. After an 11-day wait the pirates gave the shipmaster a course to steer by the stars; in the event, a gale blew him to St Malo where he nearly foundered.[12]

With no other indicators, the shipmaster could, as a last resort, obtain a rough idea of direction from a number of natural phenomena. The feel of the surrounding air usually offers not only a clue to the in-coming weather, discussed below, but also an indication of the direction from which the wind is blowing using the rule of thumb that, in northern and western European waters, warm wet winds blow from somewhere between south and west and cold dry winds from somewhere between north and east. Although the accuracy of orientation by the wind is poor in northern waters, in the Mediterranean, where winds are more consistent, they were used for orientation, and the points on a compass card were called 'winds', or *vents*, a practice which continued well into the sixteenth century.[13]

The behaviour of birds may also be used as crude pointers; in season, skeins of geese migrating between British estuaries and Iceland indicate approximately north and south. Less dramatic than the release of birds by Noah and by the Vikings, the evening return of gulls and other non-pelagic birds indicates the direction of land when that is obscured by mist or rain. Positions, rather than directions, can be determined by shipmasters who know certain waters well, for example, by observing concentrations of sea birds feeding on fish attracted by plankton carried by the North Atlantic Drift and brought to the surface by deeper, colder water or by the slope of the continental shelf. The accuracy and reliability of direction-finding by wind or by animal behaviour is uncertain and certainly poorer than by using the sun or the stars however hazily seen. Out of sight of land

---

[12] Chaucer, *Complete Works*, 'A Treatise on the Astrolabe', 2, 36, lines 6–9. *Rozmital*, pp. 162–4.
[13] The Greek *rosa ventorum* carved in the Athenian Temple of the Winds demonstrates the eight-point (45°) rose:

	Tramontano	
Maestro		Greco
Ponente	*	Levante
Africo		Scirocco
	Ostro	

Taylor, *Haven-finding Art*, pp. 7, 53–5, discusses 10- and 12-point Mediterranean roses. Barbara Obrist, 'Wind Diagrams and Medieval Cosmology', *Speculum*, 72 (1997), pp. 33–84: 'Ces quatre parties [of the world] se meuuent & sont congneues par quatre vens principaux, qui sont, Leuant, Ponant, Septentrion, & Midy'. Nicolai, *L'Art de navigver*, pp. 25–6.

and with no opportunity to see a heavenly body, a shipmaster had no alternative but to sail his ship on a course which he felt was safe even if it was not taking him to his destination.

Depth and seabed

The seabed is usually the nearest land to a ship and to know its distance and nature are indispensible components of coastal navigation. To measure shallow depths, a pole marked by coloured bands was used from the bows of boats and smaller ships; the Bayeux tapestry shows Harold's ships feeling their way into the French coast in 1064. Medieval ships intending to dry-out on a beach at low water would have felt their way in with such a pole, probably from the ship's boat rowing ahead. In depths of more than a fathom (2m) a lead-line – a weight attached to a length of cord – was indispensable; it could give an approximate position, warn of approaching underwater hazards, guide a ship into a haven, and confirm that the depth and bottom in the haven were suitable for anchoring. No documentary or archaeological evidence of the size and shape of medieval lead weights has been found except for the illustration in the Hastings MS of a ship sounding with a conical or elongated bell shaped weight suspended from a line carried in the leadsman's hand (Figure 7). References in early sailing directions to the nature of the seabed make it clear that the leads were 'armed' with tallow or pitch, pressed into a hollow in the bottom of the lead, to bring up samples. Archaeological finds of seventeenth-century leads (the earliest found) are similar in shape to that illustrated in the Hastings MS and weigh about 7lbs (*c.*3.2kg) and 14lbs (*c.*6.4kg), the latter probably for deep sea work, both with recesses at the lower end to take the tallow. The line to which the lead was attached had pieces of fabric or leather threaded through its strands as depth markers and, for coastal work, did not need to be over 50 fathoms (*c.*30m) and for deep-sea use, up to 150 fathoms (*c.*90m).

There is no reason to suppose that sounding in the Middle Ages was in any way different from today's practice. The lead is thrown as far forward as possible from the bows of the ship by a crew member who allows the line to pay out freely through his hands as the lead sinks. In deep water more men are required, standing along the side of the ship paying out the line as the ship moves forward and the weight sinks. When the line slackens the weight has reached the bottom; the run is then arrested and the line hauled back inboard, one man calling out the depth shown by the markers. Admiralty trials in the nineteenth century found that it takes about 45 seconds for a deep-sea lead to reach 100 fathoms (55m), in which time a ship travelling at five knots will have sailed over 130 yards (120m); ships therefore have to moderate their speed by heaving-to or by easing sheets if they are sailing, before deep soundings can be made. To avoid the ship drifting down-wind over the line, heaving should be from the windward side of a sailing vessel which also offers the leadsmen a better working platform on the higher side.

In the Hastings picture, the men are handling the line on the lee side and, apart from the brailed mizzen sail, the ship's speed appears not to have been moderated; artistic licence has prevailed over accuracy. There is an accurate description of sounding in *Morte Arthure*: '[the man] launchez lede apone lufe lacchene ther depez', and then, 'ffrekes mone the forestayne fakene theire coblez' that is, the sounding lead is thrown over the windward side to measure the depth and afterwards men on the foredeck coil the rope. 'Fakeing' is still the nautical term used for coiling cables on deck or in boxes, ready to run out freely again.[14]

The dramatic change of depth from the continental shelf down to the abyssal depths of the ocean was, and is, used by mariners as they come into, or go out of, 'soundings', as an indication of their distance from land. A unique example occurs in the English rutter, describing a passage from north-west Spain into the Western Approaches: 'And ye bee at capfenister [Cape Finisterre] go your cours north northest ... till ye come into Sowding [soundings], And yif ye have an C. fadome depe or else iiijxx.x than ye shall go north.'[15]

Closer in-shore, depths were used to warn of dangers ahead; from the rutter, when crossing the Channel from the South Downs: 'And yif ye turn [tack] in the Downes come not nere Godwyn than ix. fadome ne not nere the brakis [the Brake sandbank] than v. fadome.' Sailors making night passages, or caught in fog, have traditionally followed a suitable depth contour (isobathic navigation) until sure of their position. An example from the rutter reads:

> And yif ye goo fro the shelde [Cromer] to the Holmes [sandbank], and it be in the nyght ye shall go but xviij fadome fro the coste till the gesse [you estimate] that ye be past Limber and Urry [sandbanks], and to the estermare cours [hold an easterly course] till ye come to xiiij fadome ... but the moost wisedome is to abide till it be day.

Knowledge of the depth was not always sufficient however to avoid the hazards ahead; heaving-to with plenty of searoom off the coast overnight was not uncommon and ships could be seen in the Channel 'lyeing howlyng in the trowghe of the sea taryeng for the night.'[16]

Samples of the seabed brought up by the tallow on the lead gave the navigator, from his experience or from the information in sailing directions, an idea of his position. In the Western Approaches, for example, pale coloured stones found on the bottom indicate that the ship is standing closer to the dangerous French side of the Channel than to the safer English side where dark stones occur. Sailing in

---

[14] J.E. Davis, *Notes on Deep-Sea Sounding* (London, 1867), pp. 2–8.
[15] Hastings MS, fo. 138r, lines 11 ff.
[16] Hastings MS, fo. 132r, lines 20 ff. and fo. 131v, line 3 ff. G.V. Scammell, 'European Seamanship in the Great Age of Discovery', *MM* 68, 4 (1982), p. 359: PRO HCA 1/33 fo. 262.

the neighbourhead of Ushant before entering the Western Approaches, the seabed is usefully described in the *Seebuch* thus:

> Also, anyone sounding near Ushant who finds fine white sand and small shells which are white, and small white long things, will know that Ushant lies NW of him; and if he finds small long things like needles, then Ushant lies E of him.

The nature of the seabed decides the holding power of an anchor; thick seaweed has to be avoided as anchors cannot get a grip and rocks of a certain size and shape can imprison an anchor. Anchoring requires a cable of at least four times the depth to ensure a low pulling angle between the cable and the seabed as the ship is blown astern, but such a length may allow the ship to swing with tide or wind into danger. Before anchoring therefore, a shipmaster has to establish that the bottom offers good holding and that within the scope of the cable, i.e. within the radius of the circle around the ship, there are no hazards. After anchoring, the master has to keep an eye on marks ashore to ensure that the anchor is holding fast. He might also assess the state and range of the tide by measuring the variation in depth with time – necessary information if it is proposed to beach the ship to handle cargo, or to proceed further up an estuary.

Tidal times and range
The medieval shipmaster had to know the tidal characteristics of the havens and channels he used, and the off-shore tidal currents in his passages between waypoints. The importance of this information is reflected in the surviving contemporary sailing directions, about one third of which are devoted to tidal information. Although harmonic tidal prediction is an extremely complex mathematical exercise quite unknown to medieval seamen, three lunar phenomena enabled him to obtain sufficiently accurate tidal information to meet his needs. The first phenomenon is the syzygies: when the moon and sun are in line on the same side of the earth, that is, in 'conjunction', the face of the moon is unlit and invisible and said to be 'new'. When they are in line but on opposite sides of the earth, that is, in 'opposition', the face of the moon is fully illuminated and it is 'full'. The second phenomenon is that two 'heaps' of water on opposite sides of the earth are dragged by the gravitational attraction of the moon around the world from east to west in something less than 24 hours. There are therefore usually two high and two low tides in every 24-hour period, occurring at times related to the meridional passage of the moon. Approximately every 15 days, the increased gravitational attraction of the sun and moon, whether in conjunction or opposition, causes a greater range between high water and low water, a phenomenon known as 'Spring tides'. When the sun and moon are at right angles to each other, the range is reduced to give 'Neap tides'. This phenomenon was known, but probably neither understood nor quantified, from the earliest times; a newcomer to tidal phenomena, William of

Worcester, wrote an account of the tidal range at Bristol, sometime before 1480, which, translated reads:

> The height of the sea [the tidal range] in the Avon at the new flood of the sea on the first day of the moon's change [new moon], as I have seen and heard, in the lunation next before the sun's entry into Libra [the equinox] is 7 or 8 arm-breadths, in English 'fathom', and a fathom contains 6 feet, at the beacon.

William's estimate of the Spring range at Bristol, one of the largest in the world, is close to the current Admiralty figure of 12.3m at Avonmouth.[17]

High water springs might be expected to coincide with the meridional transit of the full or new moon, but because of global hydrodynamic friction, inertia, irregularities in depths and the shapes of coastlines, the tidal 'heaps' of water are impeded in their circumterrestial passage and lag behind the moon. The time between the full moon's meridional transit and the next high water springs is the 'lunitidal interval' at each location, known in the past as, variously, the 'tide-hour', 'High Water, Full and Change' (HWF&C), and the 'Establishment' of that place. This interval, assumed for general navigation work to be a constant, was formerly defined by a lunar bearing, using the moon as an analogue clock (explained below); it is now stated as a time relative to high water springs at a standard port, for example Dover, or to a secondary port.[18]

The third lunar characteristic relates to the daily retardation of high water. The earth appears to rotate around the sun faster than the moon circles the earth by between 38 and 66 minutes per day, averaging 48 minutes or 12° in a 360° rotation. Because 180° ÷ 12° = 15, the moon takes about 15 solar days to move from conjunction to opposition; and the interval between consecutive Spring tides (and between Neap tides), is therefore approximately 15 days. The 'age' of the moon on any day, counted from 'new', can be used to calculate the delay of the time of high water (HW) relative to the time of high water springs, so that [(the age of the moon in days) x 48 minutes] = the delay of HW (or LW) on that day. As a working approximation, the mediaeval shipmaster rounded down the 48 minutes to 45. Using the moon as an analogue clock, with midnight at north and midday at south (and 06.00hrs and 18.00hrs at east and west), any time can be defined by a lunar bearing, as may be seen in Figure 4 and Table 2. The approximate 45-minute daily retardation of the moon, is represented by one point on this analogue clock, and has to be subtracted for each day of the age of the moon. It was therefore

---

[17] *William Worcestre, Itineraries*, pp. 262–3. In practice, the largest tidal range is typically one or two days after the corresponding syzygy but this 'age of the tide' may be zero or negative in certain locations.
[18] 'Establishment', French *Etablissement*, was described by Admiral W.H. Smyth in his *Sailor's Word-Book* (London, 1867), as 'an awkard phrase lately lugged in to denote the tide-hour of a port'; it is, however, still in use colloquially rather than 'lunar tidal interval'.

Table 2 The moon as an analogue clock

The table gives the time corresponding to a lunar bearing when the moon is full or new, and at seven days into the lunar cycle, i.e. when the moon's 'age' is seven days. For example: in the English rutter: 'All the haunenes be full at a west southe west mone betwene the start and lisart' means that between Start Point and The Lizard, high water will be at 4.30 or 16.30 when the moon is full or new (a Spring tide), and in a week's time it will be at approximately 10.00 or 22.00. By today's assessment, high water Springs at that location is more accurately 5.00 or 17.00 – an error of 30 minutes. A compass rose, with lunar bearings, is shown in Figure 4, p. 131.

Lunar bearing on 32-point compass rose	Lunar bearing in degrees	Time of moon at 'Full and change'	Time of moon at 7 days of age
N	0°/360°	00.00/12.00	05.36/17.36
N by E	11.25°	00.45/12.45	06.21/18.21
NNE	22.5°	01.30/13.30	07.06/19.06
NE by N	33.75°	02.15/14.15	07.51/19.51
NE	45°	03.00/15.00	08.36/20.36
NE by E	56.25°	03.45/15.45	09.21/21.21
ENE	67.50°	04.30/16.30	10.06/22.06
E by N	78.75°	05.15/17.15	10.51/22.51
E	90°	06.00/18.00	11.36/23.36
E by S	101.25°	06.45/18.45	12.21/00.21
ESE	112.5°	07.30/19.30	13.06/01.06
SE by E	123.75°	08.15/20.15	13.51/01.51
SE	135°	09.00/21.00	14.36/02.36
SE by S	146.25°	09.45/21.45	15.21/03.21
SSE	157.5°	10.30/22.30	16.06/04.06
S by E	168.75°	11.15/23.15	16.51/04.51
S	180°	12.00/24.00	17.36/05.36
S by W	191.25°	12.45/00.45	18.21/06.21
SSW	202.5°	13.30/01.30	19.06/07.06
SW by S	213.75°	14.15/02.15	19.51/07.51
SW	225°	15.00/03.00	20.36/08.36
SW by W	236.25°	15.45/03.45	21.21/09.21
WSW	247.5°	16.30/04.30	22.06/10.06
W by S	258.75°	17.15/05.15	22.51/10.51
W	270°	18.00/06.00	23.36/11.36
W by N	281.25°	18.45/06.45	00.21/12.36
WNW	292.5°	19.30/07.30	01.06/13.06
NW by W	303.75°	20.15/08.15	01.51/13.51
NW	315°	21.00/09.00	02.36/14.36
NW by N	326.25°	21.45/09.45	03.21/15.21
NNW	337.5°	22.30/10.30	04.06/16.06
N by W	348.75°	23.15/11.15	04.51/16.51
N	360°	24.00/00.00	05.36/17.36

possible for a shipmaster in possession of a compass, to forecast, but only very roughly, the time of high water on any day in the lunar cycle, at any location where he knew the lunitidal interval. As an example: if high water springs occurs at a certain location at 06.00 (the lunitidal interval of that location), then four days later high water will occur at the time represented by a lunar bearing four points N of E, which is NE, or 03.00 hrs. Aware that the tidal range was greatest at Springs and least at Neaps, the shipmaster would also have been able to forecast, from the age of the moon, the approximate range and therefore the depth of water throughout the lunar cycle.

The lunitidal intervals of many havens are given in the sailing directions, always as lunar bearings: the time of high water springs at the location in the above example would have been defined in the rutter as an 'est mone maketh hiest water' and in the *Seebuch* as 'maket vulsee eyn osten mane'. Information about the direction of tidal streams and of their times of reversal is given in slightly different formulae, which are discussed below.[19]

As an alternative to the sailing directions as sources of tidal information, early coastal maps (they cannot be described as sea charts) illustrated the time of high water springs on a compass rose, at specific locations. The earliest known example of a such a diagram, in the Catalan Atlas manuscript of 1375, consists of 14 concentric circles, each for a different port in Brittany, France and England.[20]

The shipmaster's tidal calculations could incorporate an error possibly greater than an hour, and further deviation from the theoretical might be caused by a persistent wind or by high or low barometric pressure. In short, the medieval mariner with a compass was able to calculate an approximate theoretical time for high water and low water (provided he could see the moon and had kept count of its age), but his rough assessments, local factors and meteorological conditions inevitably reduced the accuracy of his forecast. It is therefore probable that when the tide was of vital importance, a fail-safe factor of an hour or more was incorporated into the shipmaster's calculations. It is possible to calculate tidal times more accurately by observation of the moon with an astrolabe, as Chaucer demonstrated in his *A Treatise on the Astrolabe*, but it could not be used on the wind-blown deck of a violently moving ship. The instrument was available ashore long before the fourteenth century but apparently seamen were not interested, presumably because of its expense and limited use – 'Ffor as moche as yche man may not have þe astrolabe'.[21]

---

[19] In relation to the stars, the sun appears to move about 1° E and the moon about 13° E each day, hence the apparent 12° 'lag'. There are several definitions of the lunar cycle; the synodic (relative to the sun) is 29.53059 days, the sidereal (relative to the stars) is 27.32166 days, the tropical (relative to the equinox) is 27.32156, and others.
[20] Derek Howse, 'Some Early Tidal Diagrams', *MM* 79, 1 (1993), pp. 27–43.
[21] Chaucer, *Complete Works*, pp. 544–63, although the authorship of these *Supplementary Propositions* is uncertain.

Illiterate shipmasters without sailing directions had to remember the tidal times for the havens they used, possibly with mnemonics to assist them of the type: 'High water London Bridge, / Half ebb in the Swin; / Low water Yarmouth Roads, / Half flood at Lynn.' The earliest tide tables known in Europe, 'of fflod at london brigge', were produced by the monks of St Albans, early in the thirteenth century. It is interesting that, as those tables show a constant 48 minutes daily correction, they appear to have been constructed from theoretical calculations rather than by empirical observation. Considerably earlier, the Chinese are known to have constructed tide tables for the bore on the river Chien-Thang, near Hangchcow, some time before the eleventh century, demonstrating their understanding of the regularity of Spring tides and the lunar influence on tides.[22]

Knowledge of the depths at the entrances to and within harbours and anchorages was valuable information for enemies and pirates and not to be shared lightly with ships from other ports. Perhaps for that reason, the early rutters are stronger on tidal streams directions, tide-hours and off-shore depths than they are about the depth of water in havens. The few harbour depths that are included in the sailing directions are usually simple statements of the minimum depth, and only rarely is any indication of the depth at several points in the tidal range given. For example, in the rutter there is a very generalised (and not entirely accurate) reference to high water times in the harbours on the south-west coast of England but with no depths. The *Seebuch*, however, is more forthcoming on the depth of water in the havens along the same stretch of coast, perhaps because for the Hansa seamen these were not home waters and there was no need for security: 'Between Falmouth and the Lizard there lies a tidal haven called Helford and whoever wants to sail in must have a quarter flood tide [i.e. 1½ hours after low water] for a ship which draws two fathoms [5.4m] and it is a good haven.' The Helford estuary is indeed a good haven, sheltered from all but easterlies with a Springs tidal range of 4.7m. Entering strange havens without information from sailing directions, the canny navigator had always to include a fail-safe margin in his calculations, or lie off for a tide to observe the time and range, unless he had hired the services of a local pilot.[23]

Tidal streams off-shore do not necessarily change direction at the times of high water and low water on the adjacent land, but the necessary information about current directions and reversal times was given in the sailing directions. No speeds of the currents could be given, however, as the measurement of the speed of a tidal

---

[22] *MM* 3 (1913), p. 319, 'Answers 81 (S.G.)'. Commander W.E. May and Captain L. Holder, *History of Marine Navigation* (Henley on Thames, 1973): British Library Add. MS 30221 (Codex Cotton, Julius DXVII, page 45b). Joseph Needham (with Wang Ling), *Science and Civilisation in China*, 3, 21, pp. 483–94 (Cambridge, 1959).

[23] Hastings MS, fo. 133r. *Admiralty Tidal Stream Atlases*, Hydrographic Office, NP 250 (English Channel), NP 251 (North Sea, Southern Part), NP 265 (France, West Coast). *Seebuch*, MS B, fo. 7v, item 1.

stream was not possible. In the *Seebuch*, the actual stream reversal times are given in terms of lunar bearings, sometimes at different distances off-shore, and in the English and French rutters they are defined as the duration of the flood or ebb after high water or low water ashore, at an unspecified distance from the coast. The time lag between high water ashore and the tidal stream change is generally described in the rutter as one tide running under the other – 'under rothir' – and was measured in quarter or half tides, i.e. 1½ hours or 3 hours. An example from the rutter reads:

> And at the schelde it floweth on the londe west north west and half strem vndir rothir be the londe till ye come to wyntirbornesse and fro wyntirbornesse til ye come to kyrkle rode it floweth on the londe northe west and quarter tide and half quarter vnder rothir.

This may be paraphrased 'And off Cromer as far as Winterbourness it flows WNW for 3 hours after high water ashore. And from Winterbourness to the Kirkley roadstead it flows NW for 2¼ hours after high water ashore'.[24]

Although not quantified, warnings of severe tidal dangers, especially around Ushant and amongst the Channel Islands, are sometimes given in the sailing directions. For its dramatic value, a somewhat later example from the 1540 French edition of the Scottish rutter of Alexander Lyndsay describing the Corrievreckan, is worth repeating:

> There is another great danger ... caused by four or five contrary tides with a great swirling of water causing a deep and noisy whirlpool. The middle is very dangerous for all ships, large and small ... and there is no other refuge but to die.

Enough, surely, to deter any mariner.[25]

The rutter and the *Seebuch* make use of every possible non-instrumental aid to navigation and often include several 'notes to mariners'; a good example from the *Seebuch* describes the approach to Hunstanton thus:

> when you arrive at the Wash with a heavy ship and want to go further in, then take a big quarter flood tide, but if you have an outward flowing stream and a westerly wind, then anchor until the stream sets inwards; when the wind blows with the sea [i.e. on the flood tide], then run in with a small sail for as long as the stream sets inwards; and if you arrive by day, anchor over-night in

---

[24] Hastings MS, fo. 131r.
[25] R.M. Ward, 'Sailing Directions for James V of Scotland', *History Scotland*, 4, 2 (March / April 2004), pp. 25–32. Spring tides race through the Corrievreckan at up to eight knots. It is navigable under sail at slack water with a favourable wind.

10 fathoms and wait for the [next] flood tide. And there is there a dangerous high stony sandbank and it is on the port side as one sails in; then you see a headland [Gore Point] and a steep cliff close by the water and you will see the two pointed high towers [possibly the Church of St Mary the Virgin] to the west of the chapel [St Edmund's chapel on St Edmund's Head].

With knowledge of the local lunar-tidal interval to calculate the time of the flood, a shipmaster had all the information he needed to approach the town. When sailing out, the shipmaster is advised to bring the two spires, which are described as 'runners' (presumably because of the parallax effect as the ship moves), a good bow-shot to the west of the chapel. Silting and erosion have radically altered the shape of this coast line so that the accuracy of the directions cannot be assessed today.[26]

Time, speed and distance made good
An accurate estimate of the time of day was of greater importance to the medieval shipmaster than to his peers ashore, most of whom lived by an elastic liturgical *horarium* marked by bells. The shipmaster was also interested in elapsed time, for example, how long his ship had been on one tack or how long a piece of wood took to float along the length of the ship. Sometime towards the end of the thirteenth century, sand-glasses, probably of a half-hour duration, began to be used on board ships for the measurement of fixed periods of time (their appearance in ships' inventories is discussed below). There still remained the problem of the estimation of variable periods of elapsed time. Guesses at the passage of time are subjective, the accuracy of the guess decreasing with the length of time estimated. Long periods of elapsed time may be measured by the difference between the time of day at the beginning and end of an event. Ashore, that was easily measured with a sundial or an astrolabe; as early as 1024 an academic in Cologne invited a friend to see his astrolabe with which he could calculate, *inter alia*, the time of day, and therefore elapsed time, and latitude. But sundials and astrolabes require a stable base for operation, a condition not available on the deck of a rolling the ship, and instruments were expensive; in daylight at sea, therefore, only midday could be judged by the sun's meridional passage (provided that a compass was available), from which rough estimates of the time of day could be extrapolated, albeit with limited accuracy.[27]

Telling the time on a clear night is an altogether easier and more accurate process. Apart from the use of the moon for tidal time calculations, medieval

---

[26] *Seebuch*, MS B, fo. 34r, item 1.
[27] Psalms, 119, 64: 'seven times a day I praise Thee for thy righteous ordinances': matins, prime, tierce, sext, none, vespers and compline (also lauds at dawn). Taylor, *Haven-finding Art*, p. 90: Ragimbold, *magister* of the schools of Cologne, invited Radolf of Liège to see his new astrolabe.

seamen used the circular movement around the Pole Star, *Polaris*, of 'the guards' of *Ursa Minor*, now known as stars β and γ of that constellation, which can be read as if they were the hands of an analogue clock. The clock, however, marks sidereal time, a 'day' of which is 3 minutes 56 seconds shorter than the mean solar day of 24 hours. The classical Mediterranean method of reading solar time from sidereal information was to imagine a 'man in the sky' over the observer's head; he was thought of as face downwards, head towards north, hands stretched out laterally east and west. To know the time, the position of the guards relative to the figure was noted, and mnemonic jingles were recited to convert that to the time, for example: 'Mid-July, midnight in the right arm. End of July, an hour before the right arm.' There is no mention in either the German or the English sailing directions of such methods of telling the time, all tidal times being related to lunar bearings. However, an experienced seaman would have had no need for the 'man in the sky' nor for the mnemonics; by mentally relating the guards as they appeared at sunset to his estimate of the time, he could follow the astral rotation through the night and instinctively 'read the time'. Such a reading of the time probably had an accuracy of no better than ± 1 hour, and then only if the reference time had been correct. The time of dawn could also be deduced from the position of the guards at any season of the year or, alternatively, Pierre de Medine's *L'Art de Navigver* suggests dividing by two the day length in hours (if that information is known), then subtracting the quotient from 12 (i.e. midnight). Interestingly, the day length examples given in the table in *L'Art de Navigver* are valid for latitude 46° 40′ N (just south of the île de Yeu in the Bay of Biscay) and the dates are in the Gregorian calendar.[28]

Short periods of time may be measured by recitation or counting. To measure in seconds, rhythmic counting was (and is still) used: 'one-and-two-and-three-and ...' and for longer periods, prayers were recited. Surviving examples from the fifteenth century include: 'And in a minute, a man may resonably say a *pater noster* and an *ave*'; a *miserere* took the length of time required to boil an egg (hard or soft is not specified, but perhaps four minutes!); and one hour is 'as longe tyme as thou may say two nocturnes of the psalter'. No doubt there were other traditional mnemonics for counting the passage of seconds, minutes and hours. To estimate a ship's speed, a floating marker could be timed down the length of her hull; the time in seconds, related to the water-line length, giving a measure of the speed through the water. A marker passing down the side of a 23-m ship would take the following approximated times:

---

[28] *L'Art de navigver*, pp. 114–15.

At a speed of 1 knot	44 seconds	e.g. a cog sailing in a light breeze (Beaufort scale 1–2)
At a speed of 3 knots	15 seconds	sailing in a gentle breeze (Beaufort scale 3)
At a speed of 5 knots	9 seconds	sailing in a fresh breeze (Beaufort scale 5)
At a speed of 6 knots	7 seconds	sailing in a strong breeze (Beaufort scale 6).

All these times are within the range of accuracy of rhythmic counting.[29]

Although some idea of the ship's progress could be obtained by multiplying the estimated average speed by the number of hours sailed, a ship's speed through the water is not necessarily the same as her speed over the ground. The precise distance covered was uncertain so long as the shipmaster was unable to measure the ship's leeway and the speed and direction of any current. Sailing at night, a shipmaster would have had to 'fail-safe' by deliberately overestimating the ship's speed and, if necessary, heave-to, to avoid reaching land before dawn, as in the example given earlier of the entrance to Hunstanton.

In the unusual event of a long passage out of sight of land, the shipmaster could measure his progress only as the number of days sailed, just as his predecessors had done hundreds of years before: Ohthere's eighth-century account of his North Cape voyage illustrates this: 'Then he travelled north close to the land: he left that west land always to starboard, and then the open sea on the port side for three days.' William of Worcester, as discussed above, did the same in the mid-fifteenth century: 'Et dicte insula Man distat per 4 kennyngs de Irlanda [and the said Isle of Man is a distance of four kennings from Ireland] id est a day and a nyght saylyng.' Given the substantial doubt that a shipmaster must have entertained about his position after a day out of sight of land, it is not surprising that he preferred to keep the coast in sight whenever possible.[30]

The introduction of instrumental aids, however primitive, allowed the first steps towards 'indirect' navigation. The aids have now evolved into a suite of instruments dependent on gyroscopes, radio waves, high-frequency sounds and geo-positioning satellites, all requiring the minimum of human intervention (or indeed, skill) to operate.

---

[29] Laurel Means, 'Popular Middle English Variations on the Compotus', Speculum 67 (1992), pp. 595–623 at p. 621: Cambridge, Trinity College, MS 0.10.21, fols. 36v–37r. Don Lepan, The Cognitive Revolution in Western Culture (London, 1989), p. 91. Albrecht Sauer, 'Segeln mit einem Rahsegel', in Die Kogge, ed. Gabriele Hoffmann and Uwe Schnall (Bremerhaven, 2003): for sailing performance of cog, see 'Sailing', chapter 7.

[30] 'Þa for he norþryhte be þaem lande: let him ealne weg þaet weste land on ðaet steorbord, ond þa widsae on ðaet baecbord þrie dagas', British Library, Add MS. 47967, 'The Voyages of Ohthere and Wulfstan', in Sweet's Anglo-Saxon Reader in Prose and Verse, ed. Dorothy Whitelock (Oxford, 1983), p. 17, lines 9–11). William Worcestre, Itineraries, pp. 302–3.

Indirect, or instrumental navigation

Magnetic compasses

North-seeking magnetic devices have been known in Europe since the twelfth century and perhaps earlier, but exactly when they began to be used at sea is not known. The earliest direction indicators were 'lodestones', pieces of a naturally magnetic mineral, magnetite (Fe_3O_4), which, suspended by a thread, would point north. The discovery that iron could be magnetised by stroking or touching with magnetite, led to the substitution of the stones by needles which, because they were of 'soft' iron, had to be frequently remagnetised. The use of such needles for direction finding was the subject of a lecture in Paris in 1180 by an English monk, Alexander Neckam. In his *De Naturis Rerum* he wrote:

> hidden by the gloom of nocturnal shadows as the world revolves, and not knowing towards which point the bow is heading, they place a needle above a magnet, which turns around continuously until, its movement ceasing, its point may indicate the north region.

It has been generally accepted that Neckam meant by this that contemporary sailors were already familiar with magnetic aids to navigation but the use of the subjunctive of 'indicate' should suggest some caution.[31]

More convincing evidence of the early use of a magnetic needle at sea may be found in the poetry of Guyot of Provins from around 1205, in which he describes sailors magnetising a needle by touching it with lodestone and then floating it, stuck through a straw, on water'. Such a compass would, however, swill about with the movement of a moving ship and was probably usable only in the calmest of seas. It is interesting that although the current Italian for a compass is *bussola* there survives the older term *calamita*, 'a frog', which might possibly be a reference to the floating needle. That remagnetisable devices were well known a century later may be adduced, by default, from *Barbour's Bruce*: 'in addition, there was no needle nor stone' in the ship in 1306 for Bruce's passage to Carrick. The need to remagnetise the compass needle is apparent over more than a century; there are several references to a needle and stone in English alliterative poetry written around 1400, the former never without the latter. Examples include a line in *Morte Arthure*: 'with the nedylle and the stone one the nyghte tydez'; and a line in *The Libelle of Englyshe Polycye* written in 1435–36: 'Men have practised by nedle and by

---

[31] The extract in full reads: 'cum caligine nocturnarum tenebrarum mundus obvolvitur, et ignorant in quem mundi cardinem proara tendat, acum super magnetem ponunt, quae circulariter circumvolvitur usque dum, ejus motu cessante, cuspis ipsius septentrionalem plagam respiciat': Taylor, *Haven Finding Art*, pp. 9 and 95–6. *Respiciat* here is the third person present subjunctive of *respicere*. Taylor cites Alexander of Neckam, *De Naturis Rerum*, ed. T. Wright, pp. xxxv–xxxix and 183.

ston.' As late as 1485, the Celys bought a piece of magnetite in order to remagnetise two compasses on their ship.[32]

Flavio Gioia of Amalfi has been credited with the invention of the graduated compass card to which a magnetised needle was attached, as early as 1302. Although a dubious claim, it is said by Amalfians to be substantiated by the motto on the city's arms, 'prima dedit nautis usum magnetis Amalfis'. As this is a line from a poem by Antonio Beccadelli who died in 1471, the provenance of the motto, and the claim, have to be regarded with some circumspection. The problem of the oscillations of a needle on a ship at sea appears to have been partially overcome sometime in the fourteenth century by pivoting it on a pin, and it is perhaps this that was the invention of Flavio. With the next step of mounting a magnetised needle under a marked card (the 'rose') pivoted on a pin, the compass evolved to become an instrument with which bearings could be read to an accuracy of one point of a 24-point rose, i.e. 15°. Further improvements in the mounting of the card allowed an accuracy of one point of a 32-point rose, or 11.25°, even at sea. This development was confirmed by Chaucer in 1391 and has been discussed above, p. 132.[33]

The manufacture of magnetic compasses, probably for use on land, flourished in Flanders from the fourteenth century but by 1394 the Hansa employed its own compass makers, no doubt for marine use. The earliest known references to magnetic direction-finding aids in English naval ships are in the 1410–12 inventory of the *Plenty*, which had on board '1 sailing piece', and the *George*, for which '12 stones, called adamants, called sailstones' were bought for 6s. in Flanders. Although it is probable that the adamants were to be used to 'stroke' the soft iron compass needles, their purpose is not known with any certainty.

The date of the introduction of magnetic devices to English merchant ships is not known. Although the *OED* gives the earliest reference to the word 'compass', in an indubitably magnetic sense, as late as 1515, the Yarmouth customs accounts show a dozen 'compas' brought in by a Netherlands ship in 1400 for unknown customers and purposes, and the naval inventories of 1422 show one 'compass' on each of the *Rodcogge* and the *Katerine Britton* (but none on the two dozen other ships of the fleet). If those 'compas' were magnetic and not geometrical instruments, which is possible, then there were remarkably few in the English fleet. Indeed, a nineteenth-century naval historian remarked that 'every vessel might not have been supplied with them, only the Admiral or leading ship of a squadron or fleet'. It is possible, however, that naval shipmasters, like mercantile mariners, had

---

[32] *Barbour's Bruce*, 3, Book V, pp. 105, l. 18. *Morte Arthure*, l. 753. *Libelle of Englyshe Policy*, chapter 10, l. 801, p. 41. Hanham, *Celys' World*, pp. 362–3.
[33] António Estácio dos Reis, *Medir Estrelas* (Lisbon, 1997), pp. 30–42. J.A. Bennett, *The Divided Circle* (Oxford, 1987), pp. 27–30. Gimballs to allow the compass bowl to swing freely were first recorded in 1537 by the Portuguese Pedro Nunes. Chaucer, *Complete Works*, pp. 544–63.

their own compasses which were not listed in the ships' inventories, as in the case of John Aborough (see p. 117).[34]

Magnetic variation (the angle subtended between lines pointing to magnetic and to geographic North) had been observed by academics ashore and by the Augsburg sundial manufacturers from early in the fourteenth century. Variation, together with compass deviation (errors due to an inherent fault in the compass or to adjacent pieces of iron), however, was not recognised, or at least not corrected, at sea until much later. Historic variation in the northern hemisphere has been calculated from palaeomagnetic evidence by two groups of researchers who, unfortunately, reached differing conclusions. The variation in the English Channel in 1450, for example, was calculated by one group to have been 2°W and, by the other group, 4°E. Although substantially different, these results suggest that the variation was not gross in either direction and certainly less than one point on a 32-point rose. Given the inaccuracies of the early compasses and the difficulties of reading a bearing on a heaving ship, such a variation would have been unnoticeable. Indeed, since the Pole Star could be used to calibrate compasses to within a degree of true North, the failure of the early navigators to notice any variation reflects the poor accuracy of their instruments.[35]

The eventual general introduction of the marine compass, whatever were the instrument's shortcomings, had a remarkable effect on sea-borne exploration and commerce. With some guarantee of the accuracy of the course, passages out of sight of land became less speculative and the efficiency of the commercial shipmaster was improved dramatically, perhaps by a factor of two. The increasing quantities of goods loaded on ships for transport around, rather than by cart

---

[34] D.W. Waters, *The Art of Navigation in England in Elizabethan and Early Stuart Times* (London, 1958), p. 25. G.V. Scammell, *The World Encompassed: The First European Maritime Empires c.800–1650* (London, 1981), pp. 22, 76: PRO E 122/150/3m. 7d. Rose, *Lancastrian Navy*, pp. 142, 155 and Appendix III, pp. 229–46. Nicolas, *Royal Navy*, II, p. 444. Burwash, *Medieval Shipping*, pp. 33–4: shipmaster John Aborough's 1533 inventory included four compasses.

[35] It was thought at one time that lines of equal variation ran north and south and could be used to estimate longitude (isogonal navigation). Columbus, in 1492, recorded the fallacy: 'En este dia, al comienzo de la noche, las agujas noruesteaban, y a la mañan nordesteaban algo tanto' (from his *Diário* in dos Reis, *Medir Estrelas*, p. 35). *Obras Completas de D. João de Castro*, ed. A Cortesão and Luis de Alburquerque (Coimbra, 1969–82): in 1538 João de Castro observed magnetic deviation induced by a cannon close to the compass. L. Hongre, G. Holst, and A. Khokhlov, 'An Analysis of the Geomagnetic Field over the Past 2000 years', *Physics of the Earth and Planetary Interiors*, 106 (1998), pp. 311–35; C.G. Constable, C.L. Johnson and S.P. Lund, 'Global Geomagnetic Field Models for the Past 3000 Years: Transient or Permanent Flux Lines?', *Philosophical Transactions of the Royal Society of London*, 358 (2000), pp. 991–1008. These two archaeomagnetic studies found, for 1450, magnetic variation of: 2°E and 5°E in northwest Spain; 3°E and 3°W at Ouessant and in the Irish Sea; 4°E and 2°W on the east coast of England; and 5°E and 1.5°W on the coast of Brittany, respectively. Magnetic variation is now ± 7°W in the English Channel.

across, Europe, has been attributed to the increasing availability of the compass; ships were at last seen to be reliable alternative carriers.[36]

Measurement of astral heights
Instruments such as the quadrant, rectangulus and cross-staff had been in use on land for measuring astral altitudes before the fourteenth century. Although sufficiently robust, compact and economic, the first two had the practical limitation of reliance on a plumbline, which was impracticable at sea. Cross- and back-staves may have been in use at sea in the fifteenth century but the first record is from 1514 and is Portuguese. The 'astrolabe', mentioned above as an instrument with which to measure azimuths and altitudes and so derive latitude, the time of day, sunrise, sunset and the sun's position in the zodiac, had been known since the eleventh century. It began to appear in commercial quantities in the fourteenth century and its operation was described by Chaucer in *A Treatise on the Astrolabe*. Its use at sea was restricted by its sophistication and cost, however, and, although it was suspended by an integral ring and was weighted in the lower arc to reduce oscillation, it was practicable only on the calmest of days. The earliest known reference to the use of an astrolabe on a ship dates from 1481 and is also Iberian, but the ship may have been in shelter and not sailing.[37]

The importance of knowing the ship's latitude while at sea had become apparent to the Portuguese early in their exploratory voyages. They began colonising the Azores in the 1430s and in repeatedly re-finding the islands, they must have practised some form of latitude estimation, although there is no record of that until a generation later. Further, by 1433 they had doubled Cape Bojador some 700 miles south of Portugal. Returning by the *volta pelo largo*, a wide swing out into the Atlantic to find wind with a southerly component, they somehow knew when to turn east for home. There is some evidence that, before measuring instruments usable at sea were available, they made very rough estimates of latitude from astral heights measured against a vertical lance or perhaps by the length of the shadow cast by the mast. The first recorded measurement of *alturas* (astral heights) at sea was off the African coast in 1455 by Alvise de Cadamosto. By 1460 Diogo Gomes,

---

[36] *Encyclopaedia Britannica* 99, 'Compass': William Barlowe, *Magnetical Advertisements*, p. 66. As late as 1616 the compass was described as 'the most admirable and useful instrument for the whole world [but] is both amongst ours and other nations for the most part, so bungerly and absurdly contrived, as nothing more': F.C. Lane, 'The Economic Meaning of the Invention of the Compass', *American Historical Review* 68, 3 (1963), pp. 605–17.

[37] Means, 'Variations on the Compotus', p. 599: Cambridge University Library MS Ll. 4.14, fo. 155r, 'The Wise Book of Astronomy and Philosophy'. Bennett, *Divided Circle*, pp. 12–19, 32–6. dos Reis, *Medir Estrelas*, p. 55, 79: the quadrant is mentioned from the thirteenth century in the Portuguese *Libros del Saber Astronomia*. Bennett, *Divided Circle*, pp. 12–19. National Maritime Museum, *The Planispheric Astrolabe* (London, 1989). Alan Stimson, 'The Mariner's Astrolabe', *HES Studies in the History of Cartography and Scientific Instruments*, 4 (Utrecht, 1988), pp. 13–44: citing the West African voyage of Diogo d'Azambjos.

sailing south on the west African coast, could write: 'And I had a quadrant when I was at those countries [places], and I wrote on the scale of the quadrant the height of the arctic pole.' With pre-calibrated instruments it was possible for Portuguese ships, with relatively unschooled navigators, to remain far off-shore for days when sailing north or south before turning east for land.[38]

The introduction of northern seamen to Portuguese methods of determining and using latitude is thought to have been effected in the sixteenth century via Pedro de Medina's *Art de Navegar*, first published in 1545 and later translated into German, French, Italian and English. The determination of latitude was therefore apparently not part of a northern European shipmaster's navigational technique until mid-sixteenth century. The Bordeaux wine ships returning to England, have generally been assumed to have sailed in-shore around the Bay of Biscay, with a victualling stop at St Matthieu. However, a section in the rutter lists depths, descriptions of the seabed, and invisible waypoints on land, with which it is possible to plot a hypothetical off-shore passage on an Admiralty chart, even without distances and course bearings, none of which are given. The information in the rutter is in the form: 'open of Pertuis Maumusson, in 12 fathoms there is stinking mud; open of the Pointe d'Arseaux, in 24 or 26 fathoms there is large gray sand and small black stones with large white shells'; and so on past the Île d'Yeu; the Loire; Belle-Île; until 'open of Ushant, in 50 or 60 fathoms there is red sand and black stones with white shells'. A course drawn through the mean positions of these soundings, with confirmation from the description of the seabed, runs north-west from the Gironde, turning north, probably off Penmarc'h, to lead, west of Ushant, into the Western Approaches. Relevant extracts from the rutter text and the hypothetical course pricked on a chart, may be seen in Figures 5 and 6. This evidence makes it very probable that English shipmasters did take this off-shore route, which would have been quicker, free of pirates and less exposed to the risks of shipwreck.[39]

But there remains the question of how the shipmaster was to know when he was 'open' of the waypoints listed, when they would have been out of sight for most of the passage. Was he to compare mentally the distance along the in-shore arc (which he knew) with the distance he had sailed on the off-shore chord (which he could measure)? Or might this section of the rutter have been the 'borrowed' depth and seabed section of a thematically organized Portuguese *roteiro* which included the *alturas* (astral heights and therefore latitudes) of the waypoints? Astral heights, not yet measurable by Englsh navigators but perhaps vaguely

---

[38] dos Reis, *Medir Estrelas*, passim.
[39] Hastings MS, fo. 137v, lines 6 ff. The counts of Léon controlled the coast from Roscoff to St Mathieu from the thirteenth century; *sceaux*, later *brefs*, were sold to merchants on passing ships as guarantees that in case of shipwreck their goods would be safe (contrary to the Breton *droits de bris*); Guyomarc'h de Léon in 1235 described the coast as 'une pierre plus précieuse qu'aucun joyau': Jean Delameau, ed., *Histoire de la Bretagne* (Toulouse, 1987), pp. 160–2.

BAY OF BISCAY

KEY
· · — — · THE HYPOTHETICAL COURSE
+   +   DEPTH AS GIVEN IN RUTTER

No.	'Open of'	Rutter Soundings (in fathoms)	Rutter description of sea-bed	Admiralty sea-bed information	Notes
1	The Gironde	12, 14 and 16	Mud and sand	Sand, shingle	Course North West
2	Pertuis Maumusson	12	Stinking mud	Sand, mud	
3	Pointe d'Arseaux	24 or 26	Large grey sand, small black stones, large white shells	Sand, shingle	Out of sight of land
4	Île d'Yeu	50 or 60	Muddy sand	Sand, mud, shingle	
5	The Loire	None given	None given		
6	Belle-Île	60 or 70 (?aberrant)	'Dial sand'	Mud, sand, shingle	'Dial sand': small, round grains (as in sand-glasses)
7	Pointe de Penmarc'h	50	Black mud	Sand	
8	Île de Sein	60	Sandy mud and black 'fishy stones'	Sand, shingle	Course North. Fish-shaped black lenticular biotite (mica)
9	Ushant	50 or 60	Red sand, black stones, white shells	Sand, shingle	

5 Hypothetical passage across the Bay of Biscay. Illustration by Ruairi Prendiville.

understood by them, may have been translated, *faute de mieux*, as 'open of', and taken to mean 'on the same east–west line'. If that hypothesis is correct, 'open of', before translation, was 'on the latitude of' and Portuguese mariners had already estimated and logged the latitudes of port towns on the Bay of Biscay.

Another item in the description of the off-shore Biscay course is of particular (and peculiar) interest: 'Opyn of the saym [the Ile de Sein] in lx fadim ther is sondi wose [mud] and blak fischey stonys amonge.' On the latitude of 48° 6′N, which is approximately the latitude of the Île de Sein, the hypothetical passage crosses a geological fault where 'mica fish', or black lenticular porphyroclasts of biotite distorted to fish shapes by tectonic stresses, might be expected. The depth of 60 fathoms (c.110m), the reference to the Île de Sein, and this geological phenomenon thus give a precise latitude fix for that point on the course.[40]

It is not known if it were simply a lack of technique, or a complacent satisfaction with their coastal routes, that explains the fifteenth-century northern seamen's lack of interest in astro-navigation. Even voyages from England to Iceland could be made by compass alone, by sailing up the Irish Sea and the Sea of the Hebrides in sight of land, and thence due north until landfall was made on the Faroes. From the north end of the Faroes the course would have been altered to WNW for Iceland, a leg of about 240 miles, with the 2000m mountains in south-east Iceland being visible as marks in clear conditions from not far past half way. Passages across the North Sea could be made in three or four days by sailing on a compass bearing with no visible waypoints, until making landfall somewhere on the Danish or Norwegian coasts. It was therefore possible for a shipmaster trading in northern waters to go about his business without any knowledge of latitude.[41]

Measurement of time
The sand-glass, the first instrument (after the lead-line, if that may be described as an instrument) to be introduced on board ship, begins to appear in the inventories of English ships from 1295 as a 'dyoll', 'horloge de mer' or 'renning glass'. Primarily used to measure day and night watches, it could also be used to mark a fixed period (that of the particular glass) for navigational purposes; for example, when the ship's course had to be altered after a certain time in order to clear a known hazard, or when a certain fraction of tide was required before attempting to enter a harbour. Both situations may be found in the early sailing directions: 'than ye must goo southe a glass or ij for cause of the rokke' in the rutter; and 'but a large

---

[40] Admiralty chart no. 20, 'Île d'Ouessant to Pointe de la Coubre'. Dr Gerald Roberts, University of London, kindly identifed the 'fishey stones'. The geological fault runs irregularly slightly north of W through the Île de Sein and out to sea. It may be seen on Google 'MapApp' from which a bathymetric profile showing the fault may be drawn from land to sea.
[41] Distance in nM = 2.072 x ($\sqrt{h_e} + \sqrt{h_h}$) where h_e and h_m are the heights in metres above sea level of eye and object.

ship must have two thirds of the tide and a ship which draws two fathoms must have one third of the tide' in the *Seebuch*.[42]

Medieval sand-glasses were too fragile and degradable to have survived, but the example above of an elapsed time as a measure of distance, confirms that the running time of a sand-glass must have had some degree of standardisation, probably of 30 minutes. Assuming a speed of five knots in the example, such a standard glass would allow the ship to travel 2½ miles. The optional second glass may have been for ships sailing in light winds or otherwise incapable of attaining a reasonable speed. The glasses were not always filled with sand but sometimes with crushed egg-shells or powdered silver or tin; whatever the powder, the neck of the instrument eroded in use, and the time measured consequently decreased. In Columbus's log of his first voyage he wrote '14 glasses each of half an hour or slightly less', illustrating this lack of accuracy due to erosion. False measurements were also obtained when the glass was turned by a cold, tired and impatient watch-keeper before the run was complete. In short, estimates of elapsed time measured by the glass were not entirely reliable, but almost certainly better than by any non-instrumental method.[43]

Assessment of speed and distance run
The methodology of measuring speed (and so calculating the distance run) was inverted by the introduction of the sand-glass. Instead of counting the time required to travel a fixed distance (for example, to time a wood chip floating the length of the hull), it became possible to measure the distance covered in a fixed time. A substantial piece of wood, the 'log', was attached to a length of line and thrown into the sea; at the same moment a short period sand-glass was turned over. The length of line pulled out by the 'log', measured in arm-spans, during the fall of the sand, gave a direct measure of the speed of the ship (assuming that the wood had not been dragged through the water). A half-minute glass represents $1/120$ of an hour and the pro rata fraction of a 5,000-foot mile (as it was then thought to be) is 41 feet 8 inches or about seven arm spans (or seven fathoms); each length of seven fathoms veered in half a minute therefore represents one mile sailed by the ship in an hour. Seven fathom lengths were later marked by knots in the line to give an immediate measure of the ship's speed in 'knots'.[44]

It is not known when the log came into general use; the first known English reference is as late as 1574:

---

[42] Waters, *Art of Navigation*, p. 36. Rose, *Lancastrian Navy*, pp. 169, 173, 177. Hastings MS, fo. 132r, lines 3–4. *Seebuch*, MS B, fo. 10r, item 1.
[43] dos Reis, *Medir Estrelas*, pp. 25–8: the log entry is for 17 Jan. 1493.
[44] In 1637, a minute of longitude at the equator (= one sea mile), was revised to 6,120 feet, the sand-glass having to be reduced from 30 to 28 seconds, or the distance between knots increased to eight fathoms. The nautical mile is now 6,080 ft (1.852 km).

> And to know the ship's way, some do use this which (as I take it) is very good; they have a piece of wood & a line to vere out overborde, with a small line of great lengthe ... In like manner they haue either a minute of an hour glasse, or else a knowne part of an houre by some number of wordes spoken.

This suggests that although the method had been known for some time, it was still not in general use amongst English shipmasters. This mention of counting the passage of time even in the late sixteenth century is interesting, and perhaps reflects a paucity of sand-glasses. However, an earlier reference, sometime in the first half of the fifteenth century, indicates the earlier use of a log in northern waters: Nikolaus von Kues (1401–64), from Mosel, measured the time, possibly by counting, required to cover a fixed distance. It is probable that if logs were in use on north German ships before the middle of the fifteenth century, then English sailors were almost certainly also using them soon after, but that cannot be confirmed.[45]

Sailing directions

By early in the fifteenth century, a literate northern shipmaster could have had access to handwritten copies of sailing directions, as *aides mémoires* to familiar waters or as pilots to new areas. Copies of these directions could be purchased, copied or simply memorised but, unsurprisingly and unfortunately, given the conditions at sea, examples which have been used on board a ship are unknown. The oldest surviving sailing directions compiled for, but not necessarily originated by, northern seamen, are a manuscript volume of two editions of a pilot in Middle Low German (the *Seebuch*), and two manuscript copies of a pilot in Middle English (the rutter). All those surviving manuscripts date from the mid-fifteenth century, but they contain material of mixed provenance attributable to the fourteenth or earlier centuries. The manuscripts of the two editions in Low German survive in Hamburg in good condition and were bound together in one volume entitled *Das Seebuch* sometime after 1474. The manuscripts of the rutter, also in good condition and textually very similar to each other, are each bound into a family library's *Grete Boke*, one now in London and the other in New York. Figure 6 shows the first folio of the Lansdowne MS copy of the rutter. Those directions are described in more detail below. Printed directions, which had a much wider distribution and of which many examples have survived, did not

---

[45] *A Regiment for the Sea and Other Writings on Navigation by William Bourne, a Gunner, 1535–82*, ed. E.G.R. Taylor, Hakluyt Society 2, 121 (London, 1963), p. 237. Sauer, *Seebuch*, p. 140, citing Arthur Breusing, *Die nautischen Instrumente bis zur Erfindung des Spiegelsextanten* (Bremen, 1890), p. 24.

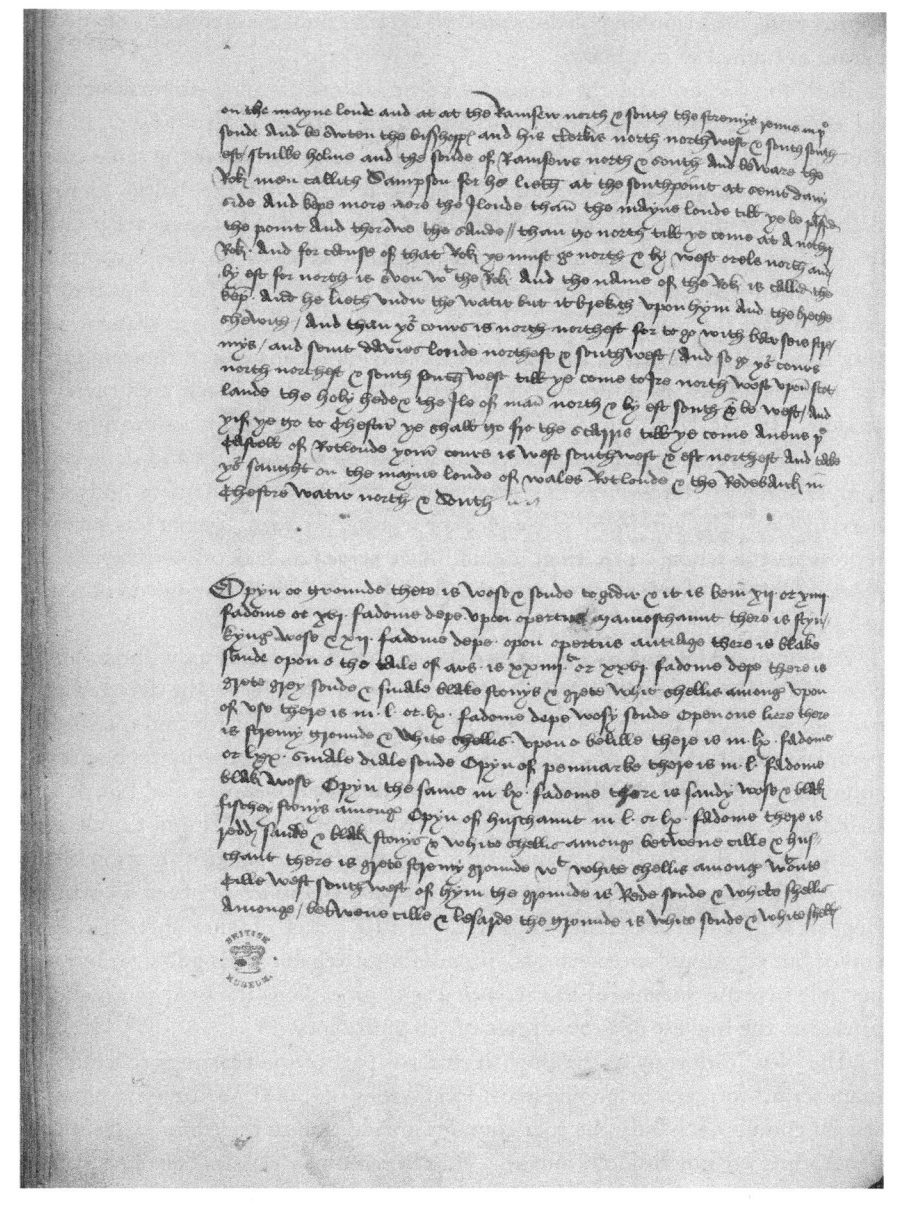

6 Folio 137v of the Lansdowne MS 285, by kind permission of the Picture Library, British Library, London.

appear until the beginning of the sixteenth century and are therefore outside the period examined in this book.[46]

Both the *Seebuch* and the rutter are compilations of some original work by the editors and a much larger quantity of eclectic borrowings from other, mostly southern European, sources which have not survived. Both cover the same coasts from eastern England to Gibraltar including Ireland, but the Baltic, German Bight and the stretch of southern Spain from Gibraltar to Cartagena are peculiar to the *Seebuch*. The English and German directions show no direct commonality in their descriptions of the various routes, havens and hazards, but they do establish that the navigational techniques practised by all northern seamen were very similar. The *Seebuch* is substantially more comprehensive and thorough than the rutter and is largely organised thematically, that is, for each area there are sections listing tidal stream directions, times of high water, compass bearings and distances between waypoints, havens and anchorages, soundings and dangers. In comparison with the *Seebuch*, the rutter is a poor thing, partly thematic and partly narrative in form, with many incomplete or missing sections. If what has survived represents the whole work, then it could have served as little more than an *aide mémoire* for the compiler or as additional notes to another, unknown collection of sailing directions.

Although the information in the two editions of the *Seebuch* was, without doubt, collated by Hansa seamen, original Hanseatic contributions can be detected only occasionally. It is particularly detailed on the coasts of Normandy and the Iberian peninsula but the areas described do not all correspond primarily to Hanseatic shipping routes, and the main sphere of Hanseatic influence – the North and Baltic Seas and the passage to Bourgneuf Bay, for example – are not dealt with in any detail. The Hamburg manuscripts have been dated by identification of the watermarks to *c.*1470, that is, during the 1469–74 conflict between Hanseatic, English and Dutch merchant ships. During that period, Hansa ships had little choice but to sail off enemy coasts, often without reliable local pilotage, and it is possible that the purpose of the *Seebuch* was to give Hanseatic merchantmen and privateers the highest possible degree of self-sufficiency.

The New York copy of the English rutter is part of the Hastings collection of manuscripts formerly belonging to Sir John Astley (d. 1486). Written on vellum in several good book hands, the *boke* contains, in addition to the rutter, a miscellany of treatises on knighthood, jousting, state ceremonial, classical texts, astrology, weather forecasting and various domestic subjects. The London copy of the rutter is in the Lansdowne collection of manuscripts formerly belonging to Sir John Paston (d. 1479); that *boke* is written in a good secretarial hand on paper, and the contents are similar to those in the Hastings collection; folios of the rutter may

---

[46] Full references are made to the *Seebuch* manuscripts and the English rutter manuscripts at the beginning of this chapter.

be seen in Figures 3 and 7 (from the Hastings MS) and 6 (from the Lansdowne MS). The two copies of the rutter differ only in scribal errors, omissions and idiosyncrasies and were probably copied from the same original.[47]

On the last folio of the Hastings MS copy of the rutter, shown in black and white in Figure 7, there is a coloured illustration of a ship taking soundings; her structure and rigging suggest that she is no earlier than mid-fifteenth century. If that illustration has always been integral with the main text, as seems probable, then the Hastings copy of the rutter may be dated to the same period. The absence of the Garter on the arms of the Earl of Hastings, reproduced on three pages of the *boke*, suggests that at least part of it was written in or before 1461 when Hastings was appointed to the Order. In the Lansdowne manuscript, the scribe William Ebesham's hand has been identified. An invoice for his work done for Sir John Paston has been found, drawn up, sadly, while he was in *seintwarye* (sanctuary) from creditors. If, as is thought likely, the invoice refers to the rutter, it establishes that the Lansdowne copy was made in or before 1468. The two copies of the English rutter, therefore, may be dated with some confidence to early in the second half of the fifteenth century and are approximately synchronous with the two editions of the *Seebuch*.[48]

The English rutter appears to have been edited by a lone shipmaster based on the east coast of England, for which detailed information is given from Berwick to the Downs, probably from his own experience. For other areas, although the rutter may be seen as a personal record of his own trading voyages, completed or planned, the contents appear to have been 'borrowed' from an assortment of other sailing directions. The rutter includes many waypoints on both sides of the Channel with bearings and distances between them, a circumnavigation of Ireland, information for a passage up the river Gironde and much about the coast of Brittany. Unlike the *Seebuch*, the information for the Iberian coast is meagre. Of particular interest are an off-shore passages from Santiago de Compostela to England which, uniquely for the early sailing directions, goes 'out of soundings', i.e. over the continental shelf; and the off-shore passage across the Bay of Biscay,

---

[47] G.A. Lester, *Sir John Paston's 'Grete Boke': A Descriptive Catalogue, with an Introduction, of British Library MS Lansdowne 285* (Woodbridge, 1984), pp. 164–6.

[48] Harold Arthur, Viscount Dillon, 'On a Manuscript Collection of Ordinances of Chivalry of the Fifteenth Century Belonging to Lord Hastings', *Archaeologia*, 2nd series, 7 (1900), pp. 29–70. A.H. Moore, 'Some 15th-Century Ship Pictures', *MM* 5 (1919), pp. 15–20; G.F. Howard, 'The Date of the Hastings Manuscript Ships'; *MM*, 63 (1977), 3, pp. 215–18. Howard concludes that the ship in the final folio may be *c*.1470 and those on the first folio, by the gun-ports on the lower deck, perhaps 1510–30; Norman Davis, ed., *The Paston Letters and Papers of the Fifteenth Century* (Oxford, 1976), II, pp. 386–7, 391–2, letters 751 (invoice) and 755 (receipt) dated between July and end of October, 1468. Curt Bühler, in 'Sir John Paston's "Grete Booke", a 15th-century "best seller"', *Modern Language Notes* 56 (1941), pp. 345–51, queries whether Ebesham's invoice was indeed for the Grete Booke or for other manuscripts in the Paston library.

which was discussed above (p. 134), as possible evidence of the early use of latitude by Portuguese navigators.

A version of approximately the first third of the text of the rutter, entitled *A Newe Routter of the Sea for the North Parties* and attributed to Richard Proude, was added to the 1541 and subsequent printed editions of Robert Copland's *The Rutter of the See* which was, in turn, a translation of *Le Routier de la mer*, attributed to Pierre Garcie, and first printed in France in 1502. Copland's translation was the first rutter to be printed in English, in 1528. The remaining two thirds of the rutter, and the two editions of the *Seebuch*, were never printed for the use of contemporary seamen.[49]

Summary of the shipmaster's navigational methods

During the hundred years between 1350 and 1450, navigation evolved from 'direct' methods reliant on the five senses to indirect methods in which instruments were used. Shipmasters relying solely on direct observation were generally restricted to in-shore routes, their off-shore navigation being necessarily of limited reliability. Shipmasters using the new technology, and in particular the magnetic compass, were able to set and steer courses, calculate the distance run, and forecast tidal conditions in channels and havens. Estimation of latitude was not used by northern seamen until the sixteenth century but that appears not to have mattered on the routes which they habitually sailed. The increasing availability of written sailing directions further improved the reliability of ships, as masters became less dependent on their memories, and on information gathered informally in dockside conversations. As a result of this improved efficiency and safety of sea transport, shipping became an increasingly attractive alternative to road transport.

---

[49] D.W. Waters, *The Rutters of the Sea* (New Haven, CT, 1967), includes facsimile copies of Garcie's and Copland's rutters.

7

The Shipmaster at Sea – Seamanship

At the end of the fourteenth or early in the fifteenth century, the design and construction of ships in northern waters benefited from technical ideas seen in ships from the Mediterranean. Carvel construction, in which the smooth hull is planked with edge-butted timbers, largely replaced traditional clinker construction in which the planking overlapped; the sail area was split over several masts and so could be increased in total area; and a fore-and-aft lateen sail was rigged on the new mizzen mast to improve the ship's performance to windward. The late medieval ship, the most complex of contemporary machinery, has attracted much scholarly attention. Its design and development, as seen in contemporary illustrations, port town seals and archaeological finds, and as described in inventories, accounts and contemporary literature, have been thoroughly examined.[1]

Less scholarly attention has been paid to medieval seamanship. The earliest surviving works on 'good marinership' date from early in the sixteenth century and tend to be didactic rather than informative in the same way as contemporary works preached 'good husbandry'. The problems presented to a ship and her crew by wind and current, at sea or at anchor, do not change, and while the development of new materials has led to very considerable improvements in the design and construction of ships and their equipment, it may safely be assumed that most basic manoeuvres were conducted in a manner similar to current practice. Being of poorer quality materials throughout, however, the medieval ship was more at the mercy of the elements; often working with little safety margin, her operational parameters were considerably narrower. Evidence of early ship and sail handling techniques is available in contemporary literature, occasional court cases, letters, and illustrations. Conclusions may also be drawn from surviving equipment lists and from ships' accounts. In some areas, educated guesses or reasonable assump-

---

[1] Landström, *Sailing Ships*, pp. 72–89; Richard W. Unger, ed., *Cogs, Caravels and Galleons* (London, 1994), pp. 29–59; Hutchinson, *Medieval Ships, passim*; Friel, *The Good Ship*, pp. 68–180; *Middle English Sea Terms*, ed. Bertil Sandahl, 3 vols (Uppsala, 1951–82); R.M. Ward, 'An Elucidation of Certain Maritime Passages in English Alliterative Poetry of the Fourteenth Century', unpublished MA thesis, Keele University, 1991.

tions have to be made, to reach a plausible account of the medieval shipmaster's methods.

Cargo handling

Although many of the goods freighted in medieval ships were loaded in small units, manhandling barrels of 252 gallons (*c*.1,147 litres) of wine weighing over one ton, and sarplars of wool weighing *c*.730lbs. (*c*.331kg) in and out of the hold, must have been a considerable challenge. Cargo might be handled in three different situations: with the ship tied-up against a dock as in Bordeaux, on a drying beach as on the Norfolk coast, or swinging to an anchor where there was neither wharf nor sand. Ships lying alongside usually had to use dockside cranes with local labour, paying dues to the local authority, but in the absence of such facilities the ship's crew (with payment of 'primage' or overtime) and her equipment were employed. When a ship was beached for handling cargo in and out of carts, or at anchor and using lighters, the men and equipment available on board had necessarily to be used. One method of hoisting cargo on board may be discerned in a detail from a painting by Hans Memling in which a horse is being lifted onto a ship from a boat alongside. The hoisting line, attached to a wide sling under the horse, passes through a block on one end of the yard, thence to another block hanging by a pendant from the mast-head, and then down the mast, to be led to the ship's windlass or capstan. A guy is attached to the other end of the yard with which it is swung to a position above the hatch by crew members on deck. The gunwales of ships must have been subjected to considerable wear and tear during cargo handling; removable wash-boards were probably unshipped when handling cargo.[2]

When the ship's equipment was to be used for cargo handling, the shipmaster had to obtain the shipping merchants' approval of his cordage and machinery and, as discussed in chapter 5, if he did not have their approval and goods were damaged due to equipment failure, he and the crew were liable. *Oleron* suggests that such compensation should be taken out of the 'guindage' or craneage charge, with additional personal contributions by the shipmaster and crew if necessary. Guindage was around 2d. per tun in the mid- and late fourteenth century, varying from port to port. If shore labour was not available, or was not obligatory, by tradition the crew were offered by the merchant shippers 'first refusal' to unload the cargo, for the payment of primage. This was generally between 1d. and 2d. per tun, a rate sometimes agreed in the charter-party. It is not known if guindage

---

[2] The 'wine gallon' of Edward III was 8lbs; a 'sarplar' was two sacks each of 364lbs of wool, a 'sack' being only a unit of account. Hans Memling, *The Seven Joys of Mary* in the Munich Pinakothek.

included primage or was a further charge on the merchants for the use of the ship's derricks.³

The internal arrangement of ships may have been modified to suit the requirements of the owner. A dedicated wine ship, for example, would have had removable deck planking so that the barrels could be lowered directly onto dunnage anywhere in the hold, the ship being moved along the quay to be under the shore-side crane. When using the ship's own lifting equipment, cargo must have been rolled, or otherwise moved, to or from the lifting fall suspended from the yard. Commodities such as salt or grain would have been loaded in sacks by crane, or in barrows by hand, probably involving every man in the crew. 'Lasts' loaded with hides or fish may have been similar to modern pallets and could have been hoisted by crane in and out of the hold. When removable deck planking (known by variations of the word *hacchis*, which evolved into the current English 'hatches'), was replaced before departure, it required nailing down and caulking to prevent sea- and rainwater spoiling the cargo. This procedure is described in the poem *Morte Arthure* in which the crew of a ship preparing to depart 'bettrede hatches' (improved the hatches). Moisture-sensitive bulk cargoes, for example salt, alum and grain, and bolts, bails and lasts of cloth and furs, would require further protection from water leaking through the deck or swilling up from the bilges. Additional freight charges were specifically authorised in *Queenborough* when waterproof covers were supplied by the ship for a cargo of salt.⁴

As discussed in chapter 5, the shipmaster and his crew were responsible for the stowage of the cargo and were liable for compensation to the merchants if goods were damaged in the hold, as in the *Oleron* example where wine is lost from a stoved-in barrel. Because there was an ever-present risk of barrels rolling off the dunnage, the amount of loss or damage acceptable to the shipping merchants was sometimes specified in the charter-party. If the agreed loss was exceeded, the crew had to pay compensation.⁵

---

3   Appendix 1, *Oleron*, article 10. *Local Customs Accounts of the Port of Exeter*, p. 6: a charge was made for the use of Topsham town crane. Harding, 'Port of London': PRO E 101/612/31, m. 1; E 101/79/5, m. 11; E 101/80/24. Reddaway, *Accounts of John Balsall*, p. 23. Appendix 3, *Coutumier*, chapters 76, 95, 97. Ships were also liable assiage (stowage), planchage (landing dues) and quillage ('keelage' or pier dues). *Local Customs Accounts of the Port of Exeter*, p. 1, fn. 2: crane dues may also have been charged, in addition to wharfage charges, when a ship's equipment was used alongside a town quay; keelage in Topsham early in the fourteenth century was 2d. *Primage* is mentioned in some versions of *Oleron*, article 10. PRO, C47/37/14, mm. 19–34, fo. 5 and mm. 49–60, fo. 10; C47/37/11, mm. 22–3, fos 1–6d, etc.
4   Tim Weski, private communication, 1996: Hanseatic merchants were organised into market groups: *Baiefahrer, Bergenfahrer, Englandfahrer*, etc.; it is probable that the layout of their ships was designed to suit their habitual cargoes; it is not known if English merchant ships were similarly specialised. *Morte Arthure*, line 3656. Appendix 2, *Queenborough*, article 6.
5   Appendix 1, *Oleron*, article 11. Twiss, *Black Book*, III, pp. 342–2: *Customs* has 14 articles concerning damage to the cargo; ibid., I, pp. 88–131. It is just possible that some ships may

Departure

The best surviving descriptions of the departures of medieval ships are in two alliterative poems written around 1400, and in a political satire of a somewhat later date (1548). The *Morte Arthure* description, modernised, reads:

> vigorously on the ship's side they weigh their anchors with the skill of the watermen of the surging waves; men on the fore-deck coil their cables … sails tight to the top [of the mast] and the luff [of the sail] turned [from the wind] … completely without damage they haul in the boats, shipmen quickly shut their ports.

And, from *Pearl*:

> They lace on the sail, fasten ropes, men at the windlass weigh their anchors, the thin bowline is attached smartly to the bowsprit, they haul the guy ropes, the great cloth falls; they lay in [with oars] on the port side and pull up to windward; they swing the sweet ship swiftly from the haven.[6]

The third description, again modernised, is from the prose *Complaynt of Scotland* :

> then the master whistled, and boldly the mariners laid the cable on the capstan, to wind and to weigh, then the mariners began to wind the cable with many a loud call, and as one called, all the rest called in the same tune, as if it had been an echo from a high cliff. And as it appeared to me, they called their words as follows: 'veer-a, veer-a (repeated). fine young lads (repeated). wind I see it (repeated). to the shackle (repeated). haul all and one (repeated). haul him up to us (repeated).' Then, when the anchor was hauled above the water, one mariner shouted and all the rest followed to the same tune 'haul the cable (repeated). stop the cable (repeated). cat the shackle (repeated).' then they made fast the shank of the anchor … Then the master whistled and shouted, 'Two men aloft to the main yard, cut the ribbands, and let the main sail fall, haul in the luff close aboard, haul aft the main sail sheet, haul out the mainsail bowline'. Then one of the mariners began to hail and to shout, and all the mariners answered with the same sound 'heave (repeated). pulpela (repeated). bowline (repeated). 'hands-on' (repeated). hard back (repeated). before the wind (repeated). God send (repeated). fair weather (repeated). many prizes (repeated). good fair land (repeated). stop (repeated). make fast and belay'. Then the master called, 'And quickly lace on a bonnet, veer the trusses, now hoist.' Then the mariners began to haul up the sail calling 'heave (repeated). like that (repeated). go (repeated).' Then the master called to the helmsman, 'rudderman, sail full and by … luff

---

have carried 'flat-pack' barrels on the outward bound voyage to Bordeaux, to be assembled by a cooper in the crew, and filled from smaller containers in the hold.

6   *Morte Arthure*, lines 3656, 740–3, 744 and 748–9. *Pearl*: 'Patience', lines 102–6 and 108.

up ... don't let her back ... harden up ... enough ... steer straight ... bear up ... like that').

A description of setting the foresail has been omitted as it is exactly as for the mainsail.[7]

From all three quotations it is clear that the sequence of events is to close all open ports in the hull, stretch the sails on the yards, secure and caulk removable deck planking, and haul on board the ship's boat. The anchor is then weighed and the sail(s) dropped and set by bringing the luff (the windward edge of the sail) close inboard, hauling the sheet (the rope led from the leeward side of the sail) aft and leading a line from the luff to the bowsprit. A bonnet (an additional strip of cloth laced below the sail) is bent on, in one case while the sail is still furled and in the other after it has been dropped and has to be hoisted again. In all the extracts, the ships are on a lee shore (for dramatic effect) and have to sail off, hard on the wind; one crew having to row on the lee side to bring their ship up sufficiently to clear an obstacle. It is clear from the Scottish extract that rhythmic calling was a feature of sailors working – the forerunner to the shanties of later generations of mariners. With an on-shore breeze a shipmaster would normally postpone departure until the wind was favourable unless there was some overriding reason not to delay. If he had to leave but was unable to sail out safely, the three possible aids available were: to warp out on the anchors, to be towed out by the ship's boat or one hired locally, or to sail out with oared assistance, as in the case of the *Pearl* ship. A ship being towed out of a haven by a boat with six oarsmen may be seen in Figure 3.

Anchors were expensive items and every effort had to be made to recover them if they became trapped in rocks. To free such an anchor, the shipmaster would try sailing back and forward across the wind to attempt to tug the anchor out. If that failed, then either from the ship or from the ship's boat, the buoy line would be pulled to try to trip the anchor, grappling with hooks if the buoy line had broken. As a last resort, the cable would have to be cut and the anchor temporarily abandoned with a marker buoy. An abandoned anchor, marked with its buoy, was inevitably a target for opportunist crews coming in later; recovering and keeping someone else's anchor was theft under criminal law, but could lead to an admiral's inquiry as a violation of maritime law.[8]

---

[7] A. Jal, *Archéologie navale*, 2 vols (Paris, 1840), pp. 529–31. *Complaynt of Scotland*.
[8] Appendix 2, *Queenborough*, articles 21 and, in a different context, 60; cutting a buoy line and so losing an anchor was also an inquiry offence, *Queenborough*, article 61.

Sails and sailing

The sails of fourteenth- and fifteenth-century northern ships were made of vertically sewn strips of cloth woven from canvas or wool, or a mixture of both, the composition of the mix being chosen to give an acceptable compromise between cost, durability and performance. Because of its organic nature, few samples of medieval sailcloth have survived and it is not possible to identify the fibre mix, cloth weight, thickness of warp and weft or alignment of weave of a typical cloth. The rough and porous sails, however made, would certainly have offered a less than ideal surface for efficient air flow. They would have stretched in use, become heavy when wet and been prone to weakening by mould growth in humid conditions when not in use. Some improvement could be made to porosity by wetting the sailcloth with buckets of water but at the expense of increased top-heaviness, but nothing could be done about the effect on the sail's aerodynamics of the cloth's hairiness, a phenomenon not then recognised. To compound the problem of poor-quality sailcloth, an incomplete understanding of a good aerofoil shape inevitably led to inefficient sail setting. Many contemporary illustrations show ships running before the wind with their courses roundly billowed and apparently almost out of control, a profile less efficient than when the sail is held firmly by sheets and tacks.[9]

The cost of replacement sails was an important item in a ship's accounts, amounting to something of the order of 5 per cent of the value of the ship, depending on the size of ship and sails. To prolong the life of the fabric for as long as possible, the cloth was frequently inspected, and repaired as necessary, probably in every harbour. Attempts would have been made to keep mildew at bay by washing the sails with fresh water and drying them as often as possible. Repairs, and even the sewing of new sails, could be effected by members of the crew; from the Celys' payments for canvas and thread and additional wages for the crew, but no payment to a sailmaker, it is apparent that the crew made and repaired their sails. In *Customs* a qualified mate has to be able to measure and cut sails, a step beyond merely sewing them, and it is quite possible that similar skills were expected of senior members of the crew on English ships. Sail-making ashore, when necessary, appears to have been supervised by shipmasters, possibly retired.[10]

---

[9] Friel, *The Good Ship*, pp. 96–9. Canvas was imported from Brittany throughout the fourteenth and fifteenth centuries. Valerie Fenwick. ed., *The Graveney Boat* (Oxford, 1978), p. 251: Woollen sails, made from a cloth called *bever* or *belver*, were used as late as the end of the fifteenth century in Kent (not 1371 as reported by Friel).

[10] Scammell, 'European Seamanship', p. 360. Billowing sails were discussed in *MM*, 3 (1913), p. 239ff; 4 (1914), p. 347ff; they may have been only artistic convention. Friel, *The Good Ship*, p. 97: sail costs from galley accounts range from £10 12s. to £17 14s. Rose, *Lancastrian Navy*, p. 250: ship costs in royal accounts range from the *Ane*, 120 tons @ c.£180 and the *George*, 120 tons @

The results of sailing trials with a full-size replica of a 23-m. Hansa cog loaded with 26 tons of ballast, have revealed something of the performance of a medieval cargo ship:

Beaufort wind scale	Wind speed	Ship's speed through the water
3	7–10 knots 'a gentle breeze'	c.3.4 knots
4	11–16 knots 'a moderate breeze'	c.4.0 knots
5	17–21 knots 'a fresh breeze'	c.5.1 knots
6	22–27 knots 'a strong breeze'	c.6.0 knots

The trials also showed that the closest to the wind the cog could sail was $c.70°$ with leeway of $15°-20°$, reducing the course made good to not much better than a right-angle to the wind. A Viking longship, on the other hand, could sail on a course of perhaps five points off the wind ($c.56°$) and make good a course of around $65°$. Fully laden ships with fouled bottoms would have achieved substantially less speed and would have had a significantly poorer windward performance, which explains much of the prolonged waiting times in harbours. A ship is said to be 'close-hauled' when she sails as close to the wind as she is able; any closer to the wind, her sails will 'back' and, if the helmsman is not quick enough to ease off downwind to fill the sails again, she will stop 'in irons'. While in irons she will begin to sail astern and violent changes of tension on the shrouds and back stays, as the sail flaps wildly, may break the mast. Towards the end of the passage from the *Complaynt of Scotland* quoted above, there is a clear picture of the anxieties of a shipmaster trying to sail his ship as close to the wind as he dare. As practical evidence of the high risks to the mast, there have been found in medieval wrecks 10 or even 14 holes in the wales to take shrouds and backstays. Although allowance has to be made for mast supports set up with a purchase requiring two securing points, confirmed by the deadeyes and lanyards found in inventories and seen in contemporary illustrations, many mast supports, particularly aft of the mast, were obviously considered necessary.[11]

When close-hauled, the luff or weather edge of a sail set athwart the ship has

---

c.£230, to the *Nicholas*, 330 ton @ £500. Hanham, *Celys' World*, p. 366. Twiss, *Black Book*, III, pp. 90–3: *Customs*, chapter xviii.

[11] Sauer, 'Segeln mit einem Rahsegel', p. 26. Hutchinson, *Medieval Ships*, p. 5. J.T. Tinniswood, 'The English Galleys 1272–1377', *MM* 35 (1949), pp. 276–315. Friel, *The Good Ship*, p. 101: backstays accounted for up to a third of headropes in fifteenth-century inventories. *Accounts of the Clerk of the King's Ships*, PRO E 372/203/36–39 (1358–59, Thomas de Snetesham): 'iiij. hausers alb' ij. par' de dedmenneshyne vnde j. cum cathena ferri exist' in quadam naue voc' la Naw seinte Marie.'

to be held forward by tack and bowline and the leeward edge has to be held back by brace and by sheet, as may be seen in Figures 3 and 7. The luff could also have had additional lines leading forward to the bowsprit and a pole was sometimes used to hold outboard the weather clue of the sail. This 'luff pole' or *betas* was a direct descendant of the Viking *beitiáss* and appears not infrequently in poetry, for example in *Morte Arthure*: 'sails tight to the top and turn the luff [with a pole]', and 'some worked the windlass, some the luff, some the *betas*'. To change tack when close-hauled, a sailing vessel has to be either 'put about' or 'weared'. The former involves turning the bow through the wind, a manoeuvre which requires readjustment of the sheets, braces, tacks and bowlines as the weather side of the ship becomes the lee side, and vice versa. As a further complication, the tension of the lee shrouds has to be released and the new windward shrouds made up as the ship changes tack, an operation over which the shipmaster has to be extremely vigilant to avoid risk to the mast. During the whole manoeuvre the ship has to maintain steerage way to avoid being trapped 'in irons' and drifting astern, out of control. Wearing involves turning the ship's stern through the wind, a less hazardous operation since it risks neither the wind backing the sail nor the ship stopping in the water. With her slow speed and poor windward performance, particularly when laden and fouled, it would often have been extremely difficult to acquire sufficient momentum to tack a laden medieval cargo ship through an angle as wide as 180°, in which circumstances it would have been preferable to wear ship. The disadvantages of wearing are that the ship has to turn downwind during the operation and a considerable amount of windward progress is lost. On a lee shore, the risks of wearing might be as great as the risks of going about. An extract from a report by a Dutch privateer in the 1470s gives a chilling description of a ship, heavy because of a leak, trying to go about:

> and weighed our anchor and handed the foresail; then the ship would not come round; then handed the main course, then the good ship would still not come round so that we were driven towards the land. Then at last God in Heaven and the great St James helped us so that the good ship came up. Then we sailed to windward as best we could.[12]

In port town seals portraying cogs, the mast generally appears to be stepped forward of the centre of lateral resistance, a position which would drive the ship out of the wind and require constant and inefficient corrective lee helm to hold

---

[12] The word 'wear' derives from 'veer', hence the apparently anomalous past participle. Sandahl, *Sea Terms*, 2, pp. 60–1, quoting from the 1472 *Hanserezesse*, 2, 6, p. 500. F. Howard, *Sailing Ships of War 1400–1860* (London, 1987), pp. 31–3: even full rigged ships of the early nineteenth century, with better windward performances than the medieval cog, had difficulties going about, especially when heavily fouled: Lords St Vincent and Exmouth and Sir E. Owen issued orders to their fleets to wear rather than tack, when not inconvenient, because the accidents and wear and tear of tacking was detrimental to the sails, spars and rigging.

her up. Paradoxically, in the sailing trials mentioned above, a full-scale replica of the 1380 cog was found to require 10–15° of weather helm as she tended always to 'luff up' to windward, a result which casts doubt on the accuracy of the illustrations in the seals, or on the configuration of the replica (which seems unlikely to be wrong).

Although there is general agreement amongst maritime historians that early in the fifteenth century northern ship rigs evolved from a single mast to three masts, there has been much discussion about the order in which the foremast and mizzen were introduced. The introduction of a lateen-rigged mizzen offered an improvement in windward performance and manoeuverability, but the long yard required by the lateen sail was labour intensive and so was frequently left furled, as in Figures 3 and 7, except when the ship was attempting to claw up-wind. The ability to make up to windward was further reduced by another late fourteenth- or early fifteenth-century innovation: a sail set on the bowsprit. The downwind leverage of this spritsail must have been so considerable that it was probably set only on long downwind passages and handed before attempting to go about.[13]

Because of unreliable equipment, medieval shipmasters had to be extremely cautious at all times. All cordage, for anchor cables and for standing and running rigging, was liable to part, and only the resourceful shipmaster with an alternative plan put quickly into operation, escaped unharmed from what might easily be a serious accident. Because his ship had such a poor windward performance, the shipmaster had to allow a large margin of safety when trying to clear headlands, reefs or harbour entrances, and he had to have the patience to wait for days or even weeks for a suitable wind for his planned voyage. His respect for the weather and the sea may often have been put to the test by impatient shipping merchants prepared, in their ignorance, to take risks in order to exploit a market. The struggle between commercial forces and maritime caution may be seen in the clauses of maritime law covering jettison, general average, delays and the delegation of responsibility for cargo handling equipment.

Sail reduction
Sometime after 1350, sail reduction by slab reefing with ties was generally abandoned in favour of using a smaller sail with extensions of sail cloth called bonnets, which were laced along the foot of the sail, when wind conditions permitted. Why bonnets replaced reefs is not known; it may have been because the main course had become too large to be reduced in slabs, even when handed on deck.

How bonnets were laced and unlaced to the course is unknown. It would have been less arduous to attach them with the foot of the course on deck, but there

---

[13] The evidence perhaps favours the mizzen, the aftermost mast in English terminology, as the first additional mast, but the French use of *misaine* for 'foremast' and *artimon* for 'mizzen' may be significant. A discussion was conducted sporadically in the *Mariner's Mirror* from 1918 to 1933 and see also Sandahl, *Sea Terms*, II, pp. 73–8].

is evidence, in the extract already quoted from the *Morte Arthure*, that the sail was trussed up to the yard (although this was perhaps because, in this case, the ship was still at anchor). Not all ships at that time were equipped with 'lifts' on the yards, so had to rely only on the halyards to raise and lower them. In those cases there would have been no direct control of the yard's angle to the horizontal, which must have complicated the bonnet handing operations. A lowered main course is mentioned in a 1440 petition to the chancellor by William Waleys, whose ship the *George* of Welles had been deliberately rammed by Richard Walter, master of the *Christofer* of Dartmouth; Waleys claimed that his ship '. lay upon the lee wyth ther corse low sett'. The addition and removal of bonnets according to the wind conditions is illustrated in another fifteenth-century poem, *Richard Redeless*: 'they bent on a bonnet and set a topsail ... and took off a bonnet before the blow came.' There is no evidence of bonnets on the lateen sails set on the mizzen mast; when the wind became too strong they would have been trussed up or dropped to the deck.[14]

Reefing points reappeared in the 1660s and bonnets became less common, again for unknown reasons, and the operation of making-up and loosing reefs was then probably very similar to that practised on square rigged ships to this day. A third and older reefing system may have persisted after the introduction of bonnets: tightening brails vertically down the belly of the sail to divide it into two sections and so destroy the aerodynamic flow. Although it put more strain on the sailcloth, the system required less physical effort from the crew. The Vikings may have used vertical brails as well as horizontal reef slabs, and a passage in the 1450 poem mentioned on pp. 160–1, appears to describe the survival of the same reefing method: 'Hoist, truss, haul in the brails! You're not hauling, by God, you fail!' From earlier in the poem, there appears to be a good breeze, the bowline and sheets having been hauled tight; the reason for now hauling tight the brails, therefore, cannot be to furl the sail but to divide it vertically. There are illustrations of ships with their courses divided by a brail in this fashion but there is no specific written evidence of the practice apart from this poem.[15]

Curiously, on none of the ships with sails set in Figures 3 and 7 can either reefing points or bonnet lacing cringles be seen, although many other details of the ships and rigging are visible and identifiable. The sail cloth in Figure 3 is clearly

---

[14] H.H. Brindley, 'Reefing Gear', *MM* 2 (1912), pp. 129–134. Landstrøm, *Sailing Ships*, pp. 72–85. Friel, *The Good Ship*, pp. 95–99. First inventory reference to' bonnet' is PRO E101/26/14: 'In j. velo j. bonett'. Some ships continued to use reefing ties after the introduction of bonnets, for example, in the c.1400 Rye town seal. Gardiner, *West Country Shipping*, citing PRO C1/43/33. Langland, *Richard Redeless* (date 1399), lines 71, 80.

[15] Sandahl, *Sea Terms*, 2, p. 89: Vikings reefed with vertical brails and horizontal slabs but Sam Svensson, *Sails Through the Centuries* (New York, 1965), p. 11 mentions only horizontal reefing with ties. Furnivall, *Pilgrims' Sea-Voyage*, p. 33.

made up of vertical strips, the usual construction, whereas in Figure 7 it appears to be sewn in horizontal lengths.

Anchoring

Before anchoring, the shipmaster would have checked the depth and the suitability of the seabed with the sounding lead and a lump of tallow. If possible, this would have been done by sailing slowly into the anchorage and making frequent soundings; if there were other ships already at anchor or space was limited, then the ship's boat would be used for the reconnaissance. When sailing in to anchor, the shipmaster had two possible options. He could either drop the anchor as the ship sailed over its chosen position, hope that it would hold, arrest the motion of the ship and swing her round into the wind. Speed was necessary to ensure that the anchor would dig well into the ground, but to sail too fast risked running up the beach, if it failed to hold. The alternative was to sail past the chosen point, come up into the wind, drop the anchor as the ship came to a standstill, and try to dig the anchor in by backing the sail and sailing astern. In both manoeuvres, if the anchor failed to hold, the shipmaster would have had to sail off to try again, and for this eventuality, the sail(s) could not be furled until the ship was secure. Anchoring in anything above a gentle breeze was therefore a potentially hazardous operation requiring both skill and a certain amount of luck; more of the former lessened the need for the latter. In order to ensure a shallow angle of pull on the anchor, the length of the cable would normally be four to five times the depth at high water; care had to be taken, therefore, that there were no dangers within the scope of the swinging ship (see also chapter 6).

A haven with confined space would normally be entered by the ship in tow, pulled by the ship's own boat or by a boat hired locally. Payment for the hire of towage, whether riverine or in harbour, was, according to *Oleron*, to be to the merchants' account; it is possible that when the ship's boat was used, the crew were given extra money, as they were when they volunteered to unload the ship. When necessary, a second anchor would be set by sending out the ship's boat with the anchor suspended over the side, to be dropped at a good angle from the first anchor; a ship lying to two anchors may be seen in Figure 3. When the ship was to dry-out on the beach on an ebbing tide, the shipmaster might send the ship's boat ashore with an anchor where it could be set manually. At high water, the ship would be brought ashore by the crew, hauling the anchor cable on the capstan or windlass. An anchor visible on the shore need not be buoyed, which explains the differentiating reference in *Oleron* to 'ancres qe ne parigent au plein'. The setting of an anchor on-shore may be seen in the Bayeux Tapestry as Harold arrives in Normandy.

Anchors had to be buoyed for three reasons: first, the cable enabled the crew

til ye come in to iiij. fadmn deep and yf it be stremy
grounde it is beleuene sufficiant and ille in the entre
of the chanel of ffaumores and soo goo yowre conrs
til ye haue sixti fadmn deep. than goo est northe est
a longe the see. +c.

7 A ship sounding, with text describing the passage from Ouessant into the Channel. Folio 138v of Hastings MS 775, reproduced with the kind permission of the Pierpont Morgan Library, New York.

to 'upset' the anchor when it is trapped in rocks; second, to warn later arrivals where an anchor had been set and so avoid a sharp anchor fluke coming through the ship's bottom as she dried out; and finally, if an unbuoyed anchor did damage to another ship, the shipmaster who laid the anchor was held responsible for the damage. Anchoring no doubt led to a certain amount of jostling when several ships arrived more or less together, perhaps from a convoy, each seeking the best position in the haven. A somewhat confused article in *Oleron* describes the situation in a crowded anchorage as the tide ebbs. Ship 'A' finds herself in danger of drifting over the anchor of ship 'B'; the crew of A asks the crew of B either to move their anchor, or to give A's crew permission to move it. Although the text is not completely clear, the article then appears to attach responsibility to B for any subsequent damage to both ships, although she was the first ship in the haven. The decision was reached, perhaps, because it has been assumed (but not stated explicitly) that B's crew, having found a good position, refused to move their anchor, or let it be moved. The full explanation is revealed at the end of the article: B's anchor was not buoyed. The importance of anchors and their buoys is underlined by two articles in *Queenborough* which order an admiral's inquiry to be held into the removal of an anchor without permission and, significantly, into the cutting of anchor buoy lines. In the inventories of the Lancastrian navy, parcels of up to 170 pieces of cork are shown in stock for the manufacture of buoys, and several ships' lists include made-up buoys and lines, sometimes specifically for the anchor.[16]

Although no clear evidence has survived of medieval rules for the avoidance of collision at sea (see 'Rule of the road', below), in both *Oleron* and the *Coutumier* there are rules defining precisely the allocation of responsibilities for collision in an anchorage. When a ship collides with another already anchored in a haven, in *Oleron* the colliding ship is described as 'hastant de sa marree', i.e. carried down by the tide and not necessarily anchored, whereas in the *Coutumier* she is dragging down either from an anchored position or while anchoring. The *Coutumier* explains that an accident can happen to any ship in such a situation so that, in principle, each ship involved should pay half the damage, in effect, a *force majeure* clause. *Oleron* suggests that an old ship might be placed deliberately in the path of more valuable incoming ships in order to benefit from the 50:50 rule, a trailblazer for insurance scams. To avoid such fraud, the *Coutumier* allows that if the stationary ship can prove fault on the part of the dragging ship's crew or equipment, then it is not an accident and the latter has to pay the whole amount. In *Oleron* the shipmaster and crew of the moving vessel must swear that the collision was not deliberate and if they refuse to do so, they are liable for all damage. The

---

[16] Appendix 1, *Oleron*, articles 13, 16. Appendix 2, *Queenborough*, articles 6, 60. Rose, *Lancastrian Navy*, variously pp. 137, 152, 161, 163, 167 etc.

effect of the *Coutumier* ruling is to accept the innocence of the dragging ship until she is proved guilty whereas *Oleron* assumes her guilt until proved innocent.[17]

Although chain cables for anchors were known well before the Middle Ages, hempen cordage was generally used in the fourteenth and fifteenth centuries no doubt because it was cheaper and easy to cut in emergencies. Because it was lighter however, it did not offer the holding resistance obtained by a length of chain lying on the bottom to reduce the angle of pull on the anchor. It is possible that some anchors had a few fathoms of chain bent on below the rope cable as a compromise solution, but there is no evidence of that. It was because of the uncertainty of the strength of the cordage and of the holding power of the anchor, that ships put out two anchors, a precaution which has been mentioned above. The loss of an anchor and its cable was not uncommon and the ship inventories of the Lancastrian navy show that most ships carried several. There is no reason to doubt that merchant ships were similarly equipped with several anchors, lengths of cable, line and reserves of cork for buoys.[18]

Rule of the road

Like Sherlock Holmes' dog that didn't bark, one of the most interesting aspects of medieval maritime law is the absence of rules for the avoidance of collision at sea. In anchorages there were rules, discussed above, but on the open sea it appears to have been 'every man for himself'. The records of a few cases concerned with collision have been found. A water bailiff of a *showt* was arrested for causing damage to a ship at Queenhithe, but no other details are known. Since one or both of the ships could have been moored or sailing, the damage might have been caused by careless cargo handling, or the crews may have been involved in a fracas on board, there is little to be learned from that case. Two promising examples from the mid-fourteenth century concern ships which were 'maliciously run down' by others, allegedly causing considerable damage, but here the charges were trespass heard before a mayoral court, rather than violation of any maritime code to be heard by an admiral. There is also a record of arbitration by *aimables compositeurs* appointed by an admiral following a collision at sea, but once again the information is inadequate. In 1437 an appeal was made for the restoration of wrongly sequestered goods which had been sold following a decision by an admiralty court

---

[17] Appendix 1, *Oleron*, article 15. Appendix 3, *Coutumier*, chapter 82.
[18] *The Gallic War*, ed. H.J. Edwards (London, 1917), IV, 23: the Veneti tribe were said by Julius Caesar to have 'ancorae pro funibus ferreis catenis revinctae', and a Veneti anchor with chain has been found at Bulbury Camp. Rose, *Lancastrian Navy*, p. 134 and *passim*: chain was held in the naval stores but apparently only to construct defensive booms, *cf.* 'thare the false mene fletyde and one flode lengede / with chefe chaynes of chare chokkode to-gedyres': *Morte Arthure* lines 3602–3.

in a collision dispute involving *le Antony* of London, carrying merchandise from Prussia, but there is no other information. None of these cases confirms or denies the existence of a 'rule of the road' but the fact that litigation had been instigated, even as trespass, suggests that there was some regulation for the avoidance of collision. As discussed in chapter 1, pleas of merchants and sailors were tried in the Bristol courts before 1241 and the city custumal specified that actions 'between merchants and ships ... or between ships and ships ... whether burgers or aliens' could be heard according to the laws and counsels of the town. The phrase 'ships and ships' might well mean that collisions, or the results of collisions, were considered in court, but that can only be conjecture. As further indirect evidence of there being a recognised 'rule of the road', a phrase from the fifteenth-century Sandwich custumal indicates rather more positively that collisions at sea could be actionable, albeit in a port town rather than an admiral's court, 'quod navis aliqua alteri navi fecerit dampnum in aqua'. The paucity and imprecision of the evidence indicate that incidents at sea leading to damage, apart from acts of violence, were not sufficiently frequent in the fourteenth and fifteenth centuries to require a legally recognised rule of the road.[19]

Meteorology

Weather forecasting in north-west Europe requires an ability to foresee and assess incoming atmospheric low- and high-pressure areas. To do that without instruments, the medieval mariner could only interpret cloud formation, feel the temperature and humidity of the air, assess the size and direction of waves, note the strength and direction of the wind and observe the behaviour of insects and animals. He instinctively and continually collected and analysed this information and, in the light of his experience and with folkloric, and often faulty, meteorology, made short-term forecasts. However reliable his methods may have been, any decision to sail had, by maritime law, to be confirmed by his crew and it is likely that any sail reduction or increase also had to be discussed on board. If the shipmaster sailed on his own initiative and against the opinion of the crew, then he became personally responsible for any damage or loss to the ship and her cargo.[20]

The Coriolis effect, and high equatorial and low Arctic temperatures, ensure that north-west Europe, and particularly the British Isles, are subject to a series of meteorological depressions progressing west to east across the north Atlantic. These depressions and their associated fronts bring warm, wet south-westerly

---

[19] PRO C1/3/30, of unknown date. *CLB*, I, no. 54, p. 27, II, no. 42, pp. 158–9. Marsden, *Select Pleas*, pp. lxix and 90–1. *CPR*, 1436–41, p. 94. Bateson, *Customs*, 2, p. 193.
[20] Appendix 1, *Oleron*, article 2.

and westerly winds while the occasional anticyclone interrupts the sequence with cold, dry north and north-easterly winds. During the Medieval Warm Period (c.1000–c.1250) the path of the depressions may have been further north than today, while early in the fourteenth century the evidence of poor crops in northern Europe suggests a mean path of the depressions further to the south. Significantly higher salt deposition found in the layers of the Greenland ice cap laid down after c.1410 points to intensification of atmospheric circulation – significantly stronger winds have persisted from that time (the onset of the Little Ice Age with cold, dry windy conditions) until the present day. However, since the driving forces of the North Atlantic weather in the Middle Ages were generally as today, although at varying latitudes and with differing wind speeds, basic meteorology may safely be discussed with reference to today's conditions.[21]

The approach of weather fronts is heralded by clouds, and their formation, dissipation, shape, position, speed and direction of drift have always been recognised by mariners as important. Long parallel streaks of high cloud (now known as cirrus), particularly if they can be seen to be moving, warn of the formation of a vigorous depression with winds up to gale force from the west or north-west to be expected within a day. Winds blow anti-clockwise around a depression and clock-wise around an anticyclone so that the passage of lows and highs is accompanied by changes in wind direction. If the direction of the surface wind 'backs', i.e. moves anti-clockwise west–south–east, then a deterioration of the weather may be expected. Practically, and probably known for as long as men have sailed, if one stands with one's back to the surface wind (indicated by the movement of the lower, more solid looking cumulus clouds) and observes the upper wind (the movement of the high cirrus clouds) moving from left to right, the weather will deteriorate. Conversely, when the wind direction veers, i.e. rotates clockwise east–south–west, the upper clouds move from right to left, and conditions will improve. In the introduction to the storm passage in the alliterative poem *Patience*, a point is made of mentioning that the winds are Eurus and Aquilon which blow from the east or south-east and from the north or north-north-east respectively. They therefore appear to be backing from south-east to north-east, indicative of a depression passing to the south of the ship. The forecast was certainly correct, Jonah and the ship suffered at least a full gale. It is not known if seamen at that time realised that often a ship sailing on starboard tack, that is with the wind on

---

[21] K.J. Kreutz et al., 'Bipolar Changes in Atmospheric Circulation During the Little Ice Age', *Science* 277 (27 Aug. 1997), pp. 1294–6. Bolton, *Medieval English Economy*, p. 182. Changing weather patterns may have affected not only harvests, disease and mortality but also sailing routes, particularly if there was a change in the prevaling wind direction. Meteorological Office, *Meteorology for Mariners* (3rd edn, London, 1978), Part III, pp. 107–31.

the starboard side, can find improving weather conditions as she sails out of the low pressure zone.[22]

Folk weather lore is a miscellany of valid conclusions drawn from generations of acute observation and from a rag-bag of wishful, or pessimistic, thinking. Cause and effect were frequently confused; for example, a hazy moon often portends rain, not because of any lunar meteorological effect but because humidity in the atmosphere reduces its transparency. At least one late medieval manual of navigation includes statements blending fact and fantasy, translated from the French: 'If the four-day old moon is red, it means high winds; if the moon is "straight up and laid-back", it means high winds: even more if it happens on the fourth day.' Although there is no scientific reason why the fourth day of lunation should have any meteorological significance, a red or copper-coloured moon may augur high winds for the same reason as a red sky in the morning, a phenomenon discussed in the next paragraph. Similarly, a Breton proverb, 'Ring round the moon, sign of rain', describes the symptons of a depression with an associated warm front marked by a procession of cloud. The phenomena move in this order: cirrus > cirrostratus (when the moon is seen to have a halo) > altostratus > nimbostratus and strato-cumulus with rain and wind from south-west to south becoming south to south-east, and strengthening within a day; in short, bad news. A maritime proverb from Picardy repeats the warning explicitly and specifically to the sailor: 'Ring round the moon, sailor, climb to the hounds [of the mast, to shorten sail].' The appearance of the moon in these folkloric previsions is, of course, symptomatic of existing atmospheric conditions, not the cause of them.[23]

Folkloric meteorology giving correct information was generally based, without understanding, on observations of the effect of the serial movement of depressions across northern Europe. There are, and were, many examples of the 'Red sky at night, shepherds' [or sailors'] delight, Red sky in the morning, shepherds' [or sailors'] warning' school. An early surviving example of this genre may be seen in Wyclif's St Matthew's Gospel of c.1395. Similarly, again from the French 'When the sun rises and there are some red clouds in front of it, and none of those clouds disperse towards the north or south, it means wind and heavy rain'; and 'If at the setting of the sun its face looks white, it means a storm during the night and it will be cold and it will blow.' A red sky in the evening, caused by the reflection of the sun's rays (which always appear to be red at sunset because of refraction) from the upper cloud layer following a receding cold or occluded front, indicates that there are no low-level clouds to the west and therefore no immediate threat

---

[22] Andrew, *Pearl*, 'Patience', lines 133–4. The poet's vocabulary and knowledge suggest a maritime background.
[23] Nicolai, *L'Art de navigver*, p. 19: Pierre de Medine suggested that this folk meteorology existed prior to Pliny's *Natural History*, book 18, chapter 45. Albert Simon, ed., *Les Dictons météorologiques de nos campagnes* (Delarge, 1978), 'Bretagne' and 'Picardy'. Lunar meteorological (and medical) myths persists to this day.

of an incoming depression with, probably, a clear night and falling temperatures. A red sky in the morning is the reverse of that situation; the sun is 'downwind' and the red refracted rays shining over a clear horizon are reflected from the face of an approaching warm front, announcing the advance of another depression. Of interest to the early wine shippers was a Gascon proverb based simply on local observation: 'Bordeaux clear, mountain hidden – the weather is stable'. Lore based on false premises survived if it was thought often enough to be valid; the prognostication for St Swithin's Day, for example, was established by the twelfth century but merely reflects the chances of a wet or dry English summer. Proverbs may survive by ambiguity, for example a Breton *dicton* warns that 'Wind during the day doubles at night, wind in the evening will drop during the day'; if that is simply a statement of the time required for a depression to pass, it is acceptable but if it refers to the diurnal effect, it would be more accurate to say that the 'wind during the day will be calm in the evening'. Also ambiguous because it does not define the direction of the horizon or the time of day is another Gascon proverb, 'Red horizon, sign of wind or rain'.[24]

Mariners have always recognised the significance of changes in animal behaviour: swallows fly high before the arrival of good weather (because they are chasing insects rising in the low humidity), and cattle and horses become restless before the onset of a thunderstorm (because atmospheric static electricity passes to earth through their hair). Similar gifts of prognostication have been attributed to bees, frogs, porpoises, seabirds and fish and natural hygrometers, such as wet seaweed and soggy biscuits, give warnings of high humidity. There are many such observed phenomena and associated conclusions collected over generations in seafaring regions from which the medieval seaman derived his weather forecast.

Many ships were lost after encountering weather beyond their capabilities. Fleet losses, as opposed to individual disasters, almost certainly occurred when the weather pattern was deceptive or fast changing and caused a collective misprognostication. Most ships were not overcome by the weather however; the recurring names in port customs accounts over periods of years indicate that most survived to continue trading. Their longevity may be attributed to the shipmasters' caution rather than their meteorological acumen; when they had any doubt about the strength or direction of the wind – and acting under the scrutiny of their crews – they did not set out.[25]

---

[24] Matthew, xvi, 2: 'The eeuenynge maad, ye seien, It shal be cleer, for the heuene is lijk to reed; and the morwe, To day tempest, for heuen shyneth heuy, or sorwful'. Nicolai, *L'Art de navigver*, pp. 18–19. Simon, *Dictons*, 'Bretagne', 'Gascogne' and 'Picardy'.
[25] Some ships in the Exeter customs accounts sailed for ten years or more, mostly on the Bordeaux run. Harding, 'Port of London', pp. 269–70: 16 shipmasters working from London in 1325–6 were still working in 1332 including two from 1312–13. Appendix 1, *Oleron*, article 2.

Pilots

Pace Chaucer's claim for his Shipman to know 'alle the havenes / as they were / Fro Gotland to Fynystere / And every cryke in Britaigne and in Spayne', it is unlikely that shipmasters were able to navigate over the whole of the North Sea, Baltic and eastern Atlantic coasts, entering any harbour they wished, without help. Without an accurate compass, charts and sailing directions, each could be confident only on the routes he knew well. As late as 1537, when navigational aids were more freely available, an Admiralty inquisition investigating the skills of the 'sayling men' in the east coast ports of England found that out of 140 men, 15 could navigate to Iceland, five to France, Bayonne and Zealand and a further 14 could handle coastal work – evidence of a high degree of specialisation.[26]

Pilots had to be taken on board, therefore, for routes and harbours not well known to the shipmaster, the costs of whom, according to *Oleron*, were to be borne by the ship for deep-sea pilotage and by the shipping merchants for local pilotage. To that rule the *Coutumier* adds a rider that when the ship has her full complement of crew and a sea pilot, any further mariners or pilots required by the merchants are to be on their account. In *Queenborough*, the relevant article is equivocal, the jurors saying that they knew of no better advice than that in *Oleron* but not defining whether they referred to responsibility *of* or *for* the pilots. What constituted local pilotage has been extracted with reasonable certainty from the confused text of *Oleron*:

> after the island of Batz on ships bound for Breton ports (presumably ships from the north and east);
> after Guernsey on ships bound for Normandy or England (presumably for ships from the west and south);
> after Calais on ships bound for Flanders (presumably for ships from the west);
> after Yarmouth on ships bound for north-east England and Scotland (presumably for ships from the south).

The question of who paid the pilots is discussed in chapter 4, pp. 89–90. The responsibility of a pilot was to conduct the ship from where he had been picked up, perhaps at the entrance to a harbour, to wherever had been stipulated. *Oleron* is particulary precise in the pilot's job description: 'And the pilot has done his duty well when he has guided the ship to safety up to the berth because up to there was where he was to guide her'. The translation of the word berth (*fourme*) is discussed in Appendix 1.[27]

---

[26] Burwash, *Medieval Shiping*, p. 28.
[27] Appendix 1, *Oleron*, article 13 and 24. Appendix 2, *Queenborough*, article 16. Appendix 3, *Coutumier*, chapters 88 and 95. Timothy J. Runyan, 'The Relationship of Northern and Southern

On sanctions against unsatisfactory pilots, *Queenborough*, largely similar to *Oleron*, deals with unskilled pilots whose actions have led to loss or death, but rules that an admiral's inquiry should be held, a more equitable rule than the summary punishment by execution advocated by *Customs*. Litigation against pilots in the fourteenth and fifteenth centuries appears to have been unusual and sporadic – or not recorded. John of Colchester, 'lodmannus' (pilot) found himself incarcerated in Dublin castle in 1307 because he maliciously and traitorously guided a ship upon Lambeye, and another anonymous pilot of Margate, hired by merchant shippers for the local pilotage to London of the *S. Juan* of Bilbao with 80 tuns of white wine, lost her off the Isle of Sheppey in the 1360s; his fate is not recorded.[28]

The necessity of a pilot on a route unknown to the shipmaster, is demonstrated by several incidents. In 1387, a shipmaster refused to sail around the North Foreland without a pilot so the Gascon merchants on board, who were freighting wine from Southampton to Sandwich, agreed to hire one. Pilotage around the North Foreland as defined in *Oleron* was 'petty', or local, and was therefore correctly a charge on the merchants, which they accepted. As it happened, the pilot defaulted and the merchants, anxious to sell their wine quickly, ordered the ship's helmsman to take the ship himself. Unfortunately he ran the ship aground off Seaford whereupon the merchants seized the shipmaster's goods in retribution, perhaps as a pre-emptive measure, and the shipmaster had to sue to recover his ship and belongings, with an unknown result. It is clear that the failure of a shipmaster to hire a deep-sea pilot could be seen as negligence. A ship carrying a group of Irish merchants shipping goods from Dublin to Flanders came to grief off Plymouth in 1382 for lack of 'good ruling' and by the negligence of the shipmaster, because no pilot had been taken on board. The merchants had expected that at least the south coast of England would be known by a competent English shipmaster and had not insisted on a pilot at the beginning of the voyage. A change of route could require a change of pilot: in 1467 the merchants on board the *Trinity* of Southampton, with a Bristol pilot aboard, set out for Iceland but were held up for four weeks by bad weather in the Scilly Isles. They changed their plans and took on a pilot in Mount's Bay to go to Ireland. Similarly, in 1387, three Hansa merchants in a German ship on passage from La Rochelle to Ireland, by lack of skill of the 'lodesman', dared not steer the ship on the high seas and so went to Falmouth to arrange a pilot who knew Irish waters; unfortunately they were attacked and robbed while doing so. In some areas, particularly for estuarine entrances to up-

---

Seafaring Traditions in Late Medieval Europe', in C. Villain-Gandossi, S. Busutil and P. Adams, eds, *Medieval Ships and the Birth of Technological Societies*, vol. 2, *The Mediterranean Area and European Integration* (Malta, 1991), p. 201.
[28] Appendix 1, *Oleron*, article 24. Appendix 2, *Queenborough*, article 47. Twiss, *Black Book*, III, pp. 428–37. *Customs*, chapter ccv: 'perdre lo cap encontinent sens tot remey' but also suggests a gratuity for the pilot. O'Neill, *Merchants and Mariners*, p. 116, citing PROI, 1A/53/27, fo. 213. CPR, 1361–1364, p. 151. *Das Seebuch*, MS B, fo. 19r.

river ports, pilots had to be taken obligatorily. An example from the *Seebuch* prior to a passage up the River Gualdiquivir to Seville reads: 'one may anchor in 6 fathoms and then by law the pilot comes on board.' Unfortunately there is insufficient evidence to establish the general practice in the fourteenth and fifteenth centuries.[29]

Little is known of the men who worked as pilots. Deep-sea pilots presumably had experience of the passages for which they offered their services implying that they were either shipmasters currently without ships of their own, or men who had retired from a full-time life at sea to take up casual work. One would expect local pilots to have been experienced shipmasters who wanted to work closer to home and their small-holding, but from the introductory description in *Oleron*, 'un bacheler est lodman dune nef', they appear to have been young men rather than old sea-dogs.[30]

The forerunner of the Trinity House Corporation of Deptford, the Guild of the Holy Trinity, is believed to have been established in the twelfth century with the aim of caring for distressed mariners and their families and, significantly, to assist in pilotage, teach navigation and provide seamarks. Pilotage on the Thames was unsatisfactory however, as in 1513 mercantile and naval shipmasters petitioned the king to incorporate the guild in order to regulate it. Young men without experience, they claimed, were imperilling lives and ships, making no effort to learn the art of pilotage, depriving men retired from the sea of work, and allowing foreigners to learn the secrets of the approaches to the Port of London. Their complaint indicates that even local pilotage was considered to be work for retired shipmasters and that younger men with less experience had rather taken over. Earlier, but less certainly, the Trinity Guild of Kingston-upon-Hull, founded in 1369, was largely devoted to religious observances and charitable work amongst seafaring folk but its full name, according to Naish, was 'The Guild or Fraternity of Masters, Pilots and Seamen of the Trinity House' suggesting that in the mid-fourteenth century, Humber pilots belonged to a recognised branch of the maritime profession.[31]

Conclusion

The introduction in the early fifteenth century of new ship design and construction methods, and the distribution of an increased sail area over several masts,

---

[29] PRO C1/3/4: Martin van Mere, shipmaster of the *Marieknyght* sued the shipping merchants for the loss of his ship. CCR, 1381–1385, p. 72. Burwash, *Merchant Shipping*, p. 28 from C1/43/275–8: John Richeman, London fishmonger, sued the widow of John Payn, the quondam shipmaster and Edmund Kervile, grocer, who may have been the widow's second husband, for taking the ship to Cork. It is curious that a Bristol pilot did not know Irish waters. CCR, 1385–1389, p. 364.
[30] Appendix 1, *Oleron*, articles 13 and 24. Appendix 3, *Coutumier*, chapter 88.
[31] Harris, *Trinity House*, p. 19 and *passim*. Naish, *Seamarks*, pp. 41–2.

improved substantially the performance of late medieval ships. The basic tenets of seamanship have remained the same until today, although with the more resilient materials now used for the sails, rigging, hull and mast, mistakes are more easily forgiven. The most obvious difference between square-rigged ships then and now is in their windward performance; a fifteenth-century ship could achieve little better than a right angle to the wind whereas a modern ship can sail within four points of the wind. This difference restricted the options open to the shipmaster in a haven or picking his way through a narrow channel, but fundamental aspects of seamanship, such as preparing for sea, anchoring and recovering a trapped anchor, presented the same problems as today. There appear to have been no rules for the avoidance of collision at sea but behaviour in anchorages, particularly where there was a drying-out beach, was meticulously defined. Meteorology enjoyed no advances and would continue to be empirical and mythic until the introduction of thermometers, hygrometers and barometers three centuries later.

Conclusion

Little is known of the personal lives, background or training of English medieval shipmasters; it has to be assumed that they went to sea as ordinary seamen, possibly with familial connections, and learned the trade 'on the job'. There was no system of apprenticeship and, in the fourteenth century, no guild to control their qualifications. Of their professional lives, once they had their own ship, rather more is known from records of their appearances in court, charter-parties and other surviving documents.

Having gained sufficient experience at sea, an ambitious seaman looking to be a shipmaster, had four options: to persuade a shipowner to take him on as a waged employee, to enter a shipowning partnership with merchants or financiers, to charter a ship on his own account, or to buy his own ship. Each option offered advantages and disadvantages, each had its own modus operandi, and in each the shipmaster's position varied under the several available codes of law.

During the period under examination, the differing views on commerce and on the master/servant relationship in common and merchant law, and the competition for business between their courts and the admiralty courts, led to considerable confusion. Although common law was absorbing from the law merchant the concepts of trust, service contract and partnership, there was always some doubt about which law would offer a shipmaster a more sympathetic hearing in cases concerned with a disruptive or non-cooperative partnership, or any commercial dispute.

Having, in some way, acquired a ship and found sufficient cargo to justify the voyage at profitable freight rates, the shipmaster was faced with a considerable amount of bureaucracy. His contract with the shipping merchants was in the form of a charter-party; this could be quite straightforward, even formulaic, but it could also be complex, with the merchant shippers demanding a flexibility of route, an impossible timetable, a mixture of currencies, and a variety of other clauses, all to be negotiated. With his charter-party, the shipmaster then had to arrange credit, without incurring accusations of usury, to fit out and victual the ship and to pay his crew for the outward voyage. He also had to agree with the crew how they were to be paid for the homeward voyage, in cash or by an allotment of cargo space for their own endeavours.

The shipmaster's relationships with the merchant shippers travelling with their cargoes, and with his crew, were largely subject to protocols laid down in two codifications of maritime law. These were the *Lex d'Oleron* and the *Inquisition of Queenborough*, both of which are records of legal decisions, establishing rules for, *inter alia*, jettison, general average, delays incurred by the merchants or the shipmaster, damage to cargo, anchoring discipline in havens, and other potentially contentious issues. Further, relating to the crew, the two codes laid down rules for the maintenance of discipline, a scale of punishment, payments, and the care of the sick and wounded.

Litigation following infraction of any part of maritime law should, ideally, have been heard before a court specialising in such matters. Throughout the fourteenth century, attempts were made to set up admiralty courts to deal with all maritime misdeeds, except felonies, but after a brief flowering towards the end of the century, the courts suffered from the effects of personal greed and increasing competition from common law courts, and went into decline. By mid-fifteenth century, they were virtually impotent and of little importance.

During the period under examination, the art of navigation advanced to become a science, with the introduction of the magnetic compass and the hour-glass. Before they had access to those instruments, navigators kept close to the coast, relying on landmarks to fix their position, the sun or *Polaris* to indicate north, and a lead-line to warn of shallows and to locate suitable places to anchor. Magnetic compasses considerably improved the efficiency and safety of shipping and contributed to the growth of the industry at the expense of road transport. Tidal times were recorded by reference to compass bearings on the lunar analogue clock and this, together with the hour-glass, meant that shipmasters could take advantage of favourable tides in channels and in havens when planning their passages.

Unlike horticulture, the techniques of medieval seamanship were not recorded in any surviving instruction manual. They can, however, be traced from information in contemporary literature, including alliterative poetry, which is characterised by accurate descriptive detail, from contemporary illustrations, and from information in the surviving sailing directions. From these sources, cargo handling, preparing for departure, sailing, reducing and augmenting sail, and anchoring have all been reconstructed.

The introduction of written sailing directions, with details of hazards, havens and tidal ephemera along trading routes, was a considerable step forward for literate shipmasters, both as *aides memoires* for local passages and also as an introduction to areas new to the shipmaster. Copies of a Low Middle German *Seebuch* and a Middle English rutter have both survived from the mid-fifteenth century with much of the material in them being at least a century older. Analyses of their contents indicate that navigational and ship-handling techniques were broadly similar for Hansa and English seamen.

This book has examined the shipmaster's craft; the legal and commercial background to his work, his options in shipowning and partnership, his responsibilities as a manager ashore and afloat, his knowledge of navigation and meteorology, and his seamanship. He had to know the law, on- and off-shore, and when to disregard it, how to read the weather and calculate his course, and memorise an atlas of tidal streams as well as tables of astronomical ephemera. He also had to remember the intricacies of harbour entrances, distances and directions between way-points and unseen hazards on his route.

Given the ever-present possibilities of disaster, commercial or maritime, the successful shipmaster had to be physically tough, courageous, commercially astute, and steady and resourceful in crisis; no doubt, caution and robust 'fail-safe' margins were essential ingredients of his commercial transactions and of his navigation. There is no way of knowing how many met that magisterial paradigm, but the evidence of the number of shipmasters who sailed the same ship for years, apparently without catastrophe, indicates that survival was not uncommon. The working life of a medieval shipmaster was difficult and dangerous, but a homeward passage before the wind, across the Bay of Biscay, with the sun on his back, a hold full of wine and not another sail in sight, surely compensated him for all the complexities and hazards of his profession.

APPENDIX 1

Transcription and translation of the MS Liber Horn *copy of the* Lex d'Oleron

The history and significance of the *Lex d'Oleron* have been discussed in chapter 1. This transcription and translation of the MS *Liber Horn* [LH] copy of the *Lex* has been prepared to correct certain errors in existing translations and to clarify the original intentions of the law-makers.[1] The first folio of the *Lex* from the *Liber Horn* MS is shown in Figure 1.

Transcription

Corrections of scribal errors and omissions have been made where grammar and / or sense indicate and where the evidence of error is sufficiently strong. Amendments have been made only after reference to other manuscripts from which textual corrections have occasionally been borrowed; all amendments have been enclosed in square brackets [ ] and noted in footnotes. The articles have been numbered in upper case roman, and punctuation has been added as sparingly as possible. All place names have been capitalised initially, abbreviations have been silently expanded and the marks / and // have been inserted at manuscript line and folio endings respectively.

[lex Oleroun][2]
[leges maris vocatae Oliron
Memorandum quod Insula de Olirun sita est in mari Austrino inter Cornubiam et Aquitanium. Et est Marchia inter Aquitanium et Peyto et continet predicta

---

[1] MS *Liber Horn*, folios 355v–360r, CLRO, The Guildhall, London [MS L]; Other manuscripts to which reference is made are those in Twiss, *Black Book*, I, pp. 88–131 including MS Bodley 462, Bodleian Library, Oxford [MS B]; MS Whitehall [MS W]; MS *Liber Memorandum*, CLRO, Guildhall, London [MS LM]; MS Rawlinson B356, Bodleian Libary, Oxford [MS R]; MS Selden B27, Bodleian Library, Oxford [MS S]; MS Cotton Vespasian B XXII, British Library, London [MS V]. Further manuscripts cited in Karl-Friedrich Krieger,ed., *Ursprung und Wurzeln de Rôles D'Oléron*, Quellen und Darstellungen zur Hansischen Geschichte, Neue Folge /Bande XV (Cologne and Vienna, 1970) are: MS Liber Rubeus, City of Bristol Archives, Bristol [MS LR] and MS 1386 Troyes, Bibliothèque de Troyes [MS T]. The texts of MSS LH, LM, LR and R are essentially the same and together with MS B are fourteenth century, as is MS T, a Norman version of the Laws, the 'Coustume de Normandie'. MSS S and V are fifteenth century and contain 35 articles.
[2] This (fo. 355v), and most of the folios which follow, are headed *lex Oleroun* or simply *Oleroun*.

APPENDIX 1

insula in longitudine unam dietam et in latitudine tertiam. Et habet in Austro civitatem vocatam Zanctonas ubi sanctus Eutropius requiescit ab ea distantem per.xij. miliria passuum et habet in Euro – est suz est – la Rochele].[3]

I   Ceo est la copie de la chartre Doliroun des iugemenz / de la meer. Primerement lem fet un home mestre dune / neef. La neef est a deus homes ou a treis. La neef se /npart de pays dount ele est et vient a Burdeaux ou a la / Rochele ou ailours et se frette a aler en pais estraunge. / Le mestre ne poet pas vendre la nef si il nad comaun /dment ou procuracioun des seignurs; mes si il ad mestier / de despenses il pout bien mettre ascun des apparailes en ga /ge par counseil de compaignouns de la nef. Et ceo est / le iugement en ceo cas./

II   Une nef est en une havene et demoere pur attendre soun / temps et quant vient a soun partir le mestre deit prendre / counseil oue ses compaignouns et lour dire, seignurs, vous / avez cest temps; ascun i auera qi dirra, le temps nest pas / bon et ascuns qi dirrount le temps est bel et bon; le mestre / est tenuz de ceo acorder oue les plus des compaignouns. / Et sil fet autrement, le mestre est tenuz a rendre la nef / et les darrees si il semperdount. Et cest le iugement en ceo cas./

III   Une nef sempert en alcun teres ou en quel leu qe ceo soit. / Les mariners sount tenu a sauver le plus kil purrount / et sil aident, le mestre est tenu a engager sil nad deniers / de ceo qil sauverount et les remener a leur teres et sil / ni aydent il nest tenuz de riens lour bailer ne de rien les / purveier, ayns perdent lur lowers quant la nef est perdue. / Et le mestre nad nul poer de vendre aparailes de la nef / sil nad comaundement ou procuracioun de seignurs mes les / deit mettre en sauve garde jesqes al taunt qil sache lur / volunte. Et si doit fere a plus loialment qil purra. Et si le / feseit altrement il est tenu damender, sil ad de quei. / Et cest le iugement en ceo cas./

IV   Une nef se part de Burdeux ou aileurs; il avient ascune foiz / qele sempire lem sauve le plus qe lem peut des vins et des / autres darrees; les marchaunz [et le mestre][4] sount en graunt debat et demaundent //[5] les marchaunz de mestre aver lour [darrees],[6] il les deyvent / bien aver paiaunt lur fret de taunt come la nef ad fet / de veyage, sil plest al mestre. Et si le mestre voet, il / poet bien adubber sa nef sil est en cas kil la puisse / adubber prestement. Et si noun, il poet lower un autre / nef et fere la veiage et auera le mestre soun fret de taunt / cum il auera des darres sauves par alcune manere. Et cest le / iugement en ceo cas.

V   Une nef se part de acun port charge ou voyde et aryve / en alcun port et les mariners ne deyvent pas issir hors / saunz conge de mestre, kar si la nef senperdoit

---

[3]   The Latin text has been written in the margin of MS LH by a later hand. The same gloss occurs in MS LM.
[4]   *et le mestre* has been added as superscript to MS LH in a later hand; it is necessary for the sense.
[5]   Folio 356r begins here.
[6]   *deniers* in MS LH is *darrees* in MSS LR and T: Krieger, *Oleron*, p. 126, footnote 583. *Darrees* is better than *deniers* in the context and therefore has been preferred.

par acun / aventure a dunc il serrount tenuz a amender [sils ont de qei; mais si la nef estoit en lieu ou ele se fut amarree de quatre amarrees il purront bien issir hors][7] et revenir / par temps a lour nef. Et cest le iugement en ceo cas./

VI   Mariners se lowent ou lour mestre et acuns deux sen issent[8] / saunz conge hors et senyverent et fount contekes et en y / a acuns qi sount naufres; le mestre nest pas tenuz a / eux fere garir ne a les purveier de rien eins les poet ben / mettre hors et lower un autre en lieu de li et sil couste plus / qe celuy, il [le mariner][9] le deit paier si le mestre troeve rien de soen;/ mes si [le mestre][10] lenvoye en acune service de la nef par soun comaun /dement et sil se blessat ou le naverat, il deit estre garries / et sauves sus le coustes de la nef. Et cest le iugement en ceo cas./

VII   Il avient qe maladie enprent a un des compaignouns ou a / deus ou a troys [et][11] il ne poet pas taunz estre malades en / la nef [en fesanz lur service de la nef].[12] Li mestre li doit mettre hors et li quere un hostiel / et li bailer crescet ou chaundeile et li bailer un de ses / valles de la nef pur li garder ou lower une femme qe / prenge garde a li. Et li deit purveier de tele viaunde / cum len use en la nef cest asaver de taunt come il prist en saunte //[13] et rien plus, si ne li plest. Et sil voet aver viaundes plus deli /ciouses le mestre nest pas tenuz a li quere, sil ne soit a ses des /penses. La nef ne deit pas demorer pur li einz se deit aler. / Et sil garist, il deit avoier[14] soun lower tot a lonc. Et / sil moert, sa femme ou ses prives deyvent avoier / pur li. Et cest le iugement en ceo cas./

VIII[15]   Une nef charge a Burdeux ou aillours et avent chose / qe torment la prent en la mer et qe il ne poent eschaper saunz / gettre darres et des vins. Le mestre est tenu de dire as mar /chaunz, seignurs, nous ne pouns eschaper saunz gettre des vins / ou des darres; les marchauns si en.j. a[16] respoundrent / lour volunte et greent bien le getisoun, par aventure les / resouns del mestre sount plus cleres.

---

[7]   The text within the brackets has been added in the margin of MS LH in a later hand, either as an amendment to the original article or as the correction of a scribal omission.
[8]   Twiss, *Black Book* I, p. 94: MS W has *yssent hors de la nef*; which makes clear the sense of going ashore.
[9]   *il* in MS LH has been corrected to *le mariner* by a later hand; the correction improves the reading.
[10]   *le mestre* has been added to MS LH, presumably to improve the reading.
[11]   *et* has been added as superscript to MS LH in a later hand; it appears to be intended as nothing more than conjunctival punctuation.
[12]   The words within the brackets have been added as superscript to MS LH in a later hand; they appear also in MSS R and T: Krieger, *Oleron*, p. 128, footnote 587.
[13]   Folio 356v begins here.
[14]   Twiss, *Black Book*, I, p. 96: MS LH has the verb *avoier* in this and the following sentence but MS W has *avoir*; neither Twiss nor Krieger remark on the alternative.
[15]   In the margin of MS LH, at the beginning of this article, the word *Jettison* is written as a subtitle, the only article to be so marked.
[16]   *si en.j.* in MS LH is followed by the *a* which is slightly larger than the surrounding script and is written in a space which is longer than normal. Krieger, *Oleron*, p. 129, footnote 589: without mentioning the additional space, believes that the *a* has been added by a later hand but, because the form of the letter *a* is very similar to those around it, and there is what appears to

APPENDIX 1

Et sil ne greent / le mestre ne deit pas lesser pur ceo kil ne gette taunt qil / verra qe bien soit, juraunt le tiers de ses compaignouns / sur les seinz evangelies quant il serra venuz a sauvete al / tere kil ne fesoit mes pur sauver les corps et la nef et les / darres et les vins. Cels qi serrount gete hors deyvent / estre aprisagez a foer de ceux qi serrount venuz a sauve /te et serrount venduz et partis livere a livere entre les mar /chaunz. Et y doit le mestre partir a countre la nef ou / soun fret a soun chois pur estorer le damage. Les ma /riners deyvent aver [chescun][17] un tonel fraunk et lautre deyvent / partir au get solonc qe [le] auera,[18] si defent en la meer / cum un homme. Et sil ne defent il ne auera riens de / fraunchise. Et en serra le mestre cru par soun serment. / Et cest le iugement en ceo cas./

IX Il avient qe le mestre dune nef coupe soun mast / par force del temps; il deit appeller les marchaunz et //[19] lour moustrer kil covient couper le mast pur sauver la nef et / les darres. Acune foiz avient qe len coupent cables et lessent / auncres pur sauver la nef et les darres, il deyvent estre countes / livere a livere come get. Et il deyvent partir les marchaunz / et paier saunz nul delai tot avaunt qe les darres serrount / mises hors de la nef. Et si la nef estoit en dur sege et le / mestre demorast pur lur debat et yl y eust corisoun le mes /tre ne doit partir. Eins si doit aver soun fret cum des autres / darres qi sount sauvez. Et cest le iugement en ceo cas./

X Un mestre dune nef vient a sauvete a sa descharge. Il / doit moustrer a marchaunz les cordes oue quei il [guidera].[20] / Et si il veit qil a amender, le mestre est tenuz a les amen /der; kar si le tonel se pert par defaute de [guide][21] ou de corda /ge, le mestre est tenuz al amender, luy et ses mariners. Et / il deyt partir le mestre pur taunt qil prent en gunyndage, / et deyt le gunyndage estre mis a restorer le damage pri /merement. Et le remenaunt deit estre parti entre eux. Mes / si cordes rumpent saunz ceo qil eut moustre as marchaunz, / il serreit tenu a rendre tut le damage. Mes si les mar /chaunz dient qe les cordes soient beles et bones et il rum /pent, chacun doit partir du damage, cest asaver les marchaunz / a ki les vins serrount taunt seulement. Et cest le / iugement en ceo cas./

XI Un [nef][22] charge a Burdeux ou ailours et leve sa veille pur ariver / ses vins et senpart et nafient pas le mestre et les mariners lur / boucle[23] sicum il dussunt et les prent mal temps en la meer / en tiele manere qe la fuistaile de leyns enfoundre

---

have been an erasure under the .j. (which is itself too large and is similar in appearance to an *l*), it is probably unnecessary to doubt the *a*. Twiss, *Black Book*, I, p. 96: MS W has *sil en y a*.

[17] *chescun* has been added as superscript to MS LH bin a later hand; the addition removes an ambiguity.

[18] MS LH reads *solonc qe me auera* which is clearly an error.

[19] Folio 357r begins here.

[20] Although MS LH has *guidera*, the context suggests that *guindera* is intended. Twiss, *Black Book*, I, p. 100: MSS W, B and V have *guyndera* whereas MS R has *guidera*.

[21] As in the note above, the MS LH *guide* is probably an error for *guindeau*.

[22] *nef* has been added as superscript to MS LH in a later hand to correct a scribal omission.

[23] Twiss, *Black Book*, I, pp. 102–3 and footnote 2: in MS W, in place of *boucle* there is written

ou tonel / ou pipe. La nef vient a sauvete, les marchaunz dient qe / lur fuistaile ad les vins perduz. Le mestre dit qe noun fist. / Si le mestre poet jurer, li et ses troys compaignouns ou / quatre de ceux, qe les marchaunz eslirunt, qe les vins ne se / perdirent pas pur lur fuistaile come les marchaunz lur met /tent sus, il en deyvent estre quites et deliveres. Et sil / ne voilent jurir, il deyvent rendre as marchaunz lur da /mages, kar il sount tenuz a affier lour boucles et lour / elores bien et certeinement avant kil se deyvent partir / del lieu ou il se chargent. Et cest le iugement en ceo cas./

XII   Un mestre lowe ses mariners et les deit tenir en pees / et estre lur juge, sil i a nul, qi endamage lautre par quei il / met payn et vin a table.[24] Celi qi dementera lautre deit / paier.iiij.d. Et le mestre sil demente nul deit paier.viij.d. / Et sil il ia nul qi demente le mestre, il doit paier a taunt cum le mestre. / Et si ensi est qe le mestre enferge un de ses mariners il deit / attendre le primere colee cum de poin ou de paume, et sil le fiert / plus, il se doit defendre. Et si le mariner fert le mestre / primer, il doit perdre.c.s. ou les poins al chois de mariner.[25]/ Et cest le iugement en ceo cas./

XIII   Une nef frette a Burdeux ou a La Rochele ou aillours et vient / a sa descharge e sunt[26] chartre partie towage et petites lod /mannage sunt sus les marchaunz; {e la coste de Bretaigne / tous ceuz qe lem prent pus qe lem ad passe les de Batz ou / sunt petit lodmaunz. Et ceus de Normaundie et dEngleterre / puis qe lempasse Caleys. Et ceus dEscoce puis qe lem passe Ger /neseye. Et ceux de flaundres puis qe lem passe Caleys. Et / ceux dEscoce puis qe lem passe Gernemue}.[27] Et cest le iugement / en ceo cas./

XIV   Contek si fet en une nef entre le mestre et ses mariners. / Le mestre deit ouster la towaile devaunt ses mariners trois / foitz avaunt qe il les [comaunde][28]

---

boude, without comment from Twiss who notes that the word is *voille* in the Norman manuscript.
[24] The sentence appears to be corrupt or incomplete towards the end.
[25] *les poins* in MS LH should probably read *le poin*; see Krieger, *Oleron*, p. 134, footnote 597: the word is singular in both MSS R and T. Further, it is probable that the MS LH *mariner* should be the plural *mariners* as in MS T. The problem of grammatical number is discussed in the translation below.
[26] Krieger, *Oleron*, p. 135, footnote 598: in place of the MS LH *sunt*, MS T has *font*. Twiss, *Black Book*, I, pp. 104–5 and footnote 3: MS W omits *chartre partie* and MS R has 'descharges et sont partie charter'. The Catalan text reads 'è hay carta partida ... segunt la costumbre de la terra'.
[27] The text between brackets { } is clearly corrupt and, according to Krieger, *Oleron*, p. 135, footnote 600, is so in all the fourteenth-century English manuscripts. The passage in MS T reads, 'en la coste de bretaingne tous ceulz que len prent puis qe len a passe lille de bast ou leon sont petis lamens. Et ceulz de normendie ou dengleterre puis qe len a passe grenesy et ceulz de flandres puis que len a passe cales. Et ceulz descosse puis que len a passe Germenie.' Twiss, *Black Book* I, p. 105, footnote 4 and III, p. 19, footnote 2: The Breton manuscript reads *Bas*.
[28] *comaunde* has been added to MS LH as superscript by a later hand over the word *menge* which has been crossed out; *comaunde* offers a satisfactory reading.

APPENDIX 1

hors. Et [si][29] le mariner ofre a fe /re les amendes a la gard des mariners qi sount a la table //[30] et le mestre soit taunt cruel kil ne voile rien fere et le met / hors, le mariner se poet aler et seure la nef jeqes al deschar /ge et [doit][31] aver autresi bon lower com il venu dedeinz a / mendaunt la forfet a la gard de la table. Et si ensink / soit qe le mestre [neust][32] autresi bon mariner cum li en la nef, / et la perde par acun aventure, le mestre est tenu de rendre le / damage de la nef et de la marchaundise qil y serra sil / ad de quei. Et cest le iugement en ceo cas.

XV Une nef est en un cuvers amarre et hastant de sa / marree un autre nef crest en sa pees. La nef est ada /mage du coup qe lautre li doune. Et y a des vins enfoun /dres, dascuns le damage deit estre prisagez et parti moite / entre les deus nefs. Et les vins qi sount dedeinz les / .ij. nefs, deyvent estre partiz pur le damage entre les mar /chaunz. Le maistre de la nef, qe ad feru lautre, est tenuz / a jurir, li et ses mariners, kil ne firent pas de gre, et est re /soun pur quei cest iugement est fet, si [ency][33] est, qe une viele nef / se mist volunters en la voie a une meilure si ele touz / ses demages pur quider aver lautre nef; mes quant ele siet / qele doit partir la moite ele se voit volunters de la voie. / Et cest le iugement en ceo cas./

XVI Une nef ou.ij. ou plus sunt en une havene ou il i a / poi de ewe. Et a [secche][34] un des nefs et[35] est trop pres de lau /tre. Le mestre de cele nef deit dire as autres mariners, / seignurs, levez vostre auncre, kar ele est trop pres de nous et / purroit fere damage. Et eus ne la voilent lever, le mestre / pur li et ses compaignouns la vount lever et esloigner de li. //[36] Et si il tolent a lever [lancre][37] et lautre lur fet damage, il sunt / tenuz al amender tut alounc. Et si ensi estoit qil y eust mis / ancre saunz boye et il fount damage, il sount tenuz al amen /der tut alounc. Et sil sunt en une havene qe asecche il sunt tenuz / al maistre balinges [as][38] ancres qe ne parigent au plein. / Et cest le iugement en ceo cas./

XVII Les mariners de la costere de Bretaigne ne deivent aver / qe une quisine

---

[29] *si* has been added to MS LH as superscript by a later hand to correct a scribal omission.
[30] Folio 358r begins here.
[31] MS LH here has *tout* which does not fit in the context. Krieger, *Oleron*, p. 136, footnote 604: MS T has *doit*; which offers a sound reading.
[32] MS LH here has *ume* which has been corrected in superscript by a later hand to something illegible. Krieger, *Oleron*, p. 136, footnote 605 reads the word to be *mettre*; MS R has *neust* which allows a satisfactory reading.
[33] *ency* has been addedin a later hand to MS LH; it improves the reading.
[34] Twiss, *Black Book*, III, p. 22 has *secche* in place of MS LH *cecche*; but *cecche* is certainly the correct reading of the text, an opinion shared with Krieger, *Oleron*, p. 137. MSS W, B, R and V all have variations of *secche*.
[35] Either *et* is superfluous or a verb has been omitted after *des nefs*.
[36] Folio 358v begins here.
[37] MS LH reads *et lautre et lautre* which appears to be a scribal error, amended here to *lancre et lautre*. Krieger, *Oleron*, p. 138, footnote 608 omits one *et lautre* and reads the other as *lancre*, justifying this correction by comparison with MSS M and R, both of which have *lancre* once. The alternatives offer similar meanings.
[38] Krieger, *Oleron*, p. 138, footnote 608: in MS LH *et* has been corrected to *as*; MS R has *as*.

le jour par la resoun qil ount beverage en / alaunt et en venaunt. Et ceus de Normandie endeyvent / aver deux le jour par la resoun qe lour mestre ne lur baile / qe ewe al aler. Mes puis qe la nef est en la tere ou le vin / crest, les mariners deyvent avoir beverage et lur deit le ma /ystre quere. Et cest le iugement en ceo cas./

XVIII   Une nef arive a sa charge a Burdeux ou aillurs. Le mais / tre est tenuz dire a ses compaignouns, seignurs, frettere vous a marrees ou liweres a fret de la nef. Ils sount tenuz / a respundre le quel il frount. Et si il elysent al fret / de la nef, tiel fret cum la nef auera, il aueround. Et sil / voilent fretter par eux il deyvent fretter en tele manere / qe la nef ne soit demoraunte. Et si il aviegne qil ne tro / event fret le mestre nad nule [blame].[39] Et il doit le mestre mous / trer lour rives[40] et lur leire. Et il deit le mestre penser de lur / mareage chescun. Et si il voilent mettre tonel de ewe [et][41] soit / gette en la meer il doit estre counte pur vin ou pur autre dar / res, livere a livere, si les mariners se puissent defendre re / sounablement en la meer. Et si ensi est qe eux se freget / tent as marchaunz [tiele franchise comes les mariners avent, doit estre as marchaunz].[42] Et cest la custume en ceo cas.[43] //[44]

XIX   Une nef vient a descharge. Les mariners voilent aver lur lou / wers. Et il i a acuns qe ne ount lich ne arche leins. Le mestre / poet retenir de soun lower pur rendre la nef la, ou il la prist / sil ne doune bone caucioun pur furnir la veyage. Et tiel est / le iugement en cest cas./

XX   Le mestre dune nef lowe ses mariners de la vile dount la nef / est, les uns a mareage, les autres a deniers. Il avient qe la nef / ne peut trover fret a venir en ses parties. Et lur covient aler plus / loins. Ceux qi sunt a mareage la doyvent suire; mes ceux qi / sount a deniers le mestre est tenuz a lur crestre lour lowers / vewe par vewe et corps par corps par la resoun kil les avoit lowe a / termine lieu. Et si ele venoit plus pres qe le covenaunt fut / pris, il deyvent aver tut lu lower. Mes il deyvent aider a ren /dre la nef la ou eus la pristrent si le mestre [veut][45] a le aven /ture [de Dyeux].[46] Et cest le iugement en ceo cas./

---

[39] *blame* has been added as superscript in MS LH in a later hand to correct a scribal omission.
[40] Krieger, *Oleron*, p. 140, footnote 611: *rives* in MS LH is *rimes* in MS T, a reading preferred by Krieger in his translation, without explanation.
[41] *et* has been added as superscript in MS LH in a later hand to improve the reading.
[42] The text between brackets has been added to MS LH in a later hand either as the correction of a scribal omission or as an amendment to the article. It is an important extension of the sailors' franchise.
[43] This and the following article are the only two in which there is a variation in the ending.
[44] Folio 359r begins here.
[45] *vent* in MS LH has been corrected to *veut*; Krieger, *Oleron*, p. 141, footnote 617 cites MS R with *sy le mestre voet* and MS T *with se le mestre veult*. The reading requires *veut* and *vent* makes no sense.
[46] *dedaunz* in MS LH has been corrected here to *de Dyeux* as in MS LR; it is also *de daunz*

APPENDIX 1

XXI Il avient qe une nef est a Burdeux ou aillurs. De tel cusine / kil auera en la nef, les.ij. mariners poent enporter un mes; mes / taunt cum [dementrers][47] ils serrent trenchez en la nef. Et tel pain cum / il i auera, il endeivent aver solunc ceo qil porrrunt manger. Et / de beiverage endeyvent eux rien aver [et deyvent revenir][48] tut aprestement / si qe le mestre ne perde ses houres de la nef; kar si le mestre / les y perdoit et il y eut damage, il serrount tenuz al amen /der; ou si un des compaignouns se blessad par bosoygne de / ayde, il sount tenuz a fere garir et amender al compaignoun / et al mestre et a ceux de la table. Et cest le iugement en ceo cas./

XXII Un mestre frette sa nef a un marchaunt et est devise entre //[49] eux et mis un terme bonement deux[50] Et le marchaunt nel / tient pas, einz tient la nef et les mariners par lespace de.xv. / jours ou plus et acune foiz enpert le mestre soun temps et sa / messioun par defaute de marchaunt, le marchaunt est tenuz / al amender a le mestre. Et en cel amender qi serra fet / les mariners[51] i deyvent partir le quart et le mestre les / trois parties par la resoun qil troeve les coustes. Et cest le / iugement en ceo cas./

XXIII Un marchaunt frette une nef a la charge et la met / en chemin et entre cele nef en une port et demoret taunt / qe deniers lur faillent. Le mestre tient bien et poet / envoyer en soun pais pur quere del argent. Mes il ne / doit mie perdre temps kar sil fet il est tenuz al amender / as marchaunz tut lur damage kil aueround. Mes le / mestre poet bien prendre des vins as marchaunz et les / vendre pur aver soun estorement. Et quant la nef serra / arive a droite descharge, les vins qe le mestre auera / pris deyvent estre a foir mis qe les autres serrount / venduz, ne a greindre foir ne a menour. Et deit le mes /tre avoir soun fret de ceux vins cum il prendra des / autres. Et cest le iugement en ceo cas./

XXIV Un bacheler est lodman dune nef et est lowe del amener jeqes / au port ou lem la deit descharger. Il avient bien qen ceste port / a formez ou lem met les nefs pur descharger. Le mestre est tenu / pur purveier sa fourme, li et ses compaignouns, et y mettre bailig /nes kil prengent au pleyn ou qe la fourme soit

---

in MS R: Krieger, *Oleron*, p. 142, footnote 618, but *de Dieu* in MSS W, B and V: Twiss, *Black Book*, I, p. 114, fn. 27; a scribal error.

[47] *mes taunt cum* has been struck out of MS LH by a later hand and *dementrers* substituted. The latter was perhaps intended to correct an omission; the words struck out and the superscription have been retained. There is no reference to the superscription in MS LH by Twiss, but MS W has *mais dementrers quilz seront trenchez*; Twiss, *Black Book*, I, 116.

[48] The text between the brackets has been added as superscript in MS LH in a later hand, apparently to correct a scribal omission.

[49] Folio 359v begins here.

[50] In MS LH *deux* is written twice and a section of text has been omitted; the sense may be surmised.

[51] *le marchaunt* here in MS LH has been struck out and corrected to *les mariners*. Krieger, *Oleron*, p. 143, footnote 623: both MSS R and T have *mariners*; the sense demands *les mariners*.

ben balig /nee, qe les marchauns neient damage, kar si il vient dama /ge le mestre est tenuz al amender si il ne dient resoun pur //[52] quei le mestre soit abatu de sa resoun. Et le / lodman ad bien fet soun dever quant il ad amene / la nef a sauvete jeqes a la fourme, kar jeqes iloeqes la devoit / amener. En avaunt le fees [est][53] sus le mestre et sus ses com /paignouns. Et cest le iugement en ceo cas.

Translation and commentary[54]

When necessary to maintain intelligibility, the grammatical tense, voice, mood and number have been altered, not always with notice. Square brackets [ ] enclose words added for grammatical reasons and round bracket ( ) those added for clarification. Text within square brackets in the transcription has been translated without comment and the brackets have not been carried forward. Comparisons have been made with the English *Rutter of the Sea* [RS], and with Twiss's English and Krieger's German translation of MS LH.[55]

Article 1: This is the copy of the Oléron charter of the judgments of the sea. First a man is appointed master of the ship. The ship belongs to two men or to three. The ship leaves the country where she is and comes to Bordeaux or La Rochelle or elsewhere and is freighted to go to a foreign country. The shipmaster may not sell the ship if he does not have an order or authority from the owners; but if he has had necessary expenses he may pledge some of the equipment with the agreement of his companions on the ship. And that is the judgment in this case.

Comment: *Oleron* is concerned here with a shipmaster who is employed by, or is the managing partner of, the owning partnership, but see the *Coutumier*, chapters 63, 64, 83 and 87. That the shipmaster has to have the crew's approval before pledging the ship's equipment suggests either that to return home the crew would require a complete ship, or that this is a surviving element of the cooperative ventures of merchant entrepreneurs, see also *Oleron* articles 2, 14 and 18.

Article 2: A ship is in a harbour and stays to await her weather and when it comes to her departure the shipmaster must consult with his companions and say to them, 'Gentlemen, you have this weather'; there will be someone there who will say 'The weather is not good' and others who will say 'The weather

---

[52] Folio 360r begins here.
[53] The textual *et* has been corrected to *est* to make sense of the sentence.
[54] The dictionaries used are listed at the end of the Bibliography.
[55] In Twiss, *Black Book*, I, pp. 89–131 the 1536 *Rutter of the See* is printed on pages opposite a transcription of MS W although not a translation of that manuscript; it is, in fact, a translation of Norman and Breton versions of the *Lex*. The Twiss transcription and translation of MS LH are printed in his *Black Book*, III, pp. 4–33; Krieger, *Oleron*, pp. 123–145.

is fair and good'. The shipmaster has to agree on this with the majority of his companions. And if he does otherwise, the shipmaster has to replace the ship and the cargo if they are lost. And that is the judgment in this case.

Comment: Vestiges of cooperative ventures are again apparent. The 1497 Hamburg *Van Schipprechte* article IX stipulates that in bad weather the shipmaster 'avereyn to tragende myt dem meisten deele' ('had to heed the views of the majority').[56] Full replacement by the shipmaster of losses appears to have been modified later; MSS Bodley, Corpus Christi and Vespasian read 'si il ad de quay' ('if he had the wherewithal')

Article 3: A ship founders on some land or in any place that she may be. The sailors are obliged to save the most they can and if they help, the shipmaster has to pledge that which they saved, if he has no money, to get them back to their homeland; and if they did not help he is not responsible for any expenses nor any rations; also they lose their wages [from] when the ship is lost. And the shipmaster has no power to sell the equipment of the ship if he does not have an order or the authority of the owners but he must put it (the equipment) in safe keeping until he knows their wishes. And he must do that, the most loyally he can. And if he does it otherwise he has to pay compensation, if he has anything. And that is the judgment in this case.

Comment: The crew's insurance against stranding far from home. Even *in extremis* the employed shipmaster could not sell any part of the ship – an extension of *Oleron* article 1. The witholding of cash and rations to unenthusiastic sailors could be fatal for them.

Article 4: A ship leaves Bordeaux or elsewhere; at some point she founders; they save the most they can of the wine and other cargo. The merchants and the shipmaster have a serious dispute and the merchants ask the shipmaster for their cargoes. If the shipmaster agrees to that, then they may well have them, paying as much of their freight charge as the ship had sailed on the voyage. And if the shipmaster wants, then he can caulk the ship, if it is the case that he is able to caulk her quickly. And if not, he can hire another ship and complete the voyage and the shipmaster will have for his freight payment as much as he would have had for the cargo however it was saved. And that is the judgment in this case.

Comment: The shipmaster's entitlement to part or full freight reflects both parties' contractual obligations; there was no *force majeure* disclaimer in charter-parties; see chapter 3, p. 000. No mention is made of additional handling charges nor of penalties for delays, a rich field for potential litigation.

---

[56] Johannes Schildhauer, *Die Hansa* (Leipzig, 1988), p. 150.

Article 5: A ship leaves from any port, laden or empty, and arrives at another port. The sailors must not leave without permission from the shipmaster, for if the ship founders by some chance, they will have to pay compensation, if they have anything; but if the ship should be in a place where she has been tied up with four cables, then they can leave and return in time to their ship.[57] And that is the judgment in this case.

Comment: Securing alongside with breast line, stern line and two springs was, and is, standard practice. *Customs* makes no such concession and advocates withholding all rations from men on overnight leave. *Oleron* article 21 halves the rations and witholds wine for sailors ashore, unless they are on ship's business. *Customs* allows men to leave the ship for pilgrimage, to fulfil a vow, to be married, and for six days to arrange their own ventures.[58] The treatment of sailors who are hurt while ashore, with or without permission, is similar in *Customs* to this and subsequent *Oleron* articles.

Article 6: Sailors hire themselves to their shipmaster and [if] any two leave without permission and get drunk and make a disturbance and in it some are hurt; the shipmaster does not have to give them shelter nor supply them with anything; also he can then throw them off [the ship] and hire others in their place and if they (the latter) cost more than they (the former) did, then the sailors (the former) must pay it [the difference] if the shipmaster finds something of theirs. But if the shipmaster sent them on some service for the ship or by his command and if they are wounded or hurt they must be given shelter and saved at the expense of the ship. And that is the judgment in this case.

Comment: None necessary.

Article 7: Sickness as a result of service on the ship happens to take one of the companions or two or three; he cannot be so ill on the ship. The shipmaster must put him ashore and find for him lodgings and supply a lamp or candle for him and provide one of the ship's boys to look after him or hire a woman who will look after him. And he (the shipmaster) must supply such food as he (the sailor) would have on board the ship, that is, as much as he took in good health and nothing more if he (the shipmaster) does not wish it. And if he (the sailor) wants to have more delicious food, the shipmaster does not have to find it for him if it is not to be at his (the sailor's) expense. The ship need not wait for him but must go. And if he is being sheltered, he must waive his wages for all that time. And if he dies, his wife or his intimates must waive [the wages] for him. And that is the judgment in this case.

---

[57] Twiss, *Black Book*, I, p. 93: the RS version reads 'where it were ankered with two or three cables' although other manuscripts generally refer to *amaree de quatre amaree*. Twiss, *Black Book*, III, p. 9 translates MS LH *amaree* as 'moored'. Anchoring, mooring and tying alongside are not the same manoeuvres.

[58] Twiss, *Black Book*, III, pp. 196–7, *Customs*, chapters xci–xcii.

Comment: Twiss and Krieger both ignore the superscript clause 'en fesanz lur service de la nef', perhaps because it was written by a later hand. RS reads 'any mariner be taken with sekenesse in the ship doying service thereto belongyng.'[59] The translation of the last two sentences of the article presents some difficulty: if the verb is *avoyer* (= *avouer*), 'to acknowledge' or 'recognise as one's own', then the intention appears to be for the sailor or his heirs to accept that his wages will be discounted during his incapacity. If the verb is *aver* (= *avoir*), 'to have', then the intention is for the sailor to have the whole of his wages. *Avouer* is perhaps more likely than *avoir* and the discount is to follow him beyond the grave. RS agrees with the payment of wages less discount; Twiss disagrees, translating the sentence as: 'he ought to have his wages for the whole voyage'; Krieger also disagrees, translating it as: 'Und wenn er geheilt ist, soll er seinen vollen Lohn haben. Und wenn er stirbt, sollen seine Frau oder Angehörigen den Lohn für ihn haben' ('And when he is cured he should have his full wages. And when he dies, his wife or relatives should have his wages').[60] In the maritime law of Rome, from which, distantly, *Oleron* was derived, a discount for care ashore is clearly defined.[61] In balance, a deduction from the wages appears to be the intention.

Article 8: A ship loads in Bordeaux or elsewhere and something happens in a storm at sea which takes her and from which she is not able to escape without jettisoning cargo and wines. The shipmaster has to say to the merchants 'Sirs, we cannot escape without jettisoning some wine or cargo'. The merchants, if they are there, confirm their willingness and so agree with the jettison, if it happens that the shipmaster's reasons are sufficiently convincing. And if they do not agree, the shipmaster must not, because of that, desist from jettisoning as much as he feels necessary, a third of his companions[62] swearing on the holy Evangelists, when they have come safely to land, that it was done only to save the bodies and the ship and the cargo and the wines. That which was thrown overboard must be valued as that which was brought to safety and was sold and [the proceeds] divided pound for pound between the merchants. And the shipmaster must contribute the ship or his freight, at his choice, as his share in the account to repair the damage. The sailors must each have a tun free and the other[s] must contribute to the jettison according to how much they had, if, while at sea they had defended like men. And if they did not defend, they will have nothing of the distribution. And the shipmaster will be believed on his oath. And that is the judgment in this case.

Comment: Inclusion of a ship and her equipment in the contribution to average

---

[59] Twiss, *Black Book*, III, p. 11; Krieger, *Oleron*, p. 128 ; Twiss, *Black Book*, I, p. 95.
[60] Twiss, *Black Book*, III, p. 11; Krieger, *Oleron*, p. 129.
[61] Twiss, *Black Book*, II, p. 441, footnote 1: citing *Digest*, xix, tit. ii, p. 38.
[62] Twiss, *Black Book*, III, p. 13 translates the phrase as 'himself and three of his companions', which is clearly incorrect.

runs contrary to Edward I's **Letter Patent** of 25 May 1285,[63] see also *Coutumier* chapter 94, and discussion in chapter 5 of this book. This article, therefore, was apparently formulated earlier than 1285 and is not relevant to the present work. *Customs* details the valuation of jettisoned items, the repayment under the rules of average and the solemnities to be observed during the repayments. It also rules that the merchant owner of the goods should throw overboard the first item, with alternative arrangements in his absence, and gives the procedure for the mariners and merchants to testify under oath after jettison or damage.[64]

> **Article 9:** It happens that the master of a ship cuts her mast because of the force of the weather; he has to call the merchants and show them that it is advisable to cut the mast to save the ship and the cargo. And any time that the cables are cut and the anchors left to save the ship, it (the cost) must be calculated pound by pound like jettison. And the merchants must contribute and pay without any delay before the cargo is taken out of the ship. And if the ship is on hard ground and the shipmaster delays because of their dispute and there should be leakage, the shipmaster need not contribute but must have his freight in with the other cargo which has been saved. And that is the judgment in this case.

Comment: Contribution to average is extended to cover the loss of the mast or anchors. The exemption of the shipmaster from contribution (see article above and *Coutumier* chapter 94b) had not yet been recognised but he is given some concession if the damage is due to delay caused by dissenting merchants. The shipmaster's right to hold the cargo as security until the contributions have been made would have been complicated if the merchants did not have full title to the goods.

> **Article 10:** A master of a ship arrives safely at his discharge. He must show the merchants the ropes with which he will crane. And if [they, the merchants][65] see that they require repair, the shipmaster has to repair them for if a tun is lost through a fault in the crane or cordage, the shipmaster must make compensation, he and his crew. And the shipmaster must contribute as much as he took in cranage charge and the cranage charge must be taken first to compensate the damage. And the remainder must be contributed by them (the shipmaster and crew). But if the ropes break without being shown to the merchants, he (the shipmaster) will be held responsible for all the damage. But if the merchants say that the ropes are good and strong and they break, each must contribute to the damage, that is to say the merchants to whom the wine belongs alone. And that is the judgment in this case.

---

[63] CPR 1281–92, pp. 168–9.
[64] Twiss, *Black Book*, III, pp. 148–57, *Customs* chapters l–liv; pp. 162–73, chapters lxvi–lxvii; pp. 644–6, chapters ccxxxix, ccl–ccli.
[65] As the phrase *et si il veit* in the original refers to the merchants, the subject is presumably 'they'.

Comment: As discussed in the transcription, it has been assumed that *guidera* and *guide* are scribal errors for *guindera* and *guindeau*; Twiss translates *guidera* as 'hoists', Krieger as *winden wird*.[66] The function of the initial *mes* in the penultimate sentence is unclear; if it means 'but', it shifts culpability from the shipmaster and crew to the shipmaster alone; however, with the second *mes* in the last sentence, it may be a form of alternatives: *mes ... mes ...* meaning 'either ... or ...'. Without the merchants' approval of the equipment, the shipmaster and crew are to be held responsible for any damage, the unloading charge to be forfeited first and thereafter the shipmaster and his crew to find the difference. *Customs* covers in a similar way the damage arising from lifting tackle failure.[67]

> **Article 11:** A ship loads at Bordeaux or elsewhere and hoists her sail to deliver her wine and sets out and the shipmaster and the sailors do not trim the sail as they should and they meet bad weather at sea in such a way that a wooden barrel or a tun or a pipe breaks open. The ship arrives safely, the merchants say that their barrel has lost the wine. The shipmaster says that it did not happen. If the shipmaster can swear, he and three companions or four of them whom the merchants have chosen, that the wine was not lost from the barrel as the merchants have reproached them, they must be cleared and free. And if they are not willing to swear, they must compensate the merchants for the damage because they ought to trim their sails and hatches well and surely before they have to leave the place where they loaded. And that is the judgment in this case.

Comment: Translation difficulties raise doubts about the cause of the damage – poor loading of the ship or negligent sail handling. As translations of *boucle* and *fuistaile de leyns*, Twiss has 'bulkheads', and Krieger has (hesitantly) *Laderaum* and *Holzverstrebungen* ('loading space' and 'dunnage').[68] RS has *sayl* in place of *boucle*, following *voille* in the Norman version, and *takelyng* (rigging or equipment) for *fuistaile*.[69] No relevant lexographic elucidation of *boucle* has been found; the word may be an error for *voille*, as in RS. *Fustaille* is recorded in *Larousse Etymologique* as thirteenth-century, *tonneau*, and this meaning of the word is confirmed by its second and third appearances, where the loss of wine is discussed. There appears to be no need to resort to dunnage or bulkheads for *boucle* nor to rigging for *fuistaile*. The problem of translation is not new; RS reads 'takelyng crusheth or smyteth out the bottom of tonne' and the seventeenth-century translation of *Oleron* taken from *Garsias, alias Ferrand* (Pierre Garcie's *Grant Routier*) attributes

---

[66] Twiss, *Black Book*, III, p. 15; Krieger, *Oleron*, p. 131.
[67] Twiss, *Black Book* III, pp. 104–5, *Customs*, chapter xxviii and pp. 342–5, chapter clxxxii.
[68] Krieger, *Oleron*, p. 132 and fn. 595: Krieger describes the translation as *dunkel*. Twiss, *Black Book*, III, p. 17.
[69] Twiss, *Black Book*, I, p. 103 with footnotes, 2, 3 and 4.

to a yard the damage to a barrel head.⁷⁰ Twiss's translation has 'do not fasten as they ought their bulkheads', then goes on to say that 'the casks within the ship crush either a tun or a pipe' and ends with 'as the merchants stowed their wines above the waterline, they ought to quit'.⁷¹ However the intention remains the same – unless the crew swear that they had done their best in handling the ship and in securing the cargo, then they are liable for any damage. The present translation is felt to be rather more in line with that intention than the suggestions of Twiss and Krieger. *Customs* deals with damage to cargo much more comprehensively: some 13 chapters cover bad stowage, negligence, damp, rats and so on.⁷²

> **Article 12:** A shipmaster hires his sailors and must hold them in peace and be their judge if there is one who damages another while he puts bread and wine on the table. He who denigrates the other must pay 4d. and if the shipmaster denigrates someone he must pay 8d. And if there is someone who denigrates the shipmaster, he must pay as much as the shipmaster. And if it is so that the shipmaster hits one of his sailors he (the latter) must take the first blow from fist or palm and if he (the former) does it more, he (the latter) must defend himself. And if the sailor strikes the shipmaster first, he must lose 100s. or his fist, at the choice of the sailors. And that is the judgment in this case.

Comment: The usual translation of *dementer* is 'to give the lie to',⁷³ but since the intention is surely to give a wider description of trouble-making; 'denigrate' or 'insult' are felt to be better. A literal translation of 'par quei il met payn et vin a table' is given by Twiss and Krieger,⁷⁴ but it is more likely that there is bread and wine already on the table, and there is no apparent reason why the act of delivery should be specified. The 'table' appeared to have a symbolic importance in the life of the ship, see also *Oleron* articles 14 and 21 and *Queenborough* article 46. The fines relate to a day's wage, the shipmaster earning twice as much as a deck-hand. As noted in the transcription, there is some doubt about the grammatical number of 'fist' and 'sailor'. As the choice of punishment would not have been left to the accused and it is unlikely to have been the loss of more than one hand, 'fist' must be singular and 'sailors' plural. In other, later, manuscripts the fine is 5s. and in Article XIV of *Old Rules for the Lord Admiral* (dated by Twiss to 1337–50) the fine is 100s. or the loss of the fist with which the assailant struck the other, subject

---

[70] George Dawes, *An Extract by way of the Ancient Laws of Oleron rendred into English etc.* (London, 1685).
[71] Twiss, *Black Book*, III, p. 17.
[72] Twiss, *Black Book* III, pp. 92–105, *Customs* chapters xviii–xxvii; pp. 138–9, ibid. chapter xlvi; pp. 242–7, ibid. chapter cxli; pp. 274–9, ibid. chapter clii; pp. 428–33, ibid. chapter cciv.
[73] Twiss, *Black Book*, I, p. 105; Krieger, *Oleron*, p. 134.
[74] Twiss, *Black Book*, III, p. 19 for RS; Twiss, *Black Book*, I, p. 103 for MS LH; Krieger, *Oleron*, p. 134.

to pardon from the king or high admiral.[75] Since any treatment of an amputation would have been difficult on a ship and, if he recovered, a one-handed man would be of little use, it is unlikely that manual abscission was ever carried out at sea, but it may have been postponed until the ship reached port. The shipmaster's responsibility as judge of his crew is restricted by *Queenborough* articles 29, 30, 45 and 46, which stipulate that admirals' inquiries should be held into a number of serious offences such as strike, mutiny, murder and mayhem, none of which, together with theft, is covered by *Oleron*.

In the punishments for disobedience, *Customs* are more precise: a mariner may be dismissed his ship, and then only after having had his rations withdrawn and other sanctions applied, for theft, quarrelling and disobedience, all of which break his signing-on oath. For the more serious offences of quarrelling with the managing owner (shipmaster), he is to lose half of his wages and portage, if armed he is to be seized and imprisoned and if he strikes the shipmaster he is to lose all his wages and portage. He must also take the first blow from the shipmaster but may then flee and may not be pursued 'beyond the chain', i.e. to the bows, and an officer may not order a man to do something which is beyond that officer's authority. *Customs* also deals with theft (loss of wages, put in irons and delivered to a magistrate) and undressing while at sea (three duckings from the yard and loss of wages after three offences), neither of which is mentioned in *Oleron*.[76]

> **Article 13**: A ship loads in Bordeaux or La Rochelle or elsewhere and arrives at her discharge and [as stated in] the charter-party, towage and petty pilotage [charges] are on the merchants; on the coast of Brittany all those who are taken on after passing the Isle of Batz or Léon are local pilots; and those of Normandy or England after passing Guernsey and those of Flanders after passing Calais; and those of Scotland after passing Yarmouth.[77] And that is the judgment in this case.

Comment: Although the geographic limits mentioned in this article are perhaps confused (it is similar in all the Anglo-Norman manuscripts), the definition of the costs to the merchants additional to those in the charter-party is clear. That the merchants should pay for local pilotage is further confirmed in the *Coutumier*, chapter 95.

---

[75] Twiss, *Black Book*, I, pp. 104–5: MS W and in Twiss, *Black Book*, I, p. 54: in *RS*; the fine is 5s.
[76] Twiss, *Black Book*, III, pp. 186–7; *Customs*, chapter lxxx, pp. 226–9 and chapters cxviii–cxx.
[77] From *on the coast of Brittany* to the end, this article is a translation of a transcription of MS T made by Krieger, *Oleron*, p. 135, footnote 600. It has been used because of the corruption in MS LH, see footnote 27.

Article 14: If a dispute occurs on a ship between the shipmaster and his sailors; the shipmaster must take away the cloth from in front of his sailors three times before he orders them off. And if the sailor offers to make amends to the satisfaction of the sailors who are at the table and the shipmaster is so merciless that he wants nothing to do with it and puts him off, the sailor may go and follow the ship until the unloading and [then] must have as good a wage as if he had arrived on board by accepting the penalty agreed by those at the table. And if it should be that the shipmaster does not have on board as good a sailor as he was and loses her (the ship) by some chance, the shipmaster is held responsible for the damage to the ship and to the merchandise, whatever it may be, if he has anything. And that is the judgment in this case.

Comment: This is an extension of *Oleron* article 12. Withdrawing the *towaile* (cloth) three times appears to be the equivalent of the current oral, written and final disciplinary warnings; it may mean that the defaulter's rations were to be withdrawn for a unspecified period.[78] The table again plays its part as the forum where the crew assess a defaulter's contrition. The involvement of the crew may have been either because they had to live and work with the accused or because the article is another survival from the days of cooperative ventures, cf. *Oleron* articles 1, 2 and 18. For the *Customs* punishments, see comments on *Oleron* article 12.

Article 15: A ship is moored in a road and, running in on the flood tide, another ship disturbs her peace; the [first] ship is damaged by a blow which the other gives her and there is wine spilled. The damage must be estimated and divided, half between the two ships. And the wine which is in the two ships must be contributed for the damage [divided] between the two merchants. The master of the ship which has hit the other must swear, he and his sailors, that they did not do it deliberately and the reason that this judgment is given is thus, that an old ship might put herself voluntarily in the way of a better if she was covered for all her damages by the other ship, but if she knows that the contribution is shared, she will willingly keep out of the way. And that is the judgment in this case.

Comment: The phrase 'hastant de sa marree' implies movement of a ship carried by the tide, a situation similar to that in *Coutumier* chapter 82, in which one ship drags onto another in an anchorage. The *Coutumier* explains that if it were an accident, which can happen to any ship, those involved should each pay half the damage. There are, however, differences in the onus of proof; in the *Coutumier*, if the stationary ship can prove fault on the part of the dragging ship's crew or equipment, then it is not an accident and the latter has to pay the whole amount. In the *Oleron* article there is no avoidance of the 50:50 rule unless the dragging ship's

---

[78] Twiss, *Black Book*, I, p. 107, footnote 3: 'M. Pardessus cites the phrase *trancher la nappe devant soy* as an ancient form of expression for excluding a person from the table.'

complement refuse to swear that the collision was not deliberate. The mention of spilled wine is peculiar to the *Oleron* article, the *Coutumier* is more concerned with damage to the ships themselves. *Customs* has similar provisions: any ship entering an anchorage, port or beach has to keep clear of other ships already anchored there. If damage is caused, the later arrival must pay compensation unless she is the victim of bad weather (in the haven), in which case the assessment of damage will be made by *prudhommes* experienced in the ways of the sea. If a ship drags through an anchorage her crew is not responsible for any damage if the weather deteriorated suddenly, provided that she had all her cable out, and her crew had been unable to obtain more. If more cable could have been acquired, if the crew had been warned of the incoming bad weather, or if they had been asked to re-anchor more securely, then they are to be held liable for any damage. If she has dragged because of equipment failure, the crew are not liable for any damage provided that they did everything possible to avert collision, and her equipment had been in sound condition.[79]

> **Article 16**: One or two or more ships are in a harbour where there is little water. And on drying out one of the ships [may be] too close to the other. The master of that (the latter) ship has to say to the other sailors (on the former ship) 'Gentlemen, lift your anchor because it is too close to us and could do damage'. And [if] they are not willing to lift it, the master himself and his companions (from the latter ship) [may] go there to lift it and to move it [away] from them. And if they refuse to lift the anchor and the other does them damage, they have to recompense everything. And so it is if she anchors without a buoy and there is damage, they have to recompense everything. And if they are in a haven which dries out they have to buoy the anchors that will not be fully visible. And that is the judgment in this case.

Comment: It is possible that in the first sentence of the text, *cecche* should be *secche*. Twiss transcribes without comment the word as *secche* and both he and Krieger, who transcribes it as *cecche*, translate it as 'dries'.[80] However, in thirteenth-century French *cacher* meant 'crowd in on' or 'constrain' which would give 'And one of the ships crowds in and is too close to another'. 'Drying' is the more likely translation because of evidence from other manuscripts, although the grammar is not altogether satisfactory. Both translations describe a crowded anchorage with an early arrival in danger of drifting over the anchor of a later arrival. The first ship to anchor has prior claim to her space and can ask the crew of a later arrival to move their anchor, or, with permission, move it for them. In the following sentence it is not clear which is the 'other ship'; if the crew of the first ship do not move the anchor of the second ship, it could be that they have to take responsibility for any

---

[79] Twiss, *Black Book*, III, pp. 282–91, *Customs*, chapters clv–clviii.
[80] Twiss, *Black Book*, III, p. 22; Krieger, *Oleron*, p. 137.

damage, or it may be a repetition of the warning to the second ship to move her anchor or they will be responsible for the damage, a more logical explanation. The importance of buoying anchors in shallow water is often stressed and *Queenborough* articles 60 and 61 order an admiral's inquiry into the removal of an anchor or the cutting of anchor buoy lines. Without an anchor buoy, it is not always possible to know where an anchor has taken up, with the danger of another ship settling on the sharp flukes on the ebb.

Article 17: Sailors from the coast of Brittany may not have more than one cooked meal per day because they have drink going and coming. And those of Normandy may have two per day because their master supplies them only with water on the way out. But after the ship has been to a country where wine grows, the sailors must have drink and the master must supply them. And that is the judgment in this case.

Comment: Since LH was a London document, it would appear that this article was copied without amendment from earlier Breton or Norman versions of *Oleron*. *Customs* also lists the rations.[81]

Article 18: A ship arrives to be loaded at Bordeaux or elsewhere. The master must say to his companions 'Gentlemen, will you take your freight as portage or will you participate in the ship's freight?' They have to reply with what they want to do. And if they choose the ship's freight, such freight as the ship has, they will have. And if they want to freight by themselves, they must freight in such a way that the ship is not delayed. And if it happens that they are not able to find freight, the master has no blame. And the master must show them their space and their weight (for their portages). And the master must think about each man's portage. And if they want to take a barrel of water and it should be thrown into the sea, it has to count as wine or other cargo, pound for pound, if the sailors were able to defend reasonably at sea. And if it is so that they freight (their portage space) for the merchants, such privileges as the sailors have, the merchants must have too. And this is the custom in that case.

Comment: The crew might be paid *a deniers* (cash), by portage or *mareage* (a defined space in the hold), or *au fret de la nef* (a share in the profits of the voyage if they make their portages available for ship's cargo).[82] At the outward port, the shipmaster is to ask his crew to choose their option. For an additional perquisite

---

[81] Twiss, *Black Book*, III, pp. 210–13, *Customs*, chapters c–ci.
[82] Studer, *Oak Book*, II, p. 487 translates *lievres a fret de la nef* as 'will you hire yourselves according to the freight of the ship'; Burwash, *Merchant Shipping*, pp. 174–6 reads, with etymological justification, *lerrez* in place of *lievres* and translates as 'will you leave your *mareage* to the freight of the ship'. MS W has *lerrez*, MS B has *lerres*, the Oak Book *loweret*, MS V has *lerrez*, MS R has *liverees*, MS 10,146 (Gascon) has *leres*, the Leghorn MS has *larres* and MSS LH and LM have *lieveres* and *liverees* respectively. In balance, Burwash appears to be correct.

attached to portage see *Oleron* article 8 and *Queenborough* article 14, and for specific portage rates see *Queenborough* articles 3–13 and table 4. *Queenborough* article 13 makes it clear that the crew are to be paid at the end of an outward voyage in order to buy their merchandise and it was probably usual to offer portages there for the return voyage (except from Calais and Flanders, see *Queenborough* articles 8 and 9). *Oleron* article 20 suggests that portages may have been offered sometimes for the outward voyage, but the weight of evidence in *Queenborough* points to portages for homeward voyages only. There is some doubt about the suggested translation of the sentence beginning 'The master must show them …' because of the words *rives* and *leire*. A fourteenth-century use of *dériver* to mean *s'écarter de la rive* is given in *Larousse Etymologique*; since *rive* in current French is 'margin' or 'boundary', it is possible that *rives* here means the area in the hold within which the sailors' portages are to be loaded. The meaning of *leire* is even more occult. It is translated in *RS* as 'the weyght of their ship meate' which, Twiss suggests, is an error for 'shipment';[83] in the present translation that meaning has been adopted as it lies happily with the perceived sense of the sentence. In his translation Twiss has 'their fares and their berths' and goes on to assume that *rives* should be *rimes* and that is cognate with *arrimer* 'to stow'; and *leire* is cognate with English *lair* 'a bed', giving 'And the master ought to show them their fare and their berths, and each ought to place there the weight of his venture.[84] Krieger translates as 'Und der Kapitän soll ihnen ihre Arbeit und ihre Kojen zeigen und jede'm seinen Anteil am Laderaum zumessen' ('And the captain should show them their work and their berths and each his share of hold space'), conjecturing that *rives* should be *rimes* and translating that as 'work'.[85] The present translation is thought to reflect the intention of the article.

In *Customs*, mariners may be given five options at the shipmaster's discretion: payment by month, by voyage or by mile; with a share in the ship's freight; or with their own venture. For the last option they are to be allowed time off the ship and paid half of their wages in the out-board port to buy their cargoes, and other members of the crew have to help with the loading. Further, those who load their 'ventures' early, enjoy some priority whereas, if they are late in delivering to the ship, they may be refused space. Subcontracting of portage space, legitimate on English ships, is not allowed in *Customs*.[86]

> **Article 19**: A ship arrives at unloading. The sailors want to have their wages. And there are some who have on board neither bed nor chest. The master may retain from their wages [as much as is required to pay them] to take the ship

---

[83] Twiss, *Black Book*, I, p. 113 and footnote 4.
[84] Twiss, *Black Book*, III, p. 25 and footnote 2.
[85] Krieger, *Oleron*, pp. 139–140.
[86] Twiss, *Black Book*, III, pp. 186–197, *Customs*, chapters lxxix, lxxxv–lxxxix, xci–xcii, c, cc.

back to whence she came, if they do not give good security to complete the voyage. And thus is the judgment in this case.

Comment: The question of where and when the crew should be paid is set out in *Oleron* article 20, and in *Queenborough*, articles 2, 13, 15 and 17. It was apparently sufficiently common for sailors to jump ship for shipmasters to require a sanction, a situation foreseen here and in *Oleron* article 20. *Queenborough* article 15 stipulates that when there is a time clause for payment of the freight in the charter-party, the crew are to receive half their wages on loading and the other half on arrival at their destination after the master or owner has been paid half the freight. *Customs* makes provisions similar to *Oleron* article 19 for payment and discouragement of desertion.[87]

> **Article 20:** The master of a ship hires his sailors in the town in which the ship is, some on portage, the others on wages. It happens that the ship is not able to find freight locally and it is convenient for them to go further. Those who are on portages must follow her but for those who are on wages the master has to increase their hire league by league and person by person because they were hired to the final place. And if they come a shorter distance than the contract had stated, they must have all their wages. But they must help to take the ship back to where they brought her from, with God's help. And that is the judgment in this case.

Comment: After *Oleron* article 18, the meaning of this article may be that the sailors are to be re-hired at the outboard port. Additional wages for extra distance for the waged men is stipulated here and in *Queenborough* article 17 but there is to be nothing additional for men with portages which is, effectively, a fixed rate. There is again here the fear of desertion, a subject dealt with in the previous article. *Queenborough* article 17 threatens 'severe punishment' if any sailor should leave the ship too soon.

> **Article 21:** There happens to be a ship in Bordeaux or elsewhere. From such cooked food that they might have on the ship, the two sailors can take away one helping, but [only] as much as they would have drawn on the ship. And such bread as there might be, they should have according to that which they can eat. And they need have nothing to drink. And they must return punctually if the master is not to lose their hours (of work) on the ship, for if the master does lose them and there is damage, they are responsible for compensation. Or if one of their companions is wounded because of lack of help [by the other], they have to shelter and compensate the companion and the master and those at the table. And that is the judgment in this case.

---

[87] Twiss, *Black Book*, III, pp. 198–203, *Customs*, chapters xciii–xciv.

APPENDIX 1

Comment: This article may expand *Oleron* articles 5 and 6, which would explain why two sailors are introduced without preamble, but it is not clear if they are on leave or on ship's duties ashore. It is an interesting provision that any sailor who does not help a man who is consequently injured has to compensate the shipmaster and crew. Apart from recreation, the crew would also have had to go ashore to arrange their portages; *Customs* specifies a period of leave for personal business.[88] The importance of the table in the crew's affairs is also discussed in *Oleron* articles 12 and 14 and *Queenborough* article 46.

> **Article 22:** A master freights his ship to a merchant and they agree between the two of them a convenient term [for loading the ship]. And the merchant does not keep to it and thus holds up the ship and the sailors for a period of 15 days or more and each time the master loses his time and the mission through the fault of the merchant, the merchant has to compensate the master. And from that compensation which has to be made, the sailors must share a quarter and the master three quarters because he has to cover the costs. And that is the judgment in this case.

Comment: In *Queenborough* there is no mention of loss arising from protracted cargo loading; the crew apparently being expected to share in the commercial risks of a dilatory merchant. In *Customs*, there are three chapters covering various delays, including the situation where a shipmaster has agreed with a merchant to wait for a certain time.[89]

> **Article 23:** A merchant freights a loaded ship and she goes on her way and that ship enters a port and is delayed there so long that their money runs out. The master would be correct and able to send to his country to look for money. But he must not lose time because he has to compensate the merchants [for] all the damages that they may have. But the master can certainly take the wine from the merchants and sell it in order to have his revictualling. And when the ship arrives at her correct [port of] unloading, the wine that the master had taken must be valued as the other which was sold, neither at a higher nor a lower value. And the master must have his freight payment for that wine as he received for the other [wine]. And that is the judgment in this case.

Comment: While this article gives the impression of being for the common good, it is clearly more beneficial to the shipmaster. Running out of money for victuals or necessary repairs appears to have been fairly common; in *Customs* there are provisions for loans by the merchants of money and victuals.[90] When the ship is to be held as security, the loans are close to bottomry.

---

[88] Twiss, *Black Book*, III, pp. 196–7, *Customs* chapters xci–xcii.
[89] Twiss, *Black Book*, III, pp. 162–3, *Customs*, chapter lx; pp. 196–7, chapter lxxix; and pp. 366–9, chapter clxxxix.
[90] Twiss, *Black Book*, III, pp. 162–5, *Customs*, chapters lxi–lxii.

Article 24: A young man is the pilot of a ship and is hired to guide her to the port where they will unload her. There is certainly in this port a berthing area where they put the ships to unload. The master has to provide his (or her) berth, he and his companions, and put buoys there to be fully visible so that the mooring may be well marked so that the merchants suffer no damage; for if damage is done the master has to make compensation if there is no justification for what the master may have given as his reason. And the pilot has done his duty well when he has guided the ship to safety up to the berth because up to there was where he was to guide her. From then on the responsibility is on the master and his companions. And that is the judgment in this case.

Comment: There are two separate activities described in this article. The pilot is responsible for bringing the ship up to her berth and the shipmaster has to anchor, moor or dock the ship after arrival there. *Coutumier* chapter 88 rules that the shipmaster is responsible for conducting his ship from the port of lading to the port of unlading and the local pilot is stationed at the entrance to the port or haven because he knows the dangers there. In this article, *Oleron* indicates more clearly that the pilot has to bring the ship up to her final position. In the second activity there is some difficulty with 'pur purveier sa fourme'. Twiss translates it as 'The master is bound to provide her berth by himself and his crew, and to place buoys that may appear above water, or to see that her berth is well buoyed, that the merchants suffer no damage.'[91] If the ship is to be anchored, then *Oleron* article 16 already obliges the shipmaster to buoy his anchors. If the intention is for the ship to be moored alongside, then buoys are not necessary and the words *bailignes* and *bailignee* have to be translated in some other way. One possibility is that, instead of being cognates of *balinge*, 'buoy', they may be forms of *balinja* meaning 'cradle'.[92] That sense, given that the current English for a dried-out ship's support is 'cradle' and the word *fourme* is no doubt cognate with the current French *forme* ('dock'), would require the shipmaster to supply supports for the ship, i.e. 'legs', as she dries on the ebb. In balance the intention is probably to anchor the ship and buoy her anchors, in which case *pur purveier sa fourme* should be translated as 'to take her to her anchoring position', requiring *purveier* to be in error for, perhaps, an early form of *poursuivre*, to proceed, as in *poursuivre son chemin*.

---

[91] Twiss, *Black Book*, III, p. 31.
[92] See *Glossarium Mediae et Infimae Latinitatis*, ed. Domino Dufresne du Cange (Paris, 1840).

APPENDIX 2

Transcription and translation of the Inquisition of Queenborough

The history of the *Inquisition of Queenborough* and its importance in English maritime law are discussed in chapter 1. The fourteenth-century Anglo-Norman text was transcribed and translated by Twiss in his edition of the *Black Book of Admiralty*.[1] Most of the articles in the Twiss translation are considered to be accurate and are reproduced either in full or in summary, depending on their relevance to the present work. Where the translation or interpretation of an article is in question, a retranslation and, if necessary, a retranscription, are given here.

Between 1375 and 1403, the Inquisition sat in three 'sessions', partially separated here as Sections 1, 2 and 3. Within each section, for continuity, the jurors' decisions have been grouped by subject.

Section 1: Terms of employment, wage rates and pilots

Article 1 (summary): If a fully victualled and paid crew bound for Bordeaux or elsewhere find anything of value at sea, the ship is to have two thirds and the crew one third.

Comment: None required.

Article 2: Item, dient des ditz jurez qune nef en alant devers Bordeaux ou ailleurs pour prendre sa charge, les mariners estantz a mengier et boire et prenants louyers et portage y prengne aucune avantage de freight en alant devers leur charge prendre sans geteson de leur last les mariners navront que stowage et levage, et se une nef prent sa plaine charge, soit il au port devant leur departir ou en leur voye, et facent geteson de leur last a cause de mesme la charge prendre chacun mariner de ce prendra demy louyer. Cest assavoir la moitie de tel louyer pour le quel il fut lovez pour le voyage du quel demy lowe et de la moitie de leur entier premier louyer les mariners seront paiez a Bordeaulx ou ailleurs, ou ses biens seront deschargiez et du tiers demi louyer seront les mariners paiez a la revenue de la nef au lieu de sa descharge limitez en sa chartre de freight ou endenture en fait; mais en cas que le maistre ou le seigneur de la nef apres la

---

[1] Twiss, *Black Book*, I, pp. 132–173.

descharge dicelle la voille avoir a lostel les mariners seront tenuz de la amener a lostel et doncques seront ilz paiez de cellui tiers demy louyer et non devant.

Translation: The aforementioned jury say that on a ship going towards Bordeaux or elsewhere to take on cargo [if] the crew, having food and drink and taking wages and portages, share in any profit from freight on the outward journey without throwing out their cargo, the crew should have only stowage and freight cost. And if a ship takes her full load whether in port before their leaving or on their voyage and they throw out their (the crew's) cargo in order to take the load, each mariner shall receive half pay. That is to say, half of such wage for which they were hired for the voyage, of which half pay and the half of their entire original wage for the voyage the crew will be paid at Bordeaux, or elsewhere where the goods are unloaded, and the third half wages will be paid to the crew on the return of the ship to the place of unloading as defined in her charter-party or indenture. However when the shipmaster or the owner of the ship wishes to sail home after unloading, the crew have to take the ship and then be paid the third half of the wages, and not before.

Comment: Untangling this article reveals that crew members whose portages have been put out to make space for ship's cargo, are to receive their wages and a 50 per cent supplement. Those who had opted for a share of the profit from the ship's freight (*au fret de la nef*), or whose portages have not been put out of the ship, must abide by their original agreements. Portages, usually offered or taken for the return voyage only, have here been offered for the outward voyage, cf. *Queenborough* article 13 and *Oleron* article 20. That the crew are to be paid the final instalment of their wages only after the ship has returned home, reflects *Queenborough* article15 and *Oleron* articles 19 and 20.

In Twiss's translation in the *Black Book*, the dumping of ballast is used to decide the crew's rate of pay, an interpretation derived from equating *last* with 'ballast' (perhaps because ballast may derive from bar + last = 'naked load' [*OED*]) but the possessive 'their' is not explained. In the translation here, 'last' has been taken to be 'cargo', i.e. the crew's portages, a decision justified by the use of the word as a unit of quantity of certain goods, for example 'lest' & dim' de quire'; it also explains the use of the possessive pronoun. Twiss proposes a half-pay punishment for the jettison of ballast but it appears to be an additional half pay in compensation for loss of portages. *Geteson* here does not mean jettison but an unloading for commercial reasons. In *Customs*, mariners who load their ventures early enjoy some priority but if they are late in bringing their goods to the ship, they may be refused lading.[2] There is no mention of unloading anything.

---

[2] Twiss, *Black Book*, I, pp. 135–137. *Rot. Parl.*, I, p. 312 no. 96 (1314–15). F.C. Lane, 'Tonnages Medieval and Modern', *EcHR*, 2nd series, 17, 2 (1964), pp. 213–33. A *last* was originally a four-wheeled cart-load and became a Hanseatic grain measure of c.2 tons or c.112 cu.ft. Twiss, *Black Book*, III, pp. 190–7: *Customs*, chapters lxxxvi–lxxxix.

APPENDIX 2

Article 3: Item, dient les ditz jures que accoustume est dancien temps ung mariner de prendre de louyer de la pole de Londres jusques a Lusshebone vint souez pour le portage dung tonnel, etc.

Translation: The said jurors say that by ancient custom a mariner is to take for wages from the Pool of London to Lisbon 20s. [and] the portage of one ton etc.[3]

Comment: The original text appears to be corrupt; by analogy with *Queenborough* articles 5–12, it probably should read 'ung mariner prendra vint souez de loyer *et le portage dung tonnel*', replacing *pour* by *et* and allowing the seamen to receive a wage for the outward voyage and portage for the homeward. It is improbable that the crew would receive 20s. for cashing-in their portages or for participating in the ship's freight. Although portages appear to have been available generally for the return voyage only, this article and *Oleron* article 20 suggest that they could sometimes be taken on the outward passage. Table 2 lists wages and portages for various voyages.

Article 4 (summary): From the Pool of London to Bayonne a mariner will take 10s. for wages [and] the portage of one ton.

Comment: As in the previous article, the translation assumes that *pour* is in error for *et*.

Article 5: Item, entre Londres, Bordeauls et la Rochelle en vendage prendra ung mariner huit souez de loyer et le portage dung tonnel et en temps de Reke sept souez de louyer et le portage dune pippe.

Translation: Between London, Bordeaux and La Rochelle at vintage time a mariner will take 8s. for wages and the portage of one ton and at rack time 7s. and the portage of one pipe.

Comment: The price of rack wine, drawn off the lees in early spring, depended on the quantity and quality of the earlier vintage wine and was sometimes more expensive than the latter.[4] The lower wage offered for the spring voyage may have been because of anticipated better weather but the reduction by half of the portage allowance is not easily explained. Wages and portages are clearly separated by *et*, not *pour*, from here on.

Article 6: Item, entre Londres et le Bay prendra ung mariner selon lancien usage cinq souez de louyer et trois quartiers de sel du portage rabatuz autant

---

[3] *de louyer* and variants have been translated as 'wages' throughout, i.e., money received for hire.
[4] André L. Simon, *History of the Wine Trade in England* (London, 1906), pp. 261–8. James, *Wine Trade*, pp. 12–13.

comme meismes les trois quartiers de sel cousterent au premier achat toutesfoiz ordonne que se aucun mariner a la charge de la nef ait ung pavillon pour garder et deffendre en partie le sel estant en la nef deaue et mellieur adoncques aura il oultre le portage dun sake du sel contenant demy quartier, etc.

Translation: Between London and [Bourgneuf] Bay a mariner will take, according to ancient usage, 5s. for wages and 3 quarters of salt as portage with the freight discounted by the price at first purchase of the 3 quarters of salt Nevertheless, it is ordained that if any mariner who is in charge of the ship has a shelter to guard and partly protect the salt on the ship from water, then he will have in addition the portage of a sack of salt containing a half quarter, etc.

Comment: The article appears to mean that the value of the portage was to be no more than the cost price of salt, which varied between 8d. per quarter in 1378 and 4s. 6d. in 1495 with a mean of about 1s. 8d.[5] The additional reward for protecting the salt was therefore about 10d. A deck shelter featured in a dispute over a 1392 charter-party in which the plaintiff's copy of the charter read 'et vous calefaiteez le tilat de la dicte barge' while the defendants' read 'et qe vous ferrez calofater la couverture de la Barge'. *Tilat* was a lean-to cabin or deckhouse whereas *couverture* implies a waterproof covering of some sort. Protection of the salt from damp was sometimes purchased by the merchant as an 'optional extra'.[6]

Article 7: Item, entre Londres et Irlande prendra ung mariner dix souez de louyer et le portage de trois dikers de cuir et sil passe la Holdeheude de Endeffelde vers le west adonques aura chascun mariner deux souez plus de regard et mesme le regard aura il silz passe Kd devers le north.

Translation: Between London and Ireland a mariner will take 10s. for wages and the portage of 3 dickers of hides and if the ship passes to the west of the Old Head of Kinsale then each mariner will have 2s. more in wages and he will have the same amount if she passes to the north of Tuskar.

Comment: The Tuskar Rock and the Old Head of Kinsale are on approximately equal radii from Lands End with the medieval ports of Kinsale, Cork, Youghal, Waterford and Wexford between the two; the choice of those two way-points (in effect, 'fare-stages') at each end of the south Irish commercial arc is therefore logical. The extra 2s. in wages are for voyages beyond Kinsale to Dingle and Galway, and beyond Tuskar to Wicklow, Dalkey, Dublin and Drogheda. A dicker of hides was half a score, giving a portage of 30 hides.

---

[5] Bridbury, *Salt Trade*, pp. 133–4 and appendix I, pp. 176–7. Thorold Roger's prices for salt from 1378 to 1495 citing *Proceedings and Ordinances of the Privy Council*, vol. iv, p. 239.
[6] *CPMR, 1381–1412*, p. 196. Bridbury, *Salt Trade*, p. 134, footnote 4, cites PRO E101/ 619/18 and Salzman, *English Trade*, p. 235 as evidence for and against the merchants providing cover for the salt.

APPENDIX 2

Article 8 (summary): Between London and Calais a mariner will take 5s. wages without portage.

Article 9 (summary): Between London and Flanders a mariner will take 6s. wages without portage.

Comment: It is not known why the crew did not have the option of portages on the return passages from Calais and Flanders; it may have been because of difficulties the crew would have in arranging their own cargoes in the Staple area. The wages quoted for the round trip are higher per mile than for most voyages – see Table 1, p. 111 – perhaps because of the risks of piracy in the Channel and the loss of the privilege of portages.

Article 10 (summary): Between London and Prussia, 20s. wages and three mariners [to share] a last of portage.

Comment: Prussia could include the ports of Elbing or Danzig, where an English factory had been in operation from before 1388. A portage in lasts indicates a cargo of pelts or fish, both Prussian exports, see Article 11.

Article 11 (summary): Between London and Sweden, 13s. 4d. wages and three mariners [to share] a last of herring for portage.

Comment: A 'last', as defined in the Statute of Herrings, was 10,000 fish.[7]

Article 12 (summary): Between London and Newcastle-on-Tyne, 4s. wages and 2 quarters of coal for portage.

Article 13: Item, entre Londres et Berewyke prendra ung mariner huit souez de louyer desquelz il sera paie illecques affin quil en pourra acheter telles marchandises come lui plaira lesquelz seront chargez en meisme la nef en la quelle prendra ledit wages pour son portage.

Translation: Between London and Berwick a mariner will take 8s. for wages which will be paid in order that he can buy such merchandise as he wishes which is to be loaded as his portage on the same ship on which he took the said wages.

Comment: This article confirms that wages were normally for the outward bound voyage and portages only for the homeward. The doubling of wages from 4s. for Newcastle to 8s. for Berwick, was perhaps because of war risks; unfortunately there is no portage allowance for comparison. Berwick was once an important trading centre, exporting wool, fells and hides; established by the thirteenth

---

[7] *Rot. Parl.*, II, p. 306a, no. 28. *Statutes*, 31 Edward III, st. 2, cs. 2 and 14.

century, it had no port town competitor between Edinburgh and Newcastle but it declined in importance after 1371.

> **Article 14:** Item, se une nef soit affretee a divers pris de frett lentier de tout la ffret sera acompte ensemble et les portages paiez aux mariners selon lafferant du frett de chascun tonnel; lun acompte comme dit est droittement avecques lautre.
>
> **Translation;** If a ship is loaded at several freight rates for the cargo, the whole freight should be added together [with] the portages [and] paid to the crew in conformance with the rate per ton. One counts rightly, so it is said, for as much as another.

Comment: The freight rates would have to be averaged only when members of the crew had subcontracted their portage space to merchants. Merchants who bought portage space acquired the crew's privileges of exemption from contribution to general average, so that space was more valuable than that in the general hold (*Oleron* articles 8 and 18). Those crew members freighting their own portage would not have taken part in this averaging of rates. Twiss has all the portages paid at the average rate, but that would be the case only if they had all been subcontracted *au fret de la nef*.

> **Article 15:** Item, une nef soit afretee devezs quelque lieu que ce soit et ait certain jour limite de paiement de son frett en endenture ou autrement les mariners seront paiez de la moitie de leurs louyers a la charge de la nef et de lautre moitie quant mesme la nef sera venue en lieu de sa descharge se le maistre ou le seigneur de la nef ny veult comme dit est avoir la nef a lostel et de leure serout ilz paiez quant la moitie dudit frett est receu.
>
> **Translation:** If a ship is freighted for anywhere whatsoever and has a fixed time limit for the payment of the freight by indenture or otherwise, the crew are to be paid half their wages on loading the ship and the other half when the ship herself has arrived at the point of unloading. If the shipmaster or the owner of the ship does not wish, as it is said, to have the ship at home, the wages will be paid when half of the said freight has been received.

Comment: The indenture would be the charter-party. The retention of half of the crew's wages until half of the freight payment has been received amplifies *Queenborough* article 2; the crew are expected to share in both commercial and marine risks. When the shipmaster or owner wished to take the ship home, *Oleron* article 19 sanctioned a lien on wages, failing any other security, to hold the crew.

> **Article 16:** Item, en droit de lodemanage dient les avant ditz jurez que leur semble en cest cas ilz ne scayvent meilleur advys ne remedie mais que ce soit desore usez et fait par manere quest contenue en le loy Doleron.

Translation: On the responsibility for pilotage the aforementioned jurors said that it seemed to them in this case that they knew of no better advice nor remedy than that it should be used and done in the manner contained in the law of Oléron.

Comment: The sense of this article depends on the meaning of *droit de lodemanage*; the phrase could imply the responsibility of the pilots, referring to *Oleron* article 24, or the responsibility for paying the pilots, as in *Oleron* article 13. The intention is probably the latter, confirmed by a marginal note in the original text 'Lodemanage to bee payed'; Twiss suggests the contrary.[8]

Article 17: Item, que toutes maneres de mariners qui sont retenuz avec aucun seigneur de nef pour luy servir a Bordeaulx ou ailleurs pour raisonnable salaire ainsi comme a este use en divers ports par tout le royalme combien que les mariners ne soit pas tenuz especialement pour servir a Bordeaulx, Bayone, Lushebon, Civile, ou autre lieux quelconques, en especial se ainsi estoit que la nef ne povoit estre frettee au premier lieu les mariners ne refuserent la nef se la nef veult aller ailleurs pour avoir son frett, pourveu toutefoiz que les mariners seront raisonnablement alovez selon lafferant de leur travail. Et se aucun mariner se voide daucune nef en tel cas il sera grevousement amerciez selon la discrecion de ladmiral et fera que ou posesseur de la nef.

Translation: That all types of mariners who are hired by any owner of a ship to serve him to Bordeaux or elsewhere for reasonable wages such as are paid in divers ports throughout the whole kingdom, the mariners are not hired specifically to serve to Bordeaux, Bayonne, Lisbon, Seville or any other place whatsoever. Especially if the ship were unable to be freighted at the first place the crew may not refuse [to work] the ship if she wants to go somewhere else to find her freight, provided always that the crew are reasonably hired in conformance with their work. And if any mariner deserts any ship, in such a case he will be severely punished at the discretion of the admiral and make [good any costs] to the ship's owner.

Comment: This implies an open-ended service commitment by the crew and is similar to *Oleron* article 20, although in the latter there is no threat of severe punishment for jumping ship. There appears to be a textual omission at the end of the article: after *fera* and in place of *que ou* there should be something along the lines of 'will make good the costs to the owner'.

---

[8] Twiss, *Black Book*, I, p. 143, footnote 1.

THE INQUISITION OF QUEENBOROUGH

Section 2: Admiralty inquiries

Articles 18 to 70 are additions to *Queenborough* made in the first decade of the fifteenth century; the articles are in the form of instructions for admirals to hold inquiries concerning a wide variety of incidents.

> **Article 18** (summary): Concerning the distribution of prizes taken in time of war in the admiral's presence; the shipmaster to have a larger share than his crew.

Comment: The distribution of spoils was intimated to the Cinque Ports in 1285 in a Letter Patent under the Great Seal, but was the subject of many disputes. The admiral's deputy's interest in prize dates from the 1360/1 appointment of Sir John Beauchamp as Lord High Admiral with judicial authority according to maritime law. The deputy's authority in prize thereafter grew while that of the King's Council, except as a court of appeal, and of the Lord Chancellor, declined. By 1426 there were four tribunals exercising a right to intervene.[9]

> **Articles 19, 20 and 58** (summaries): Inquiries concerning the activities of pirates and those who help the enemy, specifically the rebels of Wales, and outlaws.

Comment: French troops landed in Wales in 1403 to assist Owen Glendower, thus dating this section.

> **Article 21** (summary): Inquiries concerning petty felonies including theft of gold and silver, boats, oars and anchors and the unauthorised raising of nets or pots.

> **Articles 22–5, 27, 74 and 81** (summaries): Inquiries concerning non-payment of the Admiral's share of prizes, prisoners, flotsam, lagan, deodands etc.

Comment: These articles and several of the following reflect the admirals' efforts to boost their incomes. See especially *Queenborough* articles 51 and 73–80. Articles 74 and 81 properly belong to section 3, below.

> **Articles 26, 28, 38, 39 and 55–57** (summaries): Inquiries concerning weirs, fish-nets, traps, whales, porpoise, sturgeon, oysters and mussels; ineffective water bailiffs, unlawful fishing and nets.

Comment: Irrelevant to the present work.

---

[9] *Foedera*, I, part 2, p. 654: 'Pro baronibus Quinque Portuum & caetera nautis regui, de quândam ordinatione fact.' *Documents Relating to the Law and Custom of the Sea (1205–1648)*, ed. R.G. Marsden, 2 vols, Navy Records Society, 49 and 50 (London, 1916), I, pp. 69–71. *Foedera* 10, p. 367. Additionally, the admiral sometimes gave the right of prize to a ship before she sailed.

APPENDIX 2

Articles 29–34 (summaries): Inquiries into deaths on board ships, mayhems and affrays, concealing traitors' belongings, ships breaking arrest, mariners breaking impressment and deserters on king's pay.

Comment: Although *Oleron* article 12 appoints the shipmaster to be judge of his crew, this article defines the serious crimes beyond his remit, see *Queenborough* articles 45 and 46, below. Murder, mayhem, treason, and desertion after receiving the king's pay if the wages were not returned, were felonies carrying the death penalty.[10]

Articles 35–37, 40 and 44 (summaries): Inquiries concerning customs evasions, unlicensed export of the Staple goods of wool, hides, sheepskins, tin, lead, cheese and butter; and of silver and gold (except for purchase of food);[11] carrying pilgrims to Santiago de Compostela, Calais or Rome etc.; and corn, except to Calais, Bayonne or Bordeaux.

Article 41 (summary): Inquiries concerning false claims to wrecks and those who have been wrecked.

Article 43 (summary): Inquiries concerning those who bear arms and intimidate subjects.

Comment: None of these articles is relevant to the present work.

Article 45 (summary): Inquiries concerning all mariners who violently lay hands on or beat their shipmasters against the laws of the sea and the relevant statutes of Oléron.

Article 46: Item, soit enquis de tous mariners qui sont rebelles encontre les honnestes commendemants de leurs maistres et de maistres qui ne tiennent pas leurs mariners en paix a la table et ailleurs comme les statuts doleron demandent.

Translation: Let an enquiry be made of all mariners who have rebelled against the honest commands of their masters and of masters who have not held their mariners in peace at the table or otherwise as required by the statutes of Oleron.

---

[10] *Statutes* 2 Richard II, st. 1, c. 4: the punishment for desertion with the king's wages from impressment was to refund double the amount taken plus a year's imprisonment and thereafter retention for the king's service. J.G. Bellamy, *The Criminal Trial in Later Medieval England* (Stroud, 1998), murder and mayhem pp. 57–69 and *passim*; desertion p. 189. On indictments for desertion from the army see *Statutes* 18 Henry VI, c. 19.

[11] *Statutes*, 27 Edward III, st. 2. *Statutes*, 8 Henry VI, cap. 19 forbade shipmasters, native or stranger, to carry concealed Staple products unless destined for the Staple or 'Marrok' (i.e. Straits of Gibraltar). The export of silver and gold in coin or ingot was repeatedly forbidden by statute between 1381 and 1403: *Statutes* 5 Richard II st. 1, c. 2; ibid. 2 Henry IV, c. 5; ibid. 4 Henry IV, cs. 14 and 16; ibid. 5 Henry IV, c. 9.

Comment: Mutiny, which according to *Oleron* article 12 could be dealt with by the shipmaster, is to be referred to the admiral along with the felonies listed in *Queenborough* articles 29–34. The less serious crime of striking the shipmaster may also be subject to inquiry, with the provision that the inquiry is to be in both directions, that is, into the behaviour of both the shipmaster and the crew. The articles substantially reduce the shipmaster's autonomous authority and enhance the admirals'. The importance of 'the table' is discussed in *Oleron* articles 12 and 14; it appears to have had a symbolic significance.

Article 47 (summary): Inquiries into unskilled pilots whose actions have led to loss or death.

Comment: This article expands *Queenborough* article 16.

Articles 48, 49, 50 and 54 (summaries): Inquiries concerning false claimants of property, forestallers and regrators; false weights and measures.

Comment: Irrelevant to the present work.

Articles 51 and 52 (Twiss translation): Item, let an inquiry be made of all those who sue any man at the common law of the land over something belonging to the ancient right of maritime law and of all judges who hear before them any pleas belonging of right to the court of admiralty.

Comment: These articles are evidence of the struggle between the courts of admiralty, common law and merchant law; the admirals and maritime jurists here jealously define their territory, see also *Queenborough* articles 71–8, below. Just how effective an inquiry by an admiral into the actions of common law judges might have been is open to conjecture. The other side of the argument is seen in statutes of Richard II and Henry IV which offer remedy for anyone pursued wrongfully by a court of admiralty and make it clear that admirals and their deputies may deal only with anything done at sea, as it was in the time of Edward III.[12]

Articles 53, 62 and 72 (summaries): Inquiries concerning those who obstruct admiral's officers; seamen who are rebellious to commands of king or admiral; punishment of opposers to and rebels against the Office of the Court of Admiralty.

Article 59 (summary): Inquiries concerning serjeants-at-arms who have extorted silver and gold from shipowners seeking to avoid impressment.

Comment: Articles 53, 62 and 72 presumably refer only to seamen on board merchant ships impressed for service to the Crown or on royal ships. Article 59

---

[12] *Statutes* 15 Richard II, c. 3 and ibid. 2 Henry IV, c. 11.

seeks to reduce the dishonest activities of impressment officers working in distant ports. Article 72 belongs in section 3 of *Queenborough* but fits here by subject.

> **Articles 60 and 61** (Twiss translation): Item, let inquiry be made of those who have removed the anchor from any ship without warning the shipmaster or any other of the crew by which the ship has perished or there is a man dead, and if anyone has cut the buoy tied to any buoy rope tied to an anchor in the water by which the anchor has been lost or other damage has been done or suffered.

Comment: The 'in the water' qualification confirms that article 61 does not refer to theft from a ship or on land but rather the removal of an anchored ship's marker buoy. It may be assumed that article 60 also refers to anchors in use, perhaps those which have been moved and not properly re-set, in contrast with *Oleron* articles 16 and 24. The 'other damage' could be that caused to a ship drying out on the flukes of an unmarked anchor.

> **Article 63** (summary): Inquiries concerning those who turn back ships carrying victuals to England.

Comment: Irrelevant to the present work.

> **Article 64** (summary): Inquiries into shipmasters and mariners of ships who take excess salaries or portages other than was usual in ancient times.

> **Article 65** (summary): The wages of ships' carpenters to be added to the above inquiry.

Comment: Wage rates are listed in Queenbrough articles 3–13, this later article 64 shows the attempts by shipmasters and shipowners to control wages; cf. the similar situation ashore before and after the Statute of Labourers.[13]

> **Article 66** (summary): Inquiries into the use of foreign ships.

Comment: A 1382 statute of Richard II ordained that none of the king's subjects could legally ship merchandise in any other than English ships; a year later that statute was qualified to allow the use of alien ships, if no English ships were available. In 1390 the rules were again changed to allow only English ships to be used for English goods, 'to increase the navy of England, which is now greatly diminished'.[14] This article, being in the 1403 section of *Queenborough*, is concerned with the post-1390 situation and, with the last statute, is an interesting forerunner to the later Navigation Acts.

---

[13] *Statutes* 25 Edward III, st. 1, c. 3 and ibid. 34 Edward III, c. 9.
[14] *Statutes* 5 Richard II, st. 1, c. 3; ibid. 6 Richard II, st. 1, c. 8 and ibid. 14 Richard II, c. 6.

Articles 67, 68, 69 and 70 (summaries): Inquiries into the release of prisoners without passes or before investigation, into those who deal with the enemy without licence and into anything else to do with the Court of Admiralty.

Section 3: Admiralty courts' responsibilities and fees

Articles 71–81, of which 72, 74 and 81 have already been considered, were produced by a separate inquisition of unknown date.[15] They are mostly concerned with defining the admirals' rights and dues. The articles of interest are given in full below and the remainder in summary translation.

Article 71 (summary): On the duty and responsibility of the court of admiralty: first of all to do right and give justice to all parties, both plaintiffs and defendants in the court of admiralty. A summary and full record is to be made according to maritime law and the ancient customs of the sea.

Article 73 (Twiss translation): Item, to be inquired well and duly by good and sufficient inquest taken on the sea coast where the evidence will be all the articles and circumstances required by maritime law for the advantage of the king and the admiral and to offer justice to the common people; whatever may be found by inquiry to be returned to the high admiral without making a conclusion or taking action if that was not granted by special warrant of the high admiral.

Comment: Despite article 71, the Court of Admiralty did not become a court of record until the sixteenth century. The court is only to collect evidence, unless given further powers by the high admiral.

Article 75 (Twiss translation): Item, to take for the admiral his fees, that is to say, 20d. for each pound recovered (8.3 per cent) as principal in the Court of Admiralty and note that damages are included with the principal and not the costs, and to take a reasonable fine for each plea made in the court which is not prosecuted nor determined therein.

Article 76 (summary): 4d. out of every £1 of fleet wages (1.67 per cent) to be paid to the admiral when on a voyage in the king's service.

Articles 77–80 (summary): Fees to be charged in the Court of Admiralty for use of the seal and for pleas, heard or not.

Comment: After the altruistic and patriotic sentiments of *Queenborough* articles 71 and 73, articles 75–80 reveal the true cupidity of the Court of Admiralty at that time. The court is to receive 8.3 per cent of the principal recovered plus damages,

---

[15] Twiss, *Black Book*, I, p. 171, footnote 2 suggests *t.* Henry V;

but without deduction of costs in any suit heard; a fee for any plea which is lodged but not pursued; and 1.67 per cent of the fleet wage bill when travelling. The use of the admirals' seal is also to be charged, an invitation for the admirals to devise every possible bureaucratic documentation requiring their validation. With that and the catchment area which the admirals define as theirs, the jealousy of the common law courts is understandable.

APPENDIX 3

A partial transcription and translation of Les Bons Usages et les Bonnes Costumes et les Bons Jugemenz de la Commune D'Oleron[1]

The history and significance of the *Les Bons Usage et les Bonnes Costumes et les Bons Jugemenz de la Commune D'Oleron* has been discussed in chapter 1. The greater part of the *Coutumier* is unrelated to maritime matters, being concerned with the organisation and economy of the community, but a few chapters are relevant to the present work and those are discussed below. Twiss had the whole text transcribed and translated for his edition of the *Black Book* and the manuscript was also transcribed but not translated by Bémont in his *Coutumier de L'Ile D'Oleron*. In his commentary Bémont, working some 45 years after Twiss, remarked that 'it is necessary to remark that Twiss seems not to have been very familiar with Old French and that his interpretation is not always sound.'[2] This criticism of the first modern scholar to examine the manuscript may be harsh, but it does indicate that a revision of at least parts of his translation is necessary.

Where there was any doubt about a Twiss transcription, it has been compared with Bémont's and, if necessary, revised. Translations considered dubious have been revised, and are included here with chapters of acceptable translation noted as 'Twiss translation'. In the interests of continuity, chapters of interest have been grouped by subject matter. The transcriptions and translations follow the protocols used in Appendix 1.

Rates and tariffs

Chapter 34 (Twiss translation): That which is loaded on board a ship as ship's stores is not required to pay customs, nor [are] the portages of the crew.

Comment: A valuable concession to the crew if loading in the island of Oléron, in addition to their freight-free privilege.

---

[1] MS Douce 227, Bodleian Library, Oxford.
[2] Twiss, *Black Book*, II, pp. 254–401. *Coutumier, passim*.

APPENDIX 3

Chapter 55 (Twiss translation): If a man freights the ship of another in Oléron to carry wines to another country, he shall carry 21 tons for 20 [even] although that is not specifically included in the agreement.

Comment: A compulsory 5 per cent discount for exporting merchants supporting local Oléronais trade.

Partnerships

Use of assets

Chapter 63 (Twiss translation): If there are two partners with a half share [each] in a vessel and one of them employs her for a turn in his private service, the other partner shall employ her for another turn. But if the vessel is detained longer on one turn than on the other by storm or lack of wind, that shall not be counted in the partnership. And the same thing holds for several partners.

Comment: The second sentence introduces *force majeure* as a defence for returning late.

Sale of assets

Chapter 64a (Twiss translation): If there are several partners in one and the same vessel and one of the partners takes their vessel out of port with the consent of his other partners and on return takes her without the consent of his partners to a port other than that from which she was taken, he cannot put her up for a sale option until he has brought her back from whence she was taken. While the vessel is in a distant port to which the partners cannot go to see her without great costs or delay and damage to themselves and their property, unless the vessel has been taken to [that] distant port with the partners' consent, he who has seen the vessel recently could have an advantage in the sale option over him who has not seen her for a considerable time. An option for sale ought to be made communally and loyally.

Comment: As one partner could not put the whole vessel up for sale without the authority of the other partners anyway, this chapter precludes a partner, even with permission to sell the ship, doing so in a distant port. The following two sections of chapter 64 also define the restrictions on a partner selling his share.

Chapter 64b: Essec apelon en icest luec quant vns parsoners dit a lautre, ge te met lo vesseau a essec en tau manere que tu me deras tant de la meie partie ou ge te deray itant de la toe, et dit quau some, et sachez que li autres parsoners ne puet mie refuder, quar autrement ne puet mie estre vaesseas partiz sanz damage et sans la defformacion de sa premere matere. [E en totes itaus chozes qui ne puent mie estre autrement parties sanz faire essec].³ et cil qui lou recet lou deit paier dedenz terme de vii. iors apres qui lo aura retenu.

Translation: 'Sale option' is used here when one partner says to another 'I put the vessel up for sale option in such a way that either you shall give me so much for my share or I will give you so much for your share', and he names the sum; and note that the other partner cannot refuse the offer, for otherwise a vessel could never be shared without loss and without breaking up its basic structure [and so in all such things which cannot be otherwise shared without making a sale option]; and he who receives it ought to pay within a term of seven days after he has taken possession of it.

Comment: A partner who wishes to sell his share in a vessel has to offer it to his co-partners at a fair price; if they refuse the offer, he has the right to buy their shares at the offered price. Bémont suggests that 'E en totes itaus … faire essec' may have been a marginal note incorporated by a scribe; the addition, if that is what it is, substantially extends the provision. The chapter usefully explains that the sale of part of a ship is as the sale of part of any indivisible property.

Chapter 64c (Twiss translation): If one of several partners sells his share in a vessel to another, a stranger who has nothing to do with the affair (partnership), any of the other partners may claim the share sold with all the business which has been arranged,⁴ if he wishes to use it for his own service. And in the same way, if one exchanges his share another (partner) may claim it if he wants to pay the value of the exchange. And it is the same for all assets of the partnership when an asset is not divisible. Non-divisible means when neither of the partners can say nor show definitively that 'this share is mine'. And it is understood that partners should share fairly and in common amongst themselves the debits and the credits, the bad and the good, in proportion to what belongs to each as a result of the partnership.

Comment: This is a clear definition of what is now known as 'joint-ownership' of a vessel, each shareholder having a fraction of the whole in, as it were, a single registration. The alternative is 'part-ownership' in which the shares in the ship are separately registered. The chapter makes it clear that partners in joint-ownership have 'first refusal' on any shares being sold and that each partner participates in the profits and losses of the partnership. *Customs* has several chapters on shared ownership, one of which is particularly concerned with a shipmaster selling his ship without reference to the other owners.⁵

---

3   Marginal note commented on by Bémont, *Coutumier*, p. 77 but ignored by Twiss.
4   'li autres parsoners puet retenir lo marche': Twiss, *Black Book*, II, pp. 342–3 translates *retenir* as 'retain', but as one cannot retain that which is not already held, the sense must be 'to claim' or 'to restore'.
5   Twiss, *Black Book*, III, pp. 452–7, *Customs*, chapter ccxi.

Chapter 87: Si duy ou plusor sunt parconner en vne nef, chascun daus parsoners poet vendre sa partie, se il veaut, entreaus, au fayre la nef en lemprise de lor compaignie; quar chascuns hom puet sa partie vendre coma sa choze domayne. Nem pero li aucun vodrient dire que ben deit vns daus parconners aveir la partie de la nef plus tost que vns autres estranges por le fuer de autre estrange; mas ceu ne tent mie, quar avis sereit que fust aliance. E cist iugement fut rendu a Guillaume Daniau dune part et a David Lo Corre dautre, Bretonz, li quau Bretons oguirent mult de contens en Oleron sur compaignies et sur autres chozes.

Translation: If two or more are partners in a ship, each of the partners may sell his share, if he wants, amongst the others in order to keep the ship within the enterprise of their partnership, for each one may sell his share as a personal thing. Nevertheless some would want to say that one of the partners certainly ought to have the share of the ship before a stranger [but] at the price [offered by] the stranger; but that does not hold because the opinion would be that there was conspiracy.[6] And this judgment was handed down to William Daniau of one part and David Le Corre of the other, Bretons, which Bretons had many disputes in Oléron about partnerships and other matters.

Comment: Chapters 64a and b make it clear that the other partners in joint-ownership have first refusal of a share offered for sale. Chapter 87 pursues the suggestion of a sale price offered by a stranger. However, legal opinion cannot agree to the sale of the ship to a partner at a stranger's offer price because of the risk of 'price fixing'. The *essec* [sale option] still has to be offered to the other partners in any sale of shares, as set out in chapters 64a and b, but this conclusion is contrary to that of Twiss, who suggests that a public sale has to be held.[7] Such a sale, however, would be contrary to the intention of chapter 64c and would destroy the original partnership since a non-partner would become a joint- or part-owner of the partnership's vessel, a situation contrary to merchant practice. Twiss, following Roquefort, derives *aliance* from *aliencer* which he equated with *acheter*, without any etymological explanation.

Partners' responsibilities

Chapter 83: Si duy ou plusor sunt parconer en vne nef, et li vns daus parconners ne voget ou nepuchet espleiter si partie, ia por ce ne remayndra que cil qui ne veaust ou ne puet espleiter sa partie ne fornissent les couz et les missions daus marineaus et de la nef segont sa partie, ja seit ceu que [= jaçoit ce que] il ne espleite sa partie de la nef, quar por ceu nie coste mie mainz [= il ne coute pas

---

[6] Godefroy offers only *aliancer* which he translates as *allier*; it has been assumed that *aliance* in the text derives from that verb and, in this context, may be taken to mean 'conspiracy'.
[7] Twiss, *Black Book*, II, p. 384–5.

LES BONNES USAGES ET LES BONNES COUSTUMES

moins] a fornir les marineas de la nef, en autres missions. Si cil qui ne veaut espleiter sa partie ne ne puet ne ne veaut fornir les couz si cum nos avom dit, li autres qui espleitera sa partie propre de la nef fornira les couz et les missions, et len ert tenguz li cors de la nef einsi que ia neys encore, le autre ne lespleitera decique il len ait paie dreitement de sa partie. Mas or posum einsi. Luns daus parconers charget sa partie, et apres celuy qui ne veost ou ne puet charger sa partie semont, que il facet secte[8] ou couz; si cum nos avom dit, cil en segant ses couz troubet fret, et fornist sa partie einsi que mais assez gaigneret en son fret que li autre en sa charge; or vent cilz qui ha charge et dit que il veaut aver partie comme compaignon on gaig de celuy qui ha frete, et si ait sa partie on gaig de ce que celuy a gaagne de ceu, disons nos que chascun deit aver lo gaig de sa partie cestui de ce que il ha frete, quar lor compaignie est commune devise quant a celuy tor; quar li vns ha especiaument sa partie cestuy de ce que il ha charge, et celuy de ce que il ha frete, quar lor compaignie est commune devise quant a celuy tor.

Translation: If two or more are partners in a ship and one of the partners is unwilling or unable to use his share it does not follow that he who was not willing nor able to use his share [ought] not to meet the costs and expenses of the mariners and of the ship in proportion to his share, despite the fact that he is not using his share of the ship, because it does not, for that reason, cost less to provide the mariners for the ship and other expenses. If he who does not wish to use his share neither can nor wishes to meet the costs as said before, the other who does use his own share of the ship shall meet the [whole] costs and expenses and for that the hull of the ship is to be held as his security so that the other partner cannot use his share again until he has duly paid his share. But now take an example:[9] one of the partners loads his share and then invites him who is not willing or not able to load his share to follow with the costs, as is stated above. If in meeting his costs he [the latter] finds freight and furnishes his share in such a way that he gains more from his freight than the other does from his cargo, then he who has the cargo comes and says that he wants to share as a partner in the profit that he has from the freight and claims his share of the profit which the latter has made, we say that each ought to have the profit from his own share, the latter from that which he has freighted, because their partnership is divided in common for that turn, for one has specifically his share from what he has loaded and the other from what he had in freight because their partnership is divided in common for this turn.

Comment: This chapter may be a scribal amalgam of two chapters from an earlier text. The intention in the first half of the chapter is clear: a partner refusing to take part in a voyage still has to contribute to the running costs of the ship, an

---

[8] *secte* taken to be *suite* from *suivre*.
[9] The textual *posum* is perhaps cognate with *reposoir*, a roadside altar for a monstrance; hence a 'showing' or 'example'.

223

extension of the shared responsibility of partnership. If another partner accepts the defaulter's expenses, the hull may be held as security by that partner until the defaulting partner has repaid his share. The example chosen to illustrate this principle of mutual responsibility however, does not correspond well to the hypothetical situation described. The example begins with a partner who, refusing to accept his responsibilities, has his share of the expenses in the ship met by another partner. The latter obtains a lien on the hull to prevent the defaulting partner from using the ship until he has repaid his creditor, exactly the position described in the first half of the chapter. The example goes on, however, to say that if the quondam defaulting partner pays his share of the expenses and arranges freight, in other words acts as an agent for his share of the ship's cargo space, and that turns out to be more profitable than the negotiations of the other partner, then the vessel, for that particular voyage, is no longer to be regarded as in joint-ownership but in part-ownership and each partner is to take the profit he individually has made. That decision conflicts with the repeated phrase 'lor compaignie est commune devise', which implies joint-ownership of the ship and her ventures, but it is not clear how the change from joint to part-ownership could be effected within a true partnership. The apparently spontaneous appearance of a part-ownership agreement points to the possible inclusion of another chapter, the original of which has been lost, with an example in which two investors have agreed to operate in different ways, one to load his own cargo in his space and the other to sell his space in the hold to other merchants. The missing chapter perhaps defined part-ownership and how shareholders might exploit their share of the ship in different ways, even on the same voyage. The combination of two chapters would explain the verbosity of the text, particularly in the tautologous description of the defaulting partner. It is probable that some mechanism did exist to separate the interests of partners intent on disparate business methods since the distribution of profits made from different types of negotiation would have been extremely difficult to disentangle in a joint-ownership agreement, given the differing capital involvements, risks, payment terms, labour requirements and so on.

Master/servant responsibilities

Chapter 86: Si marineaus deffaut a sa nef garder, et la nef ou li avers en recevet domage, il est tenguz damander en tout lo domage. Et si est einsi que encore plusors parconers lou ait mis parsey ou marineaus, einsi comme vns met autre parsey, cis qui lo aura mis est tenguz damander en tot lo demage, et cil qui aureit recegu lou domage lo poyret demander auquau yl vodra daus dous, ou au marinea ou a celuy qui li aura mis. Mas si hom demandet lo demage a celuy qui li aura mis, lo marinea aura recors a lautre quil y avet mis. Mas, ne pero [= nempero], si cilz qui auront recegu lo damage hant recegu soceablement celuy marineau qui aura este mis, nos de disom mie que cilz qui laureit mis en soyt coupable.

Translation: If a mariner fails to protect his ship and the ship or cargo receive damage, he is bound to make amends for all the damage. And if it happens that amongst several partners one has put a mariner on board for himself and also another has put another on board for himself, he who put him (who caused the damage) on board is to make amends for all the damage and he who suffered the damage can demand it from whichever of the two he prefers, either from the mariner or from him who put him on board. But if the man demands compensation from him who put [the mariner] on board, the mariner would have recourse to the other who had put him there. But, nevertheless, if he who received the damage had recognised sociably (the fault of) that mariner who had been put on board, we say that he who put him aboard is not culpable.

Comment: The first sentence is a clear statement of the personal liability of any member of the crew who causes damage through negligence. The second sentence is confusing; it is clear that if several partners share their ship on the same voyage, each may, or perhaps has to, supply crew on his own behalf (see chapter 95). However, that the partner who placed the man who caused damage is responsible for that damage not only modifies the first sentence but is contrary to merchant law in which the master cannot be held responsible for damage caused by his servant acting on his own initiative, a precept confirmed by Edward III in 1353.[10] An alternative explanation for this anomaly is that the law practised on the island of Oléron was, in this respect, different from merchant law.

There is also some difficulty with the third sentence, possibly arising from a textual error. Twiss, without comment, translates it: 'But if a man demands compensation for damage from him who shall put the mariner on board, the latter shall have a remedy against him whom he has put on board.'[11] In other words, the master who has to pay compensation for damage can claim that from his servant, an indirect affirmation of the position at merchant law when the servant was not acting on his master's orders. The original text, however, does not support that translation unless it implies that the mariner was acting on the authority of his master who placed him on board, when any damage resulting from the sailor's actions would indeed be the responsibility of that partner. Further to confuse the issue, in the last sentence the onus of responsibility for the damage shifts back to the servant and away from his master. 'Hant recegu soceablement' may mean that the sufferer and the perpetrator of the damage have come to a mutually agreeable settlement and the responsibility no longer rests with the partner. In short, this

---

[10] *Statutes* 26 Edward III, st. 2, c. 19 (Statute of the Staple); but see the apparently anomalous decision in the master/servant case of *Pilk v. Vener(e)*, discussed in chapter 1.
[11] Twiss, *Black Book*, II, p. 383.

chapter is almost certainly a somewhat confused reaffirmation of the limitation of a master's responsibilities for the unauthorised actions of his servant. There remains the problem of the responsibility of a partner who has placed an incompetent sailor on board.

Terms of employment

Chapter 65 (Twiss translation): If a mariner, companion or other person aboard a vessel sees anything outside the vessel which he could take and put on the vessel, he is not obliged to take the thing and put it on the vessel if he does not want to. Still less if the owner of the vessel or his representative orders it does he have to, for the mariner is not bound to do anything beyond working the vessel nor to do anything for which he is not engaged.[12] But if it happens that of his own free will he does take something, he is to have half of it and the owner of the vessel the other half, unless there is another agreement between them, for it is said that a contract binds them. And it is understood that if a servant who on land lives on the bread and wine of his master and works on the vessel, his share is for his master and he is firmly bound in all ways to work for the profit of the master.

Comment: This chapter is important because it states that a mariner does not have to obey the orders of his superior beyond his terms of employment – perhaps a vestigial remnant of the cooperative ventures when the shipmaster was merely *primus inter pares* (cf. *Oleron* articles 1, 2, 14 and 18). The division of spoils, half for the sailor who takes it and half for the owner, is at variance with *Queenborough* article 1 which specifies a one third: two thirds division between crew and ship. The last sentence is a reminder of the restricted freedom of servants.

Distribution of incidental costs

Chapter 76 (Twiss translation): The ship pays for the *assiage* (stowage, including fitting bulkheads and setting dunnage), the *planchage*[13] (landing dues) and the *quillage*[14] (pier dues) at her own cost; the cargo, according to its value pays the *rivage* (tolls on the towing paths) and it is to be understood that the people of

---

[12] Twiss, *Black Book*, II, p. 345 translates *mareer* as 'to navigate' but the work of a common sailor would be 'to sail' the ship; Godefroy has *conduire le navire*.
[13] *planchage* translates as 'landing boards' but, in context, is more likely to be a charge for the use, or placing, of landing boards, i.e. a landing charge; see also *Coutumes*, chapter 97.
[14] *quillage* (or *quallage*) may be cognate with 'keel' or 'quay'; in either meaning it may have been based on ship's length or a flat rate. In *CPR, 1391–96*, p. 217 the bailiffs and 'good men' of Mousehole were granted *quayage* for five years to contribute to a wharf. Topsham charged 2d. to dock in the early fourteenth century: *Local Customs Accounts of the Port of Exeter*, p. 1, fn. 2.

Oléron do not pay *rivage* on their own goods which they bring for the service and use of the household, and as to those goods they are to be believed upon their faith and their oath; but of the other goods which they bring from abroad they pay *rivage* equally as strangers, excepting wines which a man has from his own vines and the wines from the quarters of the four lords above mentioned.

Comment: *Oleron* article 13 distributes the costs only of towage and pilotage.

Chapter 95 (Twiss translation): The ship and not her cargo [i.e. the lading merchants] pay *quillage* [pier dues] and great pilotage (sea pilot). But when the ship is well supplied with sailors and a sea pilot, from then on if the merchants want to have more sailors or pilots to have greater safety, it must be at the merchants' cost.

Comment: The division of pilotage charges is described better in *Oleron* article 13. For additional crew, see *Coutumier* chapter 86.

Chapter 97 (Twiss translation): The ship and not the cargo pays *planchage* (landing dues) because every ship ought to have her planks to board and to go ashore, to load and to unload.

Comment: This appears to be a reaffirmation of *Coutumier* chapter 76.

Collision in anchorages

Chapter 82 (Twiss translation): If two ships are anchored and in a storm one of them drags and hits the other and the dragging ship damages the other, the ship which has dragged shall pay half the damage and the other, which has been well anchored, shall pay the other half of the damage, because this is a case of accident. If, however, the ship which has been well anchored can prove, in the view of *prud'hommes* or of other assessors, that by fault of the crew or by fault of the equipment of the said ship, the said ship dragged, and the said damage has been seen and that can be proved, the well anchored ship is not liable for any of the damages. But if the anchoring [ship] met with an accident while coming down on the well anchored ship, then the ship which is well anchored must pay half the damages, because the same could happen to her, and the ship which has dragged [must pay] the other half.

Comment: The view of responsibility for damage in the first sentence of this chapter differs from the less equitable view in *Oleron* article 15; the difference has been discussed under the latter. The conclusion of the third sentence, a 50:50 partition of damages, is the same as the first but now the moving ship is attempting to anchor.

APPENDIX 3

Responsibilities of shipmaster and pilot

Chapter 88 (Twiss translation): The shipmaster must take the ship to and from her ports of lading and unlading on the bridge of the ship, and [the] so-called petty pilotage man (local pilot) is stationed at the entrance to the ports and havens, knowing the dangers of the ports and the havens.

Comment: This is the only standing instruction for a shipmaster, albeit oblique, in the whole of the surviving corpus of medieval maritime law. The silence reflects, perhaps, the master's quondam status as owner of the ship. In separating the responsibilities of shipmaster and pilot, this chapter echoes *Oleron* article 24.

General average

Chapter 94 (Twiss translation): In jettison from a ship, the hull of the ship with all her equipment and with all her stores does not contribute, nor the beds nor the chests nor the things which, briefly, are provided for storing the ship and those within her; but if there are chests and other things carried in the name of merchandise, they all contribute to the jettison.

Comment: This article is similar to article 32 of the extended *Lex d'Oleron* which amends the original *Oleron* article 8.[15] Edward I's Letter Patent of 25 May 1285 exempts the vessel and all her fittings, the shipmaster's ring, bracelet, belt and silver drinking cup and the victuals and cooking utensils of the sailors. However, all other goods on board belonging to the sailors or the merchants such as wines, merchandise, *denarii in grosso* (bullion) and beds, have to be included in the contribution towards the restitution of the items lost.[16] Sailors were to have the freight for the goods which have been saved but the shipmaster was to lose his freight for the goods cast overboard. This chapter, rather more equitably, excludes the beds and personal belongings of the crew, but the crew's portages, which are exempted in *Oleron* article 8, are mentioned in neither the chapter nor in the Letter Patent.

---

[15] Twiss, *Black Book*, I, pp. xli–lxxi and Krieger, *Oleron*, pp. 37–93: the number of articles varies from the basic 24 in MSS LH and LM to 47 in the Breton version of the *Lex*.
[16] Riley, *Liber Albus*, p. 490–1 and *CPR*, 1281–92, pp. 168–9.

APPENDIX 4

Transcription and translation of a 1323 charter-party

MS AML/M/1 at the National Maritime Museum, Greenwich is possibly the earliest English charter-party to have survived. The text consists of ten lines of Norman French (with many Gascon variants) written in a clear hand on parchment. This is one of a pair of copies of the agreement, the original parchment having been cut in two in a sinuous line, with a 'doodle' drawn across the cut for added security. The surviving half has the shipmaster's mark manual, so it may be assumed to have been the merchant's half of the indenture. A quittance has been made out in Latin on the verso, and signed by the recipient of the cargo. The parchment measures 27.4cm x 10.1cm and is in only fair condition, being badly darkened on the right side and along the bottom for about 2.5cm into the text. There is also a square-shaped hole towards the left side between the fourth and fifth lines of text, possibly made by a filing spike, and a vertical crease on the right about 4 cm from the edge. Both sides of the manuscript may be seen in Figures 2a and 2b.

It was transcribed and translated in 1906–07 by a Mr W.K. Boyd who used 'his solution' to intensify the ink in some areas; unfortunately the solution has, with time, obliterated the writing in the treated areas. The translation was published in *The Times* on 4 February 1907 over the signature of Mr G.M. Arnold, mayor of Gravesend and honorary general secretary of the Kent Archaeological Society, without acknowledgement to Boyd. As Boyd's transcription and translation require some correction, revisions were made and published in 1995 by the present author.[1]

Transcription

In the transcription, abbreviations and elisions have been expanded without notice and capital letters have been used as appropriate. Square brackets [ ] enclose supposed letters and words in unreadable areas. No punctuation has been added or removed; // indicates the end of a line.

---

[1] Ward, 'A Surviving Charter-Party'. Thanks are due to Dr Basil Greenhill who brought the charter-party to the writer's attention and to the library staff at the National Maritime Museum, Greenwich for their assistance.

Recto

Sachent tous ceuz qui ceste chartra verront et orront que Sire Hues de Berham en nom et en lu de Sire Adam de Limbergue conestable du chasteu // de Bordeus et par nostre senhor le rey dAnglaterra duc de Guyana et en [nom] et en lu dudit nostre senhor le rey et duc a afrete et cha[rge] // (?)² a Bordeus en le cogua Nostra Dame de Lim de Wauter Gifard mestre .iiij^{xx}.xiij [ton]eus et xviij. pipes de vins des queus³ sont j toneu [iiij]. pipes [de vins] // tint et xliiij toneus de flor de farina .a. aler a Niu Chasteu sur Tine de rot pour .ix. sous de bons esterlins corones dAngleterra chascun toneu de // fret pour reyson de .xxj. toneu .j. pipa pour .xx. E le demurant des pipes .ij. pour le fret de .j. toneu du quel fret le dit mestre [recona] // que estoit payes de .vij. libres .ij. sous de bons esterlins corones dAngleterra en partie de paie dudit fret et [soi] tint pour bien [paies] // E dins xv iorns contes iorn en pres autre en pres que Deus aura conduit et tramis le dite neff a sauvete a sa droite descharge [le vins] // [et] flora de farina deuent estres descharges et le mestre paies de tot son fret sens tot delay et sans tota demora toatge [et petit lomnage // sont sur les mer]chantz E quant le neff parti de Bordeus le mestre et les merchantz furent en bone peis et en bone [amour et sans toute querrele // ceste a scaver viij^a (die)⁴ die exitus Maii anno Domini M⁰ ccc ⁰ xxiij⁰ regnant Karles rey de Fransa Edw[ard regnant en] angleterra duc de Guiayna // (...?...) [archivesque de] Bordeus testes sunt Richard Esparuer Tomas Rosen P Mauran Johan de Rosorde E qe Johan Alein [notoire] public du duche de (...?...) // [de Juins le quele lavandit] P Mauran cartolari pour [volunte] de moy escrist X

Verso

Summa fretti navis // Walteri Giffard magistri // navis vocate Seintemarie // cogge de Lime liij libres xj sous // De quibus solvuntur per A de Limbergh // vij libres ij sous Et per Polhowe xlvj libres x sous // Liberavit Polhou iiij^{xx}.vj dolia vini et xliij dolia flora // deficiunt xvj dolia vini

---

² The word *abordeus* (transcribed as *a Bordeus*) is inset a short distance from the left margin and there may have been another word before it. The reading is made more difficult by the loss of the ending of the last word on the previous line, *cha[rge]*. If the transcription is correct no additional word is required.

³ *queus* is *ques* in the Boyd transcription.

⁴ The Boyd transcription has the word *die* twice; the first is now unreadable on the manuscript, the second is clear and correct. It seems probable that the repetition is either a scribal error or a misreading by Boyd for *viij^{a}die de exitus Maii*, a formulaic expression indicating that the date is to be counted from the end of the month.

Translation

The supposed readings marked by square brackets [ ] in the transcription have been translated but with the brackets retained; gaps within round brackets ( ) have been carried forward; line indications have been omitted and punctuation added.

Know all those who shall see and hear this charter that Sir Hugh de Berham, in the name and place of Sir Adam de Limbergue, constable of the castle of Bordeaux and on behalf of our lord the king of England, duke of Guienne and in [the name] and place of our said lord the king and duke, has freighted and [loaded] at Bordeaux the cog Our Lady of Lyme of Walter Giffard, the master, 93 [tuns] and 18 pipes of wine, of which one tun [4] pipes are adulterated [wine],[5] and 44 tuns of flour, to go directly to Newcastle-upon-Tyne for 9 shillings in good English sterling crowns, each tun of freight at the rate of 21 tuns 1 pipe for 20, and the remainder of the pipes, 2 for the freight of one tun. For which freight the said master [acknowledges] that he was paid in the sum of £7 2s. of good English sterling crowns in part payment of the said freight and held [himself] well [paid] thereof. And within 15 days, counting one day after another as God, he will have conducted and brought the said ship across to safety to her correct discharge. The [wine and] the flour shall be unloaded and the master paid for all his freight without any delay and without any demurrage; towage [and petty lodemanage are on the mer]chants. And when the ship left Bordeaux the master and the merchants were in good peace and in good [love and without any quarrel. That is to say the 8th day] from the end of May 1323,[6] king Charles reigning in France, Edw[ard reigning in] England, [duke] of Guienne, (...?...) [archbishop] of Bordeaux.

Witnesses are [Richard] Esparver, Thomas Rosen, P. Mauran, John de Rosorde. And that John Alein, [notary] public of the Duchy of (...) [of Juins, which the fore-mentioned] P. Mauran, registrar,[7] wrote by my [will] X.

Endorsed on the back

Sum of the freight of the ship of Walter Giffard, master, the ship called Saint Marie cog of Lyme £53 11s. Of which is cleared by A. de Limbergue £7 2s. and

---

[5] The translation of *vin(s) tint* is uncertain. Boyd had 'stock wine'; as it was a May delivery the wine would have been *reek* and *vin tint* may have been an alternative, but unknown, name for that. Alternatively, maybe 1 tun 4 pipes of the wine had been cosmetically enhanced with *vinum tinctum* (*vin teinturier*) as in Jeanine Sauvanon, *Les Métiers au Moyen Age*, (Chartres, 1993), p. 51: 'Des filous versaient aussi quelques mésures de "vinum tinctum" (vin teinturier) lorsque la récolte n'était pas bonne et produisait un vin de petite couleur.'

[6] The Boyd translation has 1322 although in his transcription is correctly $M^o\ ccc^o\ xxiij$. With the correction in fn. 4, the date of the charter-party should be 23 May 1323, not Boyd's 8 May 1322.

[7] *cartolari* is not immediately identifiable but is almost certainly cognate with Middle French *cartulaire*: 'registrar'.

APPENDIX 4

by Polhowe £46 10s. Polhou has released 86 tuns of wine and 43 tuns of flour and 16 tuns of wine are deficient

Comment

It was ambitious of Giffard to undertake to make the passage of around 1,000 nautical miles within 15 days; he apparently fulfilled his promise although, because the quittance is undated, that is uncertain. From the charter-party it is known that the wine and flour had been freighted at the king's behest. The shipping of cereal from Bordeaux to England was unusual but, in the spring and summer of 1323, the king began to collect troops in the north and was ordering victuals for them to be sent to Newcastle and Berwick. In July proclamations had been read in Westmoreland, York, Cumberland and Northumberland that everyone was to 'bake, brew and provide victuals without delay against the king's arrival in the north whither he is journeying from Yorkshire to repress the rebellion of the Scots'. At the same time old and new cereals, and other victuals, were to be sent from London, and all other ports and any ships arriving with food were to be turned round and directed to the north.[8] Ironically both the senechal and the constable of Bordeaux were told at the beginning of June, shortly after Giffard's departure, that further supplies from Gascony of wine and victuals, nobles, horses and men-at-arms would not be required and that any outstanding orders were cancelled.[9]

The missing cargo

The quantities of wine and flour loaded in Bordeaux and unloaded in Newcastle reveal substantial deficiencies. Further, the sum paid in advance and on delivery does not correspond with either the agreed freight rate per tun delivered nor with the original bargain. These discrepancies invite examination.

Flour

The flour was apparently packed in tun barrels; 44 of these were reportedly loaded, of which Polhowe identified and released only 43. There are four possible explanations for the apparent loss of one tun:
i   A tun was shipped free of charge for the use of the crew *en voyage*.
ii A tun was lost overboard or irretrievably damaged by water
iii A tun was removed from the ship by a military commander somewhere en route. Such opportunism was not unknown.[10]

---

[8] CCR, 20 July 1323 and 24 July 1323.
[9] CCR, 2 June 1323.
[10] CCR, 8 August 1322. Robert de Sexton was reported to have taken various quantities

232

iv One of the tuns was wrongly identified in either Bordeaux or Newcastle.

Wine

102 tuns were reportedly loaded of which Polhowe identified and released only 86. There are five possible explanations for the apparent loss of 16 tuns:
i to iii as for the flour with the added complication that if one of the tuns was wrongly identified but the total was correct, the wine loss was one tun more.
iv Leakage and ullage, possibly spread over several tuns
vi Two tuns were taken as *prisage* for which the royal butler would have paid the carriage. As an 'OHMS' delivery it might be expected that the cargo was exempt from duty but possibly the bureaucracy was too inflexible to recognise that privilege. There is no indication in the endorsement of *prisage* taken and the Michaelmas 1322–33 Butler's Accounts show no Newcastle *prisages*.[11]

The freight costs

The freight charge calculation is occult; the amount of money received by Giffard does not obviously correspond to any combination of possibilities. It is clear from the charter-party that the basic rate of 9s. per tun was to be discounted so that 21 tuns 1 pipe, i.e. 21½ tuns, were to be charged as 20 tuns. It is not so clear what is to be charged for the 'remaining pipes' or indeed, what were the remaining pipes. Assuming that they were all the pipe-size casks loaded, then it is necessary only to divide by two and charge the quotient as tuns; 18 pipes were loaded so there were nine tuns to be charged at either the basic rate or the discounted rate. It is perhaps just possible that the remaining pipes were those left over after the calculation, in which case they may have been charged at the basic rate. Another difficulty lies in the 1 tun 4 pipes of *vins tint* which may have been treated in the calculation as either three 'whole' tuns or as five casks of two sizes. A further complication is that if a pipe or a tun of the wine of inferior quality, together with a tun of flour, were shipped as crew's rations, those casks would have travelled free of charge.

The shilling difference shown in the endorsement between what Giffard appears to have received (£53 12s.) and what Polhowe calculated was his due (£53 11s.) also requires explanation:

---

of wheat from two ships when he was constable of Scarborough castle, the king's clerk was acquitted of the costs.
[11] Denizens' wine cargoes were subject to *Recta Prise* by which one tun was taken from cargoes of up to 19 tuns and two tuns from cargoes of 20 and over, one from before and the other from aft of the mast.

APPENDIX 4

Polhowe released 129 tuns and therefore owed Giffard for their freight
i.e. 129 tuns x 20/21.5 x 9s = £54 0s. 0d.
Giffard was paid £7 2s. up front and £46 10s. on quittance = £53 12s. 0d.
There was therefore an underpayment to Giffard of   8s. 0d.
less the overpayment in the endorsement of   1s. 0d.
leaving a nett underpayment of   7s. 0d.

As it seems unlikely that Giffard would have allowed himself to be underpaid by Polhowe, there must be more to this affair than is now apparent.

The competitiveness of Giffard's discounted freight rate of 8s. 4½d. per tun may be judged by another near-contemporary charge for an identical voyage: in 1324–25, two ships were freighted in Bordeaux for London at 10s. per tun, although that rate may have been elevated by the risks of war in Gascony and by convoy protection money.[12]

---

[12] James, *Wine Trade*, Appendix 18, p. 151, citing PRO, Exchequer, King's Remembrancer, Accounts Various (Butlerage and *prisage*), 77/23 and 77/29.

APPENDIX 5

Transcription and translation of the chapter de regimen transfretantium from Gilbertus Anglicus' Compendium Medicine[1]

Gilbertus Anglicus, a well known thirteenth-century physician,[2] travelled to the Holy Land by sea in 1240. He drew on his maritime experience to give advice for those travelling by sea; that advice makes up part of a chapter in his *Compendium Medicine*, published in 1510. Because of its relevance to health on medieval ships, it has been transcribed and translated here, perhaps for the first time,[3] using the text of a sixteenth-century printed copy of his manuscript. The health of the crew on a medieval ship is discussed in chapter 5.

Transcription

Book 7, folio ccclxij, recto, right-hand column, from line 23 to end
Abbreviations have been silently expanded; punctuation has been left unaltered; the letters *b* and *h*, printed identically, have been differentiated; the letters *u* and *v* have been changed as necessary to regularise the Latin and the letters *i* and *j* have been left as printed. Two compositor's errors have been corrected: para 1 line 2, inversion of *et* and *rectificatione*; and para 2 line 5, *sedimen* for *sedinem*.

---

[1] *Compendium medicine Gilberti anglici tam morborum universalium quam particularium nondum medicis sed et cyrurgicis utilissimum*, ed. Michael de Capella (Lyons, 1510), 7, pp. 362–3. A copy of Gilbert's manuscript is in the British Library, MS Sloane 272, *Laurea Anglicana*. The earliest known manuscript is TK3: Bruges, Belgium, Bibliothèque Publique MS 469, dated 1271. I am grateful to the librarian of the Royal Society of Medicine, whose copy of the Capella edition I used, and to Dr Tony Hunt of St Peter's College, Oxford, who so willingly helped with the translation.
[2] Chaucer, *General Prologue*, line 434: Gilbert is included in the list in the cynical description of physicians.
[3] This chapter of the *Compendium*, which also covered the reproductive system, diseases of women, how to light fires and antidotes to poisons, is omitted from all known Middle English translations, one of which has been edited by F.M. Getz, *Healing and Society in Medieval England: A Middle English Translation of the Pharmaceutical Writings of Gilbertus Anglicus* (Madison, WI, 1991); no other translation of this chapter has been found.

APPENDIX 5

De regimine transfretantium

Regimen transfretantium mare principaliter in quattuor consistit scilicet in prohibitione nausee et sedatione vomitus in rectificatione fetoris marini in sedatione sitis et rectificatione aque. Prohibitio nausee completur per usum fructuum acetosorum in ieiunio. ut citoniorum. malorum granatorum acetosorum et citrangulorum limonorum. et per potationem seminis apij. vel cerfolij. decoctionis in aqua que decoctio bibatur a ieiuno. Sedeat autem capite erecto et teneat firmiter ad trabem et non respiciat hac aut illac: et non moveatur caput nisi motu navis. Sugat autem dulcia aut comedat semina eructuativa.

Post vero vomitum si acciderit accipiat mala granata acria et dulcia et ficus et penides et non comedat quousque stomachus vel vomitus omnino sedetur. et accidentia quiescant. tunc accipiat stomatichon aut dyantos aut aliud confortatium. comedat autem cibaria digestibilia. Et quia necesse est comedere salsa et legumina comedat ea bene cocta et non quotidie, et sint salsa cocta in tribus aquis vel quattuor: et macerentur prius in aqua dulci quamvis dicant quidam aquam salsam sal sedimen extrahere. Sit autem vinum bonum oderiferum. et quotidie mane accipiat de electuarijs bonis odoriferis.

Rectificatur autem fetor maris per usum electuariorum aromaticorum confortantium cor et cerebrum et stomachum ut faciant residentiam fortem. sicut est pliris muscatum. dyanthos cum musco. dyamargariton. post cibum masticentur gariof. muscari. ambrati. et teneantur in ore. et nux muscata et huiusmodi. teneatur lapdanum in manu aut pomum ambre. aut aliud odoriferum. Eligatur locus a sentina remotus et a canalibus quibus aque fetentes projiciuntur. Caveant in quantum possunt ab oppressione hominum et membrorum. et deambulent sepius super summitates navis ad eventandum et mundificent vestimenta a spurcicijs pulicum et pediculorum. et mutent vestes et renovent prout sepius poterunt ut inde natura exhilaretur Sedatur autem sitis per frigida et humida quorum confectiones satis patent superius.

Rectificatur autem aqua per eventationem et excolationem et agitationem et motum aut per excoctionem et post per imittatur residere. et fex abijciatur aut coletur per arenam limpidam recentem. aut si fieri potest sublimetur per duplicia vasa scilicet per alembicum ad nobiles sic enim fit aqua salsa dulcis. Et dicit Avicenna quod aqua mala aceto rectificatur. ponatur ergo in aqua parum de aceto. aut limones

Assumantur autem in nave uve passe. cepe. cucumeres. mala et pira. dyadragagantum. et cum dyadragaganto distemperetur aqua aut dyanthos. et assuescat semen feniculi. et portulace masticate. destruit enim sitim.

Caveat autem in meridie a calore in nocte a frigore a nimia constipatione et solutione. et statim nocumentis supervenientibus occurrat.

Dominus autem omnia dirigat in tranquilate. Amen.

'DE REGIMEN TRANSFRETANTIUM'
Translation

Person, tense, voice and mood have been modernised and made consistent. The third person singular 'he' has been used throughout although the plural occurs in places; punctuation has been added.

Instruction for those making a sea passage
The instruction for travel by sea consists principally of four parts; namely, in the prevention of nausea and reduction of vomiting, in the rectification of marine stenches, in the assuaging of thirst and in the purification of water. The prevention of nausea is achieved by the use, while fasting, of bitter fruit such as quinces, bitter pomegranates and oranges and, as a drink, a decoction of anise or chervil, the mixture to be drunk on an empty stomach. Also, he [the patient] should sit with the head erect and hold firmly to the beams [of the ship] and not look this way or that and the head should not move except with the motion of the ship. He should suck beforehand sweetmeats or eat seeds which produce belching.

If vomiting has occurred he should afterwards take bitter pomegranate, sweetmeats, figs and a thread of sugar and should not eat until the stomach or vomiting has completely settled down and the symptoms subside. Then let him take a stomach preparation of either extract of rosemary or another strengthening agent and let him eat digestible food. And because it is necessary to eat salted foods and vegetables, he should eat them well cooked, but not every day; the salted food should be cooked in three or four washings and soaked first in fresh water, although some say salt water, to remove the salt sediment. Also, he may take a well flavoured wine and, daily, in the morning, sweet smelling pastilles.

The smell of the sea may also be reduced by the use of aromatic pastilles so that by strengthening the heart, brain and stomach they may offer a strong resistance; for example, musk pastilles, extract of rosemary with musk [and] medicinal pearl powder. He should chew after meals cloves and musk in ambergris, hold in the mouth nutmeg and anything of that kind and hold in the hand, labdanum or a pomander or some other fragrant substance. A place should be chosen remote from the bilge and the drains through which the fetid waters run. He should avoid whenever possible the oppression of men and limbs and should walk about sheltered on the highest parts of the ship for the purpose of cleansing garments of filthy fleas and lice and change and renew clothes as often as he can in order that they may be freshened naturally. Also thirst may be asssuaged by cold and humid preparations which are sufficiently clear from the above.

Furthermore, water may be purified by the process of aerating, settling out, shaking and movement or by boiling and afterwards being allowed to settle and the sediment may be thrown away or filtered through fresh, clean sand. Or, if it is possible to distill it in a double vessel, that is, an alembic, as it is known, then salt water can be made fresh. And Avicenna says: just as water may be purified by sour wine, so put in just a little vinegar or lemon.

There should also be in the ship raisins, onions, cucumbers, apples and pears, medicament of tragacanth and with the tragacanth medicament should be mixed water or extract of rosemary and, as is customary, fennel seed and shredded portulace because that destroys thirst.

Furthermore, let him avoid the heat of midday or the cold of the night, or excessive constipation or diarrhoea, then he may resist such harmful things as may befall him.

Otherwise, may God direct all in tranquillity. Amen.

Select Bibliography

Primary sources

State Papers, The National Archives – Public Record Office
Early Chancery Proceedings (C1)
Chancery Miscellanea (C47)
Gascon Rolls (C61)
Exchequer, King's Remembrancer, Accounts Various (E101)
Exchequer, King's Remembrancer, Customs Accounts (E122)
Exchequer, Lord Treasurer's Remembrancer, Enrolled Customs Accounts (E356)
Exchequer, Lord Treasurer's Remembrancer, Memoranda Roll (E358)
Exchequer, Lord Treasurer's Remembrancer, Foreign Accounts (E364)
Special Collecton, Ancient Petitions (SC8)
High Court of Admiralty, Examinations (13/11), 1536–1537

London, British Library
Additional MS. 4564 (Compotus emptionis navium que abierunt Iherosolimam)
Additional MS. 37204 (The booke of the sea carte)
Lansdowne MS 285

Corporation of The City of London Records Office, Guildhall
MS *Liber Horn*, folios 355v–360r (Lex d'Oleron).
MS *Liber Memorandum*, folios 103v–110v (Lex d'Oleron).

Greenwich, National Maritime Museum
MS AML/M/1 (Charter party, 23 May 1323)

Hamburg, Commerzbibliothek
Altes Seebuch, saeculi, ut videtur, XIV, MSS 'A' and 'B'

New York, Pierpont Morgan Library
Hastings MS 775

'Accounts and Inventories of John Starlyng, Clerk of the King's Ships to Henry IV', ed. Alan Moore, *Mariner's Mirror* 4, 1 (1914), pp. 20–6 and 4, 6 (1916), pp. 167–73.
The Accounts of John Balsall, Purser of the Trinity of Bristol, 1480–81, ed. T.F. Reddaway and A.A. Ruddock, Camden Miscellany 4th Series, XXIII (London, 1969).
The Acts of the Parliament of Scotland, vol. 1, MCXXIV–MCCCCXXIII (Edinburgh, 1844).
Admiralty chart no. 20, *Ile d'Ouessant to Pointe de la Coubre*.

SELECT BIBLIOGRAPHY

Admiralty Tidal Stream Atlas, NP250 (English Channel), NP 251 (North Sea, Southern Part) and NP265 (France, West Coast).

Admiralty Tide Tables, *NP 201* (UK) and *NP 202* (Europe).

L'Art de Navigver de Maistre Pierre de Medine, Espaignol, Traduit de Castillan en Françoys par Nicolas Nicolai du Dauphiné, Geographe du tres-Chrestien Henri II de ce nom (Lyon, 1554, facsimile edn, Milan, 1988).

Barbour's Bruce, ed. Matthew P. McDiarmid and James A.C. Stevenson, The Scottish Text Society, 3 vols (Edinburgh, 1985).

Beowulf, ed. C.L. Wren, revised W.F. Bolton (London, 1973).

The Black Book of the Admiralty, see *Monumenta Juridica*.

The Black Book of Southampton, ed. G.B.W. Chapman, 3 vols, Southampton Record Society, XIII, XIV and XVII (1912–13).

The Book of the Wanderings of Felix Faber, ed. and trans. Aubrey Stewart, 2 vols (London, 1892).

Borough Customs, ed. Mary Bateson, 2 vols, Selden Society 8 and 21 (1904–6).

Bourne, William, *A Regiment for the Sea and Other Writings on Navigation by William Bourne, Gunner, 1535–82*, ed. E.G.R. Taylor, Hakluyt Society, 2, 121 (1963).

The Brokage Book of Southampton, 1439–40, ed. B.D.M. Bunyard, Southampton Record Society, XL (1941).

The Brokage Book of Southampton 1443–44, ed. Olive Coleman, 2 vols, Southampton Record Series, IV and VI (1960–61).

Calendar of Close Rolls, 1272–1500, 47 vols (1892–1956).

A Calendar of Early Chancery Proceedings Relating to West Country Shipping, 1388–1493, ed. D.A. Gardiner, Devon and Cornwall Record Society, NS 21 (1976).

Calendar of Fine Rolls, 1272–1509, 22 vols (1911–63).

Calendar of Letter-Books Preserved Among the Archives of the Corporation of the City of London at the Guildhall, Books A–L (1275–t. Henry VII), ed. Reginald R. Sharpe (1899–1912).

Calendar of Letters from the Mayor and Corporation of the City of London, c.1350–1370, ed. Reginald R. Sharpe (1885).

Calendar of Patent Rolls, 1232–1509, 52 vols (London 1891–1916).

Calendar of Plea and Memoranda Rolls of the City of London Preserved Among the Archives of the Corporation of the City of London, 1323–1482, 6 vols, ed. A.H. Thomas (vols 1–4) and P.E. Jones (vols 5–6) (Cambridge, 1926–61).

Calendar of Wills Proved and Enrolled in the Court of Hustings, London, 1258–1688, Preserved Among the Archives of the Corporation of the City of London, 2 vols, ed. R.R. Sharpe (1889–90).

Chaucer, Geoffrey, *The Complete Works of Geoffrey Chaucer*, ed. F.N. Robinson (2nd edn, Oxford, 1979).

The Chester Customs Accounts 1301–1566, ed. K.P. Wilson, The Record Society of Lancashire and Cheshire, CXI (1969).

The Chronicles of England, France, Spain and Adjoining Countries, Sir John Froisart, ed. Thomas Johnes, 2 vols (London, 1874).

A Collection of Ordinances and Regulations for the Government of the Royal Household, The Society of Antiquaries (London, 1790).

SELECT BIBLIOGRAPHY

Compendium Medicine Gilberti anglici tam morborum universalium quam particularium nondum medicis sed et cyrgurgicis utilissimum, ed. Michael de Capella (Lyons, 1510).
The Complaynt of Scotlande wyth ane Exortatione to the Thre Estaits to be Vigilante in the Deffens of their Public Veil, 1549, 2 vols, ed. J.A.H. Murray, EETS ES 17 and 18 (London, 1872–73).
Le Coutumier de L'Ile d'Oléron, ed. M. Charles Bémont (Paris, 1919).
Dante Alighieri, *Inferno*, ed. John D. Simpson (London, 1961).
Documents relatifs au Clos des Galées de Rouen et aux armées de mer du roi de France de 1293 à 1418, ed. A. Chazelas, 2 vols (Paris, 1977–8).
Documents Relating to the Law and Custom of the Sea (1205–1648), ed. R.G. Marsden, Navy Records Society, 2 vols, 49 and 50 (London, 1916).
Expeditions to Prussia and the Holy Land Made by Henry Earl of Derby (afterwards King Henry IV) in the Years 1390–91 and 1392–93 ed. L. Toulmin-Smith, Camden Society (London, 1894).
Extracts from the Records of the Company of Hostmen of Newcastle-upon-Tyne, ed. F.W. Dendy, Surtees Society (1901).
Foedera, Conventiones, Litterae et Cujuscunque Generis Acta Publica inter Reges Angliae et Alios quosvis Imperatores, Reges, Pontifices, Principes vel Comunitates, ab Ineunte Saeculo Duodecimo, vix Anno 1101 ad nostra usque Tempora, Habita aut Tractata, 1066–1383 AD, ed. Thomas Rymer, 4 vols (London, 1816–69): 1383 AD ff., 10 vols (The Hague, 1793–1845).
The Great Red Book of Bristol, ed. E.W.W. Veale, 5 vols, Bristol Record Society II, IV, VIII, XVI, XVIII (1931–53).
Howard Accounts: Expenses of Sir John Howard etc., ed. T.H. Turner, Roxburghe Club (1841).
Hues, Robert, *Tractatus de Globis*, ed. Clements R. Markham; James Gairdner *Sailing Directions for the Circumnavigation of England and a Voyage to the Straits of Gibraltar*, Hakluyt Society, 79 (London, 1889) [Lansdowne MS 285].
Hydrographic Department, Ministry of Defence, *Underwater Handbook, Western Aproaches to the British Isles* (London, 1970).
João de Castro, *Obras completas de João de Castro*, ed. A. Cortesão and Luis de Alburquerque (Coimbra, 1969–82).
Langland, William, *Richard Redeless*, ed. W.W. Skeat, EETS OS 54 (London, 1873).
The Libelle of Englyshe Polycye, ed. Sir George Warner (Oxford, 1926).
Liber Albus, ed. Henry Thomas Riley (London, 1861).
The Lisle Letters, ed. Muriel St. Clare Byrne, 6 vols (Chicago and London, 1981).
The Little Red Book of Bristol, ed. F.B. Bickley, 2 vols (Bristol and London, 1900).
Livro de Marinharia, Códice de 1514, João de Lisboa (reprinted Lisbon, 1903).
Local Customs Accounts of the Port of Exeter, 1266–1321, ed. Maryanne Kowaleski, Devon and Cornwall Record Society, NS 36 (1993).
The Local Port Book of Southampton for 1435–36, ed. B. Foster, Southampton Record Series, VII (1963).
The Local Port Book of Southampton for 1439–40, ed. H.S. Cobb, Southampton Record Series, V (1961).

SELECT BIBLIOGRAPHY

Malory, Thomas, *Works*, ed. Eugène Vinaver (Oxford, 2nd edition, 1971).

Memorials of Henry the Fifth, King of England, ed. C.A Cole, Rolls Series XI (London, 1858).

Memorials of London and London Life in the Thirteenth, Fourteenth and Fifteenth Centuries, 1276–1419, ed. H.T. Riley (London, 1868).

Monumena Henrici: Comissão Executiva das Comerações do Quinto Centenário da Morte do Infante D. Henrique, 14 vols (Coimbra, 1960–73).

Monumenta Juridica: Black Book of the Admiralty, ed. Sir Travers Twiss, 4 vols, Rolls Series 55 (1871–76).

Morte Arthure or The Death of Arthur, ed. Edmund Brock, EETS OS 8 (1871, reprint 1961).

La Navigation dv Roy d'Escosse Iaques Cinqviesme du Nom, Avtour de son Royaume, & Isles Hebrides & Orchades, soubz la conduicte d'Alexandre Lyndsay excellent Pilote Escossois, ed. Nicolas Nicolai (Paris, 1583).

The Oak Book of Southampton c.AD 1300, ed. Paul Studer, 2 vols and supplement, Southampton Record Society X, XI, XII and supplement (1910–11).

The Poems of the Pearl Manuscript, ed. Malcolm Andrew and Ronald Waldron (London, 1978).

The Port Books of Southampton, 1427–30, ed. Paul Studer, Southampton Record Society XV (1913).

Proceedings and Ordinances of the Privy Council of England, 10 Richard II – 33 Henry VIII, ed. Sir Nicholas Nicolas, 7 vols (1834–37).

Proceedings before the Justices of the Peace in the Fourteenth and Fifteenth Centuries, Edward III to Richard III, ed. B.H. Putnam (1938).

R. Ricard, *The Maire of Bristowe is Kalendar*, ed. L. Toulmin-Smith, Camden Society, NS V (1872).

Records of Some Sessions of the Peace in Lincolnshire, ed. R. Sillem, Lincoln Record Society XXX (1936).

'Registres de grands jours de Bordeaux', 1456, 1459, ed. H.A. Barckhausen, *Les Archives historiques du départment de la Gironde*, IX (Paris and Bordeaux, 1867).

The Rhodian Sea-Law, ed. Walter Ashburner (Oxford, 1909).

Rose, Susan, ed., *The Navy of the Lancastrian Kings: Accounts and Inventories of William Soper, Keeper of the King's Ships 1422–1427*, Navy Records Society 123 (1982).

Rotuli Parliamentorum ut et Petiones et Placita in Parliamento, Edward I–Henry VII, ed. J. Strachey, 6 vols and index (1783–1832).

A Rutter of the Scottish Seas circa 1540, ed. A.B. Taylor, revd. I.H. Adams and G. Fortune, Maritime Monographs and Reports, 44 (Greenwich, 1980).

Sailing Directions for the Circumnavigation of England etc., ed., James Gairdner; see Robert Hues, *Tractatus de Globis*.

Select Cases Concerning the Law Merchant, 1239–1633, 3 vols, ed. Charles Gross and Hubert Hall, Selden Society 23, 46 and 49 (1908–32).

Select Cases in the Court of King's Bench under Edward I, II and III, ed, G.O. Sayles, 5 vols, Selden Society 55, 57, 58, 74, 76 (1936–57).

Select Pleas in the Court of Admiralty, The Court of Admiral of the West, 1390–1404 and

The High Court of Admiralty, 1527–1545, ed. R.G. Marsden, 2 vols Selden Society 6 and 15 (1892, 1894).
Select Tracts and Table Books relating to English Weights and Measures 1100–1742, ed. Hubert Hall and F.J. Nicholas, Camden Miscellany 3rd Series XV (1929).
The Ship of Fools, trans. Alexander Barclay, ed. T.H. Jamieson, 2 vols (Edinburgh and London, 1874).
The Stacions of Rome, the Pilgrims Sea-Voyage, with Clene Maydenhod, ed. F.J. Furnivall, EETS OS 25 (1867).
The Staple Court Books of Bristol, ed. E.C. Rich, Bristol Record Society V (Bristol, 1934).
The Statutes at Large from Magna Charta to the End of the Eleventh Parliament of Great Britain, Anno 1761, ed. Danby Pickering, 28 vols (Cambridge, 1762–9).
The Stewards' Book of Southampton from 1428 to 1439, ed. H.W. Gidden, 2 vols, Southampton Record Society XXXV and XXXIX (1935, 1939).
The Travels of Leo of Rozmital, ed. M. Letts, Hakluyt Society, 2nd series 108 (1957).
The Treatise on the Laws and Customs of the Realm of England, Commonly Called Glanvill, ed. and trans. George D.G. Hall (London, 1965).
Ursprung und Wurzeln des Rôles D'Oléron, ed. Karl-Friedrich Krieger, Quellen und Darstellungen zur Hansischen Geschichte, Neue Folge/Bande XV (Cologne and Vienna, 1970).
The Vision of Piers Plowman, B Text, ed. A.V.C. Schmidt (London, 1978).
The Voyages and Colonising Enterprises of Sir Humphrey Gilbert, ed. D.B. Quinn, 2 vols, Hakluyt Society (1940).
'The Voyages of Ohthere and Wulfstan', in *Sweets Anglo-Saxon Reader in Prose and Verse*, ed. Dorothy Whitelock (Oxford, 1983).
William Worcestre, Itineraries, ed. John H. Harvey (Oxford, 1969).
Year Books of Edward II, Edward III, Richard II, Henry IV, Henry V and Henry VI; variously Selden Society, Chronicles and Memorials of Great Britain and Ireland during the Middle Ages and The Ames Foundation.
The Year Books of Yorkshire Sessions of the Peace, 1361–4, ed. B.H. Putnam, Yorkshire Archaeological Society Record Series C (1939).

Secondary sources

Adam, P., ed., *Mariners and the Law of the Sea in Later Medieval England*, Commission internationale d'histoire maritime (Paris, 1981).
Arthur, Harold, Viscount Dillon, 'On a Manuscript Collection of Ordinances of Chivalry of the Fifteenth Century Belonging to Lord Hastings', *Archaeologia*, 2nd Series, 7 (1900), pp. 29–70.
Asaert, G., 'Antwerp Ships in English Harbours in the Fifteenth Century', *Acta Historiae Nederlandicae* XII (1979), pp. 29–47.
Aston, Margaret, *The Fifteenth Century* (London, 1968).
Atiyah, P.S., *The Rise and Fall of Freedom of Contract* (Oxford, 1987).

SELECT BIBLIOGRAPHY

Avery, Margaret E., 'The History of the Equitable Jurisdiction of Chancery before 1460', *Bulletin of the Institute of Historical Research* 42 (1969), pp. 129–44.

Baker, J.H., *An Introduction to English Legal History* (3rd edn, London, 1990).

Barron, Caroline and Nigel Saul, *England and the Low Countries in the Late Middle Ages* (Stroud, 1995)

Bellamy, J.G., *The Criminal Trial in Later Medieval England* (Stroud, 1998).

Bennett, J.A., *The Divided Circle* (Oxford, 1987).

Bernard, J., *Navires et gens de mer à Bordeaux (vers 1400–vers 1550)*, 3 vols (Paris, 1968).

Blair, John and Nigel Ramsay, eds, *English Medieval Industries: Craftsmen, Techniques, Products* (London, 1991).

Boiteaux, L.A., *La Fortune de mer: le besoin de securité et les débuts de l'assurance maritime*, École pratique des hautes études, VIème section, Ports-Routes-Trafics, XXIV (Paris, 1968).

Bolton, J.L., *The Medieval English Economy, 1150–1500* (London, 1980, reprint with supp., 1988).

——, ed., *The Alien Communities of London in the Fifteenth Century* (Stamford, 1998).

Bradley, H., 'The Datini Factors in London, 1380–1410', in *Trade, Devotion and Governance*, ed. D.J. Clayton, R.G. Davies and P. McNiven (Stroud, 1994).

Bridbury, A.R., *England and the Salt Trade in the Later Middle Ages* (Oxford, 1955).

——, 'The Black Death', *Economic History Review*, 2nd series 26, 4 (1973), pp. 557–92.

——, *Economic Growth; England in the Later Middle Ages* (2nd edn, Sussex, 1975).

Brindley, H.H., 'Reefing Gear', *MM* 2 (1912), pp. 129–34

——, 'Medieval Ships', *Mariner's Mirror* 12 (1926), pp. 211–16 and 14 (1928), pp. 76–7.

Britnell, R.H., *The Commercialisation of English Society 1000–1500* (Cambridge, 1992).

Brulez, W., 'Shipping Profits in the Early Modern Period', *Acta Historiae Nederlandicae*, XIV (1981), pp. 65–84.

Bühler, Curt, 'Sir John Paston's "Grete Booke", A 15th-century "Best Seller"', *Modern Language Notes* 56 (1941), pp. 345–51

Burwash, Dorothy, *English Merchant Shipping, 1460–1540* (Toronto, 1947 reprint Newton Abbot, 1969).

Camporesi, Piero, *Bread of Dreams: Food and Fantasy in Early Modern Europe* (London, 1989).

Carpenter, Christine, ed. *Kingsford's Stonor Papers and Papers 1290–1483*, Camden Classic Reprint (Cambridge, 1996).

Carpenter, Turner W.J., 'The Building of the *Holy Ghost of the Tower*, 1414–1416, and Her Subsequent History', *Mariner's Mirror* 40, 1 (1954), pp. 55–72.

Carus-Wilson, E.M., 'The Effects of the Acquisition and of the Loss of Gascony on the English Wine Trade', *Bulletin of the Institute of Historical Research*, XXI (1946–48), pp. 145–54.

——, *Medieval Merchant Venturers* (Oxford, 1954).

——, *Merchant Adventurers of Bristol in the Fifteenth Century* (Bristol, 1962).

SELECT BIBLIOGRAPHY

——, *The Overseas Trade of Bristol in the Later Middle Ages* (2nd edn, London, 1967).

—— and Olive Coleman, *England's Export Trade, 1275–1547* (Oxford, 1963).

Cave, Roy C. and Herbert H. Coulson, *A Source Book of Medieval Economic History* (New York, 1936, reprint 1965).

Cheshire and Fifoot, eds, *Furniston's Law of Contract* (13th edn, London, 1996).

Childs, Wendy R., *Anglo-Castilian Trade in the Later Middle Ages* (Manchester, 1978).

——, '"To Oure Losse and Hindraunce": English Credit to Alien Merchants in the Mid-Fifteenth Century', in *Enterprise and Individuals in Fifteenth Century England*, ed. Jennifer Kermode (Stroud, 1991).

——, 'Anglo-Portuguese Trade in the Fifteenth Century', *Transactions of the Royal Historical Society*, 6th series II (1992), pp. 195–219.

—— and John Taylor, eds, *Politics and Crisis in the Fourteenth Century* (Gloucester, 1990).

Cipolla, Carlo M., 'Currency Depreciation in Medieval Europe', *Economic History Review*, 2nd series 15, 3 (1962–3), pp. 413–27.

Constable, C.G., C.L. Johnson and S.P. Lund, 'Global Geomagnetic Field Models for the Past 3000 Years: Transient or Permanent Flux Lines?', *Philosophical Transactions of the Royal Society of London* 358 (2000), pp. 991–1008.

Constable, Olivia R., 'The Problem of Jettison in Mediterranean Maritime Law', *Journal of Medieval History* 20 (1994), pp. 207–20.

Cooper, H.A., 'The Dunwich Iceland Ships', *Mariner's Mirror* 25, 2 (1939), pp. 170–7.

Coulton, G.G., *Medieval Panorama* (Cambridge, 1937).

Cousins, Edward F. and Robert Anthony, eds, *Pease and Chitty's Law of Markets and Fairs* (4th edn, Croydon, 1993).

Cruz, António, 'Quadros da vida social e económica da cidade do Porto no século quinze', *Anais da Academia Portuguesa de História*, 2nd series 26, 2 (Lisbon, 1980), pp. 202–13.

Cutting, Charles L., *Fish Saving: A History of Fish Processing from Ancient to Modern Times* (London, 1955).

Dawes, George, *An Extract by Way of the Ancient Laws of Oleron Rendred into English etc.* (London, 1685).

Davis, J.E., *Notes on Deep-Sea Sounding* (London, 1867).

Davis, Norman, ed., *The Paston Letters and Papers of the Fifteenth Century*, 2 vols (Oxford, 1971–76).

Day, J., 'The Great Bullion Famine of the Fifteenth Century', *Past and Present* 79 (May 1978), pp. 3–54.

Delumeau, Jean, ed., *Histoire de la Bretagne* (Toulouse, 1969, 2nd edn, 1987), pp. 161–86.

Dubuy, Georges, ed., *A History of Private Life*, 2 vols (Cambridge, MA, 1988)

Duffy, Michael, Stephen Fisher, Basil Greenhill, David J. Starkey and Joyce Youings, eds, *The New Maritime History of Devon* (Exeter, 1992).

Dyer, Christopher, *Standards of Living in the Late Middle Ages: Social Change in England c.1200–1520* (Cambridge, 1989).

Edwards, C.R.W., I.A.D. Bouchier, C. Haslett, E.R. Chilvers, eds, *Davidson's Principles and Practice of Medicine* (17th edn, Edinburgh, 1995).
Ellmers, Detlev, 'The Cog as Cargo Carrier', in *Cogs, Caravels and Galleons: The Sailing Ship, 1000–1650*, ed. Richard W. Unger (London, 1994).
Fenwick, Valerie, ed., *The Graveney Boat* (Oxford, 1978).
Fischer, David H., *The Great Wave, Price Revolutions and the Rhythm of History* (Oxford, 1996).
Forte, A.D.M., 'Marine Insurance and Risk Distribution in Scotland before 1800', *Law and History Review* 5 (1967), pp. 393–412.
Friel, Ian, *The Good Ship* (London, 1995).
Fryde, E.B., 'Edward III's Wool Monopoly of 1337: A Fourteenth-Century Royal Trading Venture', *History*, NS 37 (1952).
——, *Studies in Medieval Trade and Finance* (London, 1983).
——, *Peasants and Landlords in Later Medieval England, c.1380–c.1525* (Stroud, 1996).
Gardiner, D.A., 'John Hawley of Dartmouth', *Transactions of the Devonshire Association* 98 (1966), pp. 173–205.
Gelsinger, Bruce E., 'Lodestone and Sunstone in Medieval Iceland', *Mariner's Mirror* 56, 2 (1970), pp. 219–26.
Getz, F.M., *Healing and Society in Medieval England: A Middle English Translation of the Pharmaceutical Writings of Gilbertus Anglicus* (Madison, WI, 1991).
Girtin, T., *The Triple Crowns: A Narrative History of the Drapers' Company 1364–1964* (London, 1964).
Goode, R.M., *Commercial Law* (rev. edn, London, 1995).
Gras, N.S.B., *The Early English Customs' System* (Cambridge, MA, 1918).
——, 'Capitalism – Concepts and History', *Bulletin of the Business Historical Society*, XVI, 2 (1942).
Gray, H.L., 'The Production and Export of English Woollens in the Fourteenth Century', *English Historical Review* XXXIX (1924), pp. 13–35.
Hanham, A., *The Celys and Their World, An English Merchant Family of the Fifteenth Century* (Cambridge, 1958).
——, 'Foreign Exchange and the English Wool Merchant in the Late Fifteenth Century', *Bulletin of the Institute of Historical Research* XLVI (1973), pp. 160–75.
——, ed., *The Cely Letters 1472–1488*, EETS, OS 273 (1975).
——, 'The Profits on English Wool Exports, 1477–1544', *Bulletin of the Institute of Historical Research*, LV (1982), pp. 139–47.
Harris, G.G., *The Trinity House of Deptford, 1514–1660* (London, 1969).
Hatcher, J., *Plague, Population and the English Economy, 1348–1530* (London, 1977).
——, 'Mortality in the Fifteenth Century: Some New Evidence', *Economic History Review*, 2nd Series 39, 1 (1986), pp.19–38.
——, 'England in the Aftermath of the Black Death', *Past and Present*, 144 (1994), pp. 3–35.
Hattendorf, John B., et al., *British Naval Documents, 1204–1960*, Navy Records Society, 131 (Aldershot, 1993).

SELECT BIBLIOGRAPHY

Heers, J., 'Le Prix d'assurance maritime à la fin du moyen age', *Revue d'histoire économique et sociale* 37 (1959).

Hingeston-Randolph, F.C., *The Register of John de Grandison, 1327–69*, 3 vols (London, 1894–99).

Hilton, R.H., 'Freedom and Villeinage in England', *Past and Present*, 31 (July 1965), pp. 3–19.

——, *The Decline of Serfdom in Medieval England*, The Economic History Society (1969).

——, *Bond Men Made Free: Medieval Peasant Movements and the English Rising of 1381* (London, 1973).

Hocquet, J.-C., 'Tonnages anciens et modernes: Botte de Early Modern England', *Historical Journal* 15 (1972).

Hoffmann, Gabriele and Uwe Schnall, eds, *Die Kogge, Sternstunde der deutschen Schiffsarchäologie* (Bremerhaven, 2003).

Hohesel, Wolf-Dieter, 'A Full-Scale Replica of the Hanse Cog of 1380', in *Crossroads in Ancient Shipbuilding*, ed. Christer Westerdahl, Oxbow Monograph 40 (Oxford, 1994).

Holdsworth, W.S., *A History of English Law*, ed. John Burke, 17 vols (London, 1903–72).

Hongre, L., G. Holst, and A. Khokhlov, 'An Analysis of the Geomagnetic Field over the Past 2000 years', *Physics of the Earth and Planetary Interiors* 106 (1998), pp. 311–35.

Howard, F., *Sailing Ships of War, 1400–1860*, (London, 1987).

Howard, G.F., 'The Date of the Hastings Manuscript Ships', *Mariner's Mirror* 63, 3 (1977), pp. 215–18.

Howse, H. Derek, 'Some Early Tidal Diagrams', *Mariner's Mirror* 79, 1 (1993), pp. 27–43.

Hunt, Tony, *The Medieval Surgery* (Woodbridge, 1992).

Hutchinson, Gillian, *Medieval Ships and Shipping* (London, 1994).

Jacob, E.F., *The Fifteenth Century 1399–1485* (Oxford, 1961, reprint 1988).

Jal, A., *Archéologie navale*, 2 vols (Paris, 1840).

James, M.K., 'Gilbert Maghfeld, a London Merchant of the Fourteenth Century', *Economic History Review*, 2nd series 8, 2 (1955–56), pp. 364–76.

——, *Studies in the Medieval Wine Trade*, ed. E.M. Veale (Oxford, 1971).

Jansen, H.P.H., 'Holland's Advance', *Acta Historiae Nederlandicae*, X (1978).

Johnson, Charles, *An Early Admiralty Case*, Camden Miscellany 3rd series XV (1929).

Jones, Michael, 'Two Exeter Ship Agreements of 1303 and 1310', *Mariner's Mirror* 53, 4 (1967), pp. 315–19.

Jones, Michael, 'Le Voyage de Pierre de Lesnerac en Navarre, 1386', *Mémoires de la société d'histoire et d'archéologie de Bretagne*, LXI (1984), pp. 83–104.

——, 'Roches contre Hawley: la cour anglaise de chevalerie et un cas de piraterie à Brest, 1386–1402', *Mémoires de la société d'histoire et d'archéologie de Bretagne*, LXIV (1987).

SELECT BIBLIOGRAPHY

Kerhervé, Jean, *L'Etat breton au 14e et 15e siècles. Les ducs, les hommes et l'argent*, 2 vols (Paris, 1987).

Kermode, Jennifer, ed., *Enterprise and Individuals in Fifteenth Century England* (Stroud, 1991).

——, 'Money and Credit in the 15th Century: Some Lessons from Yorkshire', *Business History Review* 65 (1991).

——, *Medieval Merchants, York, Beverley and Hull in the Later Middle Ages* (Cambridge, 1998).

Kiedel, Klaus-Peter and Uwe Schnall, eds, *The Hanse Cog of Bremen of 1380* (Bremerhaven, 1985).

Kleineke, Hannes, 'English Shipping to Guyenne in the Mid-Fifteenth Century: Edward Hull's Gascon Voyage of 1441', *Mariner's Mirror* 85, 4 (1999), pp. 472–6.

Kowaleski, Maryanne, 'Working at Sea: Maritime Recruitment and Remuneration in Medieval England', *Ricchezza del Mare, Ricchezza dal Mare, Secc. XIII – XVIII*; Atti della 'Trentasettesima Settimana di Studi', 11–15 April 2005 (Florence, 2006).

Kreutz, K.J., K.J. Mayewski, et al., 'Bipolar Changes in Atmospheric Circulation during the Little Ice Age', *Science* 277 (27 Aug. 1997), pp. 1294–6.

Labarge, Margaret W., *Medieval Travellers* (London, 1982).

Landström, Björn, *Sailing Ships* (London, 1978).

Lane, F.C., 'The Economic Meaning of the Invention of the Compass', *American Historical Review* 68, 3 (1963), pp. 605–17.

——, 'Tonnages, Medieval and Modern', *Economic History Review*, 2nd series 17, 2 (1964), pp. 213–33.

Lang, A.W., *Geschichte des Seezeichenswesens* (Bonn, 1965).

Lecky, S.T.S., *Wrinkles in Practical Navigation* (20th edn, London, 1920).

Leone, A., 'Maritime Insurance as a Source for the History of International Credit in the Middle Ages', *Journal of European Economic History*, 12, 2 (1983).

Lepan, Don, *The Cognitive Revolution in Western Culture* (London, 1989).

Lester, G.A., *Sir John Paston's 'Grete Boke': a Descriptive Catalogue, with an Introduction, of British Library MS Lansdowne 285* (Woodbridge, 1984).

Littleton, A.C. and B.S. Yarney, eds, *Studies in the History of Accounting* (London, 1956).

Lloyd, C.C., *The Health of Seamen*, The Navy Records Society 107 (1965).

——, *The British Seaman, 1200–1860: A Social Survey* (London, 1968).

Lloyd, T.H., *The English Wool Trade in the Middle Ages* (Cambridge, 1977).

Loomie, A.J., 'An Armada Pilot's Survey of the English Coastline', *Mariner's Mirror* 49, 4 (1963).

Lopez, R.S., *The Commercial Revolution of the Middle Ages, 950–1350* (New York, 1971).

Mackie, J.D., *The Earlier Tudors* (Oxford, reprint 1991).

McKisack, May, *The Fourteenth Century 1307–1399* (Oxford, 1959, reprint 1988).

Maitland, F.W., 'Trust and Corporation', in *Collected Papers*, 3 vols, III, pp. 321–404 (Cambridge, 1911).

Markus, G.J., *Conquest of the North Atlantic* (1980).

Martin, Jill E., ed., *Hanbury and Martin: Modern Equity* (14th edn, London, 1993).

SELECT BIBLIOGRAPHY

Mate, M., 'High Prices in Early Fourteenth Century England: Causes and Consequences', *Economic History Review*, 2nd series 28, 1 (1975), pp. 1–16.

Mauro, F., *Le Portugal et l'Atlantique au XVII siècle, 1570–1670* (Paris, 1960).

May, Cdr W.E., and Capt. L. Holder, *History of Marine Navigation* (Henley on Thames, 1973).

Means, Laurel, 'Popular Middle English Variations on the Compotus', *Speculum* 67 (1992), pp. 595–623.

Melikan, Rose, 'Shippers, Salvors and Sovereigns: Competing Interests in the Medieval Law of Shipwreck', *American Journal of Legal History* 11, 2 (1967), pp. 163–82.

van der Merwe, P., 'Towards a Three-Masted Ship', International Congress of Maritime Museums, 4th Congress Proceedings (Paris, 1981).

Meteorological Office, *Meteorology for Mariners* (3rd edn, London, 1978).

Miskimin, H.A., 'Monetary Movements and Market Structure', *Journal of Economic History* 24 (1964), pp. 170–90.

Mollat, Michel, ed., *Travaux du colloque international d'histoire maritime: 1e–8e* (Paris, 1957–66).

——, *Le Navire et l'économie maritime du nord des moyen-age au XVIIIe siècle* (Paris, 1960).

——, *La Vie quotidienne des gens de mer en Atlantique, IXe–XVIe siècle* (Paris, 1983).

——, *Europe and the Sea* (Oxford, 1993).

Moore, A.H., 'Some 15th-Century Ship Pictures', *Mariner's Mirror* 5 (1919), pp. 15–20.

Munro, J., *The Dawn of Modern Banking* (New Haven, CT, 1979).

Munro, J.H., *Wool, Cloth and Gold: The Struggle for Bullion in the Anglo-Burgundian Trade, 1340-1478* (Toronto 1972).

Musson, Anthony and W.M. Ormrod, *The Evolution of English Justice: Law, Politics and Society in the Fourteenth Century*, British Studies Series (Basingstoke, 1999).

Myers, A.R., *England in the Later Middle Ages* (London, 1952).

Naish, John, *Seamarks: Their History and Development* (London, 1985).

National Maritime Museum, *The Planispheric Astrolabe* (Greenwich, 1989).

Needham, Joseph, with Wang Ling, *Science and Civilisation in China*, 7 vols, III (Cambridge, 1959).

Nicholas, David, *Medieval Flanders* (London, 1992).

Nicolas, Sir Nicholas Harris, *A History of the Royal Navy from the Earliest Times to the Wars of the French Revolution*, 2 vols (London, 1847).

Nightingale, P., *The Grocers' Company and the Politics and Trade of London, 1000–1485* (London, 1995).

Obrist, Barbara, 'Wind Diagrams and Medieval Cosmology', *Speculum* 72 (1997), pp. 33–84.

Ohler, Norbert, *The Medieval Traveller* (Woodbridge, 1989).

O'Neill, Timothy, *Merchants and Mariners in Medieval Ireland* (Dublin, 1987).

Oppenheim, M.A., *History of the Administration of the Royal Navy, 1509–1660* (London, 1896).

Palmer, Robert C., *English Law in the Age of the Black Death, 1348–81: A Transformation of Governance and Law* (Chapel Hill, NC, 1993).

SELECT BIBLIOGRAPHY

Pattison, G., 'Observations on the History of the Bill of Lading', *Mariner's Mirror* 50, 4 (1964), pp. 283–95.

Paviot M.D. and J. Rieth, 'Caravel Construction at Brussels', *O Arquéologia Português*, series 6/7 (1988–9).

Penn, Simon A.C. and Christopher Dyer, 'Wages and Earnings in Late Medieval England: Evidence from the Enforcement of the Labour Laws', *Economic History Review* 2nd series 43, 3 (1990), pp. 356–70.

Peragallo, Edward, *Origin and Evolution of Double Entry Bookkeeping* (New York, 1938).

Perez-Embid, Fl., 'Navigation et commerce dans le port de Seville au bas moyen âge', *Le Moyen Age* 75 (1969), pp. 263–89 and 479–502.

Peroni, Amadeo Giulio, *The Florentine Merchant and the Profit Motive* (Washington, DC, 1968).

Phelps-Brown, E.H., 'Gregory King's Notebook and the Phelps Brown-Hopkins Price Index', *Economic History Review*, 2nd series 43, 1 (1990), pp. 99–103.

Pollock, Frederick and Frederic Maitland, *The History of English Law Before the Time of Edward I*, revd. S.F.C. Wilson (2nd edn, Cambridge, 1968).

Poos, L.R., 'The Social Context of Statute of Labourers Enforcement', *Law and History Review* 1 (1983), pp. 27–52.

Porter, Roy, *The Greatest Benefit to Mankind* (London, 1997).

Postan, M.M., 'Credit in Medieval Trade', *Economic History Review*, 1st series 1 (1928), pp. 1–5.

——, 'Some Evidence of Declining Population in the Later Middle Ages', *Economic History Review*, 2nd series, 2, 3 (1949–50), pp. 221–46.

——, *Medieval Trade and Finance* (Cambridge, 1973).

Powell, J.E. and K. Wallis, *The House of Lords in the Middle Ages* (London, 1968).

Power, E., *The Wool Trade in English Medieval History* (Oxford, 1941).

—— and M.M. Postan, eds, *Studies in English Trade in the Fifteenth Century* (London, 1933).

Prestwich, M.C., 'Edward I's Monetary Policies and their Consequences', *Economic History Review*, 2nd series 22, 3 (1969), pp. 406–16.

Putnam, B.H., *The Enforcement of the Statute of Labourers during the First Decade after the Black Death 1349–59* (New York, 1908).

Randalls, W.G.L., 'La Naissance d'un concept nouveau à l'epoque des grandes découvertes maritimes: le globe terraqué', *Revista da Universidade de Coimbra*, 'Separata' XXXIII (1985), pp. 329–38.

Rawcliffe, Carole, '"That Kindliness Should Be Cherished More and Discord Driven Out": The Settlement of Commerical Disputes by Arbitration in Later Medieval England', in *Enterprise and Individuals in Fifteenth Century England*, ed. Jennifer Kermode (Stroud, 1991), pp. 99–117.

dos Reis, António Estácio, *Medir Estrelas* (Lisbon, 1997).

Richmond, C.F., 'The Keeping of the Seas During the Hundred Years War', *History* XLIX (1964), pp. 283–98.

——, 'English Naval Power in the Fifteenth Century', *History* LII (1967), pp. 1–15.

Richmond, Colin and Isobel Harvey, eds, *Recognitions – Essays Presented to Edmund Fryde* (Aberystwyth, 1996).

Roger, James Steven, *The Early History of the Law of Bills and Notes* (Cambridge, 1995).

Rogers, Clifford J., 'The Military Revolution of the Hundred Years War', *Journal of Military History* 57 (1993), pp. 241–78.

Roover, F. Edler de, 'Early Examples of Marine Insurance', *Journal of Economic History* 5, 2 (1945), pp. 183–4.

Roover, R. de, *L'Evolution de la lettre de change XIVe–XVIIIe siècles*, Ecole pratique des hautes études, VIe section, affaires et gens d'affaires, IV (Paris, 1953).

Ruddock, A.A., 'The Method of Handling the Cargoes of Medieval Merchant Galleys', *Bulletin of the Institute of Historical Research* XIX (1942–43), pp. 140–8.

Runyan, Timothy J., 'The Laws of Oléron and the Admiralty Court in Fourteenth Century England', *American Journal of Legal History* XIX, 1 (April, 1975), pp. 95–111.

——, 'The Relationship of Northern and Southern Seafaring Traditions in Late Medieval Europe' in C. Villain-Gandossi, S. Busuttil and P. Adam, eds, *Medieval Ships and the Birth of Technological Societies*, vol. 2, *The Mediterranean Area and European Integration* (Malta, 1991).

——, 'The Cog as Warship', in *Cogs, Caravels and Galleons: The Sailing Ship, 1000–1650*, ed. Richard W. Unger (London, 1994).

Sandborn, Frederic Rockwell, *Origins of the Early English Maritime and Commercial Law* (New York and London, 1930).

Sauer, A., ed., *Das Seebuch* (Hamburg, 1996).

——, 'Segeln mit einem Rahsegel', in *Die Kogge*, ed. Gabriele Hoffmann and Uwe Schnall (Bremerhaven, 2003).

Sauvanon, Jeanine, *Les Métiers au moyen age: Leurs 'signatures' dans les vitraux, Cathédrale de Chartres* (Chartres, 1993).

Sayles, G.O., 'The English Company of 1343', *Speculum* VI (1931), pp. 177–205.

Scammell, G.V., 'English Merchant Shipping at the End of the Middle Ages; Some East Coast Evidence', *Economic History Review*, 2nd series 13, 3 (1961), pp. 327–41.

——, 'Shipowning in England c. 1450–1550', *Transactions of the Royal Historical Society*, 5th Series, 12 (1962), pp. 105–22.

——, 'Manning in the English Merchant Service in the Sixteenth Century', *Mariner's Mirror* 56, 2 (1970), 131–54.

——, *The World Encompassed: The First European Maritime Empires c.800–1650* (London, 1981).

——, 'European Seamanship in the Great Age of Discovery', *Mariner's Mirror* 68, 4 (1982), pp.357–76.

Schildhauer, Johannes, *Die Hansa* (Leipzig, 1988).

Senigallia, Leone Adolfo, 'Medieval Sources of English Maritime Law', *Mariner's Mirror* 26, 1 (1940), pp. 7–14.

Sherborne, J.W., 'The Hundred Years' War. The English Navy: Shipping and Manpower 1369–1389', *Past and Present* 37 (July 1967), pp. 163–75.

Sherborne, J.W., 'The Battle of La Rochelle and the War at Sea 1372–1375', *Bulletin of the Institute of Historical Research* XLII (1969), pp. 17–29.
Simon, Albert, ed., *Les Dictons météorologiques de nos campagnes* (Delarge, 1978).
Simon, André, *History of the Wine Trade in England* (London, 1906).
Simpson A.W.B., *A History of the Common Law* (Oxford, 1975).
Spufford, Peter, *Money and Its Uses in Medieval Europe* (Cambridge, 1988).
Squibb, G.D., *The High Court of Chivalry* (Oxford, 1970).
Stimson, Alan, *The Mariner's Astrolabe*, HES Studies in the History of Cartography and Scientific Instruments, 4 (Utrecht, 1988).
Svensson, Sam, *Sails Through the Centuries* (New York, 1965).
La Tapisserie de Bayeux (Bayeux, n.d.).
Taylor, E.G.R., *The Haven-finding Art* (London, 1956).
Thomson, John A.F., *The Transformation of Medieval England, 1370–1529* (London, 1983).
Thorpe, Benjamin, ed., *Ancient Laws and Institutes of England* (London, 1840).
Thrupp, Sylvia, *The Merchant Class of Medieval London 1300–1500* (Chicago, 1948).
——, 'The Gilds', *Cambridge Economic History of Europe*, vol. III (Cambridge, 1963).
Tinniswood, J.T., 'The English Galleys 1272–1377', *MM* 35 (1949).
Toomer, G.J., ed. and trans., *The Instruments of Ptolemy* (London, 1984).
Touchard, H., 'Les Brefs de Bretagne', *Revue d'histoire économique et sociale* XXXIV (1956), pp. 116–40.
Tracy, James D., ed., *The Rise of Merchant Empires: Long Distance Trade in the Early Modern World, 1350–1750* (Cambridge, 1990).
Unger, Richard W., *The Ship in the Medieval Economy, 600–1600* (London, 1980).
——, ed., *Cogs, Caravels and Galleons, The Sailing Ship, 1000–1650* (London, 1994).
Unwin, George, *Finance and Trade under Edward III* (London 1918, reprint 1962).
——, *The Gilds and Companies of London* (London, 1925).
Veale, E.M., *The English Fur Trade in the Later Middle Ages* (Oxford, 1966).
Villain-Gandossi, C., S. Busuttil and P. Adam, eds, *Medieval Ships and the Birth of Technological Societies*, Vol. II, *The Mediterranean area and European Integration* (Malta, 1991).
Ward, R.M., 'Cargo Handling and the Medieval Cog', *Mariner's Mirror* 80, 3 (1994), pp. 327–31.
——, 'A Surviving Charter-Party of 1323', *Mariner's Mirror* 81, 4 (1995), pp. 387–401.
——, 'English Charter-Parties in the Fourteenth and Fifteenth Centuries', Association for the History of the Northern Seas, *Yearbook 1999*, pp. 1–22.
——, 'The Earliest Known Sailing Directions in English', *Deutsches Schiffahrtsmuseumarchiv*, 27 (2004).
——, 'Sailing Directions for James V of Scotland', *History Scotland* 4, 2 (March/Apri 2004), pp. 25–32.
Waters, D.W., *The Art of Navigation in England in Elizabethan and Early Stuart Times* (London, 1958).
——, *The Rutters of the Sea* (New Haven, CT, 1967).
Wickersheimer, E., *Les Médecins de la nation anglaise* (Paris, 1913).

Wilson, K.P., ed., *The Port of Chester in the Fifteenth Century*, Transactions of the Historical Society of Lancashire and Cheshire CXVII (1965).
Winter, H., 'Who Invented the Compass?', *Mariner's Mirror* 23 (1937), pp. 95–102.
Wright, R.F., 'The High Seas and the Church in the Middle Ages', *Mariner's Mirror* 53, 1 (1967), pp. 3–31 and 2, pp. 115–35.

Unpublished theses

Harding, Vanessa, 'Port of London: Topography, Administration and Trade in the Fourteenth Century', unpublished PhD thesis, University of St Andrews (1983).
Simmons, J.J., 'The Development of External Sanitary Facilities Aboard Ships of the 15th to 19th Centuries', unpublished thesis, Texas A&M University (1985).
Ward, R.M., 'An Elucidation of Certain Maritime Passages in English Alliterative Poetry of the Fourteenth Century', unpublished MA thesis, University of Keele (1991).

Dictionaries and reference books

English
Concise Oxford Dictionary of Place Names, ed. Eilert Ekwall (4th edn, Oxford, 1981).
Handbook of British Chronology, ed. E.B. Fryde, D.E. Greenway and I. Roy (3rd edn, London, 1986).
Handbook of Medieval Exchange, Peter Spufford (London, 1986).
The Macmillan and Silk Cut Nautical Almanac, ed. Cdr R.L. Hewitt *et al.* (London, 1987).
Middle English Sea Terms, ed. Bertil Sandahl, 3 vols (Uppsala, 1951–84).
Middle English Dictionary, ed. Hans Kurath and Sherman M. Kuhn (Ann Arbor, 1952–).
The Oxford Dictionary of Nursery Rhymes, ed. Iona and Peter Opie (London, 1973).
Oxford English Dictionary, Compact Edition (Oxford, 1971).
Sailor's Word-Book, ed. Admiral W.H. Smyth (London, 1867, reprint 1996).

Dutch
Greet Nederlands–Engels Woordenboek voor Studie en Practijk, ed. Dr. H. Jansonius, 2 vols and supplement (Leiden, 1950–59).

French
Anglo-Norman Dictionary, ed. William Rothwell, Louise W. Stone, T.B.W. Reid *et al.* (London, 1992)
Cassell's French–English, English–French Dictionary, ed. Ernest A. Baker (London, 1961).
A Dictionary of the Norman or Old French Language, Robert Kelham (London, 1779).

Larousse Nouveau Dictionnaire Etymologique et Historique, ed. Albert Dauzat, Jean Dubois and Henri Mitterand (Paris, 1971).
Lexique de L'Ancien Français (Frédéric Godefroy), ed. J. Bounard and Am. Salmon (Paris, 1901).
Manual of Law French, ed. J.H. Baker (2nd edn, Aldershot, 1990).

German

Kleines Mittelhochdeutsches Wörterbuch, ed. Beate Hennig and Christa Hepfer (Tübingen, 1993).
Langenscheidt Standard German Dictionary, ed. Heinz Messinger and Gisela Türk, (Berlin, 1993).

Latin

Glossarium Mediae et Infimae Latinitatis, Domino Dufresne du Cange (Paris, 1840).
Latin-English Dictionary, ed. William Smith (London, 1877).
Promptorium Parvulorum sive Clericorum, Lexicon Anglo-Latinum Princeps, Auctore Fratre Galfrido Grammatico, AD c.1440, ed. A.L. Mayhew, EETS 102 (London, 1908).
A Revised Medieval Latin Word-List, ed. R.E. Latham (London, 1965).

Portuguese

Dicionários Acadêmicos: Inglês–Português, Português–Inglês (Oporto, 1973).

Index

Accountancy 70
Actions
   of account 10, 52
   against admiralty court decisions 42–3
   of *assumpsit* 13–14
   of covenant 14
   for damages 14
   recording of 38
   for trespass 13–14
   of torts 13
Admiral, origins of title 28
Admirals
   Alard, Gervase 28
   Arundel, Richard, earl of 33
   Barrau de Sescas 28
   Beauchamp, Sir John 32, 34
   Beaufort, Thomas, earl of Dorset 44
   Bedford, John, duke of 45
   Botetourte, John 28
   Bryan, Guy de 34, 37
   Grimaud, Reyner (acting for French king) 28
   Huntingdon, John Holland, earl of 38, 42
   Leyburn Sir William 28
   Nevill, John, lord 37
   Pavely, John de 34
   Somerset, John Beaufort, earl of 42
Agreements
   freighting 44, *see also* Charter-parties
   service 10–15, 40, 51–54, *see also* Partnerships
Aldridge, William, (ship's purser) 65
Alvise de Cadamosto (magnetic variation) 147
Amalfi, Flavio Gioia of, (invention of compass) 145
Anchoring/anchorages 125, 167–70, 199–200, 205, 216, 227
Avowry *see* Colouring

Balsal, John, (ship's purser) 74
Bayeux tapestry 133
Bayonne 28, 111
Beccadelli, Antonio (Amalfi poet) 145
Beowulf 124
Berwick 111

Bills of exchange 71–2
Biscay, Bay of 142, 148–150, 155
Bole, Henry (Lt. Gen, Court of Admiralty) 44
Bordeaux 111, 148
Bottomry 65, 73, 76, 204
Bourgneuf, Bay of 111
Bridport, John, (sleeping partner) 57, 61
Bristol 16–18, 20, 26, 29,
   Little Red Book 17
   Tolsey court 16, 18
Bruges 74

Calais 33, 110–11
   Court 55
   inquiries into spoilage 28,
   mint 69, 74
Cargo handling 158–9
Carta Mercatoria see Staple, Statute of
Catalan Atlas 138
Cely family
   bills of exchange 71–2
   credit 70
   failure 74
   magnetic compass 145
   partnership 64
   sea loan 65
   shipownership 64
Chancellor 10–11, 18–20
Charter 78ff
   bare-boat charter 63
   freight rates and cargo handling charges 84–7, 89–90
   legal clauses 82–4
   payment 84–7
   pilotage charges 89–90
   voyage time and route 87–9
   whole-ship charter 63–4, 77
   witnesses to charter-party 84
Charter-parties
   Bagot 1453 65, 83
   Copyn 1393–4 82, 91
   Giffard 1323 85, 87–90
      facsimile, transcription, translation 79, 183–205
   Lisle 1465 88–9
   Lynne 1392 86–7, 91–92

INDEX

Normant 1393 83–4, 88–9
Prophet 1387 85–6
Chaucer, Geoffrey,
  Shipman 123
  The Shipman's Tale 69, 72, 73
  A Treatise on the Astrolabe 131–2, 138
Cinque Ports 9, 23, 27, 28
Claims by, and against
  Aragon, king of 33
  Flemish 30,
    at Admiralty court 37, 41
  French 29–30, 36–7,
    at Admiralty court 32, 36, 41
    inquiries 28, 30
    at King's Council 31
  Portuguese 30, 34, 39
  Spanish 30, 32
Clerk, Walter (charterer) 52
Colouring by avowry 60
Commenda 12, 50, 53
Compaignons de marchaundie 524
Companhia das Naus, 78
Compurgation 13, 38
Conservators 45
Copland, Robert *see* Sailing Directions
Corpus juris 9
Court hearings
  Beche v Nyweman (debt) 41
  Bedon v Richardesson (rendering account) 55, 61
  Bensyn v Brennyng (disputed agreement) 84
  de Beuso v Crake (piracy) 29
  Bridport v Gyles (sale of ship) 57, 61
  Burwell v Horne (dispute between partners) 55
  Copyn v Snoke & Saylingham (freight payment) 41, 83
  Croppe v Hornbroke (breach of agreement) 61–2
  Draper v Stillard (freight contract) 41
  G. Sculte et al. v Wm. Long et Thos. Hoo (sea loan dispute) 75–6
  Gernsey v Henton (authority of local court) 40–1
  Hamely v Alveston (use of compurgation) 13, 38
  Helemes v Opright (breach of contract) 27
  Henton v Kedewelly (breaking and entering) 40
  Heyton v Bagot (dispute over law) 83
  Hornbroke v Croppe (dispute in partnership) 61–2

  Mulard v Hobbe (piracy) 28
  Normant v Lotolli (forgery, breach of contract, alien involved) 83–4
  Nocolt v Appe Hacche (disputed ownership) 41
  Pilk v Venere (theft by crew) 18–20, 33
  Roches v Hawley (spoilage involving aliens) 35
  Sampson v Curteys (authority of local court) 39
  Smale et alia v Houeel et alia (equity in admiralty court) 36
  Watertoft v Jonesson (freight contract) 44
  Yter v Haule (Hawley) (piracy) 41
Courts
  Admiralty 15, 20, 22, 26, 27–47 *passim*
  Aldermanic 9
  Chancery 9, 10–15, 28, 31–32, 39
  Chivalry (Constable and Marshall) 35
  Coram Rege 26
  County 9
  King's Bench, 8, 28, 38, 39
  markets and fairs 9, 12, 15
  manor 9
  piepowder 16
Covenant *see* Actions
Credit 69–71, 73, 75, 87, 94
Customs (Catalan) 56, 62
Custumal
  of Bristol 27
  of Fordwich and Sandwich 46

Danzig 111
Dartmouth 35, 44, 49–50, 64, 101, 103
Debt 12–16,19, 69–73, 86
Decree *ad personam* 9
Departure 86, 147, 159, 160–5
Dover Castle, constable of 28
Drying-out 158, 178, *see also* anchoring
Dublin 111, 176

Edward I 22, 25
Edward II 25, 29
Edward III 19, 23, 25, 29–30, 32–4, 37, 43
Equity 11, 13, 36, 37

Faversham 56
Flanders, 54, 110, 111, *see also* Claims
Fose, Walter of Lescluse, (killed at sea) 32
Foulk, Peter, (ship sunk in Calais) 33
France, king of 28, 29, 31, 43–4
Freight
  discount 81, 84–5, 220, 231–3
  rates and payments 84–7, 233–4

256

INDEX

Garcie, Pierre *see* Sailing Directions
General average   34, 70, 95–7, 108, 117, 195, 228
Gomes, Diogo, (latitude determination)   147–8
Gordon, John (concealed wine)   33
Grimaud Reyner (French admiral)   28
Guyot of Provins, (poet)   144

Hansa   127, 139, 145, 154
Hastings MS *see* Sailing Directions
Henry II   10, 24
Henry III   24–5
Henry IV   46
Henry VI   46
Herle, Robert de, Captain of Calais   32

Instruments,
    financial and commercial   70–72, 93–4
    navigational   122–3, 141, 144*ff*
Insurance   74–8, 87, 94
    Florentine and Genoese formulae   76–8
    in partnerships   50, 75, 78
    premium   75, 76–78
    by sea loans   72–3, 76–78
Investment, shipowning   64–7
Ipswich   46

Jettison   95–7, 100, 104, 108, 117
Joint/part ownership   55–8, 60–1

Kedwelly, John (victim of piracy)   44–5
Kelke, John (lack of counsel)   45
King's Council   9–11, 19, 40–42, 45–6
Kinsale, Old Head of   209

Lacer, Henry le (Geffrey le) (robbed abroad)   31
Lansdowne MS   *see* Sailing Directions
La Rochelle   110, 111
Law
    common   9–26, 27–47, 77, 83, 93
        commerce   12–15
        partnership   50–62, 64–66, 68
    maritime   20–6, 27–47, 82–3, 120
    merchant   15–20, 27–47, 51–66, 70
    Oleron Lex or *Roles*   16–26, 27–47, 48, 50
        anchorages   167–71, 199–200
        cargo   97–8, 158, 192, 196
        freight   204
        general average   195
        jettison   95–7, 194

crew management and relationships   66–7, 100–7, 191–3, 197, 201–3
    pilots   89, 175–7, 198–9, 205
    see also Oleron and Remuneration
Letter patent, 1285 (contribution after loss of ship)   96, 117
The Libelle of Englyshe Polycye   144
Liber Horn   see Oleron
Limbergue, Sir Alan de, Constable Bordeaux Castle   90, 230–1
Lisbon   110–11
Loans   52–5, 59, 62, 65–6, 70–6, 86–7
Lyndsay, Alexander *see* Sailing Directions

Marque, letter of   45
Maffe, Francis (merchant, robbed abroad)   31
Medine, Pierre de (author of *L'Art de Navigver*)   142
Merchants   9–121 *passim*, 192, 194–6, 198, 204, 211, 227
    Bensyn, Bernard (Bordeaux)   84
    Bokeland, Richard (London)   54
    Boys, John de (Brittany)   54
    Brennyng, Bernard (shipowner)   78
    Croppe, Thomas (shipowner)   61–2
    Denys, Harry (grocer)   89
    Denmars, Bartholomew (corder, shipowner)   49
    Genoese   29, 77
    Gunsales (Portuguese)   39
    Hatfield, John de (chandler)   56
    Heyton, John   65
    Hornbroke, Harry (shipowner)   61–2
    Lotolli, John (of Bordeaux)   83
    Lovecok, Philip, (shipowner)   59
    Lyng, John (draper)   60
    Maghfeld, Gilbert (ironmonger, shipowner)   65, 69–70
    Makenham, Arnold   88–9
    Mounier, Walter le (merchant's agent)   52, 75
    Newland, Richard (tailor)   52
    Northerne, Thomas le (vintner, shipowner)   49
    Norton, Geoffrey le   52
    Oliver, Tibbot,   73
    Payne, William (ironmonger, charterer)   82
    Pole, William de la   75
    Preston, Richard de (grocer, shipowner)   49
    Rust, Robert   98
    Sarduche, Nicholas   60

INDEX

Serland, Thomas 60
Spynule, Antonia (Genoa) 77
Venetian 29, 77
Waryn, John 80
Watere, Gamelin atte 89
Wawton, Philip 86
Meteorology 171–74 *passim*
Morte Arthure 160, 164, 166

Navigation 122–156 *passim*
   astrolabe 131, 138, 141, 147
   compass 130–1, 144–7, 154, 156
      deviation and variation 146
   depth, sounding 123–9, 133–141, 148–50,
      152, 154–5, 168
   direction 122–9, 138–44, 151–2
   distance 122–30, 148–52, 155
      distance made good 141–3, 151–2
      log 151–2
   latitude 122, 130, 141–2, 147–50, 156
      astral heights 122, 147–50, 156
   longitude 122, 130
   marks, land- and sea- 122, 124–8, 150
   meridional passage 122, 136–41
   seabed 133–5, 148
   sunstone 130
   speed
      of current 139–40
      of ship 122, 130, 133–4, 141–3, 151–2
Neckam, Alexander (author *De Naturis Rerum*) 144
Newcastle 110, 111

Oleron, *see also* Laws, Oleron
   Coutumier 24, 62, 219–28
      anchorage 227
      expenses and general average 226–8
      freight 220
      management and
         responsibility 224–6, 228
      partnership 220–4
   history of island 24–5
   Lex (*Roles*)
      Origins and variants 20, 21
      acceptance in England 20
      Liber Horn 20–22
   transcription, translation, commentary
      183–205
Ownership
   of cargo 33–4, 90
   of ships 12, 24, 41, 48–68, 81, 90

Partnership
   advantages of 62–3

commenda type 50, 53
complete partnership 53, 56–7
finance partnership 52, 53, 55
at law 11–13, 24, 26
relationships within 54–6
responsibilities within 58–62
rôles of partners 56–8
sale of share 57, 61–2, 66, 220–2
service agreement 51–4, 55, 63
Pecok, John (attorney) 77
Pedro de Medina (author *Art de Navegar*) 148
Piers Plowman 65, 69
Pilots 139, 205, 212, *see also* Laws, Oleron
   charter-party 81, 86
   payment 99–100, 112, 227, 228
   Thames 128
Piracy 16, 23, 27–47 *passim*
Plymouth 73
Polhowe (receiver of king's victuals,
   Newcastle) 86, 229–34
Prize 23, 29–47, 82, 113, 213
Proude, Richard *see* Sailing Directions

Queenborough, Inquisition of
   Admiralty inquiries 213–7
   admiral's powers 42, 217–8
   history 23–6, 37–8,
   pilotage 212
   shipmasters' responsibilities 50, 66–7
   transcription, translation 206–18
   wages 206–11, 212

Remuneration 84–7, 107–13, 192–3, 202–3,
   206–12
   *assiage, guindage, planchage, primage,
      quillage, rivage* 99, 226
   lodemanage 99, 112
   portage 5, 96–7, 103, 107–13, 201–3,
      207–10, 219
Rente, Thomas of Pontise (alleging pillage) 31
Richard Cœur de Lion 20
Richard II 11, 35, 46
Richard Redeless 166
Roger, employee of John Bridport 57
Rosa ventorum 132, n. 13
Rozmital, Leo of 132
Rule of the road 169–71, 178

Safe conducts 29, 35
Sailing directions and rutters 123–42,
   148–50, 152–6
   Copland, Robert 156

258

INDEX

Garcie, Pierre 156
Hastings MS (rutter) 124, 125, 133, 154, 168
Lansdowne MS (rutter) 152–4
Lyndsay, Alexander 140
Proude, Richard 156
Seebuch 123–6, 129, 135, 138–9, 151–6, 177
Sails 160–7, 178
   bonnets 160–1, 165
   reefs 165–6
Salvage 35, 81, 90, 97, 104
Sandwich 28, 46
Scone 111
Scriptum obligatorium 70–1
Senyor de nau 56
Seamanship 157–78 *passim*
Seville (River Gualdiquivir) 177
Shipmaster, profession of
   bureaucratic load 120–1
   discipline 104–6
   financial 69–74, 198, 226–7
   insurance 74–8
   options 50–1
   as owner/partner/employee 48–68
   relationship with merchant shippers 95, 192, 204
   responsibility
      for crew 100–7, 192, 193, 197, 199, 200–3
      for cargo 97–8, 192, 194–6
      for expenses 99–100, 192
      for ship 191, 195, 199–200, 227, 228
      offshore 95–121
      onshore 69–94
   trust 11, 50, 57–8, 66, 68, 205
Shipmasters
   Berthe, John 81
   Boudenson, James 62
   Bygge, Nicholas 66
   Dagh, Nicholas 56–7
   Ethoun, Amisio 50
   Field, Henry 80
   Fose, Walter 32
   Hobbe, Walter (alleged pirate) 28
   Maydekyn, John, 89–90
   Normant, Robert 83, 88
   Opright, Walter 27
   Pope, Arnald 98
   Pye, Roger (waterman) 63
   Richardesson, Hugh 55
   Starling, John 77
   Treyouran, John 58, 66
   White, John 65

Shipowners
   Andrewe, Matthew (charter dispute) 89
   Blakeburn, Nicholas (also shipmaster) 52
   Bagot, Clement 65
   Bedon, John 55
   Brewer, William 58, 66
   Bye, Richard 88
   Canynges, William (fleet owner) 49
   Crathom, William 64
   Dawe, William 58, 66
   Ferrantyn, Alexander 77
   Godlok, Peres (also shipmaster) 59
   Gyles, John (also shipmaster) 57
   Hawley, John (also shipmaster, allgd pirate) 48, 81, 91
   Irpe, John 50
   Lisle, Sir John (charter dispute) 88–9
   Ribald, William (also master) 50
   Sampson, Hugh (victim of piracy) 31
   Sculte, Gaspar (also shipmaster) 75–6
   Stoon, Thomas and Margaret 63
   Straunge, Robert (fleet owner) 49
   William, John (also shipmaster, merchant) 50
Shipownership
   investment 48–50, 64
   earliest recorded 48
   partnerships 51–63, 220–4
Ships
   All Saints 27
   Andreu Le 52
   Antony Le 46
   Benalee 48
   Berie La 76
   Bonan 59
   Brette La 48
   Cracher 50
   Cristofre 55
   Davy 58
   Francesse, Le 77
   Godyer (of Ipswich) 50
   Godyer (of Spalding) 50
   Gost (of Lynn) 88
   Gracedieu (of Brittany) 81
   Hardebolle 57
   Holyghost of Spain (on charter from crown) 63–4
   Jacobknight (of Sluys) 62
   James (of Ottermouth) 89
   Jesus (flag ship of crown) 50
   John (in service of crown) 50
   Julian (on charter) 65

INDEX

Katerine La, de Hope   49
Katherine Britton (in service of crown)   145
Lambord (of Bristol)   48
Lancastre Le   52
Margaret Cely   65
Margarete   59
Marie La (lighter)   63
Marie (of Boulogne)   49
Marie Le (of Exeter)   52
Mary Asshe   86
Michel Le   33
Michel (of London)   49
Nicholas (of Romene)   89
Nostra Dame alias *Sainte Marie* (of Lyme)   90
Pelarym, Le (of Flanders)   32
Portpays   31
Rodcogge   145
Sauveye, La   48
Seint Anne (of London)   77
Seint Marie Cog (of Exmouth)   49, 59
Seinte Marie   80
Swan   50
Tarryce   32
Trinity (of Bristol)   74
Thomas Le   49
Valentine (on charter from crown)   64
Sluys, battle of   29–30
Societas maris   56
Southwark   44–5
Staple,
   Statute of   19–20, 29, 71
   towns   9, 12

Strozze, Marco, (issuer of bill of assurance)   77
Sub pœna   11
Theft   17–8, 33, 104–5, 213, 216
Tides
   lunitidal interval (Establishment)   136, 138
   range   135–41
   streams   138–41
   tables   139
Time   122, 129, 137, 141–3, 147, 150–2
   astral clock   130, 142
   lunar clock   131, 136–42
Tong, William (partnership dispute)   56
Trebeel, John (pirate)   43
Trust concomitant with 'use'   10–11, 50, 57–8, 66, 68
Turn-round   98, 204
Tuskar Rock   209

Usuria occulta   59

Voyages
   delayed and frustrated   95, 110, 192, 194, 212, 220
   penalties   86–7, 91, 110, 204

Waterford   88, 111
Whitby   30
William of Worcester   129, 135–6, 143
Winchelsea   48, 57
Wool futures   69
Writs   10, 12, 16, 53
Wroth, John (partnership dispute)   56